PRODUCT-COUNTRY IMAGES: IMPACT AND ROLE IN INTERNATIONAL MARKETING

Nicolas Papadopoulos, DBA
Louise Heslop, PhD

SOME ADVANCE REVIEWS

"The book for students and researchers of what has by now emerged as an important subfield of consumer behavior and marketing management–both domestically and internationally. It covers practically everything: consumer and industrial goods, products and services, countries and events, trade and investment. . . . It will be *the* reference book for a long time."

Jean J. Boddewyn, PhD
Professor of Marketing and International Business
Baruch College (CUNY)

"State-of-the-art academic country image research, an essential reference for any researcher. . . . I was particularly impressed with both the sophisticated statistical techniques and samples used in some of the studies, which set a new standard for empirical studies in this area. . . . A must for anyone, academic or practitioner, with an interest in this field."

Phillip Niffenegger, MBA, PhD
Professor of Marketing
Murray State University

"A very welcome reference book which will be used by many researchers. An overview of this type is needed because contemporary thought in this area has tended to be very restricted in scope. Many of the chapters are excellent pieces of scientific study of the subject while others are extensive surveys of the relevant literature. Marketing scholars should welcome this publication."

Frank Bradley, PhD
R & A Bailey Professor of International Marketing
University College Dublin

I am confident this book will be well-received by academics, especially those with an interest in global marketing. It will also appeal to marketing managers for it contains numerous strategic implications. In addition to reviews of the literature and discussions of methodological issues, the text contains an up-to-date and comprehensive list of references."

Gerald M. Hampton, PhD
Professor of Marketing
San Francisco State University

NOTES FOR PROFESSIONAL LIBRARIANS AND LIBRARY USERS

This is an original book title published by International Business Press, an imprint of The Haworth Press, Inc. Unless otherwise noted in specific chapters with attribution, materials in this book have not been previously published elsewhere in any format or language.

CONSERVATION AND PRESERVATION NOTES

The paper used in this publication meets the minimum requirements of American National Standard for Information Sciences—Permanence of Paper for Printed Material, ANSI Z39.48-1984.

Product-Country Images
Impact and Role
in International Marketing

INTERNATIONAL BUSINESS PRESS
Erdener Kaynak, PhD
Executive Editor

New, Recent, and Forthcoming Titles:

International Business Handbook edited by V. H. (Manek) Kirpalani

Sociopolitical Aspects of International Marketing edited by Erdener Kaynak

How to Manage for International Competitiveness edited by Abbas J. Ali

International Business Expansion into Less-Developed Countries: How to Use the International Finance Corporation Mechanism by James C. Baker

Product-Country Images: Impact and Role in International Marketing edited by Nicolas Papadopoulos and Louise A. Heslop

The Global Business: Four Key Marketing Strategies edited by Erdener Kaynak

Multinational Strategic Alliances edited by Refik Culpan

Market Evolution in Developing Countries: The Unfolding of the Indian Market by Subhash C. Jain

Product-Country Images
Impact and Role
in International Marketing

Nicolas Papadopoulos, DBA
Louise A. Heslop, PhD
Editors

International Business Press
An Imprint of The Haworth Press, Inc.
New York • London • Norwood (Australia)

Published by

International Business Press, an imprint of The Haworth Press, Inc., 10 Alice Street, Binghamton, NY 13904-1580

Library of Congress Cataloging-in-Publication Data

Product-country images : impact and role in international marketing / Nicolas Papadopoulos, Louise A. Heslop, editors.
  p. cm.
Includes bibliographical references and index.
ISBN 1-56024-236-1 (acid free paper)–1-56024-237-X (acid free paper).
  1. Marketing. 2. Consumers' preferences–Cross-cultural studies. I. Papadopoulos, N. G. (Nicolas G.), 1946- . II. Heslop, Louise.
HF5415.122.P76   1992
382–dc20   91-35947
                                                                                            CIP

To Irinela, Anatole, and Emile.

Nicolas Papadopoulos

To Lorne, Josette, and Claire, for the many joys and challenges they provide in my life.

Louise Heslop

CONTENTS

ABOUT THE EDITORS

Dr. Nicolas Papadopoulos (MBA Washington State; DBA Athens) is Professor of Marketing and International Business at the School of Business of Carleton University. His research and professional interests focus on international marketing strategy and consumer responses to it–especially foreign market selection and entry, international corporate networks, strategies in trading blocs, and buyer perceptions of product and country images. He has published over 100 articles and monographs and six books in these and other areas, including *Canada and the European Community: An Uncomfortable Partnership?* (Institute for Research on Public Policy), and *Marketing* and *Cases in Canadian Marketing* (John Wiley & Sons, Canada).

Dr. Papadopoulos worked with Exxon, 3M, and Procter & Gamble before starting his academic career, and has kept close ties with the private sector. He lectures and consults in North America and Europe. He served for five years on the Board of Directors of the National Capital Chapter, American Marketing Association (President in 1987-1988), on the National Marketing Task Force of United Way Canada, and as VP Marketing of the Canadian Fencing Federation. Dr. Papadopoulos is a member of the Editorial Review boards of two journals, and a reviewer for journals and research agencies such as Canada's Social Sciences and Humanities Research Council. In 1984 he co-founded and has since been the Director of The International Business Study Group at Carleton University.

Dr. Louise A. Heslop (MSc Guelph; PhD Western Ontario) is Professor of Marketing at the School of Business of Carleton University, which she joined in 1983 after teaching in the Department of Consumer Studies at the University of Guelph. She has also worked as a Senior Research Officer in the Social and Economics Studies Division, Statistics Canada. Dr. Heslop specializes in consumer behavior, marketing research, international marketing, and marketing and social issues. She has published over 30 refereed articles and seven monographs and books on such subjects as product-country images, information cue usage, advertising to children, women and advertising, decision making by elderly couples, and energy consumption. Her research has been published in a wide variety of academic journals (e.g., *Journal of Consumer Research*) and practitioner-oriented periodicals (e.g., *Industrial Marketing Management*). Her studies have been funded by public and private sector sources ranging from Cana-

da's Social Sciences and Humanities Research Council and the Marketing
Science Institute in the U.S. to John Labatts, Cognos Ltd., and several
Canadian government departments and agencies.

Dr. Heslop is active in both management education and research. She
recently completed a term as Marketing area Editor for the *Canadian
Journal of Administrative Sciences*. She currently serves on the Editorial
Board of two journals and on the review panel for SSHRC's strategic
research grants area, "Managing for Global Competitiveness." Dr. Heslop
has also served as Director of Carleton's School of Business (1989-1990)
and on the executive of the Administrative Sciences Association of Canada (1987-1990). She is both a founding and current member of the executive of the Canadian Consortium of Management Schools.

CONTRIBUTING AUTHORS

Sadrudin A. Ahmed, Professor of Marketing, Faculty of Administration, University of Ottawa, Ottawa, Canada.

C. Christopher Baughn, Lecturer, Department of Management and Organization Sciences, School of Business Administration, Wayne State University, Detroit, Michigan, U.S.A.

Warren J. Bilkey, at the time of writing, Emeritus Professor of International Business, Graduate School of Business, The University of Wisconsin at Madison, Madison, Wisconsin, U.S.A.

James A. Brunner, Professor of Marketing, Department of Marketing, College of Business Administration, The University of Toledo, Toledo, Ohio, U.S.A.

Edmen Chan, Manager, Mercedes-Benz Commercial Vehicle Department, Zung Fu Co. Ltd., Hong Kong.

Cheng-Nan Chen, Professor of Marketing at the Graduate School of Business Administration, National Cheng Kung University, Tainan, Taiwan, Republic of China.

John C. Crawford, Associate Professor of Marketing, Marketing Department, College of Business Administration, University of North Texas, Denton, Texas, U.S.A.

Faramarz Damanpour, Professor of Finance and International Business, Department of Finance & Business Law, James Madison University; and President and Founder, Association for Global Business, Harrisonburg, Virginia, U.S.A.

Alain d' Astous, Professor of Marketing, Faculté d' Administration, Université de Sherbrooke, Sherbrooke, Québec, Canada.

Alan B. Flaschner, Professor of Marketing, Department of Marketing, College of Business Administration, The University of Toledo, Toledo, Ohio, U.S.A.

Françoise Graby, Maitre de Conferences, Centre de Recherche D.M.S.P., Université de Paris IX-Dauphine, Paris, France.

Eugene D. Jaffe, Visiting Professor of Marketing and International Business, Baruch College, City University of New York, New York, U.S.A.

Johny K. Johansson, Professor and McCrane/Shaker Chair of International Business and Marketing, School of Business Administration, Georgetown University, Washington, D.C., U.S.A.

John P. Liefeld, Professor, Department of Consumer Studies, University of Guelph, Guelph, Ontario, Canada.

David T.E. Lim, Director, North American Office, Singapore Economic Development Board, Singapore/U.S.A.

Xiaogang Lou, Assistant Professor of Management, Yanshan University, Qinhuangdao, People's Republic of China.

James R. Lumpkin, Gene Brauns Professor of Marketing, University of Southwestern Louisiana, Lafayette, Louisiana, U.S.A.

Gabriele Morello, Professor of Marketing, Vrije Universiteit and Istituto Superiore per Imprenditori e Dirigenti di Azienda, Amsterdam, The Netherlands, and Palermo, Italy.

Israel D. Nebenzahl, Professor of Marketing, Department of Economics and Business Administration, Bar-Ilan University, Ramat-Gan, Israel.

Erik Nes, Chairman, Department of Marketing, Oslo Business School, Norway; at the time of writing, Managing Director, Roneo Alcatel A/S, Oslo, Norway.

Sally Stewart, Senior Lecturer, Department of Management Studies, University of Hong Kong Business School, Hong Kong.

Gilbert Y.W. Tan, Senior Tutor (at the time of writing, also a doctoral candidate at the University of Pittsburgh), Faculty of Business Administration, National University of Singapore, Singapore/U.S.A.

Marjorie Wall, Associate Professor, Department of Consumer Studies, University of Guelph, Guelph, Ontario, Canada.

Chow Hou Wee, Dean, Faculty of Business Administration; Director, School of Postgraduate Management Studies; and Head, Business Policy Department, National University of Singapore, Singapore.

Attila Yaprak, Associate Professor of Marketing, Department of Marketing, School of Business Administration, Wayne State University, Detroit, Michigan, U.S.A.

Chwo-Ming Joseph Yu, Assistant Professor of Business Administration, College of Commerce and Business Administration, University of Illinois at Urbana-Champaign, Champaign, Illinois, U.S.A.

Saïd Zouiten, at the time of this writing, Instructor, Faculté d' Administration, Université de Sherbrooke, Sherbrooke, Québec, Canada.

List of Referees

The following researchers participated in reviewing the manuscripts submitted to this volume, from which those published were selected.

Gary J. Bamossy, Vrije Universiteit, The Netherlands
A. Tansu Barker, Brock University, Canada
James A. Brunner, University of Toledo, U.S.A.
James Fisher, University of Windsor, Canada
George H. Haines, Jr., Carleton University, Canada
C.L. Hung, University of Calgary, Canada
Chan-Kon Kim, Concordia University, Canada
Gurprit Kindra, University of Ottawa, Canada
David Light, University of San Diego, U.S.A.
Judith J. Marshall, Carleton University, Canada
Thomas E. Muller, McMaster University, Canada
Erik Nes, Roneo Alcatel A/S, Norway
D. Anthony Schellinck, Dalhousie University, Canada
Marjorie Wall, University of Guelph, Canada
Ugur Yavas, East Tennessee State University, U.S.A.

Foreword

Country-of-origin analysis focuses on buyers' opinions regarding the relative qualities of goods and services produced in various countries. It appears that buyers in more developed countries tend to regard most products made in less developed ones as being of lower quality than most products made in MDCs. Logically, this gives a competitive advantage to producers from more industrialized nations.

However, there are many exceptions to this rule and many more rules in this area. Studies indicate, for example, that Jamaican Blue Mountain coffee is the best available and Colombian coffee is of superior quality–and that a country can succeed in changing its image, as Japan and South Korea have done. More to the point, the time it took to accomplish the change was some 20 years for Japan but only one half of a decade for South Korea.

Understanding the role of country-of-origin and using it to advantage creates a whole new area for study and application. The "Made-in" notion is a matter of tremendous importance in international marketing strategy, public policy making, and research. It is relevant at all levels (the product, the firm, the sector, the country, and internationally), for products as well as commodities (consider the success of Colombian coffee, as just one example), services, and any other offering.

I am extremely pleased to see this first book on country-of-origin. When Erik Nes and I did our review back in 1982 we had hoped to stimulate more and better country-of-origin research, and the response has been gratifying indeed. Today, hardly an international journal issue or a conference go by without at least one country-of-origin article. The editors of this book have made many contributions through their work in Canada and many other countries and they certainly are at the forefront of advancements in those areas where earlier research had been weak.

More importantly, a lot of water has gone under the bridge since 1982. Country-of-origin has "arrived," and the time is ripe for a book to summarize current developments and provide the integrative base for new advances. Drs. Papadopoulos and Heslop have done a tremendous job of pulling together their own know-how with that of many others from several countries. I see here most of the best minds in this area–Johansson,

Morello, Nebenzahl and Jaffe, Crawford and Lumpkin, Yaprak, Liefeld and Wall, to name just a few. I also see the exciting work of many newcomers to the field–a prerequisite for a vibrant area of research.

This book will make a seminal contribution to better understanding country-of-origin, and I feel honored to have been asked to write the Foreword. As the editors correctly point out, the more international markets become, the more prominently the origin of products will figure in sellers' and buyers' decisions. I urge both practitioners and academics to take note of the numerous insights offered in this volume so as to prepare better for meeting the competitive challenges of the global marketplace.

Dr. Papadopoulos and Dr. Heslop are to be commended for their effort and persistence in bringing this fine book to fruition.

Warren J. Bilkey
University of Wisconsin-Madison
Madison, Wisconsin, U.S.A.

All of us associated with this project were saddened by the death of Dr. Warren Bilkey, author of the Foreword and a contributor to the volume, as *Product-Country Images* was going to press. During his long and productive career, Dr. Bilkey made a singular contribution to the field of international marketing and country-of-origin research. We join his colleagues around the world in mourning his loss. Dr. Bilkey's work will continue to influence the field for many years to come.

Preface

OBJECTIVES

Some call it "The BMW Effect": the aura, the feelings, the correlations, the mystique–the "image" with which producers attempt to imbue their products and/or which consumers perceive in relation to them. A product can draw its image from its design, its performance, and many other characteristics, but also from its brand name and the name of its producer and its country-of-origin.

It is often said that brand names like "McDonald's" are worth millions. If so, how many *billions* is *Germany's* image worth? Why is it worth so much more than the image, say, of, Burkina Faso, India, or even–with sincerest apologies–France? More to the point, what does this "worth" *mean* in an era when the buzzword is "international competitiveness"? What happens when we stack up German technology and industrial prowess against French perfumes, wines, and joie de vivre? Do buyers make such comparisons, and if so, what do they "receive" from them?

This book has three main objectives:

1. Research: To offer a current and comprehensive treatment of the role of product-country images in international marketing strategy and consumer behavior, for the benefit of academic and applied researchers with interests in these and related areas. Seasoned researchers who have worked on country-of-origin issues will find the contents to be a useful refresher, but will also be quick to identify many new and untrodden paths. Others will find a wealth of information that can be useful to their research in related areas or can be used to begin work on the "Made-in" effect.

2. Strategy and Policy: To provide decision makers and policy makers with practical information of immediate usefulness in formulating international strategies and policies. "Origin" information has been used for decades in both private and public sector marketing, but, more often than not, this use has occurred in a vacuum of information about its strategic and tactical implications. The contents of this book fill this vacuum and serve to raise practitioners' awareness about the importance, domestically

and abroad, of national and other "place" images in international competitiveness.

3. Study: To expose students to this important field of knowledge, the implications of which are relevant to a variety of disciplines and subdisciplines ranging from exporting, international marketing, and international business to social psychology, geography, urban and tourism planning, and international relations. A country's long-term competitiveness depends in large measure on how well-prepared its future managers are–and in this sense it is hoped that the information in this book will close a significant gap.

BACKGROUND

In a way, "country image" is to a product what "occupation" is to a new acquaintance we make at a party: we sort of *have to* ask about it (if it has not already been offered) to put our new friend in context, to see if there is some common ground, to make a value judgment, to get a conversation going or decide whether we want to have one. Some might wish things were otherwise: that other information would be more relevant in helping to assess a person's worth. But what one does for a living (and sometimes such other things as what books or movies one likes) is often seen as a more useful surrogate because of the common context for understanding that it offers–the symbols associated with it are widely known and understood in roughly similar ways.

The power of country images is well known to the tens of thousands of sellers who use it, whether as a friendly introduction, a reference point, or a unique selling proposition, to enhance their products' chances of success. It is also known to just as many sellers who try to conceal it, fearing that if it were known consumers might make a negative association and not buy the product.

Buyers, too, know a lot about images. The ceramic tiles must be Italian, the camera Japanese, and Australians are oh-so-much-fun (the Crocodile Dundee Effect). In industrial markets, few hospitals would buy axial tomography equipment from anywhere but Israel (which holds the lion's share of this market globally) and purchasing agents in most sectors would feel uneasy buying complex equipment "Made in" the former U.S.S.R. As the reader will soon see in one of the chapters that follow, Hong Kong tour operators are willing to consider buying buses "Made in Brazil" because "a country which produced a Pele in soccer can't be too bad."

This book is about the images of countries and the way these images may affect the behavior of buyers. The subject is of vital importance to

companies looking for ways to enhance their international competitiveness, whether by expanding to foreign markets or protecting their domestic consumer franchise. It is also important to academic researchers with interests in a wide range of areas, including international marketing strategy, branding, stereotyping, ethnic imagery, rules and patterns of consumer information processing and decision making, social psychology, cultural geography and anthropology, international relations at the people or country level, and many others.

ABOUT THIS BOOK

International marketing researchers have been working on the country-of-origin phenomenon intensively for over 25 years. This book brings together most of the eminent researchers in this field as well as several new colleagues who have begun to study made-in issues more recently. To ensure high quality, contributed chapters went through a double-blind refereeing process in addition to being reviewed extensively by the co-editors, and most were revised several times before final acceptance.

In more ways than one, this book is the work of those who contributed to it. However, we did not want this to be a near-random collection of readings. As editors, we went to great lengths to ensure that the major subfields within "country-of-origin" were well represented, and that the ideas of the various individual authors were presented in as reasonably smooth a flow as possible. Among other steps, we reviewed all submitted manuscripts for content, style, and consistency, made editorial changes where necessary (without, of course, affecting the essence of the authors' works), did everything we could to ensure error-free data and reference lists (although it is inevitable that some must have escaped us), and added "editors' notes" where necessary to amplify a point or cross-reference it with a related point made in another chapter.

The end result is a wide-ranging and state-of-the-art book which involves the work of 29 researchers from 11 countries, and 15 referees from four countries, ranging from Singapore to France and Israel and including both academics and practitioners. We are pleased and gratified with the outcome of this collective effort. As the reader will soon see, many contributions are original empirical studies while others offer insightful conceptual analyses. The reader remains, of course, the final judge of whether we and our colleagues have succeeded. But as far as we as editors are concerned, we feel honored to be in the company of the many noted researchers whose work appears in the following pages.

CONTENT AND ORGANIZATION

This volume goes considerably beyond what was known until now about product-country images. Individual chapters deal with such unique subjects as the impact of events of international significance on buyer behavior, the influence of culture and political "realms" on product-country images, the image of countries as "investment products" trying to attract foreign capital, and many others.

The book is divided into five main parts. Part I contains three chapters which provide an overview of the field from various perspectives. Part II contains a review and a meta-analysis which offer a critical assessment of research findings to date, using them to chart future research directions. Part III addresses various methodological and behavioral perspectives, including the influence of personality variables on origin imagery and the views of industrial buyers about products from various countries. Part IV focuses on the images of countries as corporate entities competing for exports or investment capital in the international arena. Finally, Part V contains five chapters which examine environmental influences on the formation and impact of country images, including such events as Tiananmen Square, the 1988 Seoul Olympics, and the 1989 U.S.-Canada Free Trade Agreement.

ACKNOWLEDGMENTS

We have been working together on various projects, in this and other areas, for a long time. In 1986 we managed for the first time to convince the organizers of an academic conference to schedule a "country-of-origin" panel session (earlier proposals to the same and other conferences had been rejected out of hand–the topic was not yet hot). At that first panel, the speakers were the only audience–not one of the other 250-or-so conference participants found the topic worth attending.

How quickly things change! Just four short years later, a proposal for a "Key Panel" session on our beloved theme at the 1990 Academy of International Business Conference was reviewed and approved in spite of competition from several other suitors for the few panel spots available. Attendance at that session was among the highest at the conference–suggesting that country-of-origin had come of age.

We would like to thank, first, the contributors and referees who worked with us to make this book possible. In the final analysis it is their work that matters. To get to the point where a book on country-of-origin was even conceivable, however, we have received help for our studies from many quarters since the early 1980s. We must mention, with appreciation, the financial and other support of Canada's Department of Industry, Science, and Technology; the Marketing Science Institute in the U.S.; the European Institute for Advanced Studies in Management; the Social Sciences and Humanities Research Council of Canada; and the Faculty of Graduate Studies and Research at Carleton University.

Many colleagues in the country-of-origin field have provided the hours, work, and support that are necessary to "keep going"–to explore new avenues, challenge one's assumptions, and just plain feel that there are some fellow travellers out there. We must begin by thanking Professor Erdener Kaynak (University of Pennsylvania-Harrisburg) who, as International Business Executive Editor for The Haworth Press, encouraged us to undertake this project and supported us throughout its lengthy development process.

We are grateful for the support of, and look forward to many more years of collaboration with, Professors John Liefeld and Marjorie Wall at the University of Guelph; Gary Bamossy at Vrije Universiteit in Amsterdam; Gerry Hampton at San Francisco State University; Françoise Graby at Université de Paris IX-Dauphine; and József Berács at the Budapest University of Economics. We also want to thank Professors George Avlonitis, Friedhelm Bliemel, and Petros Malliaris, who participated in our cross-national research.

Further, a great "thanks" is due to the stalwart country-of-origin aficionados who joined us in some of the more risky endeavors over the years–in particular, Professors John Crawford, Johny Johansson, John Liefeld, and Attila Yaprak, who joined us at the 1990 AIB panel, and also to thank Johny Johansson separately for his contribution to the early development work for one of our main studies. More recently, we have been fortunate to have had opportunities to exchange ideas about the issues that concern us all with such researchers as Israel Nebenzahl and Eugene Jaffe, Sadrudin Ahmed and Alain d' Astous, Attila Yaprak, David Tse of the University of British Columbia, and many others.

Country-of-origin and the electronic briefcase (of which, to the chagrin of our families, we make extensive use) notwithstanding, one's work life revolves around one's place of work. Our colleagues at The School of Business of Carleton University provide an outstandingly supportive environment for collaborative work. Intra- and inter-disciplinary "networks" exist in the school in all fields and form the basis of several broader national and international networks. We would like to thank our colleagues who make working there a special pleasure. We wish to mention especially our fellow marketers, Professors George Haines, Judith Marshall, and Roland Thomas (who also is the School's Director), and our Dean, Professor Marilyn Marshall, for their cheery dispositions and unbending support, no matter what the circumstances (and there have been many!).

"Acknowledgments" sections customarily end with thanking one's family. This being the first-ever book on country-of-origin, the work involved in developing it was well beyond what might have been the case otherwise. We are confident that the book will be "the fifth milestone" in the evolution of product-country image research (the first chapter identifies the previous four). In the meantime, there are not enough words to express our appreciation, individually and jointly, to our families. We dedicate this book to them sincerely and wholeheartedly.

Nicolas Papadopoulos and Louise Heslop
Ottawa, Canada

PART I.
THE MEANING OF PRODUCT
AND COUNTRY IMAGES

INTRODUCTION

Part I provides an overview of the field of country-of-origin through three chapters which represent various perspectives.

Chapter 1 begins by positioning country-of-origin in the context of images and stereotyping in marketing and broadens its scope to a number of related areas. It includes an historical outline of developments in practice and research to date, highlights the various dimensions of product-country images, and draws strategic, policy, and research implications.

Chapter 2 draws from a major international study to explore various facets of product and country images. It discusses such issues as the images of the "natives" (domestic producers), the "superindustrialists" (the U.S. and Japan), and the "guerillas" (smaller but important trading nations), and serves to show how various aspects of the research literature can be integrated.

Chapter 3 deals with how managers view the country-of-origin phenomenon. It discusses such questions as the credibility of research in this field and the role of country-of-origin in global markets, in relation to bi-national products (those produced in a country other than the manufacturer's own), and as an embodiment of the country-specific advantages of nations. The chapter concludes with a strong and cogent argument that, to remain competitive, firms need to pay much more attention to the influence of their origins' image on the behavior of their target markets.

Chapter 1

What Product and Country Images Are and Are Not

Nicolas Papadopoulos

INTRODUCTION

To each memorable image you attach a thought, a label, a category, a piece of the cosmic furniture, syllogisms, an enormous sorites, chains of apothegms, strings of hypallages, rosters of zeugmas, dances of hysteron proteron, apophantic logoi, hierarchic stoichea, processions of equinoxes and parallaxes, herbaria, genealogies of gymnosophists–and so on, to infinity.

Umberto Eco (1989:23)

In this passage from his recent best-seller, *Foucault's Pendulum,* Eco uses his polyglot facility with words, and his scholarly background (he is Professor of Semiotics at the University of Bologna in Italy), to describe what an "image" is and does better than most people could: in short, an image is a beautiful thing.

This book and this chapter are about a small slice of the nature and meaning of images–the part that deals with the potential role of the images of countries in marketing and buyer behavior. In other words, we focus here on the "Made-in" images of products.

However, the previous paragraph already offers evidence of the power of images–in this case, the different images that may have been evoked in each reader's mind by the words and terms used. Some clarification is necessary. "Focus on the 'Made-in' images of products" does not mean that one should think of country images in the sense of "Made-in" product *labels* alone–less so to think of the country image phenomenon as one that can or should be studied strictly within the context of marketing, or that "product" refers strictly to "goods and services." Sellers and buyers use advertising, packaging, branding, product design, and many other means, in addition to "labels," to provide and obtain information about product origins. "Product" can mean goods and services as such but also, for example, countries marketing themselves as attractive locations for tourism or foreign investment.

The more one looks into the meaning of the terms that are of interest to us, the more complex things get. Products are not necessarily made in "countries." They are made in "places," or geographic origins, which can be anything from a city to a state or province, a country, a region, a continent–or the world, in the case of "global" products. Further, unless viewed in strictly legal terms, *made-in* can mean *manufactured-in* but also *assembled-, designed-,* or *invented-in, made by a producer whose domicile is-in,* and, often, *wanting to look like it was made-*in _____ . Lastly, "buyers and sellers" can be anything from industrial and consumer users of products to national governments courting each other in the hope of establishing closer trade relations. Since the "origin" images of "products" can have so many facets, it is no surprise that they have been the object of study in disciplines ranging from political science to cultural anthropology and urban geography.

The purpose of this chapter is to portray the multifaceted dimensions of the country-of-origin images of products and place them in the broader context of other aspects of human behavior where image is a relevant issue. An overview of this type is needed primarily because contemporary thought in this area has tended to be very restricted in scope and, more often than not, misses the richness and significant strategic implications of origin images in marketing.

The chapter has four main sections. The first reviews the role of images in general and in marketing; the second outlines the evolution of the use of "Made-in" origin identifiers on products, and their study in international marketing research; the third reviews ways in which origin cues are used by buyers and sellers and highlights some of the issues that are currently being debated in this field of research; and the last section draws implications for marketing strategy and research, through an examination of the various dimensions of country images within marketing and in other contexts.

IMAGES IN SOCIETY AND IN MARKETING

The Function of Images

By unscrambling the passage by Umberto Eco, which was used to open this chapter, we get a good glimpse into the role of images in human behavior. Some of the useful functions of images include:

- the classification of objects (category);
- the development of element (stoichea) hierarchies;
- the understanding of objects through the many correlations (rosters of zeugmas) among them;
- assessments about the substitutability (hypallages) of objects;
- the symbolization (label) of elements or objects and of the bundles of attributes that characterize them (sorites), which facilitates recall;
- their use as input to syllogisms, or personal "theories" of causality (hysteron proteron)–which, in turn, permit us to interpret phenomena and act on or react to them;
- their dynamic nature, which makes it possible to change these "theories" of causality as the world evolves–while also making it difficult to discriminate between cause and effect (*dances* of hysteron proteron in Eco's words, or the chicken-and-egg dilemma);
- and, perhaps most importantly, their use as the basis for strong explanations (apophantic logoi) of, and therefore strong chains of beliefs (apothegms) about, objects and their attendant phenomena.

This partial listing of the functions of images helps to highlight their important role and the influence they can have in daily life. Thunder and lightning are real–but they were gods to the ancients who made sacrifices to them, they are a scary thing to children who close their eyes or ears to them, and they are a welcome excuse for someone looking for a reason to stay home.

The images of objects result from people's perceptions of them and of the phenomena that surround them. Assuming a basic definition of perception as "the meaning we attribute to things," and given that perception occurs at the individual level, each object has a different image for each individual observer. And, since people act on what they *believe* is true, "intrinsic reality"–whatever it may mean and however it may be determined–plays a lesser role in human affairs than "perceived reality."

Stereotyping

Inevitably, the existence of images leads to the stereotyping of objects. Stereotyping is inherent to the process of classification which people use as a means of coping with the world around them. In developmental psychology (e.g., the work of Jean Piaget), classification involves two stages. The first, "assimilation," occurs when one is exposed to a new stimulus unlike anything that he or she has been exposed to before. Such stimuli are used to create new schemata that broaden the *scope* of cognition. The second, "accommodation," involves the fitting of new stimuli within existing schemata and serves to *deepen* cognition. Piaget was able to make this distinction through his work with children, who by definition are exposed sequentially to totally new stimuli during their early development. For example, a child will *assimilate* the concept of "cheating" the first time he or she is cheated at a game by a playmate, and will *accommodate* variants of cheating within this schema as he or she becomes exposed to new experiences of this type.

Exposure to totally new stimuli of course decreases with age, and people meet new challenges by interpreting them in the context of past experience. Over time, by classifying repeated experiences of one type into a schema, and by correlating these with other experiences involving other schemata, people develop their basic internal rules of stereotyping. For example, assimilation in the formative years teaches Italian children that most people have dark hair. So, light-haired Americans will be noticed more than dark-haired Americans when visiting Italy as tourists. Therefore, "Americans have light-colored hair."

Naturally, a stereotyped generalization like that does not represent Americans of various ethnic and racial origins. In fact, readers who have visited various parts of Italy will notice that the framing of the example itself in the previous paragraph was a stereotype (a deliberate one, in this case!). Italians in the Milano-Bologna-Torino triangle, for example, have no more dark hair than Liverpool coal miners or Welsh farmers have a British stiff upper lip or nasal drone. Yet these examples point to an important principle and its corollary that are relevant to the discussion that follows: Stereotyping begins in the form of generalizations abstracted from a limited number of observations; and, if the number and scope of observations about the object (i.e., familiarity with it) increases, the stereotype is likely to move closer to "objective reality."

Stereotyped images can be useful or can result in ugly consequences, but their appropriateness is beyond the scope of this discussion. We are concerned here more with the fact that they exist and serve to influence people's behavior.

Images and Stereotypes in Marketing

The notion that "the image is the object" is behind much of the diversity, richness, and unpredictability of the human experience–and of our small corner in it, the study and practice of marketing.

In marketing, as in other aspects of life, there is no end to the different interpretations which different observers give to the same objects. The importance of images has been well recognized for decades with regard not only to products and brands but also to producers, distributors, consumers, and everything else that comprises "marketing."

From the seller's side, for example, the consumer in the detergent business still is referred to as a "she"–suggesting the lingering image of the typical buyer as a housewife and potentially affecting the nature and direction of promotional efforts undertaken by producers. In international marketing strategy, perceptions of foreign countries as places for investment or potential markets clearly have an unexpectedly strong influence in foreign expansion decisions (Vogel 1976; Johansson and Moinpour 1977; Reid 1981; Papadopoulos and Denis 1988). The image of distributors, whether as buyers (from the manufacturer's standpoint) or sellers (in procurement), also influences corporate decisions about selling to or buying from them (e.g., Panitz 1988).

From the buyer's side, sourcing a computer system from any supplier but The Big Blue is heresy to some corporate buyers, while to others IBM is a monolith less tailored to their needs than Hewlett-Packard or less innovative than Apple. Many end-consumers seek out "designer labels" in apparel as a means of boosting their personal image, others are not interested in these labels, and those in the upper social strata shun them *precisely because* wearing apparel with a visible label would make them *look as if they were attempting to create an image* for themselves (which, at that level, one is not supposed to need to do–and which is exactly what they *are* doing anyway by *not* wearing a label!).

Generally, organizational and end-buyers alike hold images of products, brands, and the companies associated with them, and these images affect their behavior. The use of stereotyped images by sellers and buyers may make their decisions easier–or may render them less effective if the distance between "perceived" and "objective" reality is great.

Their potential significance raises, among others, the question of the *content* of images. From the marketing perspective, knowing what elements individuals use in developing images would be an important input in devising means for influencing their formation.

It is widely accepted that "image" essentially represents a collection and judgment of both intrinsic and extrinsic attributes of objects and classes of objects. Intrinsic characteristics can range from the components of a product to the architectural design of a company's headquarters building and the physical appearance of a person. Similarly, extrinsic characteristics range from a product's price to a company's reputation and a person's name. Just like price may influence product quality perceptions, research in education has shown that "Elmers" get lower grades than

"Davids" from the same teachers for identical reports (Trout 1980). And Canadian banks competed for years for the distinction of having the tallest headquarters in the country, each constructing a new, taller building every time a competitor surpassed the previous record (Newman 1975).

The image of countries, in their role as origins of products, is one of the extrinsic cues that may become part of a product's total image. Known variously as the "country-of-origin" or "made-in" phenomenon, issue, effect, or cue, the subject has attracted a lot of attention in academic marketing research and is used extensively as the unique selling proposition for many brands in practice. For reasons that will become apparent in the following paragraphs, the term Product-Country Images (PCI) is felt to be broader and represent more accurately (than "country-of-origin" or "made-in") the phenomenon under study, and so will be used in the remainder of this chapter.

A BRIEF HISTORY OF PCI
IN INTERNATIONAL MARKETING

The evolution of knowledge about the role of PCI in international marketing has an interesting and perhaps "colorful," but certainly not atypical, history. The absence of interdisciplinary research is common in science, and so, like their colleagues in other areas, academic marketing researchers started their study of PCI phenomena from scratch–often reinventing knowledge which was already available in social psychology and other disciplines about such topics as the role of images, the perceptions of nations, or the correlates of cross-national stereotyping. As a result, the field went through growing pains which impeded its rate of progress before becoming established as a recognized and important area of research endeavor. Practitioners, on the other hand, often stumbled upon the use of origin messages by habit (e.g., "American Airlines" or "Norwegian Sardines") or felt their way through them by trial and error, seldom having the time to ponder the issues systematically (much less the inclination to read the results of academic research about them). The following paragraphs outline the history of origin images in practice and research.

PCI in Practice

Morello (see his chapter in this book) reports that "Made in-" labels as such have been used to identify product origins for at least 100 years. Today, origins are used more broadly, often as a matter of overall corporate strategy. As stated by Shin Ohkawara, the president of Kentucky Fried Chicken in Japan, "We sell the idea of good old America. Green pastures, fresh air, clean water" (Naisbitt and Aburdene 1990, p. 124). More generally, the use of place-of-origin to evoke the image of everything from persons to ideas and products can be traced to antiquity. From "Joseph of Arimathea" and "Greek mythology" to "Chinese silk" and "German engineering," origin has played a significant role throughout history in enabling people to identify, classify, assess, think of, and act upon phenomena and objects.

The practical use of country-of-origin identifiers specifically in relation to products can be separated into five distinct periods:

1. Antiquity to the 1800s. Until the late 1800s, production was largely localized and trade was limited to goods in which regions had resource-based comparative advantages. Origin information was relevant only at the regional level, and only in the latter part of this period did informed and wealthy consumers begin to seek specialty products from far-away places, like Chinese silk or Canadian furs.

2. 1800s-1950s. The transformation of origin images from local to national stereotypes of international significance began with the birth of the concept of the nation-state, and advances in transportation and communication, in the late eighteenth and nineteenth centuries. This transformation has had important implications. "Origin" images now encompassed larger entities farther afield, about which information was scant. As a result, the stereotyping principle mentioned above came into play to help people understand their new environment: stereotyped images of the known part were abstracted to the unknown whole. For example, the significance of Bavarian Motor Works in BMW cars was lost to German engineering, Brussels lace became Belgian lace, and a visit to New York became a visit to "the States," therefore: "all of the U.S. is full of skyscrapers," "Belgians are good with lacework," and "all German product are well-engineered."

3. 1950s-1970s. The international trade explosion that followed th cond World War brought foreign products to practically every hor place of business. Many of the country/product images which up to t if they existed at all, were held among the select few who co imported products and eclectic behaviors, now spread through p social strata. Japanese imitativeness, American ingenuity, and all became concepts known to, and influencing the attitudes or,   of millions of both end-consumers and organizational buyers. East L. ean products were shunned because of ideological differences and products from less-developed countries were shunned because they were perceived universally as poorly made, while those from industrialized countries were sought after in the prevailing spirit of internationalism. In the same spirit, national governments granted foreign products better entry terms by reducing tariffs dramatically in successive rounds of GATT negotiations.

4. 1970s-early 1980s. The protectionist sentiment that was engendered by the energy crises and global recession of this period led to three significant developments in the meaning and use of product-country image identifiers. First, national governments began to pay more attention to "rules of origin" legislation and to enforce it more carefully, as a means of protecting domestic producers. Second, both governments and producer groups became more proactive in domestic promotions of native industry. "Crafted With Pride in the U.S.A.," "Think Canadian," "Buy Greek–You Win," and "Support British Industry" are just a few examples of promotional campaigns first developed in this period for this purpose. And third, companies began to be more discriminating about the use of origin identifiers: these were emphasized for regions or countries with a reputation felt to possess certain unique characteristics (e.g., California wines, Florida orange juice, French perfume), or suppressed when producers felt that knowledge of the origin might provoke negative buyer reactions (e.g., the Japanese car manufacturers' expanded use of English-sounding names for new models).

5. 1980s and Beyond. With the end of the global recession, the resurgence of international trade, and the emergence of trade blocs, all of which have characterized the period since the early 1980s, it would be no exaggeration to say that practically everyone has "jumped into the fray" insofar as the origins of products are concerned. In addition to the ever-growing use of origin identifiers by companies in marketing their products, and by governments in protecting their manufacturers, at least three new developments are noteworthy:

   a. Governments are becoming more proactive and systematic in promoting their image *abroad*. Realization of the importance of international competitiveness has brought about a "grouping" of efforts by government agencies and industry associations, which now mount joint foreign promotion campaigns as a matter of course. Examples range from promotions at retail locations organized by embassies (e.g., "Italian Week at Bloomingdale's") to greater support for "national" appearances at industrial trade fairs (the international growth of public programs in support of exports is detailed in Seringhaus and Rosson 1991).
   b. Origins and their images have come under intense scrutiny in the context of trade blocs. Armies of international lawyers are present-

ly grappling with such issues as the value-added level at which a Toyota made in Britain becomes a "British" product, and so gains free access to the European Community (EC), or which goods are to be free-traded in the Canada-U.S. Free Trade Agreement (FTA), given that the latter (unlike the EC) does not involve a common external tariff.

c. The "globalization" of business has brought on intense debate about the merits and continuing relevance, or lack of same, of national origin identifiers. Some observers argue that origins are no longer relevant in global markets where "hybrid" products (i.e., those with components from several countries) are the norm. Others maintain that the reverse is true, since globalization will bring about specialization, and thus accentuate the strengths (real and perceived) of origin countries ("origin" defined as the country of manufacture, of design, of the producer's nationality, and so on).

PCI in Marketing Research

Academic research into the role of "country-of-origin" in international marketing has involved a multitude of researchers who have examined various facets of the PCI phenomenon, each adding to our knowledge bank about it. The relevant literature is discussed in several other chapters of this book, and so does not need to be reviewed here. Instead, this section outlines briefly the general direction taken by researchers in this area with the intent of outlining the history of PCI research, filling some gaps which are not covered elsewhere in the book, and serving as background for the discussion that follows.

The history of academic research on PCI can be traced mainly through four significant milestones marked by the work of a handful of researchers who have left an indelible mark in this field. In addition to those seminal works, certain other studies need to be mentioned separately as "firsts" in new and noteworthy research directions.[1,2] The four milestones are:

1. The First Study. The honor of the first-ever published piece of PCI research in the academic environment (1965) clearly belongs to Robert

---

1. Several of the researchers involved have carried out multiple studies. To avoid long "strings" of citations in the paragraphs that follow, no specific references are cited here (unless otherwise necessary) for those authors who are referenced extensively in the following chapters.

2. It is part and parcel of science that subsequent works improve upon the "firsts" in various ways. Inevitably, any nonexhaustive listing is bound to differ from what others might have constructed. The author apologizes in advance to those whose work may have been omitted inadvertently.

Schooler. Ernst Dichter is frequently cited by subsequent researchers, but his reference to the significance of the "made- in" information cue was made in passim (Dichter 1962). Two other studies (Opinion Research 1959; Reader's Digest 1963) also predate Schooler but were not carried out or published in the academic research context which is discussed here. By examining product stereotyping among consumers through empirical research, Schooler inaugurated a stream of studies that have resulted by now in well over 300 publications.

2. *The Semantic Differential.* Akira Nagashima popularized the use of semantic differential scales as a means of studying the origin images of products (Nagashima 1977). In one way or another, his approach was adopted and followed by the majority of subsequent researchers.

3. *The Literature Review.* By the early 1980s, there had been enough research in the area to warrant a literature review. This was done by Warren Bilkey and Erik Nes (1982), who, with their perceptive critique of earlier efforts and pointers for future researchers, turned PCI research from a fledgling to a growth industry.

4. *The Multivariate Studies.* Johny Johansson and his colleagues helped to move PCI research over the next hump–the shift from mostly descriptive to more elaborate studies, involving multivariate analyses of the attitudinal and belief structures that underlie consumers' use of origin information generally and about hybrid products.

The research that needs to be mentioned in addition to the above four milestones includes:

5. *The Interdisciplinary Perspective.* Charles Lillis and Chem Narayana (1974) were the first to cite Herbert Kelman (1965), and thus to make the much-needed lateral connection between country images as viewed in marketing and in such other fields as social psychology and political science– where much was already known about national stereotypes and the way people develop them and act upon them.

6. *The Longitudinal Perspective.* John Darling and his associates have carried out perhaps the best known research which tracks the evolution of country images through more than just two points in time, and which has made it possible to examine the relationship between images and international trade trends (e.g., see Darling and Wood 1990).

7. *Unravelling Country and Product Images.* C. Min Han and his colleagues helped to generate interest in the interface between country and product images, and also to further our understanding of their correlates in a number of areas (e.g., the influence of consumer patriotism) through a series of advanced studies. Among other contributions, Han (1989) has

posited that the country/product image interface may work in either or both of two directions: as a "halo construct" (country image used to evaluate products about which people know little) or as a "summary construct" (knowledge about a country's products abstracted into the image of the country itself).

8. *Methodological and Related Perspectives*. While adding insights to various specific aspects of the PCI phenomenon, various studies have also addressed some of the research problems that were identified in the review by Bilkey and Nes and elsewhere. One noteworthy example is the team of Louise Heslop, John Liefeld, and Marjorie Wall, who carried out several large-scale studies with representative consumer samples, often using tangible cues in multi-cue experimental settings to elicit responses about the relative importance of the origin cue, the way consumers process information, variations in country images across market segments, and other issues. Further, an eight-country consumer study by this author, Louise Heslop, Gary Bamossy, and our associates addressed questions related to the cross-national validity of commonly used research instruments and examined correlates of PCIs and consumer response patterns across several cultures. Lastly, the following significant "first" contributions must also be mentioned: Anderson and Cunningham, 1972 (role of PCI in promotion); Hampton, 1982 (PCI related to investment rather than product flows); Wang and Lamb, 1980 (country variables affecting PCI perceptions; see Wang and Lamb 1983); and Shimp and Sharma, 1987 (development of the Consumer Ethnocentrism Scale–CETSCALE).

This historical overview, coupled with the issue-oriented reviews in the first four chapters of this book, shows that PCI research has made significant strides in the past 25 years. In addition to the growing number of researchers and studies in this field, a noteworthy development is the growth of research *networks* whose size and multifaceted projects are not often encountered in other parts of international marketing research.[3] Together with growing interest in origin-related issues on the part of practitioners, growth on the academic side has turned PCI into a field that is rich with practical and theoretical insights, implications, complexity, and challenges.

At the same time, the field is also rife with debate and misunderstandings. Before turning to an examination of the strategic and research implications of product-country images, it is useful to examine the main areas of contention.

---

3. The size, composition, and studies of these networks can be examined by perusing the references lists of the chapters that follow, noting, in particular, those of the researchers mentioned in the historical analysis.

SOME CONTENTIOUS ISSUES
IN PCI PRACTICE AND RESEARCH

From "Made-in 'Labels'" to "Product and Country Images"

Proving the power of images in human perceptions, much of the debate about the relevance of product and country images stems from misunderstandings concerning what the phrase "Made-in *'label'* " means. This is often used as a short-form reference to the PCI phenomenon. As an unfortunate by-product of offering convenience in communication, its legacy is an unduly narrow view of the broader issue of origin images. To many people in both the corporate and academic environments, the term evokes such images as cloth tags affixed inconspicuously on garments or origin declarations in unreadably small print on the bottom of perfume bottles or cereal boxes. The argument is that labels more often than not go unnoticed, and therefore origins are not important.

However, whether or not buyers notice made-in *labels* as such is beside the point. Consumers will *not* notice the product's brand name, price, and other characteristics either–and even the product itself!–if the producer fails to make them visible or tries hard enough to hide them. There is no *intrinsic* reason to expect that consumers will notice a hidden origin designation any more than they would notice the brand name of bananas.

Yet in many cases consumers do notice both of these and other information cues. The key question is whether the producer *elects to emphasize* a particular cue beyond the point necessary by legal requirements. For example, the reference to the "brand name of bananas" in the previous paragraph was, of course, deliberate: *Chiquita* bananas specifically are well known because the company invests in the brand name. In this light, it is more relevant to frame the PCI question in the context of *what* origin information is available to consumers, rather than debating whether *labels* as such are noticed. While basic, this issue has not yet been addressed systematically in published PCI works.

Origin cues are available to consumers and other publics in a far broader set of circumstances than is usually realized or acknowledged. Some of the main manifestations of the origin cue can be categorized as follows:

1. Embedded directly into the brand name: e.g., Alitalia airline, Canavac home cleaning systems (Canada), France-Soir newspaper, Nippon Electric appliances (Japan).

2. *Indicated indirectly through the brand name:* e.g., Lamborghini is Italian and Toyota is Japanese, although neither brand contains the respective country's name.

3. *Indicated directly or indirectly in the producer's company name:* e.g., Nippon Steel and Sumitomo, respectively.

4. *Promoted expressly as a significant part of, or as "the," brand's unique selling proposition.* There are thousands of examples of this practice. For this discussion, the following can demonstrate the range of potential applications:

- *Direct use of country image:* Recent advertisements by Eugene de Paris, the French cosmetics manufacturer, portray an image that can be described best as "seductive elegance" under the headline: "So French. So Rare."

- *Adapting country image to company image:* IKEA couples a cartoon drawing of an animal that symbolizes Scandinavia (moose) with the slogan "The Impossible Store from Sweden," to build a playful aura around a known and respected origin image for furniture.

- *Lateral transfer of image to an unrelated product:* Lowenbraü beer uses a positive stereotype in its advertising in Canada ("Lowenbraü: Tastefully Engineered in Germany").

- *Playing on a reverse-negative stereotype:* In its British advertising, Lowenbraü portrays a German in lederhosen with the slogan: "Thankfully they sent us their lager, not their shorts."

- *Industrial marketing:* The bank Credit Suisse advertises in the U.S. with the headline "Incredibly Swiss, Incredibly American" accompanied by photographs of a Saint Bernard dog and an American Eagle, respectively.

5. *Included as the centerpiece or a part of package design:* a nation's flag, flag colors, or some other internationally recognized symbol, printed on or forming the packaging (e.g., the packaging of Moulinex small appliances have the bleu-blanc-rouge colors of the French flag).

6. *Used in connection with a company's sales force or other service people:* e.g., building on the favorable image of the U.S. among Japanese consumers, Domino's Pizza delivery personnel in Japan wear "American flag" uniforms–red, white, and blue (Naisbitt and Aburdene 1990, p. 124).

7. *Associated, directly or indirectly, with well-known representative symbols of the origin country.* This can be done in connection with any of the preceding applications (e.g., advertising, brand and corporate logos, etc.); associations can be linguistic, visual, and/or aural, and often include:

- the national flag; animals (American eagle, Australian koala, Chinese panda bear, Canadian beaver); landmarks (Eiffel Tower, Sydney Opera, the Statue of Liberty, the leaning tower of Pisa); stereotyped images of ordinary people (e.g., British-accented models promoting tea); personalities (e.g., Paul Hogan with Australia's Foster Beer, following the success of Crocodile Dundee); music (Italian arias, Spanish flamenco guitars); geographic characteristics (e.g., the Rocky Mountains in earlier promotions of Coors beer, or beaches lined with palm trees in Club Med promotions of equatorial tourism destinations); etc.

Lastly, origin information can be:

8. Written, of course, on the made-in label.

The preceding examples were limited intentionally to *country* cues provided by *suppliers.* Among the many additional cases that might be mentioned, origin information often is:

9. Related to regions, rather than countries (Eurocar rental agency), and sometimes is used as a key *descriptor* for a product category (e.g., Scotch whisky, British ale, California wines, Bohemian crystal); and,
10. Provided by third parties, such as educators (recall the geo-economic maps in grade school, which teach students at an early age the "main products" of each country), the media, cultural products (e.g., portrayal of national stereotypes in films and books), friends and associates, etc.

This list is partial but enough to make the point: product origin information is provided to consumers through hundreds of thousands of brand and company names, promotional messages, product labels, and other means, whether directly or through symbolism. In short, the images of countries and their relationships with products are an integral part of daily life.

Importance of PCI to Practitioners, Researchers, and Buyers

The question of the importance of PCIs in international marketing presents a paradox. On the one hand, thousands of practitioners employ origin images to promote their products, hundreds of researchers study them, and millions of end-consumers and industrial buyers use them to understand and make evaluations of products. Coupled with the findings of systematic research, this proves beyond a shadow of a doubt that PCIs are considered important by all concerned. On the other hand, few are willing to explicitly "admit" this importance.

In his chapter, Johansson provides a number of strong explanations for this paradox. These range from the lack of communication between practitioners and researchers to the unwillingness of buyers to admit, when asked directly in research, that their purchase decisions are influenced by what they consider as a "nonrational" criterion.

In the context of the present discussion, it should be added that many practitioners and researchers have difficulty recognizing the role of the PCI phenomenon simply because they continue to think of it in the context of made-in *labels*. This is the typical problem of one who sees all problems as nails and therefore uses only a hammer to solve them. The reason why PCI was seen as a "nail" (label) can be found in the preceding historical overview: in both practice and research, origin images were initially thought of as an isolated aspect of international marketing arising from rules-of-origin legislation, and therefore best dealt with as a legal matter (hammer). It is only recently that the broader issue of PCIs has begun to ' fused with general questions of international strategy on the practica¹ and with image and consumer behavior research on the academic ῾ will be noted later in this chapter, the principal implication of tʰ῾ is that we have barely begun to scratch the surface of the PC῾

PCI in the Era of Global Markets

Debate also exists as to whether or not the importance of origin images in buyer behavior will diminish as markets become more globalized. The available evidence suggests that, if anything, the higher the level of globalization, the greater the significance of PCI. The issue can be considered from various different viewpoints:

1. PCI in positioning strategy. Sellers are likely to use country image identifiers ever more intensively as competition increases and the standardization of production blunts product-based competitive advantages, making the definition of unique market positions more difficult. The growing presence of national governments and trade associations as competitive entities in the international arena (see periods *4.* and *5.* in the preceding historical overview) will also intensify the use of PCI information, since governments by definition will continue to use "country" image in promoting their producers.

2. Global branding. The emergence of global brands does nothing but accentuate even further the use of origin images in the marketplace. To begin with, past experience has shown that in many cases "global" brands have difficulty shedding their national images. For example, IBM (*International* Business Machines), TWA (Trans-*World* Airlines), and Coca-Cola are clearly viewed as "American," notwithstanding the fact that none promote their national affiliation.

More significantly, true "global" branding is by definition "origin" branding. This is the case, for example, with cars which are *explicitly promoted as "world brands"* (Ford's Fiesta, or the North American automakers' "Geo" and "Passport" divisions), or with "The United Colors of Benetton." In such cases, the intent clearly is to evoke a "world origin" image as distinct from a national one–but an origin image nonetheless.

3. Hybrid products. The growth in offshore production and the presence of hybrid products presents producers with even greater opportunities to be selective as to the "origin" they designate in promotional campaigns. Note that this refers to the origin identifier in *elective* parts of the marketing mix (e.g., branding and promotion) as opposed to *legally-mandated* labeling. For example, IKEA positions its products by reference to Swedish design and not to the fact that the majority are manufactured by subcontractors in many different countries. Similarly, Volkswagen uses the term German-engineered (rather than "produced") to describe its cars in advertising. Not surprisingly, in a survey of a random sample of 2,000 consumers by the "Made in the USA Foundation," a nonprofit trade organization, more than two-thirds of respondents said they believed the Volkswagen Fox is made in Germany (it is made in Brazil, a fact which was known to only 8 percent of the respondents; Ratliff 1989).

4. Regional origin identifiers. The relative decline in the importance of the nation-state as an institution also provides new opportunities which producers have been quick to capitalize upon through origin-based branding and promotion. This decline results from pressures both from above, in the form of trade blocs, and from below, from subnational ethnic, cultural, and regional groups (see Papadopoulos 1991; also Naisbitt and Aburdene 1990, p. 146). For example, in view of "Project 1992," Europe is being flooded with products branded with one or another variant of the term "Euro," labeled as "Made in the EC," and advertised with EC-related themes (e.g., new advertisements for a Mercedes-Benz truck feature the 12-star European Community flag prominently on the side of the vehicle's cargo compartment, in support of a claim of the company's pan-European base of expertise). At the other end of the scale, in earlier times regional identifiers were used only for a limited range of exclusive products (e.g., Bordeaux wines). Today, the resurgence of regional identity, coupled with competitive pressures, leads increasing numbers of producers of a broader spectrum of products to group together at the subnational level to promote common origin-based characteristics (e.g., Florida's orange and grapefruit growers, California wines and raisins, and "Silicon Valley technology"). It should be noted that it is for these reasons that the term "origin" rather than "country" is used in most of this discussion, since any "place" in addition to nations can be used in relation to a product's image.

5. *"Borrowed" origins.* The realization of the usefulness of origin images by decision makers has led to yet another way in which origin identifiers are used increasingly in today's "global" markets: the "unauthorized borrowing" of strong origin images to enhance or distinguish the image of brands which have little or no relation with the origin in real terms. While this practice could be encountered before (e.g., Buick "Le-Mans"), it occurs much more frequently today and is likely to grow in the future. Perhaps the most prominent recent example is the use of the British flag as a "symbol of distinction" by Reebok, the U.S. athletic shoe manufacturer (this particular case was contested in the courts by the British government). Similar examples include Alpenweiss and Lac des Roches wines (produced in Canada and Greece, respectively), Australian Hair Recipe shampoo and conditioner (U.S.), Infiniti cars (Nissan), etc.

To the extent that imitation is the sincerest form of flattery, this ought to please the original "owners" of the respective distinctive images–as well as those researchers who have spent a good part of their careers trying to prove that origin matters! The growth of this practice during the 1980s suggests a profound change to a fundamental tenet of traditional theories of comparative advantage: the image of origins has been disengaged from the origins themselves. Traditionally, each country "owned" the image of its comparative advantage–whether the advantage lay in its resources, the skills of its labor force, or the specialization of its capital. This simply is no longer the case. Manufacturers essentially give their products any origin image they choose, depending on their assessment of the relevant competitive environment and without regard to their real place of production.

Note that whether the borrowed image is presented by the producer as "real," and/or believed by the consumer to be "real," is beside the point of this discussion. For instance, some consumers may indeed believe that Reebok athletic shoes are of British origin, while others may know that the British flag on them is used only to add British flair. Which of the two situations (real origin vs. image enhancer) will be presented and perceived depends on such factors as the manufacturer's intent, the consumer's awareness level, and the ethical and legal aspects of the situation. Either way, in strategic terms "borrowed" images mean that manufacturers have greater choice and also that they recognize the significance of PCI–while national governments and their producers are faced with a new significant challenge in protecting their "trademark."

6. *Consumers' use of PCI in global markets.* It is clear from the preceding discussion that use of PCI by producers is likely to grow with time. What does this mean for consumers? In brief, the more producers use PCI, the more consumers will, too, at least for as long as it is seen as useful information and always subject to the meaning of "PCI" in the context of marketplace realities. For example, if multinational production diffuses the meaning of PCI in the sense of "country of manufacture," producers and/or consumers may begin placing more emphasis on "country of design," "manufacturer's home country," and so on. Either way, considering the preceding discussion about the availability of origin information, it is reasonable to assume that consumers of brands whose producers emphasize origin will be more highly sensitized to it than others. For example, origin information is more likely to be noted and used in the case of Chevrolet ("The Heartbeat of America") and Volkswagen's Jetta ("German-engineered road sedan"), than of Ford ("Quality is Job 1").

Consumers will use origin information more for three additional reasons. First, because increased exposure to foreign countries and their products through the media, the growing presence of foreign products in the market, and other sources brings about greater awareness of, familiarity with, and acceptance of these products. Second, by launching "buy domestic" campaigns, national governments and trade associations essentially accentuate the importance of origins and highlight the differences among them. And third, as the market and products become more complex, consumers increasingly seek means of simplifying information processing through "chunking"–and origin is ideally suited to this purpose, since it can be used as a surrogate indicator of product quality and status acceptability (Papadopoulos, Heslop, and Bamossy 1990).

Methodological Issues

Before concluding the discussion on current issues in PCI, some areas must be mentioned where researchers have not yet reached agreement, largely because the methodological approaches used result in different interpretations of aspects of the PCI phenomenon. Most of these areas are discussed in the chapters that follow. Therefore, the purpose of this section is to identify some of the more contentious issues and outline the relevant questions, instead of discussing them in detail. Further, the thrust of this outline is to recognize the value of approaches on either side of the various points of contention rather than to identify weaknesses in any one of them.

"Global" vs. "Product-Specific" Evaluations

Some of the research to date has obtained "global" product evaluations (i.e., has asked respondents to rate "products from country X" generally; see, for example, Nagashima 1977), while some has focused on specific product categories (e.g., Kaynak and Cavusgil 1983). The merits of either approach have been argued endlessly in the literature. Proponents of the product-specific stream argue that images vary across product categories, and therefore global evaluations are irrelevant (e.g., the fact that Japan makes good cars does not mean it can produce good wine). The reverse argument is that category-specific origin images cannot be generalized to the overall image of an origin country, and that, conversely, if the product-specific argument is carried to its logical conclusion, then the images of categories are also irrelevant in relation to specific brands.

The argument can be resolved by reference to what and how *consumers* think about it all. Research proves beyond doubt that consumers hold distinct origin images of brands, companies, product categories, and countries. Subaru XT DL Coupe is different from Toyota Camry, Subaru from Toyota, Japanese cars from Japanese wines, and Japan from Australia. The origin images of brands, companies, product categories, and all products from a given country represent various levels of abstraction. It is obvious from past research that consumers have no difficulty attaching country images to any level.

The halo/summary construct distinction posited by Han (1989) points to how these levels of image may be interrelated. Essentially, any higher-level (general) image may function as a halo for understanding objects at a lower hierarchical level, and any lower-level (specific) image may help to create a summary view of the next-up level of abstraction. For example, German cars helped to build the image of German engineering (a summary construct), and German engineering helps to enhance the image of such an unrelated product as Lowenbraü beer ("Tastefully engineered in Germany"–a halo construct).

That images may be transposed laterally in this way is supported by those studies which have examined global, product class, and product item images simultaneously (e.g., Reierson 1966; Cattin and Jolibert 1979). The image of Japanese wines certainly is different from that of Japanese cars–but the fact that Japan builds cars well means that, ceteris paribus, consumers *may also give its wines the benefit of the doubt*. Thinking of the acceptance of successive waves of often unrelated Japanese products over time (from traditional silk flowers to trinkets to cars to consumer electronics, and more recently to semiconductors, banking, shipbuilding, and fashion) makes the point that the cars-to-wine parallel is not unrealistic at all. (Whether the Japanese are interested in wine exports is, of course, another matter.) Thus, it is clear that both global and product-specific research is useful and provides important, albeit different, insights into the PCI phenomenon.

Relative Importance of the Origin Cue

Bilkey and Nes (1982) made the point that most of the studies to that time were "single-cue" (i.e., they presented respondents with various country names and asked them to evaluate their products), and that this leads to overestimation of the origin effects on buying behavior. While several studies since then have been multi-cue (i.e., origin evaluated in the context of several characteristics, such as price and brand), many continue to use origin as the only cue presented to consumers.

There is no question that any study which attempts to measure the effect of *any one* cue, independently of others, on buyers' ultimate purchase choices, will overestimate its importance. This will be true regardless of whether the single cue presented is origin, brand, price, or any other extrinsic or intrinsic product characteristic. However, whether a single- or multi-cue approach is indicated must be considered in the context of the study's *objectives*. For example, researchers interested in identifying *inputs to* origin images (e.g., Wang and Lamb 1983), or in *comparing the images of various nations* (e.g., Darling and Wood 1990), are likely to use single-cue designs. By contrast, those interested in identifying origin image *outputs* (e.g., purchase choices), or in how consumers *process* "origin" in relation to other cues, will opt for multi-cue studies. As a result, both approaches can be useful, albeit each for different purposes.

Origin Image "Effects"

Lastly, a question related to relative importance is the *type* of origin effects that researchers are, or should be, interested in. Should our interest be only in ultimate purchase choices? Or are other aspects of consumer behavior also important?

In the broad sense, the image of an origin may lead to a range of reactions, from simple awareness to attitude formation to "intention to buy." Knowing that German-made Mercedes cars are of exceptional quality does not of course mean that all consumers will rush to buy them. On the other hand, the fact that purchase will not occur certainly should *not* mean that what non-buyers *know* and *think* of Mercedes/German quality is irrelevant. As noted, Lowenbräu apparently believes that consumer views of German engineering are relevant enough to its case and uses it to promote beer (the company surely does not assume that all its customers own German cars).

Further, the origin cue may impact the behavior of the consumer who holds the image or of others, and the effect may be direct or indirect, immediate or latent, and so on. A consumer may assess a stimulus by word of mouth (e.g., learning from a friend that jeans from X are inexpensive but poorly made) or based on direct personal experience (e.g., an inexpensive pair of jeans from country X, assessed as poorly-made during trial or after purchase). Either may lead to the belief that "jeans from X are of poor quality–no wonder they're so cheap." This same thought, mentioned to a friend of lesser means, in fact may unwittingly create a potential buyer of X's products. Concerning latent effects, a teacher showing a film to pupils about the famine in Ethiopia may help to create a generation of future consumers who will shun Ethiopian products ("How can such a poor and uneducated people produce good products?").

In the context of PCI, therefore, as in other contexts, any aspect of consumer behavior can be relevant in the marketplace and so should be of interest to both researchers and practitioners. The attitudes of an individual may not lead him or her to a particular course of action today–but may influence his or her behavior in general, or that of another individual, immediately or later. As with the previous parts of this section, this discussion leads to the inevitable conclusion that research into any aspect of the PCI phenomenon can be useful–and that the potential effects of origin images are many, varied, and complex. Against this background, the next section discusses PCI implications for strategy and research.

STRATEGIC AND RESEARCH IMPLICATIONS OF PCI

In a typical "Cathy" cartoon, Cathy complains that "it takes a man to inspire an international debt" by comparing her down-to-earth necessities ("a sweat suit," "fast food and diet soda," and "watching sitcoms") to a long litany of "origin"-brand products she must buy for her boyfriend (cited, among others, are New Zealand blue cod, Armenian cracker bread, Belgian chocolates, Beaujolais Nouveau, a Shiatsu massage video, Portuguese cutwork linens, Casablanca lilies from Holland, subscribing to the Brazilian Performing Arts series, and "a Tibetan cashmere sweater to frame a makeup system from Switzerland").

The range of products mentioned, the very fact that this cartoon was created and published, and the distinction between economy-minded Cathy (at least in this sequence!) and her label-minded boyfriend, all combine to portray what the PCI phenomenon is all about: a pervasive influence, of more interest to some than to others, growing in importance as consumers become more discriminating, based on long-standing and deeply-held beliefs about the images of countries and places in general.

Indeed, in the continuation of the passage that was used to open this chapter, the characters in Umberto Eco's novel conclude that unlike a computer, which ". . . can perform on himself precise local suicides, temporai ⁄ amnesias, painless aphasias . . . ," humans cannot forget the images they hold:

> . . . we couldn't come up with rules for forgetting. It's impossible . . . we are at the mercy of random natural processes, like stroke and amnesia, and such self-interventions as drugs, alcohol, or suicide. (1989:23)

The images of countries which we learn starting from the formative years and throughout life, whether through education, friends, products, and/or other experiences, influence the way we think and act. In the marketing context, learning about these images through research and accounting for them in strategy have become urgent necessities.

Earlier research has provided numerous insights in this area, and the chapters in this book will help to bring about another leap forward in this field of endeavor. The purpose of this section is to highlight the main implications of the PCI phenomenon for strategy and research, and point to the potential directions in which these implications may lead us.

Strategic Implications

At the most basic level, PCI is a matter of international marketing strategy. The challenge facing marketers is to ascertain the images foreign consumers hold about them and their origin countries, and, armed with this knowledge, decide whether any relevant action is indicated. Such action may be steps to suppress the origin image, to simply present it, to enhance it, or to aggressively promote it.

In essence, each of the issues that were touched upon in the previous two sections represents an aspect of PCI that marketing practitioners need to grapple with. Perhaps the best way of summarizing these issues is to view them from the perspective of the following nine main dimensions.

1. Exporters vs. Importers

Origin images are of the most immediate interest in the case of products which are marketed in a country other than the one in which they are produced. Exporters face established country images regardless of whether or not they have taken an active part in creating them. These images can act as significant barriers to or facilitators of entry into foreign markets. For example, many consumers would have less difficulty choosing a low-risk product (e.g., T-shirt) than a high-risk one (e.g., camera, pharmaceutical) from a less developed country. In deciding what market penetration strategies to use, exporters need to know what images consumers hold about the origin country, what the components of these images are, and how they compare to the images of competing producers.

Importers face similar challenges, but in many cases they have a greater amount of latitude since they can be selective as to the suppliers with whom they choose to do business. Where variants of the same product can be procured from different countries, assessing the images of these countries can serve as a significant input to sourcing decisions and determining appropriate tradeoffs among intrinsic features, price, brand name, origin, and so on.

2. Foreign vs. Domestic Producers

The conflicting interests of foreign and domestic producers have been detailed repeatedly in the literature and do not need elaboration here. Essentially, the former's gains are the latter's losses, and vice versa. Foreign producers whose origin countries enjoy a favorable image may have an advantage over domestic manufacturers, especially because in many cases the latter traditionally have been uninterested in developing and promoting an "origin" image within their home country.

Past research and recent developments lead to two basic conclusions concerning the foreign/domestic dimension. First, domestic producers cannot expect to enjoy a de facto preference on the part of consumers simply because of patriotism and nationalism (Han 1988; Papadopoulos, Heslop, and Bamossy 1990). Second, the increasing use of origin identifiers is likely to bring about some form of backlash against foreign suppliers, at least on the part of governments, domestic producers, and their associations who have only recently begun to appreciate the significance of "origin" in promotion (as opposed to, simply, on legally-mandated labels). For example, the Made in the USA Foundation is lobbying "to have legislation passed by Congress to require *disclosure* in car *advertis-*

ing of the *countries in which cars are built"* (Ratliff 1989; emphasis added). The intent is to guard against "borrowed" or "hybrid" origin images. These and other matters related to protectionism need to be addressed by both foreign and domestic suppliers, whether through lobbying, marketing strategies, or other means.

3. Developed vs. Developing Country Producers

There is enough research evidence to demonstrate that whether a supplier's origin is a "First," "Second," or "Third" World country makes a difference in how it is perceived. Producers from each of these types of origins face different strategic problems. For example:

Developed Nations (First World). While presently holding an enviable position, manufacturers from developed countries face ever-growing challenges to their dominance in markets and customers' minds. There is no reason to believe that the examples of Japan, South Korea, and Taiwan will not soon be followed by countries ranging from Brazil to Malaysia as the latter develop their ability to compete in global markets. The main issue facing developed nation producers is building on their competitive advantages to protect and enhance their existing strong origin images.

Eastern ex-Socialist Nations (Second World). The collapse of East European communist regimes at the end of the previous decade is rapidly changing the way these countries are viewed. On the one hand, these are fairly advanced countries which can be significant competitors to producers from other developed and developing nations. On the other, as has been noted throughout this chapter, old images die hard. The perceptual barrier of ideology may not exist any more among Western consumers on the surface, but what may have replaced the old images is unclear. If anything, media portrayals of ex-socialist economies in ruin may be helping to create "less developed" national stereotypes for these countries. Their producers and governments need to assess the recently-revised images consumers hold about them, and to take any necessary steps to correct them.

Less Developed and Developing Nations (Third World). Japan, South Korea, Taiwan, and a handful of other countries have shown one way to success in enhancing the origin images of their products: penetration-priced, medium-quality, low value-added products, gradually moving towards high-quality and higher-priced products involving greater (and ever-increasing) degrees of technological sophistication. Whether this model can or should be followed by other nations requires careful analysis of the subject country's existing image, its indigenous strengths, the type of image it wishes to attain, and the strategies needed to attain it.

4. Exporting vs. Local Production

Shifts in the location of production, which, more often than not, used to occur from high-cost to low-cost labor countries, often necessitate changes in the origin identifiers used. Whether the net effect of such moves will be positive or negative depends on balancing the savings realized from lower-cost labor against the potential need to discount the product's price because of the shift. Earlier studies and two chapters in this book (Nebenzahl and Jaffe, and Stewart and Chan) address this issue in detail and suggest that substantial discounting may be required in such cases. Either way, what is important is the need to realize that the effect of origin on brand value must be taken into account in making such decisions.

Conversely, companies shifting their production to where the markets are often do so to soothe nationalist feelings in host countries and prevent protectionism and trade barriers. In doing so, many companies simply move their production facilities and do little else to assuage fears of foreign domination. By contrast, in 1988 Mitsubishi Electric undertook an advertising campaign through business magazines to portray a positive image as a "competitor done good." The top two-thirds of the page in the advertisement were left blank, except for a tiny "Made in Japan" plate appearing in the middle. The bottom third started with the large-typeface headline "And California. And North Carolina. And Georgia. And Ohio." and went on to explain that, rather than being threatening, Mitsubishi in fact "employs 3,000 Americans," sources materials and parts locally, and so on.

This campaign is a typical example of how the origin identification and its benefits can be retained (the "Made in Japan" label) while also taking a proactive role in portraying a locally responsible image. Other producers in similar situations may do well to consider similar actions, rather than limiting their "good behavior" to unannounced transfers of machinery.

5. Owners vs. Part-Owners vs. Borrowers of PCI

The image of a country may be used by its "legitimate" owners, whose products are produced fully in it; by part-owners, whose hybrid products may use some components from the country; or by "borrowers," who have no direct connection with it. A typical example is the recognized strength of Italian design in cars. Ferrari is an owner; Volvo's Bertone

Coupe model is a part-owner (built by Volvo but designed by Italy's Bertone studios); and Nissan's Infiniti is a borrower. In the past, origin-based brand names and advertising themes were selected almost habitually to reflect real origins (e.g., the original entrepreneur's name, such as Buick or Honda, which by definition sounded "domestic," or symbols such as the North American Indian name "Pontiac"). The growing practice of "borrowed" origin identifiers has catapulted the PCI phenomenon square-ly into the midst of questions about branding, advertising, packaging, and other marketing strategies. Owners, part-owners, and borrowers need to rethink these strategies in terms of the potential opportunities (broader choice range) and threats ("stealing" of comparative advantage by com-petitors) which this phenomenon represents.

6. Uninterested vs. Disinterested vs. Interested Targets

In a general sense, origins are of interest to all buyers. However, some believe that origins are not important, others may use the information if it were readily available, and still others seek it deliberately and take it into account in purchase decisions. The challenge confronting marketers in this area is not much unlike the situation with branding: some buyers will purchase nothing but Crest, and others will purchase any toothpaste with fluoride, any brand carried by their favorite supermarket, or any brand that happens to be on sale. Similarly, some consumers will buy nothing but Dutch Gouda while others do not care where the cheese is made as long as it is cheap or tastes good.

While academic researchers have made some significant strides in de-lineating consumer characteristics in relation to origin images, marketing decision makers often have seen PCI as "just another theme" which can be tagged on to an advertisement or used in branding, and which does not warrant a separate research effort. Clearly, the strength of the images which origins evoke, and the consumers' various potential reactions to them, suggest the need for image research before undertaking origin-re-lated strategies.

7. Private vs. Public Sector Marketing

To the extent that governments and trade organizations are interested in the welfare of their producers and members, most of the implications discussed thus far are also relevant to public organizations of various kinds. Three additional implications need to be mentioned separately here:

a. Need to develop national image. As noted, many governments already are taking steps to promote the collective image of their manufacturers abroad. However, few have well-coordinated strategies such as those that can be found in Italy, France, or Japan. Essentially, nations need to evolve an understanding of themselves as "corporate entities" in order to compete effectively in the international arena (the chapters by Graby and Morello discuss some of the relevant issues).

b. Summary vs. halo constructs. The attitude of most governments toward whether or not domestic manufacturers use country identifiers in international strategies is indifferent: the nation has an image, and its use is up to the producers. This view, however, is based on the implicit assumption of the "halo construct" (national image is transposed to products) and does not account for the possibility that the "summary construct" hypothesis may be more relevant in some cases. The latter states that a positive image of the country may evolve from the image of products with which consumers are familiar, and that this image may in turn facilitate the export expansion of other domestic producers. This, of course, presupposes that the "products with which consumers are familiar" carry a recognizable national image. If they do not, as is frequently the case, the potential advantage is lost. Yet few nations take active steps to encourage their manufacturers to identify themselves with their origin. With due attention to considerations of government interference in the private sector, it is possible that incentive and other programs (e.g., greater support for trade fair participation to companies "waving the flag") might help to change this in cases where it is felt that such action could help.

c. "Borrowed" PCIs. The increasing use of borrowed origin images can have negative implications for the unwitting "lender" (who loses control over its national image), and, should governments act upon this, also for the "borrower" (whose unauthorized use of foreign images may be restricted). The British government had not, as of this writing, won its case against Reebok, but earlier experiences in this issue suggest that some legal protection of place images may be possible (e.g., France's Champagne and Cognac). The issue can have such far-reaching implications that both governments and companies are likely to begin addressing it soon.

8. *"Country" vs. "Place" Images*

As noted previously, origin identifiers need not be restricted to country images. London Fog, Paris-Match, Cretan Wines, California Raisins, and the "I Love N.Y." slogan all point to a broad range of opportunities for using origin identifiers related to cities, locales, regions, areas, states, provinces, continents, trade blocs, and so on, in international marketing strategy. While other place origins have not been used as extensively as countries to date, this may change as competition intensifies and companies look for new ways to position their products internationally.

9. Product vs. "Product" Images

The majority of the preceding discussion has referred to products largely in the traditional sense of goods and services that are for sale. Yet, as pointed out in the introduction of this chapter, a number of other entities can be seen as "products" that carry origin images, which, in turn, may influence the way they are perceived. For example:

a. The producers of goods and services are themselves "products." The origin image may influence perceptions of the supplier's reliability as much as it influences perceptions of the product's quality.

b. Buyers also are "products." As reported in earlier research, sellers may avoid doing business with certain buyers because of perceptions concerning the latter's country image. For instance, an exporter may not sell to a distributor in a country for which the exporter has a negative stereotype (e.g., "they're unreliable in payments").

c. Countries are investment "products" from the perspective of foreign investors. Where a company will invest depends very much on the images held by its decision makers about various alternative locations (see chapter by Wee, Lim, and Tan; also Vogel 1976, and Johansson and Moinpour 1977). The point has not been lost to the governments of many U.S. states, which frequently promote themselves in *Fortune* and other business magazines as attractive investment locations. One such advertisement portrays the torso of a man who pulls his business suit and shirt open to reveal a T-shirt inscribed with the words "MADE IN MISSOURI." The body copy is devoted to answering the following question, which is posed in the ad's headline: "Why do 106 Fortune 500 Companies Have It Made in Missouri?").

d. Countries are tourism "products" from the perspective of foreign and domestic travellers. Like investors, tourists choose destinations as much (if not more) on image as on "hard" information.

e. Lastly, *groups* of countries also can be seen as "products" in the international arena. For instance, the European Community and its members have benefited enormously from the positive publicity surrounding Project 1992. At the same time, images of a potential "Fortress Europe" have had an effect on, among other things, the policies which non-European governments evolved for dealing with the Community at various international negotiating fora (e.g., the 1990 GATT dispute). As with any image, the "Fortress" conception is part truth and part stereotype based on incomplete observations.

Most of the PCI implications outlined by the preceding nine dimensions are relevant to cases such as these and many more like them. In brief, the need to research origin images among target markets, and to incorporate the findings in the development of international marketing strategies, exists whether one thinks of products and services, companies, product categories, and industrial sectors, or subnational, national, or supranational governments.

Research Implications

Bilkey and Nes (1982) must feel gratified by the extent to which researchers took their advice and worked to minimize the weaknesses and enhance the strengths of research in product and country images. Generally, research in this area has made significant advances and is now well established.

The chapters in this book represent these advances, and many go well beyond the state-of-the-art by addressing questions that have not been discussed before in the PCI field–such as the images of countries as corporate entities (Graby, Morello), the management-research dichotomy (Johansson), meta-analysis of past research (Liefeld), countries as investment "products" (Wee, Lim, and Tan), the impact of culture realm on image perceptions (Crawford and Lumpkin), and PCIs in relation to events (Brunner, Flaschner, and Xiaogang Lou; Jaffe and Nebenzahl; Heslop and Wall).

This and the other chapters of this book point to several additional areas where future research can be useful. For example, each of the implications for practitioners in the previous section represents an area of opportunity for new theoretical or applied research. Of the various areas identified throughout this chapter, four need to be singled out and discussed separately. As with the applied implications, these will be presented in the form of dichotomies.

1. "Labels" vs. "PCIs"

Perhaps the single most important limiting factor in PCI research to date has been the narrow focus on "labels" as encapsulating the concept of country images. This view brings to mind one of the tales of Nashrudin, Syria's popular layman hero. He was found by a friend, at night, kneeling on the sidewalk under a streetlamp and looking for something. "What are you looking for?" the friend asked. "My keys," Nashrudin replied. The friend kneeled down to help find the keys. After a few more minutes of a fruitless search, he asked again: "Are you sure you lost them here?" "No," said Nashrudin, "I lost them inside the house." "Then why are you looking for them out here?" asked the perplexed friend. "There's more light under the streetlamp," Nashrudin naturally replied.

For a good part of the past 25 years we have been looking at PCI where there was more light–at the little "Made-in" label which started it all. Needless to say, this does not mean that researchers and practitioners are unaware of other manifestations of origin image identifiers. What it does mean is that the prevailing frame of reference in research has been the label and not other aspects of origin images, wherever and however they might be observed. As a result, with few exceptions (e.g., Dunn 1976; Head 1987), which have dealt with origin image advertising and related themes, the majority of past research is either mute on this question or deals explicitly with labels.

One practical implication of this, for example, is that in research design we have often deliberately *avoided* studying the views of consumers who may have been exposed to strong PCI messages (e.g., in experimental studies). Yet consumers, as pointed out earlier, by definition will have less interest in origin images in cases where the producers concerned have not promoted them. Another implication is that we have yet to develop a complete inventory of the conditions, ways, frequency, and so on, where origin image identifiers appear. As a result, we do not yet have systematic knowledge of the various shapes and forms that PCIs take. Clearly, new research that focuses explicitly on origin aspects other than the made-in label will be very useful and is sorely needed.

2. Products vs. "Products" and Country vs. "Place" Images

The vast majority of marketing research on PCIs has dealt with the origin images of *products*. In many ways, both this and the "label" focus in (*1.*) above are a reflection of the contemporary tendency toward over-specialization. Several chapters in this book deal with the images of *countries* as distinct entities, but further expansion is needed to examine the images of other "products," such as international salesforces, firms, tourism destinations, and so on. With reference to a passing comment made earlier, the origin image issue can be viewed even from the perspective of groups of employers (the "product") trying to attract qualified employees.

For instance, how might the image of California's Silicon Valley, Ottawa's Silicon Valley North, and Massachusetts' Golden Mile highway affect the decision of a young electronics engineer as to where to apply for a job?

Research has also been limited to the origin images of countries as opposed to other "places." And yet, as noted earlier, sub- or supra-national entities also have strong origin images which influence consumer views of various products. Perhaps more significantly, subnational place images can have a significant effect on *domestic* marketing as well. We are aware of only one study which has studied interregional image perceptions (El-beik 1985). For geographically dispersed countries like the U.S., Canada, the former Soviet Union, or Brazil, regional images can be an important competitive factor (e.g., Florida vs. California in the fruit and vegetable market). New studies into the images of places other than "countries" can add to our understanding of PCIs, whether these studies may be performed from an international or domestic perspective.

3. Marketing vs. Image Research

As mentioned in the historical overview of PCI research, Lillis and Narayana (1974) were the first to make a parallel excursion into a field other than marketing (social psychology and political science, based on Kelman 1965) when discussing country images. Unfortunately, that first glimpse at what others already knew was not pursued in PCI *marketing* research as much as one might have expected or hoped. Most subsequent studies were limited to re-citing Kelman and none attempted to update the relevant literature since 1965. This began to change only recently, when Wang and Lamb (1983) dealt with the environmental influences on image formation, and we began to address the images of countries and their people as distinct from those of their products (e.g., Bamossy et al. 1988; Papadopoulos and Heslop 1989).

Yet there clearly is tremendous scope for cross-fertilization of ideas and findings among various disciplines which study the images of countries and other places from a variety of perspectives. Some of the main ones, and their relationship with marketing, are briefly highlighted below.

a. Ethnocentrism. The phenomenon of a preference for one's "kind" and concomitant dislike of others, as expressed in the concepts of ethnocentrism and xenophobia, is the subject of a distinct stream of research within such fields as cross-cultural psychology, social psychology, and political science (Campbell and Levine 1972; Malliaris 1980; Aboud and Skerry 1984). Knowledge in this field can offer valuable insights for the study of patriotism as a factor in product evaluations. To date, the only major example of "fusion" between the ethnocentrism and international marketing literatures is Shimp and Sharma (1987).

b. National images. A related stream, also dealt with in social and cross-cultural psychology, studies the ways in which people cognitively represent nations (e.g., Tajfel 1981; Forgas and O'Driscoll 1984). Research findings in this area can help us develop a better understanding of national images, how they are formed, what their content is, and so on.

c. Stereotyping. Although the link between stereotyping and PCI is direct and immediately obvious, marketing researchers, surprisingly, have not drawn upon the literature on the former to help in explaining the latter. This research stream encompasses hundreds of studies in psychology, sociology, and other disciplines which deal with the stereotyping of persons (Kelley 1950; Ellis, Olson, and Zanna 1981), social groups (Snyder, Tanke, and Berscheid 1977), and other objects.

d. Decision making. Another concept which is closely related to PCI research is the means which consumers use to facilitate decision making. Somewhat surprisingly, while marketing researchers have dealt with the PCI issue from the related viewpoint of information processing, no studies have been framed in the context of decision making theory. In consumer behavior, concepts related to decisions with regard to PCI include Howard and Sheth's (1969) distinction between routinized and non-routinized behavior, and the suggestion by Zaltman, LeMasters, and Heffring (1982) that consumers explain and act upon phenomena based on the "theories-in-use" (or, stereotyped "if-then" syllogisms) which they hold. Other subfields in decision making, beyond the marketing area, could also be useful; for example, "habitual domains" research is perhaps among the most relevant to the PCI issue (since it deals explicitly with nontrivial problems, in which the influence of origin images is likely to be greater, and implicitly with stereotypes; e.g., see Yu 1981).

e. Geography and tourism. Urban, cultural, and human geographers have been dealing for years with the images of "places" and their effects on various aspects of human behavior (e.g., see Svart 1976; De Blij and Muller 1986). As well, researchers from various disciplines with interests in tourism issues have also been studying place images for a long time (Olsson 1965). Findings from these fields of research can be of great interest since their focus is precisely the images of origins/places and the ways in which they influence behavior in such direct and important ways as migratory behavior, urbanization, social organization, tourism travel, and so on.

4. Cross-National Research

Lastly, the need for more multi-country studies should be pointed out. Sekaran (1983) states that, while useful, one- or two-country studies tend to be "opportunistic" and "arbitrary" and their results cannot be generalized beyond the country(ies) sampled. In their review, Bilkey and Nes (1982) had also pointed to the need for broader-based cross-cultural studies. Yet most PCI research continues to be carried out in a limited number of countries. This limitation is especially significant in the context of the "global" marketplace. Replications of existing research in new cultural contexts, and/or new studies involving several countries, are urgently needed for both theoretical reasons (e.g., the need to understand information processing of origin cues cross-culturally) and practical considerations (e.g., researching the cross-national stability of origin images, comparative examinations of various national images, etc.).

CONCLUSION

A television commercial created on behalf of the Cadillac Southeast Dealer Marketing Association in the U.S. "opens with vintage Second World War footage" and "shows a Cadillac firing bullets from its grille and gunning down Japanese Zero fighter planes." Part of the copy states: "From the Land of the Rising Sun comes the land of rising prices . . . . Compared to Cadillac, our competition are real Zeros." ("New Ad May Be the Cadillac of Japan Bashing" 1990).

Hopefully things will not come to this type of all-out war among manufacturers from competing origins–but the image battle certainly is heating up internationally. This chapter has attempted to portray the richness, diversity, and complexity of the PCI phenomenon, and to outline the many significant implications that arise from it for both practitioners and researchers.

As mentioned in the introduction, "an image is a beautiful thing." It is encouraging to see the increasing number of researchers who work in this area and the growth of national and international networks among them. It is hoped that this interest in the origin images of products will be expanded and broadened over the next few years, so that PCI research will continue to advance our understanding of consumer behavior and international marketing strategy. The work of the many researchers who have contributed the following chapters of this first "dedicated" PCI book will certainly act as a catalyst in bringing about this advancement.

REFERENCES

Aboud, F. and S. Skerry (1984), "The Development of Ethnic Attitudes." *Journal of Cross-Cultural Psychology*, 15, 3-34.

Anderson, W.T. and W.H. Cunningham (1972), "Gauging Foreign Product Promotion." *Journal of Advertising Research*, 12, 1 (February) 29-34.

Bamossy, Gary J., József Berács, Louise A. Heslop, and Nicolas Papadopoulos (1988), "East Meets West: A Country of Origin Analysis of Western Products by Hungarian and Dutch Consumers." *Second International Marketing Development Conference* (Budapest: Association of Consumer Research; July) 149-152.

Bilkey, Warren J. and Erik Nes (1982), "Country-of-Origin Effects on Product Evaluations." *Journal of International Business Studies*, 8(1), (Spring/Summer) 89-99.

Campbell, D. and R. Levine (1972), *Ethnocentrism: Theories of Conflict, Ethnic Attitudes and Group Behavior*. New York: John Wiley & Sons.

Cattin, Philippe and Alain Jolibert (1979), "An American vs. French Cross-Cultural Study of Five 'made-in' Concepts." *Proceedings, 1979 Educators' Conference* (Chicago, IL: American Marketing Association) 450-454.

Darling, John R. and Van R. Wood (1990), "A Longitudinal Study Comparing Perceptions of U.S. and Japanese Consumer Products in a Third/Neutral Country: Finland 1975 to 1985." *Journal of International Business Studies* (Third Quarter) 427-450.

De Blij, Harm J. and Peter O. Muller (1986), *Human Geography: Culture, Society, and Space*. New York: John Wiley & Sons.

Dichter, Ernest (1962), "The World Customer." *Harvard Business Review*, 40 (July-August) 113-122.

Dunn, S. Watson (1976), "Effect of National Identity on Multinational Promotional Strategy in Europe." *Journal of Marketing* (October) 50-57.

Eco, Umberto (1989), *Foucault's Pendulum*. New York: Ballantine.

Elbeik, M.A. (1985), "Consumer Preference for Intra-National Product Origin as a Product Evaluative Criterion." In J.C. Chebat (ed.), *Marketing*, vol. 6 (Montreal: Administrative Sciences Association of Canada, May) 108-117.

Ellis, Robert J., James M. Olson, and Mark P. Zanna (1981), "The Physical Attractiveness Stereotype: Personality Inferences Following Objective vs. Subjective Judgements of Beauty." *Working Paper*. Wilfrid Laurier University, Waterloo, Canada.

Forgas, J.P. and M. O'Driscoll (1984), "Cross-Cultural and Demographic Differences in the Perception of Nations." *Journal of Cross-Cultural Psychology*, 15, 199-222.

Hampton, Gerry M. (1982), "Attitudes About Pacific Rim Investment in the American Pacific Northwest." *Journal of Contemporary Business* (August) 49-56.

Han, Min C. (1988), "The Role of Consumer Patriotism in the Choice of Domestic versus Foreign Products." *Journal of Advertising Research*, 28(3), (June-July) 25-32.

Han, Min C. (1989), "Country Image: Halo or Summary Construct?" *Journal of Marketing Research*, XXVI: (May) 222-229.

Head, D. (1987), "Advertising Slogans and the "Made-in" Concept." *International Journal of Advertising* (July) 237-252.

Howard, John A. and Jagdish N. Sheth (1969), *The Theory of Buyer Behavior.* New York: John Wiley & Sons.

Johansson, Johny K. and R. Moinpour (1977), "Objective and Perceived Similarity of Pacific Rim Countries." *Columbia Journal of World Business*, (Winter) 65-76.

Kaynak, Erdener and S. Tamer Cavusgil (1983), "Consumer Attitudes Towards Products of Foreign Origin: Do They Vary Across Product Classes?" *International Journal of Advertising*, 2 (April/June) 147-157.

Kelley, H.H. (1950), "The Warm-cold Variable in First Impressions of Persons." *Journal of Personality*, 18, 431-439.

Kelman, Herbert C., ed. (1965), *International Behavior.* New York: Holt, Rinehart, Winston.

Lillis, Charles M. and Chem L. Narayana (1974), "Analysis of 'Made- in' Product Images–An Exploratory Study." *Journal of International Business Studies*, (Spring) 119-127.

Malliaris, Petros (1980), *Xenophilic Consumer Behaviour: Theoretical Dimensions and Measurement.* PhD Dissertation, University of Oklahoma.

Nagashima, Akira (1977), "A Comparative 'Made In' Product Image Survey Among Japanese Businessmen." *Journal of Marketing*, 41, (July) 95-100.

Naisbitt, John and Patricia Aburdene (1990), *Megatrends 2000.* New York: Avon.

"New Ad May Be the Cadillac of Japan Bashing" (1990, July 30), *The Globe and Mail*, B5.

Newman, Peter C. (1975), *The Canadian Establishment.* Toronto: MacClelland and Stewart-Bantam Limited.

Olsson, G. (1965), *Distance and Human Interaction: A Review and Bibliography.* Philadelphia: Regional Science Research Institute, Bibliography Series, no. 2.

Opinion Research Corporation (1959), "American Firms and Brands in the European Common Market." *Public Opinion Index for Industry* (Princeton).

Panitz, Eric (1988), "Distributor Image and Marketing Strategy." *Industrial Marketing Management*, 17, 4, 315-324.

Papadopoulos, Nicolas (1992), "Trade Blocs and Marketing: Antecedents, Trends, and Implications." *Journal of Global Marketing*, 5, 3, 1-29.

Papadopoulos, Nicolas and Jean-Emile Denis (1988), "Inventory, Taxonomy and Assessment of Methods for International Market Selection." *International Marketing Review*, 5, 3, 38-51.

Papadopoulos, Nicolas and Louise A. Heslop (1989), "As Others See Us: The Image of Canadian Products Abroad." *Canadian Business Review*, 16, 4 (Winter) 27-31.

Papadopoulos, Nicolas, Louise A. Heslop, and Gary J. Bamossy (1990), "A Comparative Analysis of Domestic Versus Imported Products." *International Journal of Research in Marketing*, 7, 4 (December).

Ratliff, R. (1989, November 11), "Where's That New Car Made? Many Americans Don't Know." *The Ottawa Citizen*, D13. (Report on study by Made in the USA Foundation, Inc.).

Reader's Digest Corporation (1963), *European Common Market and Britain*. New York.

Reid, Stanley D. (1981), "The Decision-Maker and Export Entry and Expansion." *Journal of International Business Studies* (Fall), 101-112.

Reierson, Curtis C. (1966), "Are Foreign Products Seen as National Stereotypes." *Journal of Retailing*, 42, 3 (Fall), 33-40.

Schooler, Robert D. (1965), "Product Bias in the Central American Common Market." *Journal of Marketing Research*, II: (November) 394-397.

Sekaran, U. (1983), "Methodological and Theoretical Issues and Advancements in Cross-Cultural Research." *Journal of International Business Studies* (Fall) 61-73.

Seringhaus, F.H. Rolf and Philip J. Rosson (1991), *Export Development and Promotion: The Role of Public Organizations*. Boston: Kluwer Academic Publishers.

Shimp, T.A. and S. Sharma (1987), "Consumer Ethnocentrism: Construction and Validation of the CETSCALE." *Journal of Marketing Research*, XXIV: (August) 280-289.

Snyder, M., E.D. Tanke, and E. Berscheid (1977), "Social Perception and Interpersonal Behavior: On the Self-fulfilling Nature of Social Stereotypes." *Journal of Personality and Social Psychology*, 35, 656-666.

Svart, L. (1976), "Environmental Preference Migration: A Review." *Geographical Review*, 66, 314-330.

Tajfel, H. (1981), *Human Groups and Social Categories*. Cambridge University Press.

Trout, Jack (1980), *Positioning*. New York: Avon.

Vogel, Robert H. (1976), "Uses of Managerial Perceptions in Clustering Countries." *Journal of International Business Studies* (Spring), 91-99.

Wang, Chih-Kang and Charles W. Lamb (1983), "The Impact of Selected Environmental Forces Upon Consumers' Willingness to Buy Foreign Products." *Journal of the Academy of Marketing Science*, 11(2): (Winter) 71-84.

Yu, Po L. (1981), "Behavior Bases and Habitual Domains of Human Decision/ Behavior–An Integration of Psychology, Optimization Theory and Common Wisdom." *International Journal of Systems, Measurement and Decisions*, 1, 39-62.

Zaltman, Gerald, Karen LeMasters, and Michael P. Heffring (1982), *Theory Construction in Marketing: Some Thoughts on Thinking*. New York: John Wiley & Sons.

Chapter 2

"But Who Knows Where or When": Reflections on the Images of Countries and Their Products

Louise A. Heslop
Nicolas Papadopoulos

INTRODUCTION

We have been involved in several research projects on product-country images over the last ten years. This experience and the study of the well-over 300 publications on the topic have led us to several strongly held views about important dimensions, aspects, and relations of the country-of-origin phenomenon. We would like to share these views in order to encourage others to do so, to stimulate application of the knowledge pool that has been developed, and to advocate more and better research in the future.

Interest in the effect of country-of-origin, or what we have come to refer to as product-country image (PCI), on buyers' reactions to products has risen dramatically in recent years. This interest first emerged directly about 20 years ago with the work by Nagashima (1970). The trickle of studies which followed his revealing findings about the United States and Japan has turned into a flood of research, or at least what could be referred to as a steady stream.

At first, interest in the topic was restricted to a handful of international marketing practitioners and academics. Country-of-origin effects were judged by "mainstream" marketing academicians as too practical for inclusion in the more theoretical discipline of consumer behavior. Proposals by us and our colleagues to organize sessions on the topic were repeatedly rejected by the Association for Consumer Research for their conference because the topic was judged to be too applied and practical (this changed with the ACR's 1992 conference in Amsterdam). Indeed, as is common with new research fields, country-of-origin studies were largely atheoretical and descriptive until the last five years. Now, however, the renewed interest in semiotics and symbolism, stereotypes and halos, and the increased sophistication of PCI research itself, has legitimized the topic as worthy of in-depth analysis and serious consideration.

The research on product and country images is reviewed extensively by Papadopoulos (historical overview), Johansson (managerial significance), Baughn and Yaprak (literature review), and Liefeld (meta-analysis of experimental works) elsewhere in this book, and individual aspects of it are further dealt with in each of the other chapters. So, no additional outlining of the research in the field is needed here. Also, other reports in this volume and elsewhere have critiqued the many shortcomings of the research methodologies and approaches. There is a tremendous amount of descriptive information about views of people in a range of countries concerning products in a range of other countries, taken at one or two points in time. The resulting data sets provide a collection of isolated snapshots rather than any comprehensive picture or rich portrait of the entire scene (rather like the set of photos taken at a family picnic or company party–you'd have to have been there to really appreciate them).

But we must be careful not to "throw out the baby with the bath water." These studies have made a tremendous contribution that should not be underrated. They have provided a useful base of research on which to build. Together, they can be mined through such means as literature reviews, insightful summaries, and meta-analysis to yield some generalities. They have provided, and as replicated can continue to provide, immediate information for decision makers in business and government.

In addition, it is important to note that the descriptive base of research is now being enriched extensively through the development and testing of models of effects and models of processes. For example, through a series of correlation analyses, Johansson and Nebenzahl (1987) were able to show that, rather than directly affecting attitudes, the impact of PCI is often primarily through beliefs held by consumers to effects on overall attitudes. Their study did not fully and directly test the multistage model that they proposed. However, it did test for predicted relationships between successive model elements. Garland, Barker, and Crawford (1987) tested a multi-variable model using LISREL analysis and, although their model was rather weakly specified in terms of measurement and complexity, found support for a two-stage interactive elements model of effects. Finally, in other multivariate analysis studies (Erickson, Johansson, and Chao 1984; Johansson, Douglas, and Nonaka 1985; Yaprak and Parameswaran 1986) researchers have observed that there seem to be "halo effects" of attitudes on beliefs, as well as impacts of beliefs on attitudes.

Even more encouraging for the future of knowledge development on this topic is the size of the researcher pool and the sustained stream of work by several researchers working on various aspects of PCI. Several eminent researchers have conducted multiple studies in the field, and single- or multi-country networks of these and other researchers (see opening chapter) provide opportunities for cross-fertilization and movement forward. The value of teamwork spanning two or more countries particularly in this kind of research endeavor cannot be overrated. The generalities about the PCI phenomenon will derive from complex, multinational data bases. The most effective, cost-efficient way to gather such data is through international networks of researchers who have a hands-on feel for and access to local populations, whether they be consumers or industrial buyers, and a global view of marketing. To illustrate what can be done, we will review the experiences we had in such a multinational study and the directions our data analysis has allowed us to explore.

THE EIGHT-COUNTRY STUDY

Our international study of country and product images is the largest research project of its kind, and one of the largest in international marketing generally, to date. Consumer surveys were carried out with a team of nine noted researchers[1] in North America, Western Europe and Eastern Europe. The samples were drawn from large cities in Canada, the United

---

1. Our seven co-researchers, to whom we would like to express our sincere appreciation for their contribution, are listed below in alphabetical order (affiliation at the time of the study, if different from the current one, is given in parentheses): Professors George Avlonitis, Athens Graduate School of Economics and Business Sciences, Greece (University of Strathclyde, U.K.); Gary Bamossy, Vrije Universiteit, The Netherlands; József Berács, Budapest University of Economics, Hungary (previously "Karl Marx University of Economics"); Friedhelm Bliemel (Queen's University, Canada, and Koblenz Management School, West Germany); Françoise Graby, Université de Paris IX-Dauphine, France; Gerry Hampton, San Francisco State University (Seattle University); and Petros Malliaris, Piraeus Graduate School of Industrial Studies, Greece.

States, Great Britain, France, West Germany, the Netherlands, Hungary and Greece. Identical questionnaires were used as translated in all locations. The questionnaires collected information on views of products from five countries, the countries themselves, and their people; top-of-mind recall of, and relative preferences for, products from these countries; travel experience with the countries; assessments of the relative importance of country-of-origin as a purchasing criterion; and demographic variables.

Overall, the study collected responses from over 2200 consumers in the eight countries, through five versions of the questionnaire administered in each of six languages (including two versions of English spelling!). Those who worked on managing the overall project[2] took extensive steps to avoid the common methodological weaknesses which are encountered in trans-national projects of this type (see Douglas and Craig 1983; Albaum and Peterson 1984). These steps included:

- *questionnaire design*–e.g., ensuring language, functional, conceptual, and measurement equivalence; accounting for scale sensitivity; avoiding "courtesy" and "sucker" bias; ordering of sections and multiple rotations of items within questionnaires; translation and back-translation; de-briefing of local research administrators after data collection;
- *sampling and field work*–e.g., care in selecting sampling frames and samples; sampling procedures (the drop-off/pick-up technique was used); timing and replacing not-at-homes; cultural sensitivity to administration techniques; avoidance of the Heizenberg effect; training of interviewers; and,
- *data analysis*–e.g., appropriateness of statistical techniques used; emic and etic explanations of findings (the study design by definition was an "imposed" etic, but both emic and "emerged" etic explanations were used in analysis; as will be seen below, in etic analyses care was taken to avoid "parochial," "ethnocentric," and other pseudo-etic explanations).

The resulting data set is very large and allows for many approaches to answering questions about, for example, differences across the sampled

---

2. Papadopoulos was the overall project coordinator, Heslop did the statistical data analysis, and the bulk of the analysis and presentation of results once the data was collected was done by ourselves and Bamossy. Hampton and Graby participated in developing the main research instrument. All co-researchers took part in adapting the questionnaire to their respective national cultures, leading to the final common version, and in sampling methodology. The main aspects of project organization have been described in Papadopoulos (1986).

countries in how they see the products of one origin country, differences within sampled countries as to how they view different origin countries, differences based on demographic factors and experiences with countries, the patterns of interactions of beliefs about products and countries, and so on. We have reported on this data set and what it reveals in a number of other publications which are referenced in various chapters of this book under citations with Bamossy, Heslop, or Papadopoulos as principal authors.

The framework for the study, which began to take shape back in 1983, built on the descriptive tradition of the time and went well beyond the areas that had been charted until then. The questionnaire relied largely on lists of bi-polar adjective scales which respondents used to rate products in general from a set of countries. Products from five countries were rated–the respondent's own plus a common set comprising the United States, Canada (of special interest to us), Japan, and Sweden, and also Great Britain in those cases (U.S. and Canada) where the home country was specified in the common list. These origins were selected to allow for comparison across a representative range of levels of industrialization and presence in foreign markets among major exporting nations. The decision was made to not include any newly industrialized nations in this project since research has consistently shown that products from these countries are given lower ratings than products from the home and other industrialized countries.

To evaluate products from each country, respondents were presented with 21 bipolar adjective scale items. These were selected with considerable care. The aim in selecting was not just to replicate earlier research, but rather to assimilate the findings of this research into observable patterns. So, an underlying model of effects was posited. Then the model was used to select scale items which (1) would measure the dimensions of the model, (2) had previously been used extensively so there was some comparability with other studies, and (3) from the results of previous research, appeared to be free of varying cultural interpretations.

Further, the research took a direction which had not been explored by the existing studies of the time, and indeed has not as yet been replicated. This area involves trying to understand the link between views of *countries and their people* with views of *products* that are produced in those countries. The model that had been developed postulated some relationships between the two sets of attitudes. Therefore, 11 items to measure "country" and "people" attitude components were developed and included in the questionnaire after pretesting. The development of this scale is discussed later in the chapter.

The top-of-mind country-product associations were obtained by asking respondents to name up to four brands, products, or companies that came to mind at the mention of each of the five origin countries. Product sourcing preferences for a range of products were obtained by asking respondents to select the "most" and "least" preferred source among the five origins. The relative importance of country-of-origin and other common purchasing criteria (e.g., price, quality, style) was measured through a set of bipolar rating scale items. Lastly, in addition to demographic data, respondents were asked to provide information on the frequency of foreign travel in general and whether or not they had visited any of the five origin countries under study.

So, overall, the information obtained from respondents in some cases enabled a multinational replication and extension of previous research (e.g., product assessments along bipolar scales) while in others it provided an opportunity to move into new areas (e.g., country/people assessments, correlation with travel experiences, top-of-mind product recall, and identification of preferred sources for buying specific products). The following paragraphs highlight some of the main findings and relate them to other research in this field.

WHAT WE HAVE BEEN ABLE TO SAY
ABOUT VIEWS OF PRODUCTS

In presenting the results of this research to our peers, we first concentrated on updating the descriptive information available about views of countries along several dimensions.

Domestic vs. Foreign Products

Several researchers over the years have reported that respondents in their studies preferred domestic products to imported ones. Darling and Kraft (1977) found this for Finnish consumers; Gaedeke (1973), Lillis and Narayana (1974), and Dickerson (1986) for Americans; Baumgartner and Jolibert (1977) for the French. These findings have led to a general acceptance of a home-country bias by other researchers reporting summaries of what is known about PCI. However, such a conclusion is simplistic and largely erroneous.

Other research indicates that domestic preference is not universal, nor can it be counted on to be resistant to marketplace changes. Americans' relative views of their own products have fluctuated over the last few years, being quite negative at times (see, for example, ASQC 1980; Seaton and Vogel 1981; Sternquist and Tolbert 1986) and have been found to differ across socioeconomic groups (Han 1988). Also, British (Bannister and Saunders 1978), Canadian (Heslop and Wall 1985; 1986), and Japanese (Nagashima 1970; 1977) respondents have reported more positive attitudes and preferences for products from countries other than their own.

Our data set allowed for a thorough analysis of whether or not consumers always (or even usually) preferred domestic products. A summated score of the 21-item product attitude scale was developed. It showed that consumers from most of the countries tested did give quite high ratings and first or second ranking to domestic products. However, respondents in only two countries (France and West Germany) expressed a clear preference for their own products–and in a third country (the Netherlands) they said their home products were best, but that Japanese products were just as good. American and British respondents ranked their own products as second to those of Japan, and in the Canadian sample domestic and American products were tied behind Japan. Greek and Hungarian respondents actually rated their products at the bottom of the five origins, sometimes tied with those of other countries.

So, our conclusion is that universal domestic preference is a fallacy. Comparing respondents' views across the eight countries from most to least developed industrially (U.S. and Germany to Greece and Hungary), it likely does not exist for most countries and, where it does, it is vulnerable to attack over time. The factors affecting it appear to be:

1. the particular strength of nationalism of the peoples involved–e.g., German and French consumers are known for their strong nationalistic sentiments, whereas Canadians are known for their willingness to accept that others may "do it better";
2. level of industrialization–domestic preference will be lower in countries that are not fully developed industrially because production technologies are less advanced;
3. market development–domestic preference will be lower where the market is filled with the products of foreign manufacturers (i.e., "open" economies), especially if these manufacturers provide good market support and after-sales service;
4. economic vulnerability as perceived by consumers–domestic preference will be higher if consumers perceive that foreign goods threaten the domestic economy.

In any given situation, then, consumers will make a number of different observations, and these will not necessarily lead to the same conclusions about whether domestic or foreign goods are preferable. Which attitude they will in fact operationalize in purchasing is not immediately clear. What *is* clear is that domestic manufacturers *cannot* trust their local consumers to grant them any favor over imported goods as a matter of course. Consumption is fast becoming a global phenomenon. Local suppliers have no guaranteed special status.

The Superindustrialists

Marketers and researchers have been particularly interested in two countries, the United States and Japan, because of their powerful roles as major industrial leaders and world traders. Nagashima (1970, 1977) was one of the first researchers to recognize the importance of the two countries. Almost all future PCI studies have included one or both of them as origins which respondents are asked about. Research results over time indicate that the earlier preference for American products has been eroded and replaced by a very clear preference for Japanese products. Nagashima found such a shift occurring between the time of his first and second studies (1967 and 1975).

Our own study provides a clear opportunity to compare the views of the relative strengths of the two countries. In terms of a summated score across the 21 attitude items, Japan is the clear winner in all eight countries. The consistency of the results is probably its most dramatic statement. In North America and Western and Eastern Europe, across countries with dramatically different cultures, languages, and political ideologies, the Japanese have been successful in marketing their products and building a very positive product image.

Japanese products are the only ones which consistently outshine domestic ones except in the three cases noted above–Germany, France, and the Netherlands. Even in those staunchly nationalistic countries, Japanese products follow closely on the heels of domestic products (differences of an average of 0.0 to 0.2 points on the 1-7 point semantic differential scale).

Products from the United States are rated higher overall than domestic products only by the Hungarians and Greeks, both of whom rate domestic products very low relative to all other countries tested. Also, Canadians rate American and domestic products as equals.

A further look at individual scale items reveals that Japanese products are strongly placed to hold and even expand their dominance. While some may argue along the lines of "we knew that," it is interesting to obtain confirmation of the strength of consumer attitudes from such a widely dispersed sample–and it is very important to be able to obtain measures of the *individual areas* where Japanese products are perceived as being particularly strong. Respondents in five of the eight countries (all except Germany, the Netherlands, and Greece) rated Japanese products as the best of all countries tested (and, we have no doubt, in the world) on *technical performance*. Furthermore, all but two countries (Greece and Hungary) gave Japanese products the highest rating on scales dealing with price-value. In contrast, only the Greek respondents gave top rating to U.S. products on technical performance, while most other countries rated American products in third or even fourth place among the five origins. The same general results pertain to scales dealing with price and value, where American products are seen as among the least competitive among the countries tested.

In those scales which ask consumers about the market presence of, and their familiarity with, products from different countries, again Japanese products fared better than American ones in all countries but Canada and Greece.

Finally, consumers in all countries but Hungary are most likely to "buy" and be most "satisfied with" their own products. This is quite natural and does not negate our previously-stated view that the assumption of a universal or de facto *preference* for domestic goods is fallacious. Even in markets that are highly penetrated by imports, domestic goods are more widely available and frequently bought on the whole (one rarely buys imported bread–yet). However, consumers in Great Britain, West Germany, the Netherlands, Greece, and even the United States rank Japanese products as a close second on these scales. Only Canadians (U.S. products ranked second) and the French (American products rated equal to Japanese) do not give second spot solely to Japanese products.

The ray of sunshine for the American producers lies in one scale item where American products are viewed rather consistently as superior: innovativeness. In contrast, Japanese products are seen as more imitative. This finding is fascinating in that it proves that old images die hard. Such images can help, or haunt, a country's products long after the reality behind them has changed. Whether viewed broadly or technically, Japanese products certainly have graduated from their early approach to strict imitations of "Western" innovations. Yet consumers in five of the eight countries just do not think so; they gave them statistically significant lower ratings, with a mean score of as low as 3.9 on the 1-7 imitative-innovative scale in the Netherlands (the exceptions were Canada and Germany, where the United States and Japan were rated as equal, and Hungary, where Japanese products were rated higher).

This "strategic window" of attitude preferences can be seen as a competitive strength that can be capitalized upon by American producers, but also as an opportunity that can be lost quickly. The Japanese are trying ever harder in recent years to develop their own creative market solutions, though often by teaming up with or buying American ingenuity. For example, one of Sony's more recent successful product introductions was "My First Sony," a children's version of the Walkman for preschoolers; however, the idea for and development of this product came from Sony's American subsidiary, not Japan. American companies often seem more than willing to sell scientific and other product breakthroughs to the Japanese at earlier and earlier stages of development in order to beat out competitors who may be considering doing the same thing. In the long run, this may lead to the loss of this one remaining USP that American manufacturers are as yet seen to hold.

Niche Marketing

In contrast to the intense interest in the images of Japan and the United States, numerous isolated studies have focused attention on a range of countries with much more limited trading power, wealth, and industrial capabilities. Often these studies are undertaken because the researcher resides in the country of interest and the intent is to contribute information of direct interest to local manufacturers and government policy makers (see, for example, the studies of Canada by Heslop and Wall 1985, and Barker and Robinson 1987; of Saudi Arabia by Yavas and Tuncalp 1984; of Denmark by Damanpour and Hallaq 1981; and several chapters in this book). Other times the focus is on comparing developed to developing countries (see, for example, Lumpkin and Crawford 1985).

There are very strong indications that consumers generally devalue goods produced in developing countries in such areas as South America, Africa, the Far East, and Southeast Asia. The general image and specific beliefs towards various aspects of the products are negative overall. Products are often seen as poorly made, lacking durability, low in technology, of low price but lower value, and unreliably serviced. On the basis of this information and under these circumstances, there would seem to be little hope for these countries to ever make significant gains in exports. Consumers seem to be biased strongly against products from countries that are considerably less developed than their own.

However, to draw this conclusion seems counterintuitive. Where was Japan in the eyes of consumers 30 years ago, and South Korea just five years ago? Almost exactly in that position. Despite the same odds, these countries have become monumentally successful in generating export markets. There are at least three lessons to be learned here: things change over time, penetration pricing and other incentives can help to overcome initial consumer resistance, and a focused overall plan for market development is a must. With aggressive, well-planned, and targeted marketing, Japan has moved in the view of consumers from being a producer of cheap, nondurable knick-knacks, to a sophisticated (albeit still less "innovative" than the U.S.), high technology maker of complex, durable, high value products, especially cameras, home entertainment equipment, and automobiles. The range of products is relatively narrow but very high value-added, and the image seems to be transferrable to some extent to products that share the same characteristics as well as to totally unrelated areas (e.g., from shipbuilding to fashion). South Korea seems to be targeting a somewhat similar path to an improved worldwide image.

A different situation exists for the many smaller developed countries that have been studied. These countries do not show up as top-ranked on total assessments of products. However, a closer examination of certain variables in the long lists of product attitude scales, or of preference sources for certain products, reveals areas of unique advantage held by many countries.

In our own data set we examined Canada and Sweden, two small industrialized countries that have a great deal in common in terms of geographic location, population size, industrial development, and political orientation (viewed as more "neutral" than the superpowers). Neither (with the exception of Canada in the domestic sample) ever scored among the top three origins in overall product assessments. That is, they were not seen to have a strong overall international market position. However, a closer examination of individual scale items reveals some unusually high ratings which can be the basis of important marketing strength.

In the case of Swedish products, almost all respondent countries gave them the highest or second highest ratings on the scales dealing with reliability, workmanship, performance, and overall quality. They were also most frequently seen to be luxury products and were given the lowest rating on the price-related scales in five countries, and the lowest or second-lowest rating on scales dealing with availability. Except among French consumers, the promotion of Swedish goods was seen to be among the most credible. So, Sweden stands in a very enviable position to market very high quality, high performance products. Marketing of these products will be accepted and believed, and consumers who can will be willing to pay for them. While producers from a country like Sweden in general cannot expect that unit volumes will be high, premium pricing will make their efforts entirely worthwhile in many cases. Further, the success of companies like IKEA (all the benefits of Sweden at an affordable price) shows that hybrid strategies by specialized producers are also possible.

For a country like Canada, the good news requires more in-depth analysis and is more subtle. Its products are not well known but it has a strong and clear overall *country* image (e.g., unlike Sweden, Canada is a G-7 member and, given its geographic location, is seen as part of North America and both the Atlantic and Pacific Triangles). The product ratings overall and on specific scales in our study consistently placed Canada as fourth or fifth among the five origins studied. Canadian products are particularly poorly known abroad (e.g., mean ratings as low as 2.0 on the 1-7 "unrecognizable-recognizable brands" scale). Yet despite this lack of visibility, consumers in other countries said that they thought Canadian products were well above the midpoint on the scales dealing with product performance. Why would this be so? How can consumers be saying, "we don't know anything about your products, they're quite good"?

An examination of the "country" and "people" image scale will be touched on here for some insight. (Later in this chapter, we will explore this in more depth.) In expressing their attitudes towards countries and their people in the study, respondents gave consistently high ratings to *Canadians*. They saw them as trustworthy and likeable people, and they wished to see closer investment and social ties with *Canada*. It would appear that Canada has significant opportunities to exploit through personal selling and expansion of its international market presence, translating such people-strengths as "trustworthiness" to such product-strengths as "reliability." Assuming good overall "objective" product quality, a country like Canada essentially needs to drape its product with its positive image and take it "on the road."

So there is significant evidence from this study and others that one does not have to be big to be successful. The identification and exploitation of niches is a strong route to success. However, this strategy requires a concerted, coordinated effort on the part of marketers and their governments. A clear, consistent, repeated message must be sent over a period of time to make the impression needed to solidify the image. For maximum effectiveness, the image proposed should be close to the image held by consumers so that the message is not rejected.[3] Modifications may take the form of de-emphasizing any negative aspects or connotations of the image, and emphasizing strongly the value of the positive.

---

3. Ed. note: See the chapter by Morello for an elaboration of this theme.

Strong vs. Diffuse Images

Probably harder to deal with than a negative image is having a diffuse or weak image or no image at all. As we examined data from the respondents in the eight very different countries, one of the most striking things was to observe the singular image of Japan. It was a generally positive image, but, more significantly, it was the same image everywhere. We can examine the clarity of the PCI phenomenon through several sections of the questionnaire, starting with Japan to illustrate the point.

The summated score rating of the products of Japan was the highest or tied for highest in six of the eight countries tested, and second to home country in the remaining two (France and West Germany). So, no matter where we measured the image of Japanese products, they were solidly positioned at or very near the top. Looking at different components of the overall scale reveals the depth of strength of the Japanese position.

For the set of scale items about product workmanship, reliability, technological advancement, performance, and quality, Japanese goods were rated as highest by consumers in five countries and second highest (by 0.2-0.4 points) in two others (Germany and Greece). Only in the Netherlands did Japanese products fall to third spot, behind the home country and its very close neighbor, Sweden. Average scale scores ranged from 4.9 to 6.1. Looking at the scales concerning the expensiveness, price, and luxuriousness of products, again Japan scored highest or tied for second-highest value. So, Japanese products are seen as reasonably priced, excellent performers in every country.

A third dimension is even more revealing to international marketers: the group of scale items which deals with how well brands are known, how easy they are to find, and how much they are advertised. One might expect that goods manufactured in the home country would be rated at the top here. After all, they do have the "native" advantage. In fact, Japanese products were given the highest rating in four countries (Great Britain, the Netherlands, Hungary, and tied for first in Germany), and the second-highest rating in the remaining ones. Japanese goods have achieved a universally high presence through competent, aggressive distribution systems and promotion so that consumers know them and can find them.

However, this does not mean that consumers think all products from Japan are the most desirable. Rather, the examination of other results of the survey reveals the very distinctive product basis of this strength. Respondents were asked near the beginning of the questionnaire to name up to four products that came to mind when thinking of each country. Looking at the three most common responses reveals that only four products were mentioned for Japan by our eight samples–cars, cameras, home entertainment products, and computers. In contrast, for the United States more than 14 product types were mentioned (cars, fruits and vegetables, clothing, computers, soft drinks, large appliances, fast food, wheat, aircraft, military products, cigarettes, entertainment products, aerospace, and other advanced technology products). For Great Britain more than 16 different response categories were given (clothing, textiles, glass/china, cars, wine, fruits and vegetables, tobacco products, farm machinery, cosmetics, wheat, beer, computers, steel, natural gas, other technology products, and general luxury products). The contrast between the tightly focused image of Japanese products, as world leaders in a narrow range of products, and the diffuse images of British and American producers in an unconnected range of products that are evaluated less positively by consumers, is evident.

As noted previously, consumers were also asked for their most- and least-preferred source countries among the five origins for a list of products. The list was designed to be parsimonious (limited to 13 products, to avoid overtaxing the respondents) but also to cover a range of products selected on the basis of five dimensions:

- nondurable (cheese, canned salmon), semi-durable (shoes and four types of apparel, camping equipment) and durable goods (cars, cameras, telephones, home computers, furniture);
- branding important-not important (e.g., cameras vs. cheese);
- products usually available from domestic-foreign suppliers (e.g., furniture vs. furs);
- various levels of technology (e.g., canned salmon vs. home computers);
- various levels of purchase risk (e.g., cheese vs. camping equipment vs. cars).

The intent here was to ascertain whether common assumptions about international stereotypes in fact exist among consumers, and whether such stereotypes would in fact be carried over from awareness to action. For example, in their studies, PCI researchers often cite examples of country-product associations (e.g., France-wines, Japan-cameras). Apart from simply making such associations, would consumers also designate the commonly-*known* origins as the preferred source from which they would in fact *buy?*

As might be expected, consumers in most countries preferred to source at home for most of the 13 products (e.g., cheese, apparel). However, there were several interesting exceptions to this rule. First, for the narrow range of Japanese products that consumers have at the *top-of-mind*–cameras, cars, computers–there was also a very strong *purchase* preference. Over two-thirds of respondents in *all* countries preferred cameras from Japan. Japanese cars were preferred by the largest number of respondents in four countries, *including the United States and Canada*. Home computers from Japan were most preferred by the largest number of respondents in six of the eight countries. (Do country images carry over? *At the time of the study, Japanese home computers were virtually nonexistent in all of the markets studied*.)

Of additional interest is the pattern of responses for the *least* preferred source country for the products listed. For most of the products–shoes, clothing, fur coats, cheese, camping equipment, canned salmon, furniture– the largest single response given for *least*-preferred source country was *Japan*. This somewhat surprising finding may be due partly to the presence of market segments which will *not* "buy Japanese," for whatever reason. An additional likely explanation is that Japan's strengths are viewed in the focused context of certain product categories, as mentioned above. While Japan has expanded greatly the range of products it exports over time, this expansion has been sequential, each new "building block" relying heavily on the established success of the previous one. For example, the move into computer products was not made until after consumer electronic products (such as stereos and TVs) were perfected and firmly entrenched. Either way, this presents another strategic opportunity window for Japan's international competitors–whether among buyers who continue to shun Japanese products or in sectors which Japan has not yet entered.

To summarize then, there is a clear, crisp, widely spread image of Japan as "tops" in what it does well, and that is a narrow range of products which depend on complex, precision, technology-based mass manufacturing. Although the present product range may appear somewhat limiting, the scope for development and the future growth potential are immense. Opportunities are tremendous for Japan to move laterally from this base of expertise. The profits accruing from this kind of product because of the high value added also make the product type appealing as a base for a country's industrial strategy. From the point of view of balancing payments in international trade, the emphasis on such high-value-added products is advantageous, and focusing production on such technologically sophisticated products augurs well for the stability of employment in a skilled labor force.

However, it is not only large exporters who can take advantage of such focused images. Other exceptions to the "home preference" rule prove the presence of international stereotypes, and reinforce the preceding comments about producers from various types of countries and the strategies they should or could employ. For example, Canadian products are not well known–but Canadian fur coats were most preferred in six countries and Canadian salmon in five, pointing to this country's niche position in global markets.

Sweden, in particular, appears to be rather widely perceived in a uniquely superior way. As mentioned earlier, Swedish products overall are seen as high-quality, exclusive, and expensive. Regarding product categories, respondents consistently mentioned wood and wood furniture, cars, and glass/china, occasionally fish, and rarely anything else. Sweden was rarely mentioned as a most- or least-preferred country for sourcing products by more than about 15 percent of respondents, except for furniture (most-preferred in four countries, second in the remaining four) and salmon (most-preferred by about a third of the Hungarians and French). Therefore, Sweden can take advantage of a very positive image as a niche marketer in such product categories as luxury home furnishings and cars.

In contrast to Sweden, views about American, Canadian, and British products vary widely from country to country. American products were generally ranked lower on the product attribute scales (e.g., quality, workmanship), in third or fourth place in five countries, first in only one, and tied for second place in two countries. On scales about price, U.S. products were ranked second in Canada, third at home and fourth or fifth in the remaining countries. In terms of market presence, American products were at the top of foreign goods in Canada and Greece, but second in two other countries and third in the remaining. With the occasional exception of some clothing products in isolated cases, American products were not selected as "most- preferred" by large numbers of respondents in any of the foreign countries. And, as mentioned earlier, the top-of-mind awareness list of products made-in-the U.S. was extensive and widely varied. The overall conclusion is that American products have a more diffuse image than Japanese ones, which does, however, include strengths in some categories (e.g., from soft drinks to jeans and aerospace).

Canadian products were generally ranked weakly on most product dimensions, coming out in fifth or fourth spot. There certainly is a narrow range of products that consumers around the world think of when they think of Canada, and these are wheat, wood, furs, fish, and maple syrup–all natural resources with minimal processing. It is no doubt a challenge to build an industrial strategy for competing in foreign markets on this base which, though narrow, appears to be very weak. In the three countries where British goods were also evaluated (Canada, U.S., and "home" sample), they "competed" essentially for third-to-fifth place with Canadian and/or American goods and, as previously mentioned, had a diffuse image much like the one of American products.

So, there is a great deal of information available to marketers and policymakers from simply examining the scale ratings provided by the respondents, and their top-of-mind recollections and source country preferences. The preceding discussion clearly indicates the range of useful questions that can be asked by practitioners and/or academic researchers. The former are likely to be interested in various different source country, target country, and product combinations, depending on their specific sector of activity. The latter are likely to focus on developing more in-depth means of analyses for understanding the PCI phenomenon in general and allowing our data to "live" and contribute beyond a short period after its collection. In both cases, the generalizations that are made possible by the consistency of findings from this multicultural data set points to the value of gathering comparative data from several countries.

EXAMINING THE STRUCTURE OF PCI

The kinds of analyses overviewed above rely mainly on simple comparisons of descriptive data–means, standard deviations, t-tests. Much of what is revealed through such analyses is of immediate usefulness to decision makers. We have only brushed over the surface in the previous section. Much more can be done by looking for differences in views across different segments of the samples (e.g., different sex, age, income groups, those with and without travel experience) and so on. We have reported on some of these elsewhere.

However, we were also very interested in taking the opportunity supplied by this large data set to examine for *patterns* in the use of the product image scales across different countries. Such scales had been in use in many other studies for a long time with only limited testing for validity and reliability. Various authors had combined various scale items to form subgroups, using sometimes only intuitive logic and sometimes formal analytical procedures (see for example, Nagashima 1970, 1977; Narayana 1981; Erickson, Johansson, and Chao 1984; Johansson, and Nebenzahl 1986, 1987; White 1979). Never had there been any systematic look at a group of scales across more than two countries (e.g., Narayana 1981 compared Japanese and American consumers, and Cattin, Jolibert, and Lohnes 1982 studied American and French purchasing agents).

Of the 21 bipolar adjective items used in our eight-country study, 14 were those used by Nagashima (1977). Six of his scale items were not used for various reasons (consistent translations into all the languages needed for our study could not be obtained; the meaning of the polar ends of the scale did not work in pretests, e.g., mass produced/hand made, etc.). Niffenegger, White, and Marmet (1980) reported the same interpretation difficulties in using some of the scales. All but one of the items dropped were used in fewer than ten studies, so they are the less popular of Nagashima's scale items. However, despite the deletion of items, all the subgroupings proposed by Nagashima (1977) were well represented. We used four of the six items on price and value (a fifth was used in the country-people scale, which is discussed later), three of five on service and engineering, all three on advertising-reputation, two of three in design and style, and two of three on consumers' profile).

Seven scale items were added. Two of these were developed to measure attitudes to product-related marketing functions: honesty of promotion (before sales) and strength of warranty and service (after sales). Two dealt with exposure to the products of the country being rated: difficult/easy to find and know a little/a lot about. And another three measured global evaluations of overall quality, frequency of purchase, and overall satisfaction. In all, based on the results of the work of Nagashima and others (who do not totally support Nagashima's original proposed grouping) it was expected that the 21 items on the final scale would form six summary variables as follows:

- *Engineering/Design:* Un-/Reliable; Poor/Good Workmanship; Not-/ Technically Advanced; Imitative/Innovative; More Concerned with Appearance/-Performance; Poor/Good Quality.
- *Price-Value:* Un-/Reasonable Price; Necessity/Luxury; Expensive/ Inexpensive.
- *Marketing Integrity:* Not-/Honest Promotion; Poor/Good Service and Warranties.
- *Market Presence:* Narrow/Wide Choice of Models and Sizes; Un-/ Recognizable Brands; Little/Much Advertising; Difficult/ Easy to Find.
- *Prestige:* More for Lower/Upper Class; More for Old/Young; Not-/ Proud to Own.
- *Experience:* Know A Little/A Lot About; Usually Buy Few/Many; Overall Not-/Satisfied With.

To test the extent to which the set of scale items work together as a scale and/or form consistent subgroups, which reveal different dimensions of consumer evaluations, we began with a factor analysis of the data. The extent to which items load together would suggest the extent to which consumers see a commonality in the scales. The 40 sets (eight respondent countries rating five countries each) of 21 items were analyzed using Principal Components Analysis with Varimax rotation. Factoring was stopped according to the criterion of a minimum eigenvalue of one, and the resulting factors were examined using scree plots to determine when additional factors no longer added significantly to reducing variance. The outcome was generally consistent in leading to a five-factor solution.

In Table 1 the results are summarized for all 40 country ratings, noting for each scale item the frequency with which it loaded at the 0.40 level or higher on each of the five factors. An examination of this table indicates which items are most likely to load on each factor.

The findings do not completely support the prior beliefs concerning the six subscales which, based on the earlier studies, we had speculated might exist within the set of items tested. For example, the engineering dimension seems to absorb at least one of the two marketing integrity variables. The price-value dimension exists but may not contain the "Necessity/ Luxury" variable. Pride of ownership does not fit very well with the other two items in Prestige, nor do "Know Little/A Lot" and "Buy Few/Many" fit well with "Satisfaction" in Experience.

Given the above, we reexamined the data using the factor analysis results, but also 12 other scale item combinations which were posited based on intuitive logic, historical research, and/or a comparison of the individual factor structures of the respondent countries; we then tested for internal consistency with reliability analysis (Cronbach's alpha). This additional step is important since, if a group of items do not load together consistently, this would suggest that there is no basis for a subscale. Believing otherwise, as has been the case in some other studies, would lead to adding the scores of items in the subscale–which would, in turn, only serve to *hide* the varying scores consumers give the country on each item in the subscale (i.e., an imposed pseudo-etic explanation of the data).

Based on this second analysis, four items were dropped from further consideration because they did not fit well and consistently with the others. The remaining 17 items were grouped into the revised set of four summary dimensions shown in Table 2. The table summarizes the frequencies with which the items in the suggested subscales load together across the 40 observation points, and shows their composition. The fol-

Table 1. Factor Loadings of 21 Bi-polar Adjective Scales

Scale (b)	Frequency of Loading on Factor at the .40 Level or Above (a) Factors				
	1	2	3	4	5
Engineering and Design					
Unreliable/Reliable	30	2	6	1	5
Poor/Good Workmanship	35	7	5	1	2
Technically Not--/Advanced	19	13	7	3	1
Imitative/Innovative	23	8	4	4	2
Appearance/Performance	7	0	4	5	7
Poor/Good Quality	34	9	2	2	2
Price-Value					
Expensive/Inexpensive	4	9	11	12	4
Unreasonable/Reasonable Price	5	7	12	11	7
Necessity/Luxury	2	8	8	11	10
Marketing Integrity					
Not Honest/Honest Promotion	20	2	9	7	5
Poor/Good Service & Warranties	24	4	5	4	11
Market Presence					
Limited/Wide Choice	4	4	10	8	11
Un--/Recognizeable Brands	3	17	8	4	5
Little/Much Advertising	0	8	7	9	12
Difficult/Easy to Find	1	15	11	4	11
Prestige					
For Lower/Upper Class	5	8	9	10	8
For Older/Younger People	3	6	5	7	13
Not Proud/Proud to Own	22	11	8	3	2
Experience					
Know A Little/A Lot About	3	18	9	5	3
Buy Few/Many	8	19	9	5	2
Not Satisfied/Satisfied	31	10	9	3	1
Mean percent of variance explained	22	11	8	7	6

(a) Total may be greater than 40 because some scales may load on more than one factor in an analysis.
(b) The six summary item groups reflect the originally expected classification.

lowing paragraphs outline the base logic for this classification by tracing the main results from the factor analysis.

The first factor accounts for an average of 22.3 percent of the variance among the scale responses. It is most likely to contain the scale items on reliability, workmanship, innovativeness, quality, service, pride in ownership, and overall satisfaction, and to a slightly lesser extent, honest promotion and technical advancement (Table 1). This is clearly a Product Integrity dimension (Cronbach's alpha = .80) which is a broader form of the engineering/design or product quality dimension that had been identified previously.[4] The fact that after-sales service and also honesty of promotion usually load here suggests that consumers see marketing integrity as an integral part of product performance. So, those who provide quality products also are honest and supportive of them, and this altogether likely results in satisfaction and pride of ownership.

The second factor explains only about half as much of the variance (10.8 percent) as the first. It is most likely to include the scales on purchase frequency, knowledge, recognizability of brands, and ease of finding the Below weproducts. This appears to be a Market Presence dimension. It is interesting that buying preference loads most frequently here, rather than with the product integrity dimension. Apparently, consumers may be more likely to buy on the basis of familiarity and availability.

The third factor explains an average of 8.1 percent of the variance. It tends to include two sets of items. The most common are two of the Price-Value variables: reasonable price and expensive/inexpensive. However, the variables of availability and level of choice of brands and models, and the four response variables of proud, know, buy, and satisfied are almost as likely to appear in this factor. This might suggest that price and choice elements are equally important at this third level, depending on the country rating and the country being rated. Also, there may be a distinct Response dimension that combines the cognitive (know), affective (proud, satisfied), and conative (buy) items.

The fourth factor, explaining on average 6.5 percent of the variance, is quite clearly a price dimension, including all three price-value scales and

---

4. Nagashima's "Appearance/Performance" variable was also included in Product Integrity (Table 2), although its factor loading pattern across the eight countries was not as consistent as that of other variables. The decision to include it was based on the results from the other analyses used to arrive at the summary dimensions (extent of usage in past studies, individual factor structure of country, and reliability analysis). Nonetheless, it is possible that this scale item represents two different variables (appearance, or some other measure of "design quality," and product performance).

"More for Lower/Upper Class." Nagashima did not classify this item in the price subgroup, but included it in a consumer profile dimension.

The fifth factor explains on average only 5.6 percent of the variance and does not have any clear characteristics. Six scale items load here more than a quarter of the time, but they are a mixed group including choice level, service, amount of advertising, ability to find, necessity/luxury goods, and "More for Old/Young People." This factor is the weakest and does not seem to have a clear definition at all. As explained earlier, the usefulness of a fifth or sixth dimension to the attitude structure is highly questionable.

Therefore, it can be suggested at this point that at least three different dimensions can be identified within the set of variables (Product Integrity, Price-Value, Market Presence), and possibly a fourth Response dimension.[5] This solution is, of course, an etic, since the intent was to examine common response patterns across all eight of the countries sampled. As noted, the four summary dimensions were determined by examining several possible combinations of variables in various ways. Therefore, their composition (Table 2) does not always follow the composite picture of variable loadings from the factor analysis alone, which was shown in Table 1 and used to frame the preceding discussion.[6]

Based on this extensive analysis, we feel that at least these four different dimensions can and should be measured in PCI studies. As well, we would suggest that additional work be done to explore the prestige or "consumer profile" aspect of PCI by testing new scales developed for this purpose. Further, there may be an important aesthetic design dimension that would be useful. It can certainly be expected to be important if specific products like fashionwear and cars are being assessed.

The development of the four subscales of product and country images allows for the reporting of the results from all eight respondent countries on each of the five origin countries in some reasonably readable form, as shown in Table 3. This data was used to make the observations presented in the previous section of this paper concerning the relative positions of products from the different countries. We recognize the imperfections of

---

5. The Cronbach's alpha for Market Presence, Price-Value, and Response ranged from 0.50 to 0.60. While this is not as high as might be expected, it is satisfactory since the items in each of the dimensions were not developed so as to have the internal reliability of an index (which is what Cronbach's alpha measures).

6. The summary of factor loadings for all 40 observation points (8 samples × 5 origins) in Table 1 is useful as a starting point for examining cross-cultural similarities. Researchers interested, instead, in emic analysis, would consider the results separately for each individual country of interest (as we have done elsewhere).

this classification; some individual item scores still are "hidden" in the summary dimension means, examination of individual scale item scores will always be necessary, and better classifications are likely to emerge as new research adds to the current knowledge bank. But, we suggest that these four dimensions are a far better reflection of consumers' thought structures concerning PCIs than the intuitive subgroups that predominated in earlier research.

Table 2. Factor Loading Pattern of Summary Dimensions

Measure Name	Number of scales	Incidence of Scales in Measure Loading in Same Factor Number of scales	Number of times
PRODUCT DIMENSIONS			(max.=40)
Product Integrity (technically advanced, innovative, workmanship, quality, reliability, performance, service)	7	3-4 5-7	17 23
Price/Value (inexpensive, reasonable price)	2	2	37
Market Presence (model/size choice, recognizable brands, advertising level, easy to find)	4	2 3-4	22 16
Response (know, buy, proud, satisfied)	4	2 3-4	17 23
COUNTRY-PEOPLE DIMENSIONS			(max.=32)
Belief (managing economy well, technically advanced, industrious)	3	2 3	17 22
Affect (role in world politics, taste, trustworthiness, likeability)	4	2 3-4	19 21
Link (more investment, closer ties)	2	2	28

Table 3. Mean Scores - Summary Dimensions

	Origins						Origins				
	Home	CDN	US	J	S	GB	Home	CDN	US	J	S	GB
Evaluators	a. Product Integrity						b. Price-Value					
Canada	4.7	-	4.8	**5.5**	4.9	4.5	3.8	-	4.0	**4.5**	3.4	3.6
U.S.	4.7	4.3	-	**5.4**	4.8	4.2	3.4	4.0	-	**4.8**	3.3	3.3
Great Britain	4.5	4.4	4.6	**5.1**	**5.0**	-	3.8	3.9	3.7	**4.9**	3.1	-
France	4.9	4.3	4.9	**5.3**	4.9	-	3.8	3.9	3.3	**4.7**	3.5	-
W. Germany	**5.8**	4.5	4.6	5.4	5.2	-	3.8	3.9	3.5	**5.3**	3.5	-
Netherlands	5.2	4.5	4.5	4.9	**5.4**	-	4.0	4.0	3.5	**5.1**	3.5	-
Greece	3.6	5.2	**5.5**	5.3	5.2	-	**4.1**	3.7	3.1	3.8	3.8	-
Hungary	3.5	4.8	5.1	**6.1**	5.1	-	2.8	**3.6**	3.1	3.4	3.4	-
	c. Market Presence						d. Response					
Canada	5.0	-	**5.8**	5.3	3.4	3.9	**5.6**	-	4.8	4.7	3.6	4.0
U.S.	**6.0**	3.7	-	5.7	3.5	3.4	**5.4**	3.7	-	5.1	3.7	3.4
Great Britain	**5.5**	3.2	5.2	**5.5**	3.3	-	**5.2**	3.4	4.0	4.4	3.5	-
France	**5.7**	3.1	5.2	5.3	3.5	-	**5.9**	3.2	4.4	4.4	3.4	-
W. Germany	**5.6**	3.3	5.3	**5.6**	3.9	-	**5.7**	2.8	3.7	4.4	3.4	-
Netherlands	5.3	3.5	5.4	**5.8**	4.1	-	**5.3**	3.1	3.9	4.1	3.8	-
Greece	5.1	3.8	**5.5**	5.2	3.8	-	**5.4**	3.2	3.7	4.9	3.3	-
Hungary	3.7	3.8	4.5	**4.7**	4.0	-	4.8	3.5	4.0	**4.9**	3.7	-

Note. The origin(s) with the highest mean score is underlined. All differences between the highest and next-highest scores are statistically significant at a<0.05 based on paired T-test comparisons.

Legend. CDN=Canada, US=United States, J=Japan, S=Sweden, GB=Great Britain.

THE SOURCES OF CONSUMERS' PRODUCT IMAGES

Despite the great effort that has been expended on PCI research, comparatively little is known about *why* people hold the views they do concerning products from different countries and *how* they develop them. General learning theories would suggest that the sources are likely to be many and complex, including general knowledge about countries picked up everywhere from geography class in elementary school to daily newspapers and TV documentaries, friends and co-workers (especially those who have visited or lived in the country, including immigrants), and direct experiences from visits to the country. This knowledge, coupled with any prior experiences from using a country's products, can be applied to evaluating future purchases.

Personal Background

Several studies have examined the relationship of demographic variables to PCIs. The results of this work have been quite mixed. Schooler

(1971) and Bannister and Saunders (1978) found that women gave higher ratings than men to imports. Heslop and Wall (1985) found similar results when the country being rated was noted for producing high quality fashion goods. Some studies have found that older consumers are more likely to give higher ratings to foreign than domestic goods (Schooler 1971), while others have not found such a relationship (Wang 1978; Wall and Heslop 1986). Wang (1978) found a positive correlation between income and rating of foreign goods, but Wall and Heslop (1986) found that higher income consumers were more critical of both domestic and foreign goods. However, many studies have not uncovered any demographic correlates of PCI.

One of the reasons for the observed differences may be the framing of the studies. When the study asks about products in general, consumers with different backgrounds and product usage patterns may bring to mind different products on which to base their overall assessments. For example, Heslop and Wall (1985) noted a stronger correlation of overall country ratings by women with their ratings of the countries as producers of apparel goods. Ratings by men were more highly correlated with their ratings of the countries as producers of non-apparel goods, such as cars. Support for this proposition can be derived also from an earlier section of this chapter which noted considerable differences in the number and range of top-of-mind country-product associations by consumers. If consumers in the sample for a study are using different products as a reference point for judgments, they will likely arrive at different judgments.

Socialization

Renwick and Renwick (1988) observed that social contact with foreigners affected importers' evaluations of foreign goods. If the social linkages developed with foreigners were positive, then the importers' views of products from the country were more favorable. Similarly, perceived similarities of interests and beliefs have been found to be related to more positive attitudes towards the country and its products (Hill and Stull 1981; Taormina and Messick 1983; Tims and Miller 1983; Tongberg 1972).

Travel experiences may be another factor affecting PCI formation. In 1986 we reported on a part of our data set which looked at the relationship of travel to PCI (Papadopoulos and Heslop 1986). We found that consumers who had travelled to a country did have different views from those who had not. Differences were observed in the rating of products from the country, but were even more pronounced for ratings of the country itself and its people. Sometimes the shifts in views associated with travel were positive, and sometimes negative. The shifts appear to be in the direction of closing any gaps between previously held perceptions and the reality visitors experience on travelling to the country.

Attitudes to Countries and People

Attitudes to the countries and people producing the products have rarely been included in research on PCI in the past. The notable exception is the study by Wang and Lamb (1983) which found that willingness to buy foreign products was related to the economic, political, and cultural environment of the origin country.

In our eight-country study, we wanted to investigate more thoroughly the linkages between views of countries and their people with views of products. To do this we included in the questionnaire a list of 11 bipolar adjective scales dealing with country and people, to investigate these as possible explanatory variables for product attitudes.

We consider this to be one of the most noteworthy contributions of this research to the existing knowledge about PCI. Since this area has not been discussed in the marketing literature before, it seems useful to provide some detail on the development of the relevant scales. Given the absence of any prior marketing research in this area, in developing the scales we had to go to literature bases outside marketing that deal with international images. One excellent source was Kelman (1965), who summarized the research to date on the effects of a number of variables on nation images, including social, psychological, and cultural correlates, and the effects of international events and of contacts with the people and country through travel. Several studies in the social psychology literature have studied the dimensions used by people in comparing, evaluating, and cognitively representing nations. The dimensions found have varied slightly depending on the sample countries studied. However, the following dimensions have been found with some consistency: politics, economic development, cultural development, geographic location, and race or ethnicity (see, for example, Forgas and O'Driscoll 1984; Jones and Ashmore 1973; Robinson and Hefner 1967; Wish, Deutsch, and Biener 1970).

In determining the individual items to include as measures of country-people images, we devised or chose from earlier studies a measure on each of these dimensions with two exceptions. Geography and race were not included since all the origin countries studied in our research are similar in these dimensions (all are "Triad" countries; the only exception was race in the case of Japan). The communist/capitalist dichotomy was excluded for the same reason, but perception of the countries' roles in world politics was addressed with a question about how "admirable" each origin country's role is. Economic development was operationalized by focusing on the industriousness of the people, the economic management of the country, and its technological advancement, agricultural vs. industrial orientation, and industrial vs. consumer goods manufacturing base. The cultural dimension was examined through the variable "refined taste," again because of the similarity of shared culture among the target countries.

Except for "taste" and "role in world politics," the above scales can be considered to be measuring the belief components of a country-people attitude. Further, we were interested in measuring the affective and conative components of attitude. Affect was measured by the "taste" and "politics" items, and two more variables dealing with overall liking and trustworthiness of the people. Of these, liking made intuitive sense for inclusion; trustworthiness was identified through research into the variables used in EUROBAROMETER[7] when assessing the views of European peoples toward each other. Lastly, the behavioral aspect was measured through two scales regarding the preferred source of foreign investment among the five origin countries in the study, and the respondent's willingness to see closer ties between his/her own country and each of the five origins. Of course, these last two scales were not used to measure attitudes towards one's home country.

Overall, then, there were 11 country-people scale items for each foreign country and nine for the home country. As with the product image scale, we used factor analysis and Cronbach's alpha tests to search for the dimensions within the scale, and for similarities in these dimensions across sampled and origin countries. Between two and four significant factors emerged for each country (32 observation points in total). Various combinations of the variables were examined based on general attitude structure research and the country image literature previously cited.

Our conclusion from this analysis is that there appear to be three rather consistent dimensions. Two of the scales (agriculture/manufacturing and industrial/consumer goods) did not load well with the others, partly because there is little variance in how this set of countries is seen and partly because the bipolar adjectives used are unclear in meaning, and were dropped from further analysis. As expected, of the remaining items, four were most frequently associated together and formed one dimension

---

7. Semi-annual opinion survey in the European Community by EUROSTAT (the EC's central statistical bureau).

which we have termed "Affect": refined taste, trustworthiness, role in world politics, and likeable people. The three items on industriousness of the people, management of the economy, and technological advancement of the country loaded together and were identified as a "Belief" dimension concerning industrial development. Lastly, the two conative variables did load together very consistently and the dimension was called "Link." The relevant summary from the factor analysis is shown in Table 2, presented earlier.[8]

To examine the association between the attitudes toward country and people and the attitudes toward products from these countries, correlation coefficients were generated for all combinations of the three country and four product dimensions. The means of these coefficients are shown in Table 4.

Once again, we are tempted to call the findings "fascinating." Significant and high correlations are found for all three country dimensions with views on Product Integrity and Response. Also, the correlation between Market Presence and Beliefs just managed to reach significance, yet at the 0.01 level. All other correlations are not significant. That is, views of the country and its people are not related to assessments of the price and value of products or generally their market presence. However, they are strongly associated with judgments about the performance of the products and with willingness to buy, satisfaction, and pride of ownership. The highest associations are found between beliefs about the country (economic performance, technical advancement, industriousness of the people) and the

Table 4. Mean Correlations:
Country-People Attitudes and Product Attitudes

Product Dimensions	Country-People Dimensions		
	Belief	Affect	Link (a)
Product Integrity	.42+	.34+	.26+
Price-Value	.10	.10	.09
Market Presence	.16+	.10	.07
Response	.24+	.27+	.22+

(a) Means for Link based on foreign countries only.
+ Correlations of .16 and above are significant at the .01 level

---

8. The Cronbach's alpha for these three dimensions also ranged from 0.50 to 0.60. See footnote 6.

performance of its products. So, good products are seen to come from well managed, technologically advanced nations with hard-working people. While perhaps not a surprising finding, this result is the first empirical confirmation of the presence of explicit correlations between country and product image measures among consumers. This finding also provides empirical validation for Han's (1989) findings concerning the potential role of country images as halos for, or abstracted summaries from, product assessments.

More importantly, this research points to the role of affect in product evaluations, and the behavioral implications of consumer predispositions. Good products are seen to be produced by people who have refined taste, and are likeable, trustworthy, and admirable for their role in world politics. Overall, then, good products come from countries whose industrial prowess we respect and whose people we like and admire. Finally, there is a desire for closer links, both generally and in terms of investment flows, with countries that produce good products.

Although correlations for individual countries are not shown in Table 4, it is interesting to note that the association of affect and product integrity is particularly strong for Canada (0.39) and much weaker for Japan (0.26). Those who like Canada and Canadians will rate their products positively. However, Japanese product ratings are less tied to the liking of Japan and the Japanese.

We would also mention that overall associations between country-people images and the product dimensions of Product Integrity and Response are slightly higher than average for the home country. Further, the correlation of these two dimensions for Japan was relatively low compared to the other countries (0.29), suggesting that beliefs about Japanese products are more independent of the views of the country and the people (i.e., they stand more on their own). Japan also stands out when the market presence and belief dimensions are examined. The overall mean correlation is barely significant (at the alpha = .01 level). The mean correlation is not significant for any of the target countries individually except for Japan (0.26), perhaps suggesting that knowledge of Japan and the Japanese is more closely tied to the presence of its products in foreign markets.

Finally, the association between the overall response to foreign products, on the one hand, and the affective response to the producing countries and their people, on the other, is slightly stronger than is the link of this response to beliefs about their economy and industrial system. This suggests that liking a country and its people may be more important to ultimate choice than knowing how productive it is. Of course, the reverse direction of effects would suggest that buying and being satisfied with and proud of products will lead to greater appreciation of the people and the country, with somewhat less impact on changing views about its industry and economy.

Before closing this discussion on the country-people variables, we will briefly look at the intercorrelations among the three country-people dimensions. The dimensions are strongly associated among themselves. This should be expected from general attitude consistency theory. The average correlation of the belief and affect dimensions is 0.44, with Japan notably lower at 0.31. Again, positive views about Japan's industrial and economic capabilities are less closely associated with positive views of the country itself. The average correlation of "Link" is 0.31 with "Belief" and 0.40 with "Affect." So, the interest in linkages with countries is somewhat more closely associated with emotional reactions to the country (i.e., how much it is liked), than to how economically and industrially advanced it is seen to be.

In summary, two statements can be made from this analysis. First, the direction of effects (country image affecting product image, or vice-versa) is not clear. Undoubtedly it is not one-way, although for certain countries at certain times one direction may dominate. Neither is it clear whether intervening third factors are involved. Our experience with a tentative LISREL model, developed from a part of the data set, would suggest an answer in the affirmative (see Papadopoulos, Marshall, and Heslop 1988). Second, it is clear that country images are useful predictors of product images, especially regarding assessments of product performance and overall response to the products from the countries. New research will hopefully shed more light on these relationships.

WHERE AND WHEN
PRODUCT-COUNTRY IMAGES ARE IMPORTANT

Frequently in this book, the general question posed is "How important is the country image effect?" Is it important? The clear and resounding answer must be YES, but that is just the simple answer. Just as clearly, the importance and level at which the country-of-origin of a product matters will vary, and the challenge for researchers and marketers is to determine what the controlling factors are. In the eight-country study, country-of-origin generally was rated lower than other product attributes in the importance scales. In explaining this finding, we would side with Johansson's conclusion (see his chapter in this book): there is enough evidence to confirm that origin does matter–but, for reasons we have yet to understand fully, people do not like to admit that it does.

From our studies, those we have done with others, and the collective body of research, we would propose the framework shown in Table 5 for classifying the "wheres," "whens," and also the "whys" and "hows" of the importance of origin in product assessments.

The first column of Table 5 lists a number of factors which have been shown to be related to country-product images or to the use of information cues, including characteristics of the product, the decision criteria considered important in the decision, the decision process itself, and individual characteristics. In each case, alternatives are proposed which would enhance the direct or indirect importance of the country-of-origin of the product and information about it. For example, if the product is complex, then the country-of-origin is likely to be more important. This has been found by several researchers (e.g., Heslop, Liefeld, and Wall 1987). For complex products, consumers can be expected to seek more information to reduce risk (see type of effect column in the Table 5). Consumers will be more positive toward products from countries which they perceive to be more industrially developed (Country Dimension column), because these countries are judged to produce goods with greater "product integrity" (Product Dimension column), which they are seeking. This country-of-origin effect will thus affect consumers in their behavior directly and also will similarly affect buyers and suppliers (Who and How columns).

There are several unique, product-specific characteristics which may be linked strongly to country-of-origin and, therefore, greatly affect consumer decision making and buyer sourcing decisions. These characteristics may involve specific design or workmanship skills which have been linked historically to certain countries, and, to the extent that these skills have not been diffused over time, they will be used by consumers to reduce risk in purchasing (for example, the skills associated with the production of Persian carpets, Belgian lace, Scandinavian design in furnishings, French or Italian design in clothing, etc.). Sometimes it is the raw materials that a country produces, because of geography or geology or climate conditions, which suit it particularly well for the production of certain products (e.g., Colombian coffee, Canadian furs, French wine, or South African diamonds). Finally, the product characteristic being sought may be linked to closely held technology or knowledge which is country-specific, at least in the short run (e.g., computer software and military equipment from the U.S., biogenetic engineering in agriculture from Canada, or high-speed inter-urban transport systems from France).

The decision criteria used by consumers, even when they are not expressed as country-of-origin, may lead to country-related choices. For example, consumers seeking a low-cost product may say that they do not care where it comes from, as long as it is cheap. In this case, the country effect may directly act on buyers or suppliers who choose to source the product where production costs are low, often because of low wage rates paid to industrious laborers. Even if the consumer does not check to see where the product is made when buying, the consumer's choice is affected

Table 5. A Framework of Product/Country Image Effects

Factor	Who	How	Product Dimension	Country Dimension	Type of Effect
Product Characteristics					
Complexity	B,C	D	Product Integrity	Belief	Reduce risk
Uniqueness (of country)					
- design & workmanship	B,C	D	Performance/ Appearance; Product Integrity	Cultural similarity; Affect; Industriousness	Reduce risk
- technology	B,C	D	Product Integrity	Belief	Reduce risk
- resources	B,C C	D I	Product Integrity	Geography; Resources	Reduce risk
Decision Criteria					
Price (low)	B	D	Price-Value	Industriousness	Reduce cost
	C	I	Price-Value	Industriousness	Reduce cost
Performance	B,C	D	Product Integrity	Belief	Surrogate measure
Status	C	D	Response (Proud)	Affect (Taste)	Symbol
After-sales service	B,C	D	Market Presence	Belief	Reduce risk
Decision Process					
Search time (limited)	C	I	Market Presence	Belief	Reduce effort
Information processing	C	I	Product Integrity; Market Presence	Belief; Affect	Summary construct
Quality judgment	B,C	D,I	Product Integrity	Belief	Summary construct
Choice	B,C	D,I	Product Integrity	Affect; Belief	Summary construct or Halo effect
Purchase	B,C	D,I	Market Presence	Affect; Belief	Halo effect or Summary construct
Individual Characteristics					
Ethnicity and ethnocentrism	C	D	Response	Affect; Link	Stereotype
Travel	C	D	Response	Affect; Link	Stereotype
Nationalism	C	D	Response	Affect; Link	Stereotype
Sex	C	D	Product Integrity Response	Affect; Belief Link	Stereotype

Legend. B = organizational Buyer; C = Consumer (end-user)
D = Direct effect; I = Indirect effect
Product Integrity, Price-Value, Market Presence, Response, Belief, Affect, and Link: as defined in-text.

by the supplier's sourcing decisions in a price competitive environment. So, in this case the country effect is direct for the buyers or suppliers and indirect on consumers.

In another case, consumers may be looking for a high status product. Often the status will be directly derived from the country of manufacture (cameras from Japan; cars from Italy, Germany or Sweden; wines from France). The product image dimension of the country involved in this case is a response component of pride of ownership and is associated with the exquisiteness or high-class taste of the source country. The country-of-origin serves directly as a status symbol.

If performance is a key criterion, country-of-origin may serve as a surrogate measure of quality because of the beliefs held about the level of industrial development and quality of products produced in a country. This country effect will be direct both on consumers and on suppliers or buyers of products.

Elements of the decision process will also be related to the extent and mechanisms involved in the country effect. If decision time is short, the market presence dimension will likely be important. Consumers will buy products which they find most readily available. Producers with wide distribution, easily remembered brand names, and heavy advertising will benefit from their efforts under this situation. The country effect will be an indirect one affecting consumers who would not have said that country was important in their decision. Nevertheless, the marketplace reality will be that it plays an important role in what was chosen. When consumers are processing information about products, particularly in complex environments, country-of-origin is one type of information that is often used as a summary construct to encapsulate knowledge about product performance or price/value. Again, consumers may not say that country-of-origin is important, but they may nevertheless use it indirectly to help process information.

It is not possible, of course, to discuss the framework in Table 5 exhaustively here. Further, the framework is not meant to be "finished" and all-inclusive. Rather, we propose it as a tool that we hope will be useful in generating discussion and suggesting avenues for further research.

The country-of-origin phenomenon is a very complex one. Its manifestation may be subtle or obvious, directly or indirectly experienced by consumers or suppliers of goods and services, operant because of decision criteria used or decision process stage conditions, and related to individual and product characteristics and use situations. In the future, continuous monitoring of product-country images through more highly validated measures of both product and country-people images is needed. The structure of these images needs further investigation, as do the interactions among the dimensions. But even more strongly, we would encourage researchers to explore the conditions, bases, and reasons for country image effects. Like the verse from the 1950s' song which was used as part of this chapter's title, we must try to learn the "wheres" and "whens"–and more. The intent must be to ascertain under what conditions, when, for whom, why, where, and through what mechanisms do product-country images affect consumption–because they do!

REFERENCES

Albaum, Gerald and Robert A. Peterson (1984), "Empirical Research in International Marketing 1976-1982." *Journal of International Business Studies* (Spring/Summer) 161-173.

ASQC (American Society for Quality Control) (1980), *Consumer Attitudes on Quality in the U.S.* Milwaukee, WI: ASQC.

Bannister, J.P. and J.A. Saunders (1978), "U.K. Consumers' Attitudes Towards Imports: The Measurement of National Stereotype Image." *European Journal of Marketing*, 12, 8, 562- 570.

Barker, Tansu A. and T. Robinson (1987), "Saskatchewan Consumers' Perceptions of Domestic and Imported Products." In R.E Turner, ed., *Marketing*, Vol. 8 (Toronto, Ont.: Proceedings of the Administrative Sciences of Canada–Marketing Division, June), 186-195.

Baumgartner, Gary, and Alain Jolibert (1977), "The Perception of Foreign Products in France." In H.K. Hunt, ed., *Advances in Consumer Research*, vol. V (Ann Arbor, Michigan: Association for Consumer Research), 603-605.

Cattin, Philippe, Alain Jolibert, and Colleen Lohnes (1982), "A Cross-Cultural Study of 'Made In' Concepts." *Journal of International Business Studies* (Winter) 131-141.

Damanpour, Faramarz and John H. Hallaq (1981), "A Survey to Evaluate 'Made In' Product Images of Industrial Countries: A Comparison of U.S. and Danish Consumers' Perceptions." Paper presented to the *Conference of The Academy of International Business* (Montreal, Canada, October) 15-17.

Darling, John R. and Frederic B. Kraft (1977), "A Competitive Profile of Products and Associated Marketing Practices of Selected European and non-European Countries." *European Journal of Marketing*, 11, 7, 519-531.

Dickerson, Kitty G. (1986, November 7), "Consumers rate U.S. clothes higher than imports." *Marketing News*, 30.

Douglas, Susan P. and Samuel Craig (1983), *International Marketing Research*. Englewood Cliffs, NJ: Prentice-Hall.

Erickson, Gary M., Johny K. Johansson, and Paul Chao (1984), "Image Variables in Multi-Attribute Product Evaluations: Country-of-Origin Effects." *Journal of Consumer Research*, 11: (September) 694-699.

Forgas, J.P. and M. O'Driscoll (1984), "Cross-Cultural and Demographic Differences in the Perception of Nations." *Journal of Cross-Cultural Psychology*, 15, 199-222.

Gaedeke, Ralph (1973), "Consumer Attitudes Toward Products 'Made In' Developing Countries." *Journal of Retailing*, 49(2) (Summer), 13-24.

Garland, Barbara C., Tansu A. Barker, and John C. Crawford (1987), "A Cross-National Test of a Conceptual Framework of Willingness to Buy Products of Foreign Origin." In K.D. Bahn and M.J. Sirgy (eds.), *Third World Marketing Congress* (Barcelona: Academy of Marketing Science, August) 124-130.

Han, Min C. (1988), "The Role of Consumer Patriotism in the Choice of Domestic versus Foreign Products." *Journal of Advertising Research*, 28(3) (June-July), 25-32.

Han, Min C. (1989), "Country Image: Halo or Summary Construct?" *Journal of Marketing Research*, XXVI: (May) 222-229.

Heslop, Louise A. and Marjorie Wall (1985), "Differences Between Men and Women in the Formation of Country-of-Origin Product Images." In J.C. Chebat (ed.), *Marketing*, Vol. 6 (Montreal: Administrative Sciences Association of Canada–Marketing Division, May) 148-157.

Heslop, Louise A. and Marjorie Wall (1986), "Two Views of the World: Differences Between Men and Women on Perceptions of Countries as Producers of Consumer Goods." In T.E. Muller (ed.), *Marketing*, Vol. 7 (Whistler, B.C.: Proceedings, Administrative Sciences Association of Canada–Marketing Division, June) 179-185.

Heslop, Louise A., John P. Liefeld, and Marjorie Wall (1987), "An Experimental Study of the Impact of Country-of-Origin Information." In R.E. Turner (ed.), *Marketing*, Vol. 8 (Toronto, Ont.: Proceedings, Administrative Sciences Association of Canada–Marketing Division, June) 179-185.

Hill, C.E. and D.E. Stull (1981), "Sex Differences in Effects of Social Value Similarity in Same Sex Friendship." *Journal of Personality and Social Psychology*, 78, 165-171.

Johansson, Johny K. and Israel D. Nebenzahl (1986), "Multinational Production: Effect on Brand Value." *Journal of International Business Studies*, 17, 3 (Fall) 101-126.

Johansson, Johny K. and Israel D. Nebenzahl (1987), "Country-of-Origin, Social Norms and Behavioral Intentions." *Advances in International Marketing*, vol. 2, 65-79.

Johansson, Johny K., Susan P. Douglas, and Ikujiro Nonaka (1985), "Assessing the Impact of Country of Origin on Product Evaluations: A New Methodological Perspective." *Journal of Marketing Research*, XXII: (November) 388-96.

Jones, R.A. and R.D. Ashmore (1973), "The Structure of Intergroup Perception." *Journal of Personality and Social Psychology*, 25, 428-438.

Kelman, Herbert C., ed. (1965), *International Behavior*. New York: Holt, Rinehart, Winston.

Lillis, Charles M. and Chem L. Narayana (1974), "Analysis of 'Made-in' Product Images–An Exploratory Study." *Journal of International Business Studies* (Spring), 119-127.

Lumpkin, James R. and John C. Crawford (1985), "Consumer Perceptions of Developing Countries." In N.K. Malhotra (ed.), *Developments in Marketing Science,* VIII (Miami, FL: Academy of Marketing Science) 95-99.

Nagashima, Akira (1970), "A Comparison of Japanese and U.S. Attitudes Towards Foreign Products." *Journal of Marketing,* 34 (January) 68-74.

Nagashima, Akira (1977), "A Comparative 'Made In' Product Image Survey Among Japanese Businessmen." *Journal of Marketing,* 41 (July), 95-100.

Narayana, Chem L. (1981), "Aggregate Images of American and Japanese Products: Implications on International Marketing." *Columbia Journal of World Business,* 16 (Summer), 31-35.

Niffenegger, P., J. White, and G. Marmet (1980), "How British Retail Managers View French and American Products." *European Journal of Marketing,* 14, 8, 493-498.

Papadopoulos, Nicolas (1986), "Development and Organization of a Cross-national Study: The Country-of-Origin Effect." In M.F. Bradley and Nicolas Papadopoulos (eds.), *Proceedings, Workshop on International Marketing Strategy* (Brussels: European Institute for Advanced Studies in Management) 42-56.

Papadopoulos, Nicolas and Louise A. Heslop (1986), "Travel as a Correlate of Product and Country Images." In T.E. Muller (ed.), *Marketing,* vol. 7 (Whistler, B.C.: Administrative Sciences Association of Canada–Marketing Division, May) 191- 200.

Papadopoulos, Nicolas, Judith J. Marshall, and Louise A. Heslop (1988), "Strategic Implications of Product and Country Images: A Modelling Approach." *Marketing Productivity* (European Society for Opinion and Marketing Research, 41st Research Congress, Lisbon, September) 69-90.

Renwick, Frank and Rebecca Renwick (1988), "Country of Origin Images: Influence of Purchasing Experience and Social Linkages Upon Cross-Cultural Stereotyping." *Working Paper,* University College of Cape Breton (Cape Bretton, Canada).

Robinson, J.P. and R. Hefner (1967), "Multidimensional Differences in Public and Academic Perceptions of Nations." *Journal of Personality and Social Psychology,* 25, 428-438.

Schooler, Robert D. (1971), "Bias Phenomena Attendant to the Marketing of Foreign Goods in the U.S." *Journal of International Business Studies,* 2: (Spring) 71-80.

Seaton, Bruce and Robert H. Vogel (1981), "International Dimensions and Price as Factors in Consumer Perceptions of Autos." Paper presented at the *Conference of The Academy of International Business* (Montreal, October).

Sternquist, B. and S. Tolbert (1986, May 23), "Survey: Retailers Shun Apparel Industry's Buy American Program." *Marketing News,* 8.

Taormina, R.J. and D. Messick (1983), "Deservingness for Foreign Aid: Effects of Need, Similarity, and Estimated Effectiveness." *Journal of Applied Social Psychology,* 13, 371- 391.

Tims, A.R. and M.M. Miller (1983), "Another Look at What Affects Attitudes

Toward Foreign Countries." Paper presented to the *American Association of Public Opinion Research Annual Convention* (Buck Hill Falls, Pennsylvania).

Tongberg, R.C. (1972), *An Empirical Study of Relationships Between Dogmatism and Consumer Attitudes Towards Foreign Products.* PhD Dissertation, Pennsylvania State University.

Wall, Marjorie and Louise A. Heslop (1986), "Consumer Attitudes toward Canadian-made versus Imported Products." *Journal of the Academy of Marketing Science,* 14(2): 27-36.

Wang, Chih-Kang (1978), *The Effect of Foreign Economic, Political and Cultural Environment on Consumers' Willingness to Buy Foreign Products.* PhD Dissertation, Texas A & M University.

Wang, Chih-Kang and Charles W. Lamb (1983), "The Impact of Selected Environmental Forces Upon Consumers' Willingness to Buy Foreign Products." *Journal of the Academy of Marketing Science,* 11(2): (Winter) 71-84.

White, Phillip D. (1979), "Attitudes of U.S. Purchasing Managers Toward Industrial Products Manufactured In Selected Western European Nations." *Journal of International Business Studies,* 20 (Spring-Summer), 81-90.

Wish, M., M. Deutsch, and L. Biener (1970), "Differences in Concpetual Structures of Nations: An Exploratory Study." *Journal of Personality and Social Psychology,* 16, 361-373.

Yaprak, Attila and R. Parameswaran (1986), "Strategy Formulation in Multinational Marketing: A Deductive, Paradigm-Integrating Approach." *Advances in International Marketing,* 1: 21-45.

Yavas, Ugur and Secil Tuncalp (1984), "Exporting Saudi-Arabia: The Power of the 'Made-in' Label." *International Marketing Review,* 1,4, 40-46.

Chapter 3

Missing a Strategic Opportunity: Managers' Denial of Country-of-Origin Effects

Johny K. Johansson

INTRODUCTION

At the cash register, you don't care about country-of-origin or country of residence. . . . You don't worry about where the product was made. . . . All you care about is the product quality, price, design, value, and appeal to you as a consumer.

This stinging quote is from a *Harvard Business Review* article on global strategy by Kenichi Ohmae, McKinsey's leader in Japan (Ohmae 1989, p. 144). In this commentary, I want to take issue with the statement and show how and why Ohmae is completely wrong. I will then identify what I see as the strategic role of country-of-origin (CO) research.

A RATIONAL DENIAL?

As those of the readers who know Ohmae's work already realize, his opinions are largely just that, his opinions. Nevertheless, his opinions very often reflect the thinking of senior managers–usually less of those in Japan and more of the Western managers he advises–and thus reflect a quite

A preliminary version of this paper was presented at the 1990 Academy of International Business Conference in Toronto (October), as part of the Key Panel on Product and Country Images organized by the editors of this book.

common misconception. Why do people persist in not believing our research?

A Misinterpretation

The simplest answer is that managers misinterpret the research findings. Even we in the CO field can agree that, yes, many people might buy for the reasons Ohmae mentions, rather than because they like or dislike a country. But this does not mean that country-of-origin has no effect. Rather, the country-of-origin helps the consumer make the desired evaluations. To exemplify, how does the consumer know that the product possesses "high quality, a reasonable price, attractive design, good value, and special appeal to you as a consumer?" We have shown that these characteristics often flow from the product's country-of-origin. "High quality" is often associated with countries such as Germany and Japan, "reasonable price" with American products, "attractive design" with Italian products, "good value" with Japan and South Korea, and "special appeal" with countries such as France and Switzerland. How the matching is done depends of course on what products one is looking at. But if the consumer sees a strange design, and is told it is from Italy, he or she is prone to reassess initial impressions. If it is from Taiwan, no such effort is undertaken.

Country-of-origin is, in fact, used by consumers to reinforce, create, and bias initial perceptions of products. In most instances this influence is not misleading–if it were, it would soon be ignored (as Ohmae suggests it is). But when BMW asks its component supplier Bosch to source from its Japanese subsidiary for BMW cars, it is not because BMW likes Japan–it is because the Bosch subsidiary in Japan produces better components than its German plants. And the next time BMW has a choice, the company would rather have the Japanese subsidiary supply other components as well, sight unseen. It is of course only natural–BMW assumes that the Japanese subsidiary does a better job.

The CO effects are not minor or incidental. They are simply antecedents of the more "intrinsic" characteristics we as consumers like to think we use to evaluate products. This is perhaps easiest to see when we are negatively surprised. Most products cannot be completely evaluated before a purchase, despite Ohmae's statement. When we buy a camera, a car, a stereo, even a simple product like coffee, we often want the support from a well established brand name–and a reasonable country-of-origin. Learning that their GM pickup truck was built in Mexico or their Folgers coffee is not from Colombia will shake some consumers up. The country-of-origin is sometimes taken for granted–and therefore we as consumers do not pay attention to it. But as such experiences will teach us, the latent effect can be quite significant.

Lack of Credibility

There could be other reasons for the denial of the empirical evidence. Executives might not misinterpret our research, rather they simply do not pay attention to it. But Ohmae's awareness of the issue belies that. If he finds it worthwhile to try to debunk it, the word must have gotten out somehow.

It seems more valid to argue that our credibility is low. From a methodological viewpoint, one could say that the external validity of CO research is low and this type of consumer behavior research is often dismissed because the subjects are students. If this is what is going on, the executives miss the point in two ways. First of all, most of the big and important studies do work with samples from real-life populations–I can think of the big study by *Reader's Digest* in the early 1960s (Reader's Digest 1963), for example, and Nicolas and Louise's study[1] (1989) with some 2,200 consumers in eight countries (Papadopoulos, Heslop, and Bamossy 1989). Real people show the CO influence as well.

Second, when the country-of-origin effect is inferred from estimated relationships between variables, the use of convenience samples is not a very serious drawback. Even if the levels of attitude items and preferences are not typical of the population at large, the correlation between them may well be valid and accurate for the larger population. As Liefeld (1990) shows, the use of student samples really is not an important issue.[2]

If external validity is not a problem–and I think it is not–what about internal validity? Here I think we have some possible problems (the issue of whether the country-of-origin influence appears because other factors are omitted, for example), but I also think that managers are not very sensitive to such technical matters. Liefeld's meta-analysis suggests that surveys tend to overestimate the country-of-origin effect (Liefeld 1990). But a closer examination of the surveys analyzed suggests that this is a problem of a certain subset of the surveys in which country-of-origin is a particularly salient cue (Han and Qualls 1985). When the multiple variety of influences are accounted for so that internal validity is not a problem, the studies, whether experiments or surveys, still show a systematic and strong effect from the country-of-origin.

---

1. Ed. note: The main findings from that study are presented in Chapter 2.
2. Ed. note: Also see Chapter 5 by Liefeld.

The major problem might be the measurement. The managers do not believe it is possible to trust the responses given–the measurement is simply not trustworthy. They have not studied exactly how the research is done, but might have the kind of knee-jerk reaction to the studies as economists display with respect to any survey research: "People are lying."

The problem with this line of argument is that most studies which ask directly whether country-of-origin is an important factor in respondents' purchase decisions *find that it is not!* In my own studies, I find that the respondents, when asked explicitly about it, consistently play down the role of country-of-origin in their recorded product evaluations. Despite this, the inferred CO effect is still strong.

This is a reflection of the same kind of counter-bias that seems to afflict the managers. It goes well with the notion that one should be tolerant of people from other countries, in itself a negative demand bias in the surveys. This is counter to the findings by Liefeld (1990), who shows that there seems to be a positive demand bias in surveys. This seems to be due to a "home country" bias, however, with respondents willing to support their own country's products, at least in name (Liefeld 1990). Judging other countries' products on the basis of origin, by contrast, is less socially acceptable.

When the assessment of country-of-origin effects is done by simply asking people to associate brands or products and countries, the measurement problem is acute. This calls the country-of-origin into saliency much more than warranted in a real purchasing situation, where the made-in label is often unnoticed. The point about such studies is that they are to be interpreted simply as perceptual associations between country and product images. They say nothing directly about how important these country-of-origin images are for the final purchasing decisions–the level at which Ohmae's criticism is aimed. If one presents them as speaking about the importance of the cues, one plays right into Ohmae's hands–in that respect the studies do in fact suffer from clear measurement error. The fact that someone perceives German cars to be well engineered does not mean that he or she will buy a German car because of it.

The Convergence Notion

There might be another reason why practitioners deny the CO effect. There might be a sense that the world is converging, becoming "one," and in the process national differences will disappear. As people grow more understanding of foreign cultures, they will jettison their perceived stereotypes, and the country-of-origin effect will vanish.

The problem with this thinking is the implicit–and sometimes explicit–assumption that the stereotypes are unwarranted biases. They may of course be; and to the extent they are, increased understanding between countries will lead to a more global mindset with more accurate perceptions. But this does not mean that the actual and the perceived differences between countries will diminish.

Most evidence we have suggests that, on balance, increased globalization is leading to a greater appreciation of the actual differences between countries and peoples. It is not until one visits Japan to experience their personal service that the differences with the U.S. really stand out. It is not until one really investigates what goes into the building of a Mercedes, and the assembly of a Cadillac, that one realizes the magnitude of the American auto problem. And, to cite a recent example, it was not until the Berlin Wall was down that one could recognize how deep the economic problems facing the formerly Communist countries really were.

It is in fact the people who know little about a country who seem to be most prone to argue that "they are really the same as we." We may be, as human beings, but we surely are not as citizens in different countries. And for those who would argue that economic growth, technology, and communication will create convergence (the globalization argument of Levitt 1983), the answer emerging is that, "Yes, perhaps, in the really long term–but only on the supply side, not on the demand side."

The CO effect is a supply side effect. It derives from the differing capabilities of different countries to produce high quality products. And over time, as economic growth occurs and is shared through international trade, it is more likely that countries specialize in what they do best. Consumers already recognize that. Rather than fight this phenomenon, arguing that CO effects wash out, managers should realize that in the future, if anything, CO effects will become more pronounced–as, in fact, our research suggests.

AN EMOTIONAL PROBLEM?

So, where are we left? The denial is probably more emotional than logical. That is, there is no factual underpinning for denying the country-of-origin role, except one's own opinions–just the level that Ohmae is satisfied with. The managers he talks to obviously want to be seen as rational, objective decision makers, choosing suppliers and products on intrinsic quality grounds, not extrinsic cues such as made-in labels. It is not good for their company and for the people at large to be prejudiced against a country, and it does not look good to the people at large. These managers know it, as do their lawyers.

The denial is strikingly phony. Not only does the evidence of our research show the effects from country-of-origin to be strong, but the denial also ignores the fact that these same managers talk about the quality (or lack of it) of "American" products, the reliability of "Japanese" products, the workmanship of "German" products. These same individuals who deny the influence of country-of-origin pass sweeping judgments about the manufacturing skills of the Japanese, the hard work of the Koreans, the entrepreneurial flair of the Hong Kong Chinese. Rather than being wrong, such assessments are often based on real evidence–just as our evidence is that customers judge products against these country stereotypes.

When the managers are placed in the role of customers and are forced to own up to their denial, our predictions bear out wonderfully. Finding out that their Saville Row suit is made in Hong Kong, they revolt. Learning that the Chryslers in their car fleet are built in Mexico, they don't like it a bit. When their Volkswagen Rabbit is built in Pennsylvania, they turn away. When told that the new Canon camera they bought for the vacation is actually made in Taiwan, they feel cheated.

The point about this all is not that managers and other people are unfairly prejudiced against foreign countries and refuse to acknowledge it. Rather, the point is that the prejudice is very often–though not always–based on correctly identified underlying differences in capabilities, summarized in the country-of-origin cue. Unless manufacturing is completely standardized, it is generally wise to assume that there is a difference between products from different countries. Customers know this, use the cue accordingly, but will deny it because of the behavioral norms they face. They say–and think–that they can critically evaluate complicated products such as cars and tractors and television sets, when in fact most information has to be taken on faith. This faith is based on the manufacturer's brand, the dealer–and the country-of-origin.

COUNTRY-OF-ORIGIN EFFECTS AND STRATEGY

If managers deny the effect of CO cues because of ethical predispositions, little more need be said. On the other hand, to the extent the denial is a result of the sense that nothing can be done about it anyway, it will be important for us as researchers to further develop the managerial implications in some depth. So, we have found a strong country-of-origin effect–

what difference does it make for the executive trying to develop the marketing strategy for a new brand?

Country-of-origin does in fact have several strategic implications. Which country to manufacture in can be chosen, as is done in the typical foreign direct investment (FDI) case. Further, where manufacturing and assembly is geographically dispersed, as in the typical case of the multinational company, which country is featured is also a matter of choice (although circumscribed by international legal conventions). Then there is the communication strategy choice of what to do with the CO cue: whether to feature it prominently, or whether to play it down. This latter issue impacts not only advertising, but also packaging, and, of course, branding.

The promotional use of the CO is the most obvious application but also in a strategic sense the least interesting one. To advertise that a particular product has been manufactured abroad ("imported beer" or "Japanese quality") can be done "on the sly," as it were, without necessarily basing the whole marketing strategy on the CO affiliation. Accordingly, the decision can be made at the functional middle management level without much strategic input.

The FDI case is actually the more fundamental and important one. Research has shown two things. The first finding is that the shift of manufacturing to a country with more favorable image will in fact translate into some advantage–more specifically, into a higher evaluative product rating (see, for example, Johansson and Nebenzahl 1986). One would also expect that moving into a low-wage country with weaker image would be a negative factor, but this shift is mitigated by the fact that such strategic relocations often are limited to simpler products (leisure apparel, inexpensive watches, cheaper running shoes, etc.) where the manufacturing process can be standardized (see, for example, Chao 1989).

A second finding is that for products manufactured away from home, a strong brand name may override the country-of-origin effect. A Sony manufactured in Hong Kong is basically still a Sony, albeit with some slightly tarnished image (see Tse and Lee 1989). It seems that the established brand name may provide the insurance needed to accept a low-wage country–after all, an H-P calculator manufactured in Singapore is still backed by the H-P warranty. Nevertheless, when the perceived distance between alternative production sites is large, consumers may expect to find a significant price differential between high-wage and low-wage countries.[3]

These findings are also relevant for the multinational "assembly" case,

---

3. Ed. note: See Chapter 6 by Nebenzahl and Jaffe.

where the dispersed manufacturing generates so-called "hybrid" products. The research on hybrid products is still in its infancy, having yet to solve the problem of how to deal with the stimulus complexity resulting from multiple country sourcing (see, for example, Czepiec and Gottko 1984). Nevertheless, given what we know about overseas production locations, one would expect a strong brand name again to compensate for a foreign manufacturing location.

Such findings also suggest that well-established brand names have clear "home" countries. A Hewlett-Packard calculator is "American," a Sony TV is Japanese, et cetera, regardless of where they have actually been manufactured. This can be good news to companies in developed countries, since manufacturing locations overseas will be acceptable. By the same token, however, it may be bad news for developing countries. Companies from the third world might well plan to associate their products with a more advantageous location by assembly in a developed market country. Such an effort might be much less economical than the OEM path of associating the firm with an established host country brand, at least in the short and medium term. Creating one's own brand name–as, for example, Goldstar is now doing in the United States–would seem a viable option only if a very long-term view is adopted, regardless of the successful Japanese examples. Perhaps an intermediate step should be considered, with the adoption of a Western-sounding brand name. Sony, the great pathbreaker for the Japanese, was, after all, long perceived to be "American," even in the Japanese home market (the evidence here is weak, but personal interviews tend to confirm this "myth"; see, for example, Ohsone 1986).

These findings about the strength of the brand name would seem at first glance to reduce the strategic relevance of the country-of-origin. As long as the firm can have some confidence in managing their manufacturing process abroad, the manufacturing can be shifted to a low-wage country. The negative marketing impact can be countered by a brand name campaign backed by the requisite service and warranty offers, and the effect from shifting manufacturing overseas can be rendered negligible.

But for those who see this argument as suggesting that the brand name "wipes out" the country-of-origin effect, one can suggest the opposite. One simply has to ask oneself the question of whether Toyota means "Toyota"–or whether Toyota means "Japanese?" Judging from the findings we have, the answer is, in fact, the latter. As recent research on the Japanese auto successes overseas shows, the country effect completely dominates the brand effect (Hanssens and Johansson 1988).

A company like Toyota knows this well, insisting on using Japanese-sounding brand names (such as the Toyota "Camry") instead of easier to pronounce Western names–even though many use the Western names in the *home* market (such as the Toyota "Crown," the model which inspired the Camry name, "Camry" being Japanese for "Crown"). They want their products to be identifiably "Japanese." Only when it deems that the Japanese connotation no longer is beneficial, but on the contrary detracts from the positioning strategy, will the company adopt a more Western-sounding name (such as the Lexus). The Honda counterexample is also instructive. As is well known, Honda's use of Western names like the Accord and the Civic was used to differentiate the company away from the dominant Japanese competitors in overseas markets, while the name "Honda" itself was still recognizably Japanese (Sakiya 1982).

CONCLUDING COMMENTS

As long as executives deny the CO research findings and avoid facing up to their strategic implications, we can have but little impact on the companies' global marketing strategies. The same holds true, of course, for the impact on our own colleagues in the profession, who do not connect the CO research to the larger issues. In the final analysis, it is of course our own job to establish the connections. As academic researchers, showing an empirical effect using scientific methodology and explaining it theoretically might seem the most important work. But once we are convinced that the effect is true and important, we also have to turn to the dissemination of the knowledge to the relevant decision makers. If we want to avoid having businesspeople like Ohmae speak badly of us, we have to connect to strategy when we present our country-of-origin findings.

As argued above, the links between CO and strategy are several and quite obvious. In presenting them to the practicing manager or our professional colleagues, it may be best to emphasize from the outset that CO effects have essentially the same characteristics as country-specific advantages. The made-in label identifying the country-of-origin represents the country-specific advantages in precisely the same way that a brand name represents the firm-specific advantages.

Thus the made-in label can be made to carry exactly the same cachet as a good brand name does. To deny this strategic possibility is tantamount to denying the power of branding, an untenable position in this day of designer brands, brand extensions, and brand equity. To repeat, the reason the CO effect exists is that the made-in label in fact embodies the very "product quality, price, design, value, and appeal" characteristics that

Ohmae values so highly. This is not as bad as the ethically conscious person might think. It is not unwarranted prejudice. We are simply using the available information quite efficiently. That's why, even if we are not buying "American," we are buying "Japanese."

REFERENCES

Chao, Paul (1989), "Export versus Reverse Investment: Strategic Implications for Newly Industrialized Countries." *Journal of International Business Studies* (Spring) 75-91.

Czepiec, H. and J. Gottko (1984), "Impact of Consumer Orientations on Perceptions of Hybrid Product Quality." Paper presented at the *Conference of The Academy of International Business* (Cleveland, Ohio, October).

Han, Min C., and William J. Qualls (1985), "Country-of-Origin Effects and their Impact Upon Consumers' Perception of Quality." In C.T. Tan and J. Sheth (eds.), *Historical Perspectives in Consumer Research: National and International Perspectives* (Association for Consumer Research, School of Management, University of Singapore).

Hanssens, D.M. and J.K. Johansson (1988), "Synergy or Rivalry? The Japanese Autos' Success in Overseas Markets." Paper presented at the *European International Business Association Conference* (Berlin, December).

Johansson, Johny K. and Israel D. Nebenzahl (1986), "Multinational Production: Effect on Brand Value." *Journal of International Business Studies*, 17, 3 (Fall) 101-126.

Levitt, Theodore (1983), "The Globalization of Markets." *Harvard Business Review* (May-June), 92-102.

Liefeld, John P. (1990), "Issues in Country-of-origin Experimental Research: A Meta Analysis." Paper presented at the *Conference of The Academy of International Business* (Toronto, October).

Ohmae, K. (1989), "The Global Logic of Strategic Alliances." *Harvard Business Review* (March-April), 143-154.

Ohsone, M. (1986), head of the Sony Discman development group, Sony Headquarters, Shinagawa, Tokyo. *Personal interview.*

Papadopoulos, Nicolas, Louise A. Heslop, and Gary J. Bamossy (1989), "International Competitiveness of American and Japanese Products." In Nicolas Papadopoulos (ed.), *Dimensions of International Business,* 2 (Ottawa, Canada: International Business Study Group, Carleton University).

Reader's Digest Corporation (1963), *European Common Market and Britain.* New York.

Sakiya, Tetsuo (1982), *Honda Motor: The Men, the Management, and the Machines.* Tokyo: Kodansha.

Tse, D. and W. Lee (1989). "Evaluating Products of Multiple Countries-of-Origin Effect: Effects of Component Origin, Assembly Origin, and Brand." *Working Paper,* Faculty of Commerce, University of British Columbia, Vancouver, Canada.

PART II.
AN OVERVIEW OF RESEARCH

INTRODUCTION

Part II consists of two chapters whose purpose is to point to new directions by outlining and critically reviewing the findings of past research into product and country images.

Chapter 4 offers a "map" of the international marketing literature on country-of-origin by synthesizing the findings of studies in five key areas, ranging from perceptions of national characteristics to methodological issues.

Chapter 5 provides a unique perspective on country-of-origin research to date through a method which has not been utilized before in the product/country image research field: a quantitative meta-analysis of the size-of-effects estimates from past experimental studies. The chapter focuses on such issues as the use of student vs. consumer samples or intangible vs. tangible cues in experimental research and compares between-subject experiments to within-subject experiments and surveys.

By re-assessing and integrating the findings of past research, these two chapters draw significant implications that are likely to influence the course of future country-of-origin research for some time.

Chapter 4

Mapping Country-of-Origin Research: Recent Developments and Emerging Avenues

C. Christopher Baughn
Attila Yaprak

INTRODUCTION

The globalization of markets and multinational production within the last two decades have underscored the need for greater proficiency in understanding the impact of product and country image on cross-national consumer behavior. Research on country-of-origin (CO) effects, for example, has shown that such proficiency can contribute to the development of effective global marketing programs by synthesizing the attitudinal constructs observed in different national markets with strategy formulation (Yaprak and Parameswaran 1986). Indeed, research spanning the past 25 years has demonstrated that both industrial buyers and consumers develop stereotyped images of countries and/or their outputs and that these can affect behavior (Bilkey and Nes 1982; Yaprak 1987; Hooley, Shipley, and Krieger 1988; Schooler 1965).

This research has further shown that negative evaluations by consumers on the basis of country images constitute significant market barriers for firms from less developed countries (Schooler, Wildt, and Jones 1987); that multinational firms manufacturing abroad may also risk potential loss in brand name value (Johansson and Nebenzahl 1986); and that country images affect the positioning strategies of firms competing in their home market against foreign rivals (Hooley, Shipley, and Krieger 1988).

As Bilkey and Nes (1982) underscored in their extensive review of the country-of-origin literature, however, insufficient theoretical underpinnings and methodological deficiencies have limited the utility of past CO studies. For example, the vast majority of pre-Bilkey and Nes studies have been single-cue works. They have also focused on product perceptions rather than product experiences of consumers. Further, the methodological properties of variables used in these studies have not been properly accounted for.

The dramatic transformation of the world economy within the last decade has also reduced the applicability of pre-Bilkey and Nes research. Intensifying global competition and rapid growth in global sourcing and production configurations, for example, have led to "hybrid" products (products that contain components or ingredients made in various countries). Also, the explosive growth in global strategic alliances and countertrade arrangements have resulted in a proliferation of world markets with truly "multinational" goods and services.

These developments bring forward significant questions about the way consumers acquire, process and use image cues, the interrelationships between these and other product cues (e.g., price, styling), and changes in consumer perceptions and attitudes. They also underscore the significance of country information as a reference in the competitive positioning of brands and as a surrogate indicator of product quality.

Fortunately, since Bilkey and Nes' seminal review, many studies have enhanced our understanding of the role country and product images play in the formulation of global marketing strategies. In this context, contributions include empirical research in cue processing and usage, experimentation on country images as a surrogate, summary or halo construct, the use of multiattribute modeling to isolate the independent effects of country image on purchase behavior, and investigations of the effects of multinational sourcing and production on brand name value.

The increasing complexity of the field may itself limit our ability to understand and utilize the strategic implications of product and country images. The purpose of this chapter is to synthesize the post-Bilkey and Nes contributions into a meaningful foundation and to inspire a new wave of studies more relevant to the strategic requirements of the 1990s. To achieve this purpose, the chapter maps out the current contributions into five areas which facilitate the effective formulation of international marketing strategy. These include:

1. understanding of the national characteristics associated with the image of a country's products;
2. assessing the integration of country-of-origin information with other cues used by the consumer in assessing product quality;

3. establishing reliable relationships between CO perceptions and actionable segmentation variables based on consumer characteristics;
4. relating CO cues to our understanding of information processing and attitude formation; and
5. overcoming methodological limitations in CO research.

UNDERSTANDING THE NATIONAL CHARACTERISTICS OF ORIGIN COUNTRIES

The impact of the origin cue has been related to characteristics of the producing country. Bilkey and Nes (1982), for example, described a "hierarchy of biases" relating positive product evaluations to the economic development of the source country (p. 90). Their review also noted that a source country's political climate may lead to lower product evaluations by consumers of other countries than would be predicted solely on the basis of the CO's level of economic development.

Specifically, Bannister and Saunders (1978) as well as Wang (1978) noted lower product evaluations for products of Eastern European countries than those countries' levels of economic development would indicate. Wang and Lamb (1983) also found that consumer willingness to purchase products was related to the economic, political, and cultural characteristics of the product's origin. Given the changing political climate in Eastern Europe and in other areas of the world, we might anticipate significant shifts in such perceptions.

Based on a large scale study involving consumers from eight countries, Papadopoulos, Heslop, and Bamossy (1989, 1990) suggest that perceptions of the sourcing country entail (1) cognitions, including the country's degree of industrial development and technological advancement; (2) affect, regarding the country's people; and (3) a conative component relating to the consumer's desired level of interaction with the source country. While CO research has frequently presented such country perceptions as leading to the development of specific product images, these authors note that a consumer's image of a people with whom they are not familiar may well be formed upon the basis of knowledge about that people's products. For example, their study showed a high level of positive affect toward the Japanese people in the consuming countries, despite limited travel or other exposure to the Japanese other than through Japanese products.

Research on country-of-origin effects is just beginning to address the increasing complexity of multinational inputs in the manufacturing process. Products may well incorporate critical components sourced from countries other than the home country of the manufacturer. Production location for a single product may vary, potentially leading to shifts in product perception (Johansson and Nebenzahl 1986). The burgeoning rate of international joint ventures and other cross-national cooperative linkages (Auster 1987) increases the likelihood that various combinations of country-of-design, component sourcing, and assembly will serve as potential stimuli in influencing consumer evaluations.

In this context, Khanna (1986) reports that consumers in India were quite insistent in purchasing color TV sets (assembled in India) that had picture tubes made in West Germany rather than in South Korea.[1] In consumer electronics purchases, consumers in Singapore have shown similar sensitivity as to the production location (Japan vs. Malaysia) of Japanese-branded products. Indeed, a current issue in the U.S. involves the marked consumer preference for Japanese-branded cars rather than their American "clones," which are manufactured on the same assembly line through joint ventures in the United States ("This Week . . . " 1990).

The prevalence of such "hybrid" products has led to investigations of the relationship between images of the country of manufacture and those of the country of national origin. Seaton and Vogel (1981), for example, found that the preference utility for a German car such as the VW Rabbit declines significantly when its production location shifts to the U.S. In the same vein, Johansson and Nebenzahl (1986) used joint space mapping to chart the image effects resulting from production shifts to several different countries for different brands of automobiles. Production location had an impact on the perceived attributes of the car, the overall attitude toward it, and the price that the consumer would be willing to pay.

This recent research on hybrid products suggests several interesting research questions. A promising research avenue involves studying the nature of the evolution of country image as the product travels through its production path. Under what conditions does the product's design location, assembly center, or sourcing point become the dominant reference for origin information, for example? Is a Japanese firm's advantage in "country-of-design" image neutralized relative to that of an Indian firm, if both assemble the product in Mexico for sale in the U.S.? How can a Malaysian firm marketing its products in the U.S. wisely use origin information along its product's production path (sourcing, prototype assembly, final assembly, etc.) to establish a differential advantage over its

---

1. Ed. note: Related findings are reported in the chapters by Jaffe and Nebenzahl (Seoul Olympics) and Nebenzahl and Jaffe (demand functions from country-of-origin effect).

Japanese competitor in the U.S. market? These types of questions can generate a set of research hypotheses that would lead to fruitful new research.

INTEGRATING COUNTRY-OF-ORIGIN WITH OTHER INFORMATION CUES

Bilkey and Nes (1982) suggested that origin effects could be approached as an information cue question. In this context, production (or design, etc.) location is viewed as one of an array of information cues available to the consumer in evaluating a product. Consumers' use of both intrinsic cues (taste, design, performance) and extrinsic cues (price, brand name, warranties, country-of-origin) in evaluating products has been studied and reported in the literature extensively (see Han 1988a; Zeithaml 1988). Yet a review of the early studies of country-of-origin effects reveals that, generally, these have presented production location as the only cue on which subjects were to base their product evaluations. Not only does this limitation make it hard to estimate the size of the CO effect (Bilkey and Nes 1982), but it also fails to provide information on how or whether the origin effect can be offset by other cues.

These limitations of single-cue models have been demonstrated in research involving price cues. While early single-cue studies have shown a significant impact of price on perceived quality, later studies reveal that, when included with other image variables, the price effect is markedly attenuated (Erickson, Johansson, and Chao 1984). Similarly, the origin effect may be overstated in single-cue studies (Johansson, Douglas, and Nonaka 1985). Since such cues as price may be correlated with the product's origin, multiattribute studies are needed to assess the unique effects of related cues.

A comparison of single-cue treatments (country-of-origin information only) and multi-cue treatments (inclusion of price and brand information with the CO cue) was conducted in a recent experimental study using a consumer sample (Heslop, Liefeld, and Wall 1987). Using tangible products (shirt, billfold, and telephone), the researchers found a stronger origin effect on product quality ratings of their test products when the country-of-origin cue was presented without price and brand information. While not as strong, significant origin effects were, nonetheless, found in the multi-cue treatments for both the billfold and the telephone. Noting the strongest relationships in ratings of the telephone, the researchers suggested that the country-of-origin effect may be more powerful as product complexity and risk increase, and as purchase frequency of that product decreases. With diminished ability to form judgments, consumers appeared to rely more heavily on extrinsic cues such as brand name and country-of-origin.

In this context, Ettenson, Wagner, and Gaeth (1988) assessed the relative impact of such characteristics as price, country-of-origin (People's Republic of China vs. U.S.), brand, style, and fiber content on consumer purchase preference by manipulating levels of product-related stimuli for wearing apparel. Using conjoint analysis, these researchers found that fiber content and price were more important factors than the origin country in the purchase decision. This finding held when the study was rerun following national introduction of a "Made in the U.S.A." campaign.

In assessing the importance of origin country relative to brand name, Nes (1981) found that the negative evaluation of products made in less developed countries was not overcome by a well-known brand name.[2] Brand name was more important, however, in explaining variance in product evaluations than was the country designation. Han and Terpstra (1988) extended this research in investigating source country versus brand name effects for bi-national and uni-national products (Korean, U.S., German, and Japanese TV sets and automobiles). They concluded that sourcing country stimuli had a more powerful effect than brand name on consumer evaluations of bi- national products.

Research integrating origin country with other extrinsic cues is also necessary in assessing the extent to which the effect of production location may require (or allow) different promotional strategies. Bilkey and Nes (1982), for example, suggested that products evaluated negatively on the basis of country-of-origin may require such risk relievers as guarantees by third parties and tests by independent laboratories. Schooler, Wildt, and Jones (1987) assessed the impact of various combinations of price, warranties, and endorsements in developing marketing strategies to overcome consumer bias against foreign products. They found a particularly strong impact of product warranty in influencing choice between a foreign and domestic product. This fits well with the research by Hampton (1977), who found a general increase in perceived risk for products made abroad. Country images have also been found to affect the allowable price differential between domestic and foreign products (Johansson and Nebenzahl 1986; Schooler and Wildt 1968).

Recent studies have expanded the pioneering research of Reierson (1967), who suggested that images of foreign products could be enhanced through the use of promotional material, including association with presti-

---

2. Ed. note: The main findings from Dr. Nes's dissertation are presented in this book (Chapter 7, by Nes and Bilkey).

gious retailers. In this context, Chao (1989) integrated source country, price, and distribution conditions in a study rating the perceived believability of product attribute claims for consumer electronic products. His findings revealed both main and interaction effects which differed by product type. Certain foreign product attribute claims were perceived as more credible when distributed through a prestigious domestic retailer. The credibility effects were not only product-specific, but attribute-specific as well.

In sum, recent research in this avenue has shown that country-of-origin information is, in fact, integrated with other informational cues in forming attitudes towards the product and in expressing purchase intent. Studies assessing the combined effect of various extrinsic cues on product evaluation should continue in the years ahead, as single-cue studies are unlikely to represent adequately the informational environment within which product evaluations take place.

CONSUMER CHARACTERISTICS

In their review, Bilkey and Nes traced several studies which demonstrated that country stereotypes vary as a function of the country in which they are measured. National differences in consumers' evaluation of products from other countries may reflect differential use of criteria in evaluating imports. National differences in attribute importance structures have been found, for example, in studies of industrial buyers (Green, Cunningham, and Cunningham 1975; Lehman and O'Shaughnessy 1974) and consumers (Garland, Barker, and Crawford 1987). In a study comparing U.S. and Japanese consumers' evaluations of attribute importance, Narayana (1981) reported that while both nations' consumers appeared to emphasize quality, recognition, and prestige as important, Japanese consumers also emphasized popularity and functionality–in contrast to U.S. consumers, who indicated that mass production and product expansiveness were favorable attributes.

National differences in response to country-of-origin information may also reflect the level of knowledge that a country's consumers hold regarding products of the producing nation (Yaprak and Parameswaran 1986), as well as the level of international amity or animosity between the specific producer and consumer countries (Schooler 1965). Research studying the effect of country-of-origin cues on Bahraini and Saudi Arabian subjects' evaluations of general product attributes, for example, indicated that cultural proximity among consuming nations was related to similar perceptions regarding "made in" labels (Yavas and Alpay 1984).

Country-of-origin research has often documented a tendency for consumers to prefer their own country's products. Such preference is by no means inevitable for all products, however. For example, current studies of U.S. consumers' perceptions of automobiles indicate a significantly more favorable impression of Japanese as compared to American cars (Erickson, Johansson, and Chao 1984; Johansson, Douglas, and Nonaka 1985; Johansson and Nebenzahl 1986). Indeed, the eight-country study that was previously mentioned found that consumers from Canada, the United States, Great Britain, Greece, and Hungary all provided higher overall ratings for Japanese products than for those produced in their own country (Papadopoulos, Heslop, and Bamossy 1989; also see Heslop et al. 1987, and Papadopoulos, Heslop, and Berács 1990). Of the consumers surveyed, only those from France and West Germany rated their own country's products higher than those of Japan; in those two countries, Japanese products were rated as a close second to domestic goods. In another study of Canadian consumers, the quality of Italian shoes was rated as exceeding that of all other countries in quality, including those made in Canada (Wall and Heslop 1989).

Nonetheless, some degree of "home country preference" has been found among French, West German, U.S., Japanese, Dutch, and Finnish consumers (see review by Hooley, Shipley, and Krieger 1988). In their research, Papadopoulos and his colleagues point out that domestic products were rated as a strong second in most (though not all) of those cases where Japanese goods received the highest rating. While these findings may be related to availability, familiarity, and perceived serviceability of domestic products (Han 1988a; Hooley, Shipley, and Krieger 1988), most research attempting to differentiate among consumers on the basis of their foreign product acceptance has focused on definitive consumer characteristics such as socioeconomic variables, consumer nationalism, and product familiarity.

Socioeconomic Correlates

In general, age and educational variables have been found to be associated with foreign product acceptance. Most studies have found younger consumers to demonstrate more positive attitudes toward foreign products (Dornoff, Tankersley, and White 1974; Han 1988a; Schooler 1971; Schooler and Sunoo 1969; Wall and Heslop 1986). The impact of age on foreign product acceptance may also be related to specific product areas and countries (Bannister and Saunders 1978; Johansson, Douglas, and Nonaka 1985; Tongberg 1972).

Higher levels of education have been associated generally with more positive attitudes toward foreign products (Anderson and Cunningham 1972; Dornoff, Tankersley, and White 1974; Schooler 1971; Wall and Heslop 1986; Wall, Hofstra, and Heslop 1990; Wang 1978). Some studies, however, have not found a significant relationship with educational levels (Han 1988a; Schooler, Wildt, and Jones 1987; Tongberg 1972). As with consumer age, there is some evidence that education may have differential effects as a function of the nature of the product and its source country. Consumers with higher education (as well as higher income and employment status) were found to be particularly critical of apparel and footwear from low-wage countries (Wall and Heslop 1989).

Studies attempting to relate the sex of the consumer to their responses to origin stimuli have often produced mixed results. These studies have shown that males and females may respond differently to origin cues as a function of the particular source countries, products, and attributes under study (Bannister and Saunders 1978; Hester and Yuen 1986; Johansson, Douglas, and Nonaka 1985; Wall and Heslop 1986). In a more recent study, Wall, Heslop, and Hofstra (1989) showed, for a Canadian sample, that men and women use different sets of criteria to position countries on a quality continuum. Men tended to emphasize a country's technological development while women found geographic proximity to be more salient. The specific operationalization of the dependent variable may also be important in this regard. While Wall and Heslop (1986) found females to provide generally more positive ratings of foreign countries' products than did males, females were also more likely to favor purchase of domestic products.

In studies focusing on income, Wang (1978), Wall and Heslop (1986), and Wall, Hofstra, and Heslop (1990) found significant positive relationships between income and favorable attitudes toward foreign products. In contrast to these studies, others have failed to demonstrate a significant effect of income on the impact of country-of-origin (Anderson and Cunningham 1972; Johansson, Douglas, and Nonaka 1985; Schooler, Wildt, and Jones 1987; Han 1988a). Both Han (1988a) and Shimp and Sharma (1987) did find that socioeconomic status was related to consumer nationalism.

Consumer Nationalism

Perhaps one of the more significant advances in the country-of-origin literature in the late 1980s was in the development and operationalization of the construct of consumer nationalism. This construct is based on the notion that consumers' patriotic emotions have significant effects on attitudes and purchase intentions. Consumer nationalism reflects a willingness to make a sacrifice in order to purchase a domestic brand and may be associated with acceptance of advertising aimed at arousing consumers' patriotic emotions and obligation to buy domestic brands (Han 1988a).

In their study of Canadian consumers, Wall and Heslop (1986) found that close to half of the respondents indicated that they would be willing to purchase Canadian products at a higher price than foreign-made products if the quality was equal to that of imports. The respondents indicated that advantages of purchasing domestic products included helping the economy, increasing domestic employment, and national pride. Such consumer nationalism among American consumers may also explain the negative reaction to the discovery that Chrysler manufactures K-cars in Mexico. Even consumers happy with their car's performance may have felt that their sense of having "helped America" by purchasing an American car had been betrayed (Johansson and Nebenzahl 1986, p. 102).

Shimp and Sharma (1987) use the term "consumer ethnocentricism" to represent the beliefs held by consumers about the appropriateness and morality of purchasing foreign-made products. From the perspective of ethnocentric consumers, purchasing imported products is wrong because it hurts the domestic economy, causes loss of jobs, and is unpatriotic. Measuring this construct with a 17-item scale (CETSCALE), Shimp and Sharma found significant negative correlations between consumer ethnocentricism and evaluations of foreign product characteristics as well as attitudes toward, and purchase of, foreign automobiles. Highly ethnocentric consumers were inclined to accentuate the positive aspects of domestic products and to discount the virtues of foreign-made items.

Consumer nationalism appears to affect consumer choice both through product attribute evaluation and through direct affective factors regarding the purchase itself. Through modeling based on LISREL analysis, Han (1988a) found that consumer patriotism does effect cognitive evaluations of products, but affects purchase intent to a greater degree.

Shimp and Sharma (1987) emphasize the role of threat in eliciting consumer ethnocentric tendencies. They provide evidence that consumers in socioeconomic strata vulnerable to job displacement (upper-lower and lower-middle classes), as well as residents of geographic areas where foreign competition is acute, demonstrate higher levels of consumer ethnocentrism. A telephone survey conducted by Daser and Meric (1986) also suggests that consumers in geographic regions hard hit by import-induced unemployment favor protectionism and respond favorably to "Buy Domestic" themes. In their survey, 42 percent of the respondents in the

Winston-Salem region of North Carolina (whose employment is affected by textile imports) stated that they consciously sought "American-made" labels. In a separate study which questioned consumers just after their purchase of apparel, 39 percent of New York consumers and 19 percent of consumers from Alberta indicated a concern with the country-of-origin of their product (Hester and Yuen 1986).

The construct of consumer nationalism may be readily integrated in the network of country-of-origin relationships. Scores on the Shimp and Sharma (1987) CETSCALE were strongly correlated with measures of conservatism and dogmatism, both of which have been found to be related to preference for domestic products in previous studies (Anderson and Cunningham 1972; Tongberg 1972). Tongberg, for example, found that consumer dogmatism interacted with the value dissimilarity between the source and the consumer country in predicting evaluation of product attributes.

Regional differences in acceptance of foreign products also give rise to the notion that consumer nationalism may be influenced by local social norms. If so, this construct may be linked to Fishbein's behavioral intention model, which incorporates a normative or social component as well as a product-based attitudinal component (Ajzen and Fishbein 1980). That is, pressure from one's reference group to purchase a domestic product may override specific product attribute beliefs in influencing the purchase decision.

Differential acceptance of foreign products on a national level may also reflect levels of a country's consumer nationalism. Darling and Kraft (1977) have suggested that Finnish consumers' higher rating of domestic products relative to foreign goods reflected the "intense national loyalty and pride of the Finnish people" (p. 529). Similarly, Baumgartner and Jolibert (1977) attributed the strong preference for domestic products by French consumers to values of nationalism and individualism. In a more recent study, French, German, and Dutch consumers were found to have the most positive views about their home products, while consumers in the U.S., Canada, and Great Britain viewed their domestic products as better than foreign ones on some dimensions but as worse on others (Papadopoulos, Heslop, and Bamossy 1990).

Familiarity

Current research also suggests that familiarity and other factors affecting information or experience with a product should be taken into consideration in addition to nationality and other demographic characteristics

(Johansson, Douglas, and Nonaka 1985). Variables related to familiarity emerged as a distinct construct through factor and reliability analyses in the eight-country study (Papadopoulos, Heslop, and Bamossy 1989), and a tentative LISREL model of the data suggests that they have a direct influence on product evaluations (Papadopoulos, Marshall, and Heslop 1988). The manner in and extent to which CO information will be utilized appears to be related to the consumer's familiarity with the product area.

Yaprak and Parameswaran (1986), for example, noted a greater utilization of country/product image variables as determinants of purchase behavior in those product categories where specific product information had not achieved a sufficient level of diffusion in the markets studied. This supports arguments that consumers use origin stimuli as surrogates for evaluating specific product attributes when information about a product is not readily available to them (Bilkey and Nes 1982). This finding parallels those of studies demonstrating that consumers are more likely to use price in product evaluations when they are not familiar with the product (Han 1989a).

The possibility that country-of-origin cues may play dual roles, both as a surrogate and as a summary construct, has recently been suggested by Han (1989a). While country-of-origin information may serve as a surrogate for other information when buyers are not familiar with products, increasing familiarity may lead to abstracting, summarizing, and storing information based on the origin cue.

Another aspect of familiarity in the formation of cognitive and affective constructs regarding a country's products is the consumer's familiarity with the sourcing country itself. Papadopoulos and Heslop (1986) studied the effect that travel to a foreign country may have on consumer evaluations of that country's products. Comparing the evaluations of Canadian consumers who had visited the country whose products they were evaluating with those who had not, they found that visiting a country "reduces the gap" between the more global, prevailing public image of the country and specific national product capabilities. Consumers who had not visited Japan, for example, tended to have a particularly high regard for Japan's electronic and automotive products, consistent with the public view of Japan emphasizing its strengths in technology and manufacturing quality. While visitors to Japan also held positive views about Japan's technological strength, they were less favorably disposed to Japanese cars, but more impressed (than non-visitors) with Japan's accomplishments in other products (fashion apparel, for example) for which Japan has not yet gained wide recognition. Travel to Great Britain tended to offset the negative publicity concerning that country's economic and labor problems, while visitors to Sweden and the U.S. tended to come away with somewhat more negative images than those held by non-visitors.

In sum, recent research in this area has built upon the findings reported by Bilkey and Nes (1982) that country images may vary from one market country to another and that there may be a tendency for consumers to prefer their own countries' products (as noted, this tendency does not apply to all consumer groups or countries). With the continued development of research linking consumer characteristics to the use of origin cues, greater attention will undoubtedly be given to underlying processes by which such characteristics are linked to consumer response to country-of-origin information. Such characteristics as age, sex, and income may covary with differences in attribute importance structures, product/country familiarity, or the perceived economic threat of foreign products. Through delineation of such linkages, researchers may facilitate the development of marketing strategies for specific country-product-target market combinations.

INFORMATION PROCESSING AND ATTITUDE FORMATION

Han's (1989a) finding that the origin country cue may, like brand name, serve as a summary of specific product information as well as a basis for inferential beliefs about product quality, has been accompanied by other research attempting to delineate the process by which country-of-origin is processed and incorporated in attitude formation. Johansson, Douglas, and Nonaka (1985), for example, present a conceptual model linking country-of-origin both to consumer evaluations of specific beliefs about product attributes as well as to overall attitude (affect) regarding the product. Their model also incorporates a reciprocal link from affect back to beliefs about product attributes (halo effect), suggesting that beliefs are also influenced by overall evaluations.

Using a system of simultaneous equations with automobiles as the target product, Johansson, Douglas, and Nonaka (1985) noted the presence of a halo effect, in that the overall evaluation of the car appeared to influence ratings on specific attributes. Origin effects occurred predominantly in relation to evaluation of specific attributes rather than overall evaluations, a finding consistent with those of Yaprak (1978).

A recent study of cognitive processes associated with the effects of country-of-origin and other product attributes (Hong and Wyer 1989) suggested that in addition to a direct effect, the origin cue stimulated extensive thoughts about other product attribute information. Eroglu and Machleit (1989) have also presented recently a conceptual framework in which country-of-origin is one of many cues (each with its own subjective predictive value) used by the consumer in attempting to evaluate product quality. Their research suggests that the predictive value of any cue, including country-of-origin, is affected by such non-cue related variables as product involvement, technical complexity of the product, consumer experience, and consumer ability to detect interbrand differences.

The research cited above suggests that there are several avenues by which the country-of-origin cue may have an impact on consumer attitudes and behavior. This cue may be related to specific beliefs about product attributes, to overall attitude toward the product or purchase, and to halo effects, in which general attitude affects specific attribute beliefs.

Among the factors influencing the impact of the avenues of CO influence, consumer involvement with the product itself may be particularly critical. Recent conceptualizations of country-of-origin effects have been founded on information processing and attitude formation, often using automobiles and other high-involvement products as objects (Erickson, Johansson, and Chao 1984; Han 1988a, 1989a; Johansson, Douglas, and Nonaka 1985). Many products, however, do not elicit a high level of consumer involvement (whether based on value-expressive attributes of the products, status or price, or risk of purchase). Numerous studies outside of the country-of-origin field have demonstrated the differential use of informational message cues as a function of involvement with the message and the centrality of the product area to the individual's concerns (Batra 1984; Laurent and Kapferer 1985; Petty and Cacioppo 1980; Petty, Cacioppo and Schuman 1983). Various alternative models have been proposed (Ray 1976; Park and Mittal 1985) linking affect, product trial, and cognitive processes under low-involvement conditions.

This line of research suggests that origin cues may be utilized differently as a function of consumers' levels of product involvement. Future studies attempting to model decision-making processes regarding the country-of-origin influence may need to incorporate a wider sampling of target products than has been found in recent research.

METHODOLOGICAL ISSUES

Among the methodological issues which have received research attention recently are concerns regarding sampling and measurement. Along with concerns regarding the adequacy in sampling of target products, there has been concern about the sampling of subjects. Wall and Heslop (1986) and Papadopoulos, Heslop, and Bamossy (1990), among others, have complained of the "almost universal use of atypical populations," such as students or small consumer samples selected in a non-random, non-representative basis. While consumer samples have been used far more extensively in country-of-origin studies over the past five years as compared to the pre-Bilkey and Nes period, an additional concern has been the possibility that within-country regional differences might affect the research outcomes (Chao 1989). Although neither Reierson (1966) in the U.S. nor Bannister and Saunders (1978) in the U.K. found regional differences in the perception of country images, regional differences have been noted among Canadian as well as U.S. consumers (Wall and Heslop 1989; Shimp and Sharma 1987). Further, differential levels of acceptance of certain foreign products (such as imported autos in different regions of the U.S.) are well known. Such differences can restrict the variance of foreign product ownership in certain regions, thereby attenuating correlations relating country-of-origin predictors to ownership (Shimp and Sharma 1987). As the adequacy of the sampling procedures affects the generalizability of research findings, it must be carefully considered in designing origin-related research.

Using a U.S. consumer sample, Han and Qualls (1985) found significant differences in country-of-origin effects as a function of the data collection mode used in the research (personal interview, telephone, self-administered survey). It appeared that the data collection mode affected social desirability bias, demand characteristics, or involvement to yield differing responses. Subjects rated attributes of foreign products less favorably than U.S. products in telephone interviews. They also showed stronger intentions to buy U.S. products in this mode than in the other two.

The issue of response bias in origin studies has been raised by a number of researchers attempting to assess the tendency of consumers to report a preference for domestic over imported products (Daser and Meric 1986; Hester and Yuen 1986; Wall and Heslop 1986). In Hester and Yuen's (1986) study, for example, 39 percent of the subjects in their New York sample indicated a concern with whether the garment they had just purchased was imported or made domestically. Only 20 percent, however, indicated that they actually knew the country-of-origin of the garment. In total, only about 11 percent of the sample indicated both a concern with *and* a knowledge of the country-of-origin of the apparel product they had just bought.

Country-of-origin studies have contributed to the substantial growth of international marketing research. This growth has led to increasing concerns about methodological issues such as the need for evaluation of the psychometric properties of cross-national research measures. Construct and functional equivalence of the phenomena being studied across nations, reliability differences, and the comparability of the samples in each nation have received increasing attention (Seaton 1988). Parameswaran and Yaprak (1987), for example, demonstrated that the reliability of scale ratings of product attributes not only differed among consuming countries, but also within a consumer country when rating different products of other nations. Cattin, Jolibert, and Lohnes (1982) found it necessary to correct for national differences in response sets before proceeding to data analysis.

The increasing use of data analytic techniques capable of capturing the interrelationships among origin country and other extrinsic cues, affect, attribute evaluations, and outcomes has added to the richness of this research area (e.g., Han 1989b; Hooley, Shipley, and Krieger 1988; Johansson and Nebenzahl 1986; Johansson, Douglas, and Nonaka 1985). Such techniques comprise current "state-of-the-art" approaches in market research. A valuable addition to this stream of research has been provided by the inclusion of "true" levels of product attributes (such as gas mileage and repair record) based on published sources (Erickson, Johansson, and Chao 1984; Johansson, Douglas, and Nonaka 1985). This allows examination of the impact of "true scores" on attribute beliefs and country image effects, and a comparison of beliefs regarding product attributes with independent measures based on product trial. Erickson, Johansson, and Chao (1984), for example, found that certain product attributes for automobiles (such as economy ratings for Japanese cars) could be biased by the country-of-origin image. Similarly, using a sample of U.S. and Japanese students, Johansson, Douglas, and Nonaka (1985) found that U.S. cars were overrated on horsepower.

As country-of-origin research has now achieved a 25-year history, it is becoming possible to track changes in consumer product images over time. Past research has demonstrated increasingly positive evaluations of product attributes for both Japanese (Nagashima 1970, 1977) and South Korean (Khera and Wise 1986; Khera 1987) products. A longitudinal study conducted in Finland indicated an increase over time in positive attitude among Finnish consumers for goods produced in the U.S. between 1975 and 1985. The increase in appreciation of Japanese products (already rated higher by Finnish consumers in 1975) was greater, however. Finnish appreciation for British products appeared to have declined during the same time period (Darling 1987; Darling and Arnold 1988).

The preceding discussion of recent research streams in country-of-origin demonstrates the richness as well as the complexity surrounding the country-of-origin cue in cross-national purchase behavior. It has also underscored the fertility of the field and its potential for exciting discoveries. The next sections provide an overview of significant developments in the country-of-origin literature and highlight anticipated developments which spring from the research issues explored thus far.

THE STATE OF THE ART: A SYNTHESIS

The Bilkey and Nes review included research on the country-of-origin phenomenon up to 1980. They noted several concerns with the research to that point, including an overreliance on single-cue studies, absence of a tangible product, considerations of scale reliability, and a need to further ascertain determinants of origin "biases." Our review indicates that researchers during the past ten years have not only heeded many of these concerns, but have also extended the scope of research into areas not charted by Bilkey and Nes. For example, in the section dealing with the integration of the origin cue with other extrinsic cues, we cited several studies which have attempted recently to address the limitations of single-cue studies (Chao 1989; Ettenson, Wagner, and Gaeth 1988; Han and Terpstra 1988; Heslop, Liefeld, and Wall 1987; Schooler, Wildt, and Jones 1987). This line of research suggests a differential importance of the origin cue as a function of the product under consideration and the informational environment within which the evaluation takes place. For complex, infrequently purchased items, the origin country appears to have a significant effect on product evaluation in a multi-cue context (Han and Terpstra 1988; Heslop, Liefeld, and Wall 1987), while that effect seems to be smaller for such items as wearing apparel (Ettenson, Wagner, and Gaeth 1988; Heslop, Liefeld, and Wall 1987; Hester and Yuen 1986). Chao's (1989) study also demonstrates the importance of product and attribute specificity on the believability of product attribute claims.

The use of verbal ("made in") cues rather than tangible products remains the norm in this field of research, although a few recent experimental studies have combined tangible products with multiple extrinsic cues (Eroglu and Machleit 1989; Heslop, Liefeld, and Wall 1987). In addition, some recent studies tracking actual purchases and concomitant knowledge and attitudes have incorporated actual products (Hester and Yuen 1986; Shimp and Sharma 1987; Wall, Hofstra, and Heslop 1990).

Early research involving national product image stereotypes tended to be descriptive, relying on such scales as Nagashima's (1970, 1977) and providing mostly simple product profiles for various combinations of source and consumer countries. This tradition continues, though with increasing concern for scale properties. Items from the Nagashima scale have been factor analyzed in creating product evaluation dimensions for subsequent studies (Han and Terpstra 1988; Han 1989b). Shimp and Sharma (1987) and Han (1988a) have developed survey-based measures of consumer nationalism. And the eight-nation study by Papadopoulos, Heslop, Bamossy, and their colleagues has involved the development and assessment of scales for use in several different countries measuring perceptions of countries' products and affect towards their people.

The latter study used factor analysis, reliability analysis, and historical research to delineate four product-related and three country-related image constructs that comprise the main underlying dimensions along which countries and their products are evaluated by consumers. The product constructs are product integrity, price-value, market presence, and consumer response, while the country constructs are beliefs about the country, affect towards its people, and desired level of linkages between the source and destination countries. In addition to ascertaining the presence of these seven constructs, this research team has also explored the potential associative and causal links among them through various methods including LISREL analysis (Bamossy and Papadopoulos 1987a, 1987b; Papadopoulos, Marshall, and Heslop 1988).

Lastly, another noteworthy trend in CO research since the Bilkey and Nes review has been the increased attention to the process by which origin information is incorporated in attitude formation and related purchase intent. As indicated previously in the section devoted to studies in this area (Erickson, Johansson, and Chao 1984; Han 1988b, 1989a; Johansson, Douglas, and Nonaka 1985), this line of research had few precursors before 1980. Given the relatively limited depth in this area of the literature, it is not surprising that country-of-origin studies involving the experimental or quasi-experimental designs useful in assessing cue integration and other attitudinal processes tend to be limited to samples drawn from a single nation. Sufficient levels of international research collaboration may be developing, however, to allow for cross-national replication and extension of studies in this area as well.

FUTURE RESEARCH AVENUES

With the increasing attention given to such constructs as consumer patriotism (Han 1988a) and ethnocentricism (Shimp and Sharma 1987), empirical studies linking source country characteristics to consumer purchase resistance on the basis of national loyalty would be particularly timely. Direct assessment of the impact of consumer nationalism in other countries would also contribute to our understanding of cross-national consumer behavior. As noted earlier, substantial political shifts in several countries, as well as heightened sensitivity to economic balances between the U.S. and other developed economies, have added to the saliency of this issue. Future research may address the extent to which consumer nationalism is time-specific: to what extent is it likely to intensify during periods of intense import penetration? Future studies may also address the extent to which consumer nationalism differs across product categories and interacts with perceptions regarding specific producing countries.

Researchers have responded to findings that attitudes toward specific products of a country may differ from national stereotypes (Etzel and Walker 1974; Halfhill 1980; Yaprak and Parameswaran 1986) by using specific products as the stimuli to be evaluated. While this is likely to yield greater fidelity in research findings, care must be taken to sample product types adequately before coming to conclusions regarding origin effects or the relative impact of belief structures and affective halo effects in generating responses to the country image cue. As Zeithaml (1988) has pointed out in discussing the use of extrinsic cues, products differ in the extent to which quality can be identified prior to (and even after) the actual purchase. This may result in differential reliance on extrinsic cues, whether those cues involve price, advertising, brand name, or country-of-origin.

The integration of the country image literature with research on information processing and attitude formation suggests various avenues through which the origin cue may affect attitude and subsequent purchase. The impact of origin information on overall vs. attribute-specific product evaluations requires further investigation, as does the role of familiarity in moderating this impact. Researchers should also note the distinction between attitudes toward products and purchase intent, which may reflect social and normative influences associated with foreign product purchase. Han (1988a), for example, found that consumer patriotism affects purchase intent, but has little direct effect on product attribute cognitions. Consumers in a multi-cue experimental setting demonstrated use of country-of-origin in assessing product quality, but not in stating purchase intentions (Wall, Liefeld, and Heslop 1989). As discussed regarding the relationship between consumer sex and the influence of product origin, clear differentiation among the dependent variables used may provide a greater understanding of the network of country-of-origin relationships.

The incorporation of "true" product attribute levels in this field of research still is relatively rare. In recent years marketing researchers have debated the use of "objective quality" measures, such as published quality ratings from *Consumer Reports,* on methodological grounds. Essentially, researchers are concerned that experts and consumers may not agree on the selection of attributes and weights to measure objective quality (see Zeithaml 1988, for a review of this point). However, determination of specific country-of-origin biases (insofar as "bias" represents systematic error in evaluation) makes the most sense with the inclusion of such measures. Preference for a product produced by a particular country need not represent bias if that country does indeed produce the product with the higher levels of quality and reliability.

Findings indicating that halo processes may occur when consumers are unfamiliar with a country's products suggest that a country's initial exports (e.g., Yugo cars in the case of Yugoslavia) and highly publicized products (e.g., the Anglo-French Concord) may stimulate spillover perceptions for other products associated with that country. Longitudinal studies tracking changes in country image over time could provide invaluable information about such processes. Such research could have implications for industry association and government level policy (see Han, 1989a, for a discussion of this issue).

Longitudinal studies monitoring consumer awareness of production location for various products as well as changes in consumer nationalism will also facilitate our understanding of the processes by which a country's products gain acceptance or meet with consumer resistance over time. In tracking such awareness and acceptance, methods which incorporate behavioral responses, or test verifiable knowledge (such as in Hester and Yuen's 1986 post-purchase intercept surveys) would help to address issues of response bias and attitude-behavior discrepancies.

Tracking the diffusion of acceptance of a country's product offerings across product types may also provide insight regarding the processes by which inferences are made in incorporating country-of-origin cues. A study involving Dutch consumers, for example, found a high positive regard for Japanese products in general. However, Japan was also rated as the least preferred sourcing country for certain products, including clothing, furniture, and sports equipment–products for which Japan has not achieved a great deal of recognition. On the other hand, that country's strong reputation in electronics apparently led Japan to being rated as the most preferred sourcing country for computers, despite the fact that the PC market in Holland at the time of the study was dominated by American, Dutch, and Italian products (Bamossy et al. 1988).

Knowledge of the images held of a country's products facilitates the development of international marketing strategy models incorporating origin and other cues (e.g., Morello 1984; Schooler, Wildt, and Jones 1987;

Yaprak and Parameswaran 1986). To the extent that the country-of-origin cue provides a favorable basis for product differentiation it may be systematically promoted, as in Lowenbraü's "Tastefully Engineered in Germany" advertisements in Canada (Papadopoulos et al. 1987). While research regarding the effectiveness of patriotic appeals in promoting domestic products is not particularly encouraging (Ettenson, Wagner, and Gaeth 1988; Wall, Liefeld, and Heslop 1989; Papadopoulos, Heslop and Bamossy 1990), such "buy domestic" programs may resonate well with particular market segments (Daser and Meric 1986; Shimp and Sharma 1987). An interesting variation on this theme was demonstrated in Volvo's advertising campaign in the U.K., stressing good economic ties with the U.K. and the fact that Sweden purchased a great quantity of British auto components for use in producing the Volvo. The ad slogan, "Support the British Motor Industry, buy a Volvo" allowed nationalistic sentiments to operate in favor of a foreign firm (Morello 1984). Further, as previously noted, country images may affect the allowable price differential between domestic and foreign products and may suggest differential needs for warranty and distribution considerations.

The explosive growth in globalization over recent decades has become one of the most pervasive influences in business today (Darling and Arnold 1988; Levitt 1983). As consumers increasingly come into contact with product offerings from other countries, and as domestic firms seek to expand their markets overseas, issues of national product image become ever more salient. Country-of-origin research, now with a 25-year history, has blossomed and matured during this period as well. We anticipate that the exciting research streams identified in this discussion will continue to enrich the field and support the development of more effective international marketing strategies in the years to come.

REFERENCES

Ajzen, I. and M. Fishbein (1980), *Understanding Attitudes and Predicting Social Behavior.* Englewood Cliffs, NJ: Prentice- Hall.

Anderson, W.T. and W.H. Cunningham (1972), "Gauging Foreign Product Promotion." *Journal of Advertising Research,* 12, 1 (February) 29-34.

Auster, E.R. (1987), "International Corporate Linkages: Dynamic Forms in Changing Environments." *Columbia Journal of World Business* 22(2), 3-6.

Bamossy, Gary J. and Nicolas Papadopoulos (1987a), "Nationality Stereotyping and Shifting Perceptions: Methodological Issues in the Measurement of the Country-of-Origin Construct." In P. Leeflang and M. Rice, eds., *Contemporary Research in Marketing* (Toronto, Ont.: European Marketing Academy, June) K59-K70.

Bamossy, Gary J., and Nicolas Papadopoulos (1987b), "An Assessment of Reliability for Product Evaluation Scales Used in country-of-origin Research." In K. Bahn and M. Sirgy, eds., *Third World Marketing Congress* (Barcelona, Spain: Academy of Marketing Science, International Conference Series, vol. III) 135-142.

Bamossy, Gary J., József Berács, Louise A. Heslop and Nicolas Papadopoulos (1988), "East Meets West: A country-of-origin Analysis of Western Products by Hungarian and Dutch Consumers." *Second International Marketing Development Conference* (Budapest: Association of Consumer Research; July) 149-152.

Bannister, J.P. and J.A. Saunders (1978), "U.K. Consumers' Attitudes Towards Imports: The Measurement of National Stereotype Image." *European Journal of Marketing*, 12, 8, 562- 570.

Batra, R. (1984), "Understanding the Likability/Involvement Interaction: The 'Override' Model." In T. Kinnear (ed.), *Advances in Consumer Research*, 12 (Provo, UT: Association for Consumer Research) 362-367.

Baumgartner, Gary, and Alain Jolibert (1977), "The Perception of Foreign Products in France." In H.K. Hunt, ed., *Advances in Consumer Research*, vol. V (Ann Arbor, MI: Association for Consumer Research) 603-605.

Bilkey, Warren J. and Erik Nes (1982), "Country-of-Origin Effects on Product Evaluations." *Journal of International Business Studies*, 8(1) (Spring/Summer), 89-99.

Cattin, Philippe, Alain Jolibert, and Colleen Lohnes (1982), "A Cross-Cultural Study of 'Made In' Concepts." *Journal of International Business Studies* (Winter) 131-141.

Chao, Paul (1989), "Export versus Reverse Investment: Strategic Implications for Newly Industrialized Countries." *Journal of International Business Studies* (Spring) 75-91.

Darling, John R. (1987), "A Longitudinal Analysis of the Competitive Profile of Products and Associated Marketing Practices of Selected European and non-European Countries." *European Journal of Marketing*, 21, 3, 17-29.

Darling, John R. and D. R. Arnold (1988), "Foreign Consumers' Perspective of the Products and Marketing Practices of the United States versus Selected European Countries." *Journal of Business Research*, 17: 237-248.

Darling, John R. and Frederic B. Kraft (1977), "A Competitive Profile of Products and Associated Marketing Practices of Selected European and non-European Countries." *European Journal of Marketing*, 11, 7, 519-531.

Daser, S. and H.J. Meric (1986), "Does Patriotism Have Any Marketing Value—Exploratory Finding for the 'Crafted with Pride in the U.S.A.' Campaign." In M. Wallendorf and P. Anderson (eds.), *Advances in Consumer Research*, vol. XIV (Association for Consumer Research) 536-537.

Dornoff, Ronald J., Clint B. Tankersley, and Gregory P. White (1974), "Consumers' Perceptions of Imports." *Akron Business and Economic Review*, 5(2) (Summer), 26-29.

Erickson, Gary M., Johny K. Johansson, and Paul Chao (1984), "Image Variables in Multi-Attribute Product Evaluations: Country-of-Origin Effects." *Journal of Consumer Research*, 11: (September) 694-699.

Eroglu, S.A. and K.A. Machleit (1989), "Effects of Individual and Product-specific Variables on Utilising Country of Origin as a Product Quality Cue." *International Marketing Review* 6(6), 27-41.

Ettenson, Richard, Janet Wagner, and Gary Gaeth (1988), "Evaluating the Effect of Country of Origin and the 'Made in U.S.A.' Campaign: A Conjoint Approach." *Journal of Retailing*, 64(1): 85-100.

Etzel, Michael J. and Bruce J. Walker (1974), "Advertising Strategy for Foreign Products." *Journal of Advertising Research*, 14(3) 41-44.

Garland, Barbara C., Tansu A. Barker, and John C. Crawford (1987), "A Cross-National Test of a Conceptual Framework of Willingness to Buy Products of Foreign Origin." In K.D. Bahn and M.J. Sirgy (eds.), *Third World Marketing Congress* (Barcelona: Academy of Marketing Science, August) 124-130.

Green R.T., W.H. Cunningham, and I. Cunningham (1975), "The Effectiveness of Standardized Global Advertising." *Journal of Advertising*, 4(3): 25-30.

Halfhill, D.S. (1980), "Multinational Marketing Strategy: Implications of Attitudes Toward Country of Origin." *Management International Review*, 20(4): 26-30.

Hampton, Gerry M. (1977), "Perceived Risk in Buying Products Made Abroad by American Firms." *Baylor Business Studies* (October) 53-64.

Han, Min C. (1988a), "The Effects of Cue Familiarity on Cue Utilization: The Case of Country of Origin." Paper presented to the *Conference of The Academy of International Business* (San Diego, CA).

Han, Min C. (1988b), "The Role of Consumer Patriotism in the Choice of Domestic versus Foreign Products." *Journal of Advertising Research*, 28(3) (June-July), 25-32.

Han, Min C. (1989a), "Country Image: Halo or Summary Construct?" *Journal of Marketing Research*, XXVI: (May) 222-229.

Han, Min C. (1989b), "The Choice of Data Collection Mode in Country Image Studies." *Working paper.* Wayne State University.

Han, Min C., and Vern Terpstra (1988), "Country-of-Origin Effects for Uni-National and Bi-National Products." *Journal of International Business Studies* (Summer) 235-54.

Heslop, Louise A., John P. Liefeld, and Marjorie Wall (1987), "An Experimental Study of the Impact of Country-of-Origin Information." In R.E. Turner (ed.), *Marketing*, Vol. 8 (Toronto, Ont.: Proceedings, Administrative Sciences Association of Canada–Marketing Division, June) 179-185.

Heslop, Louise A., Nicolas Papadopoulos, George Avlonitis, Gary J. Bamossy, József Berács, Friedhelm Bliemel, Françoise Graby, Gerry Hampton, and Petros Malliaris (1987), "A Cross-National Study of Consumer Views about Domestic vs. Imported Products." In P. Leeflang and M. Rice, eds., *Contemporary Research in Marketing* (Toronto, Ont.: European Marketing Academy, June) K39-K58.

Hester, S.B. and M. Yuen (1986), "The Influence of Country of Origin on Consumer Attitude and Buying Behavior in the United States and Canada." In M. Wallendorf and P. Anderson (eds.), *Advances in Consumer Research* (Association for Consumer Research) 538-542.

Hong, Sung-Tai and Robert S. Wyer, Jr. (1989), "Effects of Country-of-Origin and Product-Attribute Information on Product Evaluation: An Information Processing Perspective." *Journal of Consumer Research,* 16: (September) 175-187.

Hooley, G.J., D. Shipley and N. Krieger (1988), "A Method for Modelling Consumer Perceptions of Country of Origin." *International Marketing Review,* 6, 1 (Autumn) 67-76.

Johansson, Johny K. and Israel D. Nebenzahl (1986), "Multinational Production: Effect on Brand Value." *Journal of International Business Studies,* 17, 3 (Fall) 101-126.

Johansson, Johny K., Susan P. Douglas, and Ikujiro Nonaka (1985), "Assessing the Impact of Country of Origin on Product Evaluations: A New Methodological Perspective." *Journal of Marketing Research,* XXII: (November) 388-96.

Khanna, S. (1986), "Asian Companies and the Country Stereotype Paradox: An Empirical Study." *Columbia Journal of World Business* (Summer) 29-38.

Khera, Inder (1987), "A Broadening Base of U.S. Consumer Acceptance of Korean Products." *Third Bi-Annual World Marketing Congress* (Academy of Marketing Science, Barcelona, Spain).

Khera, Inder and Gordon Wise (1986), "U.S. Consumers' Perceptions of South Korean Products." In M.F. Bradley and Nicolas Papadopoulos (eds.), *Workshop on International Marketing Strategy* (Brussels: European Institute for Advanced Studies in Management) 57-67.

Laurent G. and J. Kapferer (1985), "Measuring Consumer Involvement Profiles." *Journal of Marketing Research,* XXII (February) 41-53.

Lehman, D.R. and J. O'Shaughnessy (1974), "Difference in Attribute Importance for Different Industrial Products." *Journal of Marketing,* 38: 36-42.

Levitt, Theodore (1983), "The Globalization of Markets." *Harvard Business Review,* (May-June) 92-102.

Morello, Gabriele (1984), "The 'Made-In' Issue–A Comparative Research on the Image of Domestic and Foreign Products." *European Research* (July) 95-100.

Nagashima, Akira (1970), "A Comparison of Japanese and U.S. Attitudes Towards Foreign Products." *Journal of Marketing,* 34 (January) 68-74.

Nagashima, Akira (1977), "A Comparative 'Made In' Product Image Survey Among Japanese Businessmen." *Journal of Marketing,* 41 (July) 95-100.

Narayana, Chem L. (1981), "Aggregate Images of American and Japanese Products: Implications on International Marketing." *Columbia Journal of World Business,* 16 (Summer) 31-35.

Nes, Erik B. (1981), *Consumer Perceptions of Product Risk and Quality for Goods Manufactured in Developing Versus Industrialized Nations."* PhD Dissertation, University of Wisconsin, Madison, WI.

Papadopoulos, Nicolas and Louise A. Heslop (1986), "Travel as a Correlate of Product and Country Images." In T.E. Muller (ed.), *Marketing,* vol. 7 (Whistler, B.C.: Administrative Sciences Association of Canada–Marketing Division, May) 191- 200.

Papadopoulos, Nicolas, Louise A. Heslop, and Gary J. Bamossy (1989), "International Competitiveness of American and Japanese Products." In Nicolas Papadopoulos (ed.), *Dimensions of International Business*, 2, (Ottawa, Canada: International Business Study Group, Carleton University).

Papadopoulos, Nicolas, Louise A. Heslop, and Gary J. Bamossy (1990), "A Comparative Analysis of Domestic Versus Imported Products." *International Journal of Research in Marketing*, 7, 4 (December).

Papadopoulos, Nicolas, Louise A. Heslop, and József Berács (1990), "National Stereotyping and Product Evaluations: An Empirical Investigation of Consumers in a Socialist Country." *International Marketing Review*, 7, 1 (Spring) 32-47.

Papadopoulos, Nicolas, Judith J. Marshall, and Louise A. Heslop (1988), "Strategic Implications of Product and Country Images: A Modelling Approach." *Marketing Productivity* (European Society for Opinion and Marketing Research, 41st Research Congress, Lisbon, September) 69-90.

Papadopoulos, Nicolas, Louise A. Heslop, Françoise Graby, and George Avlonitis (1987), "Does Country-of-Origin Matter? Some Findings from a Cross-Cultural Study of Consumer Views About Foreign Products." *Working Paper #87-104, Marketing Science Institute*, Cambridge, MA.

Parameswaran, R. and Attila Yaprak (1987), "A Cross-national Comparison of Consumer Research Measures." *Journal of International Business Studies* (Winter), 35-49.

Park, C. and B. Mittal (1985), "A Theory of Involvement in Consumer Behavior: Problems and Issues." In J. Sheth (ed.), *Research in Consumer Behavior*, 1: 201-232.

Petty, R. and J. Cacioppo (1980), "Issue Involvement as a Moderator of the Effects on Attitude of Advertising: Content and Context." In K. Monroe (ed.), *Advances in Consumer Research*, 8 (Ann Arbor, MI: Association for Consumer Research) 20-24.

Petty, R., J. Cacioppo, and D. Schuman (1983), "Central and Peripheral Routes to Advertising Effectiveness: The Moderating Role of Involvement." *Journal of Consumer Research*, 10, 135- 146.

Ray, M. (1976), "When Does Consumer Information Processing Research Actually Have Anything to Do with Consumer Information Processing?" In W.D. Perreault (ed.), *Advances in Consumer Research*, 4: (Ann Arbor, MI: Association for Consumer Research) 372-375.

Reierson, Curtis C. (1966), "Are Foreign Products Seen as National Stereotypes?" *Journal of Retailing*, 42, 3 (Fall), 33-40.

Reierson, Curtis C. (1967), "Attitude Change Toward Foreign Products." *Journal of Marketing Research*, IV: (November) 385- 87.

Schooler, Robert D. (1965), "Product Bias in the Central American Common Market." *Journal of Marketing Research*, II: (November) 394-397.

Schooler, Robert D. (1971), "Bias Phenomena Attendant to the Marketing of

Foreign Goods in the U.S." *Journal of International Business Studies*, 2: (Spring) 71-80.

Schooler, Robert D. and Don H. Sunoo (1969), "Consumer Perceptions of International Products: Regional vs. National Labelling." *Social Science Quarterly*, (March) 886-890.

Schooler, Robert D. and Albert R. Wildt (1968), "Elasticity of Product Bias." *Journal of Marketing Research*, V: (February) 78- 81.

Schooler, Robert D., Albert R. Wildt, and J. Jones (1987), "Strategy Development for Manufactured Exports of Third World Countries to Developed Countries." *Journal of Global Marketing*, 1(1-2): 53-67.

Seaton, Bruce (1988), "An Investigation into Scale Equivalence in a Cross-national Context." Paper submitted to the *Conference of The Academy of International Business* (San Diego, CA).

Seaton, Bruce and Robert H. Vogel (1981), "International Dimensions and Price as Factors in Consumer Perceptions of Autos." Paper presented at the *Conference of The Academy of International Business* (Montreal, October).

Shimp, T.A. and S. Sharma (1987), "Consumer Ethnocentrism: Construction and Validation of the CETSCALE." *Journal of Marketing Research*, XXIV: (August) 280-289.

"This Week with David Brinkley" (1990, March 4). *ABC News Transcript*. New York: Journal Graphics, Inc.

Tongberg, R.C. (1972), *An Empirical Study of Relationships Between Dogmatism and Consumer Attitudes Towards Foreign Products*. PhD Dissertation, Pennsylvania State University.

Wall, Marjorie and Louise A. Heslop (1986), "Consumer Attitudes toward Canadian-made versus Imported Products." *Journal of the Academy of Marketing Science*, 14(2): 27-36.

Wall, Marjorie and Louise A. Heslop (1989), "Consumer Attitudes Towards the Quality of Domestic and Imported Apparel and Footwear." *Journal of Consumer Studies and Home Economics*, 13: 377-358.

Wall, Marjorie, G. Hofstra, and Louise A. Heslop (1990), "Imported vs. Domestic Car Owners: Demographic Characteristics and Attitudes." Paper presented at the *Conference of the Administrative Sciences Association of Canada* (Whistler, B.C.).

Wall, Marjorie, Louise A. Heslop, and G. Hofstra (1989), "Male and Female Viewpoints of Countries as Producers of Consumer Goods." *Journal of International Consumer Marketing*, 1(1): 1-25.

Wall, Marjorie, John P. Liefeld, and Louise A. Heslop (1989), "Impact of Country-of-Origin Cues and Patriotic Appeals on Consumer Judgments: Covariance Analysis." In Alain d'Astous (ed.), *Marketing*, vol. 10 (Montreal: Administrative Sciences Association of Canada–Marketing Division, June) 306-315.

Wang, Chih-Kang (1978), *The Effect of Foreign Economic, Political and Cultural Environment on Consumers' Willingness to Buy Foreign Products*. PhD Dissertation, Texas A & M University.

Wang, Chih-Kang and Charles W. Lamb (1983), "The Impact of Selected Environmental Forces Upon Consumers' Willingness to Buy Foreign Products." *Journal of the Academy of Marketing Science*, 11(2): (Winter) 71-84.

Yaprak, Attila (1978), *Formulating a Multinational Marketing Strategy: A Deductive, Cross-national Consumer Behavior Model.* PhD Dissertation, Georgia State University.

Yaprak, Attila (1987), "The Country of Origin Paradigm in Cross-national Consumer Behavior: The State of the Art." In K. Bahn and M. Sirgy (eds.), *Third World Marketing Congress* (Barcelona, Spain: Academy of Marketing Science, International Conference Series).

Yaprak, Attila and R. Parameswaran (1986), "Strategy Formulation in Multinational Marketing: A Deductive, Paradigm-Integrating Approach." *Advances in International Marketing*, 1: 21-45.

Yavas, Ugur and Guven Alpay (1984), "Does an Exporting Nation Enjoy the Same Cross-national Commercial Image?" *International Journal of Advertising*, 5, 2, 109-119.

Zeithaml, Valerie A. (1988), "Consumer Perceptions of Price, Quality, and Value: A Means-End Model and Synthesis of Evidence." *Journal of Marketing*, 52: (July) 2-22.

Chapter 5

Experiments on Country-of-Origin Effects: Review and Meta-Analysis of Effect Size

John P. Liefeld

INTRODUCTION

Consumers employ cognitive and affective processes when evaluating products; establishing feelings, attitudes, and intentions towards them; and making product or brand choices (Fishbein and Ajzen 1975; Rosenberg 1956; Zajonc and Markus 1982; Holbrook 1990). These processes involve consumer perceptions of and response to both extrinsic and intrinsic product cues (Olson and Jacoby 1972; Olson 1977).[1]

Prior to the 1950s, empirical investigation of consumer cue use in product evaluation and choice processes was focused almost exclusively on the extrinsic cues of price and brand, and employed survey research methods, which by their nature elicit response from the cognitive domain. In the 1960s, the research was broadened by including a greater variety of extrinsic cues such as packaging, seller, and country-of-origin. Also in the 1960s, the first research investigating consumer cue usage employing experimental research methods, which elicit response from both the cognitive and affective domains, was reported. In that period, with increasing international trade in consumer goods, the country-of-origin cue became more important (Schooler 1965, 1971; Reierson 1966; Schleifer and Dunn 1968; Schooler and Wildt 1968; Schooler and Sunoo 1969; Hakansson and Wootz 1975; White and Cundiff 1978). Most of these experiments were single cue designs relying on intangible presentations of product

---

1. Intrinsic cues involve the physical composition of the product; e.g., flavor, color, texture, etc. Extrinsic cues are external to the product itself but related to it; e.g., price, brand, country of manufacture, etc.

stimuli (descriptions of products rather than the products themselves). In the 1980s, country-of-origin cue experiments were broadened by employing multi-cue experimental designs and the use of tangible products rather than product descriptions (Nes 1981; Schellinck 1986, 1989b; Heslop, Liefeld and Wall 1987; Wall, Liefeld, and Heslop 1989, 1990). During this period researchers continued to conduct and report survey method investigations of country-of-origin cue usage (Johansson, Douglas, and Nonaka 1985; Wall and Heslop 1986; Heimbach, Johansson, and MacLachlan 1989; Papadopoulos et al. 1987; Han 1989). With a few exceptions (Heslop and Liefeld 1987), reports of country-of-origin cue usage research employing ethnographic, semiotic, or qualitative (Post-Positivistic) methods have not been reported in the literature.

The purpose of this chapter is to review the results of experimental research on country-of-origin effects. The focus will be on determining country-of-origin effect sizes and how these are related to factors within the study design. The analysis has relevance to research design as well as to determining the variables which are related to the use of the country-of-origin cue in forming judgments about products.

In taking stock of the current state of knowledge generated by experiments, this chapter first discusses selected attributes of the experimental form of inquiry. This discussion is desirable for two reasons: the recent flurry of debate regarding research philosophy and method in marketing and consumer behavior (Hirschman 1986; Holbrook 1990; Fischer 1990; Anderson 1986; Hudson and Ozanne 1988; etc.), and the need to have readers examine the evidence from a similar starting point. Well-designed experiments provide both positivistic empirical and qualitative revelation of the cognitive and the emotional and semiotic qualities of consumer judgments and choice. But specific experiments differ greatly in their achievement of these revelations.

Data collection methods should possess mundane realism (external validity). Well-designed experiments can avoid many threats to external validity. In a well-designed experiment, the interest and purpose of the researcher is hidden from the subjects. While aware that their behaviors and thoughts are being probed, subjects are unable to discern what the study object(s) is/are, and which behaviors and thoughts are of interest to the researcher. In experiments, subjects are asked to respond to situations behaviorally and do not need to remember past events and thoughts and express them in linguistic forms. Their responses to the experimental stimuli can include their affective as well as cognitive reactions to those stimuli, and do not need to be reformatted as sequential linguistic expositions. Rather, they can be expressed through the same behavioral gestalt as experienced in the marketplace. Finally, the researcher can use tangible products and situations of the marketplace as stimuli, rather than intangible descriptions of these realities.

Experiments vary in the degree to which they achieve mundane realism. In general, however, the experiment form of data collection provides excellent potential for external validity, even when some or even many of the ideal conditions are not met (Levin et al. 1983). Ideally, for external validity experiments should be multi-cue rather than single-cue and employ tangible rather than intangible product stimuli.[2]

If the treatment conditions of an experiment are well designed and executed, then behavioral product choice measures are all that are needed in order to infer the effects of the independent variables on consumer evaluation and choice of product alternatives. This is possible because experiments can deal with two of the three conditions which John Stuart Mill (1930) set out as prerequisite for proof of causality. These are: (1) precedence; and (2) statistical association. The third requirement, invalidation of competing hypotheses, can only be achieved with appropriate tests of all competing hypotheses.

Most country-of-origin experiments have relied on linguistic rather than behavioral dependent variables. The dependent variables have been rating scales for perceived quality, risk, value, likelihood of purchase, or willingness to purchase. Clearly this is an aspect of experimentation in country-of-origin effects which requires attention in the future.

Holbrook (1990) argued that the reality that emotion and affect lie at the heart of the consumption experience is rapidly being accepted by consumer researchers. Emotion and affect are not easily amenable to cognitive manipulation and linguistic expression. After all, emotion is, by definition, an affective and not a cognitive experience. Thus to the extent that affect and emotion play major roles in consumer evaluation and choice, measurement methods which rely on asking consumers questions may miss the heart of consumer experience. Well-designed experiments may reveal affect and emotion in consumer evaluation and choice with careful attention to the design and presentation of treatment stimuli. Affect and emotion are imbedded in a consumer's reaction to the intrinsic properties of products, sellers, and and choice situations contained in the experiment stimuli. The style, color, and appearance of a product, the consumer's

---

2. A number of studies in areas other than country-of-origin, such as Pincus and Waters (1975), Szbillo and Jacoby (1974), and Smead, Wilcox, and Wilkes (1981), have reported that intrinsic cues available when assessing a tangible product have major effects on consumer evaluations and choice, which are generally greater than the effects of extrinsic cues such as price, brand, store reputation, etc.

experience or impressions of the qualities of stores or sellers, the mood of the consumer at the time of evaluation and choice, are all amenable to experimental manipulation. Gardner (1988), for example, demonstrated that even the mood of consumers can be experimentally manipulated. Thus experimental measurement of consumer response to product and situation contexts combines both the cognitive and the affective/emotional responses to stimuli. When the researcher develops a theory and incorporates affect and emotional conditions into the experimental treatment conditions, their separate and interactive effects can be known.

Although experimentation may be a powerful and efficient form of inquiry, the quality of experiments varies widely as will be seen in the next section of this chapter. The question of whether poorly-designed experiments are, more often than not, still more accurate, reliable, or valid than well designed surveys or qualitative studies is an important but difficult question which will not be addressed here.

This chapter has three main parts. Part I reviews findings reported in experimental research designed to measure the impact of country-of-origin cues on consumer product evaluations. Part II reports a meta-analysis of the magnitude of effect size estimates of country-of-origin effects on product quality evaluations. The independent variables employed in the meta-analysis are: single- vs. multi-cue, tangible vs. intangible stimuli, student vs. consumer samples, country of subjects, consumers vs. purchasing agents, and between- vs. within-subject designs. The final part of the chapter discusses the implications of the accumulated evidence and the meta-analysis for producers, importers, consumers, and future research into country-of-origin cue usage.

PART I:
EXPERIMENTAL EVIDENCE
ON COUNTRY-OF-ORIGIN CUE USAGE

Experiment Selection Criteria

What distinguishes experiments from surveys, case studies, or other empirical data collection methods? There is little agreement among consumer and marketing researchers or philosophers of science about the defining boundaries between surveys and experiments (Campbell and Stanley 1963; Kaplan 1964; Rosenthal and Rosnow 1984). For the purposes of this chapter, however, it is necessary to decide which of the many studies reported in the literature are experiments and should be included in this review.

Campbell and Stanley (1963, p. 1) define experiments as "that portion of research in which variables are manipulated and their effects upon other variables observed." Rosenthal and Rosnow (1984, p. 62) suggest that in many areas of behavioral science the experiment is characterized by "controlled manipulation of independent variables." More specifically, they employ the term "experimental research" to denote that case in which the primary interest of the investigator involves introducing some feature into the environment for some of the research participants, and then comparing their reactions with those of subjects who have not been exposed to the feature.

For the purpose of this chapter, any country-of-origin investigation employing "manipulation of independent variables" and using "between subject" designs was unconditionally accepted. Investigations employing "manipulation of independent variables" but using "within-subject" designs were accepted, only if the data collection procedures were explicitly designed to: (1) prevent a "reactive" or "interactive" effect of testing, in which the experimental procedure would sensitize subjects to the experimental variable; and (2) prevent multiple treatment interference which can occur when multiple treatments are applied to the same respondents, and order and sequence are not randomized. Employing these criteria, several investigations reported as experiments by the authors, or those which used multivariate modelling analysis techniques on survey data, were not considered experiments for the purposes of this review (e.g., Erickson, Johansson, and Chao 1984; Han and Terpstra 1988; Han 1989; Heimbach, Johansson, and MacLachlan 1989; Johansson, Douglas, and Nonaka 1985; Wang and Lamb 1983).

Twenty-two experimental investigations of country-of-origin cue effects on consumer judgments and choice were chosen from the literature.[3,4] Two of these studies report effects for industrial buyers, not consumers. The first experiment was published in 1965 (Schooler). Twenty-seven researchers have been involved in producing these studies.

The characteristics of the experiments accepted for review vary considerably. Five of the studies employed single-cue designs. Thirteen used intangible product stimuli rather than tangible products. Twelve studies

---

3. One study contained three experiments, each with separate analysis and reporting (Heslop, Liefeld, and Wall 1987; Wall, Liefeld, and Heslop 1989 and 1990). These analyses are considered as three separate experiments for the purposes of this review.

4. The author attempted to cover as many literature bases as possible to identify reported experiments on country-of-origin effects. He apologizes in advance for the inevitable event in which a reported experiment has been missed.

employed university students as subjects, no doubt reducing the cost of the research but possibly limiting the generalizability to young, well-educated consumers. All but two experimenters employed linguistic rating scales for measures of response to the experimental stimuli, including ratings of quality, risk in purchase, value, likelihood of purchase, and intention to purchase. Only Schellinck (1989a) and Hakansson and Wootz (1975) employed behavioral measures of response. ANOVA was the most common form of analysis approach, although recently, conjoint analysis has also been employed as an analytical tool. Table 1 summarizes the main characteristics and findings of the 22 experiments.

General Observations

These observations are presented in descending order of confidence in their robustness.

1. Country-of-Origin Effects Are Real

In all but two of the experiments, country-of-origin was found to be statistically related to consumer product evaluations or choices. In one exception (Schooler and Sunoo 1969), the independent experiment variable was world region-of-origin, not specific countries, and hence this one exception may be attributable to an independent variable that is too general. In the second exception (Schleifer and Dunn 1968), the experiment was designed to measure the effects of advertising from different countries or reference groups, and this experiment, while enlightening, did not assess country-of-origin effects on product evaluations or choice. Although country-of-origin is reported to be related to product evaluations, the strength of the association varies considerably between products and for different experiment characteristics.

2. Country-of-Origin Effects Occur over a Wide Range of Consumer and Industrial Products

These consistent findings of country-of-origin effects are found over a wide variety of products: cars; personal computers; VCRs, CD players, SLR cameras, pocket pagers, telephones, wrist watches; wearing apparel from socks to blouses and dress shirts; desk pens; leather wallets; glassware; fruit juice and coffee beans; cigarette brands; sanitary pads; and industrial products such as lift trucks, dictation equipment, and paint.

Table 1. Summary of Country of Origin Experimental Studies

1.A. SINGLE CUE -- INTANGIBLE STIMULI*

Author(s)/ Date	Subjects & Type of Design	Products	Cues	Countries	Dependent Variables	Analysis/ Variables**	r/φ/H***	Major Findings
Hong & Toner 1989	32 female & 32 male undergrad. students in U.S. Between Subjects	Automobile Sanitary pad SLR camera	Country	Japan, Sweden W. Germany Korea, Taiwan Mexico	Quality	A-0	0.226 0.224	Use of country cue depends on general product knowledge. Product attribute information has more effect than country.
Schooler 1971	866 adults in 83 counties in Missouri and St.Louis Between Subjects	Fabric Desk pen Goblet	Country World regions	U.S., W. Germ. W. & E. Europe Czechoslovakia N. & L. America Chile, India, Asia, Nigeria, Africa	Quality	A-1	0.175 0.127	Region affects ratings. Effects are product related. Stimulus type affects results. Country effects related to gender, age, race, education, but not occupation.

1.B. SINGLE CUE -- TANGIBLE STIMULI*

Author(s)/ Date	Subjects & Type of Design	Products	Cues	Countries	Dependent Variables	Analysis/ Variables**	r/φ/H***	Major Findings
Schooler 1965	200 univ students in Guatemala Between Subjects	Fruit juice Fabric	Country	Guatemala El Salvador Mexico, Costa Rica	Quality	A-0	0.380	Country effect.
Schooler & Sunoo 1969	200 undergrad. & 120 grad. >35 students in U.S. Between Subjects	Goblet Fabric	World regions	Africa Asia S. America W. Europe	Quality	A-I	0.152	No difference in ratings of products between developed & developing regions. No age effects.
Wall, Liefeld & Heslop 1989	120 adult shoppers in Canada, mall intercept Between Subjects	Knit Polo shirt Leather wallet Telephone	Country	Canada U.S. Italy S. Korea Hong Kong Taiwan	Quality Risk Price Likelihood of purchase	A-7	0.240 0.237 0.322	Country cue only moderately important. Effect varied by product type. Consumer characteristics accounted for as much variance as country treatment. No effect of "Think Canadian" hang tag.

* Within each category of studies in this table (Single/Multi-Cue, Intangible/Tangible Stimuli), Within Subjects designs are reported first, Between Subjects designs second.

** Analysis/Variables: "A" for ANOVA (variety of) or "O" for Other, followed by the number of other variables included in the analysis.

*** Magnitude of Effect estimates for evaluations of QUALITY. Pearson's Product Moment correlation (r), the Phi coefficient (φ) associated with X^2, and Eta (H) which is associated with the F statistic, are equivalent indices of correlation. "NA" = Insufficient information provided to calculate a size of effect estimate.

TABLE 1 (continued)

1.C. MULTICUE -- INTANGIBLE STIMULI*

Author(s)/ Date	Subjects & Type of Design	Products	Cues	Countries	Dependent Variables	Analysis/ Variables**	r/φ/H***	Major Findings
Kincaid 1970	73 undergrad. students in U.S. Within Subjects	Razor blades Typewriters Car, Shaver TV sets	Brands Country	U.S. Gr. Britain W. Germany Japan, Italy	20 attribute scales	0-2	NA	Differences in brand ratings if they are perceived as foreign.
Hakansson & Wootz 1975	43 industrial purchasing agents in Sweden Within Subjects	A standard screw Standard paint	Country Supplier size Purchase situations (2 low & 2 high need uncertainty)	Sweden England W. Germany Italy France	Ranking of supplier bids Simulated purchase of one of the bids	0-2	0.707 0.707 0.707 0.497	Country and supplier size effects, no interaction between the two factors. Thus, buyers use both factors the same way in making decisions. Country effect larger than supplier size effect, accounting for approx. 50% of the variance.
Johansson & Nebenzahl 1986	320 adult shoppers in U.S. Within Subjects	Automobiles	Brand Country	U.S., Japan W. Germany Mexico, S. Korea Philippines	14 attribute scales	0-2	NA	Focused on hybrid products. Significant effects of country of manufacture on brand ratings. Country-brand interactions.
Schellinck 1986	208 undergrad. students in Canada Within Subjects	Pocket pagers SLR cameras	Country 8 product attributes 7 other characteristics--e.g. store, brand, price, user testimonial	U.S., U.K. Japan W. Germany Taiwan	Quality Predictive & confidence value of country cue Propensity to select country cue	0-7	NA	Country cue had low predictive value but high confidence value. Country cue selected less often than most other cues.
Schellinck 1989a	32 undergrad. students in Canada Within Subjects	CD players	Country Stores (3) CSA approval[1] (present/ absent)	Japan Belgium Brazil	Most likely purchase Quality of sound & components Variety of options Pride of ownership	0-1	0.12 0.18	Country important in some dimensions of product evaluation, but store more important for all dimensions of product evaluation.

1. CSA = Canadian Standards Association
Other notes and explanation of symbols: See beginning of Table.

Author(s)/ Date	Subjects & Type of Design	Products	Cues	Countries	Dependent Variables	Analysis/ Variables**	r/φ/H***	Major Findings
Reierson[2] 1967	1,000 university students in U.S. Between Subjects	Italian & Japanese products	Country Store	Italy Japan	24 item summated ratings scale	0-1	NA	Four media treatments affected image of Italian products, one of Japanese products.
Schleifer & Dunn[3] 1968	190 university students in U.S. Between Subjects	Soft drink Men's toiletry Wrist watch Cigarette brand	Product origin Advertisement country attribution Reference grp opinion (other Americans)	U.S. Egypt	15-point attitude scales	A-2	0.149 0.118	Advertisement country effect significant, but product origin only approaching significance. So origin of seller more important than place of manufacture. Reference group effect significant.
White & Cundiff 1978	236 members of the U.S. Purchasing Mgmt Assoc. Between Subjects	Lift truck Dictation system Metal working machine tool	Country Price	U.S. W. Germany Brazil Japan	Quality	A-1	0.247 0.273 0.522	Country effect significant for all products. Price and country interaction effects not significant.
Eitenson, Wagner & Gaelh 1988	106 undergrad. students in U.S. 18 adult professionals in Wash,D.C. Between Subjects	32 women's blouses, 32 men's dress shirts (written descriptions)	Country Style Quality Fiber content Price, Brand	U.S. China	Likelihood of purchase	A-5	0.245 0.316	Conjoint task. Fiber and price had greatest effects. Style and country explained only 6% of the variance each. No effect of "Made in USA" ad.
Obermiller & Spangenberg 1988	199 undergrad. students in U.S. Between Subjects	Coffee beans Backpacking stoves	Country Brand	Kenya, Columbia Costa Rica Mexico, France S. Korea	5 attributes of coffee and of stoves (incl. quality)	0-2	NA	Partial support of a test of an information processing model of country effects (model supported in the case of coffee but not stoves).
Hong & Wyer 1989	128 undergrad. students in U.S. Between Subjects	Personal computer VCR	Country 21 product attributes	W. Germany Mexico Japan S. Korea	Quality Info. recall Attrib. ratings Favorableness	A-21	0.239	Order of presentation of country information affected how it was used and its effect on the use of other attribute information.

2. This research was directed at discovery of the influence of various communication media on the foreign product images held by American consumers.
3. The primary purpose of this experiment was to examine factors that may influence the successful or unsuccessful transfer of advertising campaigns from one country to another. However, it includes an estimate of the impact of the country-of-origin of the products in the advertisement and thus is included in this review.
Other notes and explanation of symbols: See beginning of Table.

TABLE 1 (continued)

1.D. MULTI CUE -- TANGIBLE STIMULI*

Author(s)/ Date	Subjects & Type of Design	Products	Cues	Countries	Dependent Variables	Analysis/ Variables**	r/φ/H***	Major Findings
Schooler & Wildt 1968	236 university students in U.S. Within Subjects	Glassware	Country Price	U.S. Japan	8-item quality score	0-1	NA	Country effects moderated by price differentials.
Nes 1981	96 adults in U.S. Within Subjects	Flashlight Glue, Towel Toothbrush El. drill, Radio Hair dryer Car tire	Country 4 low-risk, 4 high-risk products	24 countries varying on per capita income	Risk Quality	A-2	0.109	Country effect against low GNP countries, not completely compensated by a high quality brand name. Magnitude of bias against low GNP countries does not depend on product risk level.
Dickerson 1987	122 females & 65 males from 4 U.S. cities selected from commercial panels Within Subjects	Women's dresses Men's dress shirt	Country Price Care Quality Style	U.S. Italy Taiwan	Scale of "Most--" to "Least want to buy"	0-4	NA	Country effect stronger than other cues, including quality.
Schellinck 1989b	69 adult shoppers in Canada, mall intercept Within Subjects	Socks	Country Brand, Store Fiber content Product features	U.K. Canada Poland Taiwan S. Korea	Use or non use of cue info. provided on cards	0-5	NA	Country cue ranked 4th in use. Country ratings related to patriotism, age, and education, but not to use of country cue.
Heslop, Liefeld & Wall 1987	300 females, 300 males in Canada, mall intercept Between Subjects	Knit Polo shirt Leather wallet Telephone	Country Price Brand	Canada, U.S. Italy, Taiwan S. Korea Hong Kong	Quality, Risk in purchase Value, Willing-ness to buy	A-2	0.207 0.247 0.329	Country effect in single cue design, but less effect in multi-cue design. No consistent price and brand effects.
Wall, Liefeld & Heslop 1990 (same data set but different analysis from 1987)	300 females & 300 males in Canada, mall intercept Between Subjects	Knit Polo shirt Leather wallet Telephone	Country Price, Brand Covariates: age, sex education, perceived ability to judge	Canada U.S. Italy S. Korea Taiwan	Quality Risk in purchase, Value, Willingness to buy	A-7	0.132 0.073 0.071	Intrinsic product cues and consumer characteristics have greater impact on consumer judgments than extrinsic cues.

Other notes and explanation of symbols: See beginning of Table.

3. Domestic Products Almost Always Seen as Highest in Quality

The grass is always greener in the home country in these experiments. Schooler (1965), with a sample of Guatemalan students, found that the Guatemalan juice or fabric was perceived to be of better quality than the same juice or fabric from Mexico, Costa Rica, or El Salvador. Wall, Liefeld, and Heslop (1989) and Heslop, Liefeld, and Wall (1987) found that Canadian-made products were perceived by Canadian consumers to be higher in quality than Italian, Japanese, Taiwanese or Hong Kong products, but not statistically different from American ones. Hakansson and Wootz (1975) reported that Swedish purchasing agents rated Swedish products higher in quality than German, French, or Italian ones. Similarly, American studies report that products made in the U.S. were rated higher than, or as high as, those from any other country. The only exception to this rule was found by Schellinck (1989b), who reported that Canadian consumers considered British socks to be higher in quality than Canadian socks.

4. Country Hierarchy

Several researchers report a hierarchy of countries. Based on the views of respondents in the studies, products made in the U.S. were perceived to be highest in quality; products from West Germany or Japan (depending on the product class) are perceived next highest in quality; and products from other North European countries were next in line, followed by Southern Europe, other Pacific Rim countries, Eastern Europe, South American, other Asian, and finally African countries (Schooler and Wildt 1968; Schooler 1971; Wall, Liefeld, and Heslop 1989, 1990; Hakansson and Wootz 1975; Schellinck 1986, 1989a, 1989b; Dickerson 1987).

5. The Magnitude of Effect Appears to Be Related to the Nature of the Product

The products used in these experiments vary on many dimensions including price (economic risk), technical complexity, fashion (social risk), male-female dominance, etc. There is an indication that the magnitude of country-of-origin effects is related to product type. Specifically, the eta values[5] for technically complex products, fashion-oriented products, and expensive products appear to be larger than those for products

---

5. Eta is a measure summarizing the magnitude of strength of relationship between variables and is associated with the F statistic.

low in technical complexity, inexpensive, or not fashion-oriented (Wall, Liefeld, and Heslop 1989, telephone vs. leather wallet and knit polo shirt; Ettenson, Wagner, and Gaeth 1988, blouses and dress shirts (fashion); Hong and Wyer 1989, personal computers and VCRs; and White and Cundiff 1978, metal working machine tool vs. standard paint or screws). Obermiller and Spangenberg (1988), to the contrary, found a country-of-origin effect for coffee beans but not for the technically more complex product, backpacking stoves.

6. The Country Effect is Related to the Nature of the Stimulus Employed in the Experiment

One researcher (Schooler 1971) reported that the magnitude of the country-of-origin effect was affected by the nature of the product stimulus employed in the experiment. Specifically, the effects were greater when intangible product descriptions were used compared to tangible product stimuli. This consideration is discussed in more detail in Part II, which reports a meta-analysis of effect sizes.

7. Country-of-Origin Effects Are Related to Some Consumer Demographic Characteristics

Schooler (1971) reported that country-of-origin effects were related to several consumer demographic characteristics. Older, male, less educated, and white consumers rated foreign products from less developed countries less favorably. Wall, Liefeld, and Heslop (1989, 1990) reported that country-of-origin effects were variously related to age, sex, perceptions of ability to judge the product, and number of trips outside of Canada. Schellinck (1989b) found that use of the country-of-origin cue was inversely related to age and education, and those who travelled more often were less likely to rate countries differently. Dickerson (1987) reported that men and women differed in their preferences for various attributes, including country-of-origin.

8. Prior Product Knowledge, Beliefs, Familiarity, and Prior Purchasing Experience

Hong and Toner (1989) reported that males used country-of-origin more to judge female products and females employed country-of-origin more to judge male products. The authors attributed this effect to differences between males and females with respect to product knowledge and product experience. They found that in the overall product evaluations, larger differences were found in the use of product attribute information rather than the use of country-of-origin information, between the subjects who had much knowledge (used central route of information processing) and subjects who did not (using peripheral route of processing). Wall, Liefeld, and Heslop (1990) reported that prior experience in purchasing a product type was not related to product evaluations and did not interact with country-of-origin effects.

9. Country-of-Origin Effects Diminish
in the Presence of Other Cues

Several researchers found that when more information cues were present in the choice or evaluation situation, the country-of-origin effect diminished in magnitude (Hong and Toner 1989; Wall, Liefeld, and Heslop 1989, 1990; Schellinck 1986, 1989a, 1989b; Ettenson, Wagner, and Gaeth 1988). Dickerson (1982) speculated that the reason country-of-origin effects were stronger than quality rating information could be that information normally present in a store choice situation had been removed from the products for the purposes of the experiment, thus forcing the subjects to place greater than expected emphasis on country-of-origin.

The decrease in magnitude of effect size, in the presence of other extrinsic and information cues, or conversely the possibility of overestimating effect size when the experiment uses too few cues, will be discussed further in Part II.

10. Effects Decrease Even More
When "Behavioral" Variables
Are Employed to Measure Them

Schellinck (1986) employed an experimental design in which information cues were provided only when subjects decided to examine the cue by turning over a card, or pulling a tab in a brochure. This is similar to the IDB (Information Display Board) approach to consumer decision process studies, in which the researcher is interested more in what information cues are accessed, and the sequence of accessing them, than in their effects. In Schellinck's 1986 experiments, the country-of-origin cue was accessed infrequently compared to other information cues. Schellinck also asked subjects which cues they used in making their decisions. The number of subjects reporting using country-of-origin cues was always much less that the number who had accessed it. But this is a survey measure, not an experimental measure. In another study, Schellinck (1989a) found that country-of-origin cues were accessed extensively with regard to the quality of components of CD players, but accessed less than other cues for assessing the quality of sound of the CD players. Finally, in a further experiment with real consumers evaluating real products (socks) in a shopping mall, Schellinck (1989b) found that 38 percent of the sample accessed country-of-origin information compared to 92 percent accessing material composition, 64 percent features (washability, shrinkage), 41 percent brand name, and 34 percent "store sold at." Given the low cost and simple nature of the product (socks) employed in the experiment, caution should be taken in extrapolating the low level of country-of-origin effect to more costly or complex products.

11. Perceived Risk, Predictive Value, and Confidence Values of Information Cues and/or Product Attributes

For industrial goods, Hakansson and Wootz (1975) found that industrial purchasing agents were more sensitive to the country-of-origin of suppliers in high need uncertainty situations and more sensitive to price in low need uncertainty situations. Schellinck (1986) reported that for pocket pagers and cameras subjects rated country-of-origin lowest in predictive value but, in contradiction, high in confidence value (a survey, not an experiment measure). In his 1989a experiment, Schellinck presents evidence to extend this finding that the predictive value of a cue is a good predictor of its use in consumer judgments.

12. Role of Information Processing Modes and Prior Beliefs

Hong and Wyer (1989) employed four information processing hypotheses (encoding, heuristic, primacy-recency, and cognitive elaboration), under both impression formation and comprehension conditions, to hypothesize the magnitude of effects of product attribute and country-of-origin information on overall product evaluations, recall of information, and ratings of individual attributes. Their results support the cognitive elaboration hypothesis which predicts that product attribute information will have a pronounced effect on product quality evaluations, except under comprehension conditions, when the country-of-origin information is presented last. This study opens up a new area for research by revealing that the country-of-origin effects can be related to information processing modes used by consumers, and thus suggesting a future blending of decision making and cue usage research traditions.

Obermiller and Spangenberg (1988) reported mixed support for the hypothesis that country-of-origin effects would be stronger when consumers formed prior beliefs about country and brand variations in coffee beans and backpacking stoves.

Country-of-Origin Effects for Industrial Products

Two experiments examining the effects of country-of-origin on industrial purchasing agent product evaluations and choices have been reported (Hakansson and Wootz 1975; White and Cundiff 1978). The findings of both experiments are similar to those reported for consumer products and consumer evaluations of quality in which intangible product stimuli are employed. The country-of-origin effects appear to be large. The home country quality ratings are highest, developed countries such as Germany and England are rated highly, and developing countries are given the lowest quality ratings. Also, as observed for the consumer product experiments, the within-subjects design resulted in estimating stronger effects for country-of-origin than did the between-subjects design. There is a distinct possibility that the within-subjects design revealed the researchers' interest and purpose to the subjects, thus increasing the possibility of yea-saying and other forms of response biases.

Country-of-Origin and Promotion

Two experiments examined the effect of promotion on consumer evaluations. Schleifer and Dunn (1968) employed advertisements as a treatment variable. They reported that country-of-origin of the advertisements had a stronger effect on product attitudes than did the country-of-origin of the products. Reierson (1967) found that four of five types of media presentations significantly altered student attitudes towards Italian products, but only one of the five types of media affected student attitudes towards Japanese products.

Summary

Country-of-origin does appear to affect consumer judgments of product quality, value, risk, likelihood of purchase, and other mediating variables. These effects have been found over a wide range of consumer and industrial products. Generally, products from the "home" country are perceived to be of better quality, and the perceptions of quality are positively related to the degree of economic development of the country of manufacture. The nature and strength of these effects appears to be related to: product category; the product stimulus employed in the research; the demographic characteristics of the respondents; consumer prior knowledge; experience and beliefs with the product category; the number of information cues included in the experiment; and consumer information processing styles.

PART II:
META-ANALYSIS OF EFFECT SIZES

Introduction

One method of generalization is a literature review. It lists studies in an area and contrasts them in terms of methods, results and other factors. Conclusions about the general nature of results are drawn by inspection and classification of content into what seem to be useful categories. Other ways to generalize include aggregation of probability values, averaging and/or counting, programmed research, triangulation, and analytical generalization (Farley and Lehman 1986). Analytical generalization, called Meta-Analysis, can be a useful and powerful addition to the classical literature review.

Meta-analysis is "nothing more than the attitude of data analysis applied to quantitative summaries of individual experiments" (Farley and Lehman 1986, p. 5). It requires that the key output of the studies being summarized is quantitative, and that there are sufficient numbers of observations available either through the number of studies or components within studies. Meta-analysis employs quantitative measures of Size of Effect such as r^2, U, Wilks Lambda, beta (β) coefficients, and elasticities or various correlation coefficients such as: the Pearson correlation coefficient (r); the Phi coefficient (ϕ) associated with Chi Square; or the eta coefficient (H) associated with the F statistic.[6]

Purpose

Almost all of the experiments reviewed in Part I report a country-of-origin effect on consumer product evaluations. Many of the authors, howev-

---

6. The fundamental relationship, as described by Rosenthal and Rosnow (1984), is: Significance test = Size of Effect × Size of Study. Meta-analysis is the study of Size of Effect measures across studies.

er, speculate that their results may have overestimated the country-of-origin effect due to characteristics of the experiment, such as limited numbers of cues in the treatment tasks, intangible rather than tangible product stimuli, subject artifacts generated when the subjects become aware of the purposes of the research, etc. In addition, in any one experiment, the analysis can detect statistical significance, but the magnitude of effects cannot be assessed except in reference to the magnitudes of effect found by other researchers in similar and dissimilar studies. Effect size is a term used to refer to the strength of a relationship or the magnitude of a difference between variables (Peterson, Albaum, and Beltramini 1985).

The purposes of the meta-analysis reported here were to discover if the reported effect sizes are related to characteristics of experiments, and to compare the effect sizes estimated in experiments with between-subject designs to surveys with within-subject designs. The findings should be useful in helping to interpret the absolute importance of the country-of-origin cue, and in suggesting ways in which the qualities of experiments on cue usage can be improved in the future.

Method

The process of meta-analysis is the same as in the design of any data analytic study.

1. Choose the dependent variable for the meta-analysis. The most commonly employed dependent variable across the experiments was "perceived product quality."[7] As the quantitative measure for the analysis, the indices of size selected were H, r, and ϕ.

When a size of effect estimate is not reported in a study, it can be computed from the significance test statistics: F, t (Z), or X^2. The appropriate relationships are given by Rosenthal and Rosnow (1984). First, it is known that Pearson r, eta, and Phi are equivalent indices of magnitude of effect, although H is not limited to linear relationships. These indices of size of effect can be determined from their related significance test statistic by the following formulae:

---

7. Other dependent variables reported in some studies were: perceived "likelihood of purchase," "risk in purchase," and "value;" and "selection" of the country-of-origin cue. Unfortunately, an insufficient number of studies employed these types of dependent variables and thus there were too few data points for a meta-analysis.

$$\phi = \frac{Z}{\sqrt{N}}$$

$$\phi^2 = \sqrt{\frac{X^2\,(1)}{N}}$$

$$r = \sqrt{\frac{t^2}{t^2 + (N_1 + N_2 - 2)}}$$

$$H = \sqrt{\frac{F \times dfBtwn}{F \times dfBtwn + df \times Err}}$$

2. Identify the theoretically important elements of the natural experiment (i.e., the independent variables). For this analysis, five independent variables were chosen: single- vs. multi-cue, intangible vs. tangible product stimuli, student vs. consumer samples, American vs. Canadian vs. Industrial samples, and within-subject vs. between-subject measurement. For the last comparison, it was necessary to obtain size-of-effect measures for "perceived quality" from a sample of "near experiment" and survey studies in which "within-subject" data collection procedures were employed. The convenience sample of studies chosen for this sample is identified in Table 2.[8]

3. Analyze the natural experiment for singularity, extreme imbalance, non-orthogonality, and limitations in degrees of freedom. The major problems faced in this analysis were problems of imbalance in sample sizes, but in no case were subsamples more than 20 percent different. The sample sizes were relatively small (24 data points from the experiments plus seven data points from an industrial product experiment, and 15 data points from the surveys and near experiments). These smallish sample sizes make it less likely to make a Type 1 and more likely to make a Type 2 error, which at least is a conservative strategy.

4. Perform the analysis. In this case, four separate F tests for "HO:

---

8. Convenience in this instance means that reports of the studies were widely available and accessible, statistical test results were reported, and there was little value in building the sample size for surveys out of proportion to the sample size of experiments at hand.

variances equal" were employed, one for each of the first three comparisons: single- /multi-cue, intangible/tangible, and student/consumer samples. For the comparison of American vs. Canadian vs. Purchasing Agent samples, a one-way ANOVA with two planned comparisons was employed. Ideally, a four-factor ANOVA with tests for interactions would be used for this analysis, but the limited number of data points precluded this possibility and, given the results, proved to be unnecessary. A simple F' test was employed for the within-subject vs. between-subject comparison, which involved comparing size of effect estimates for perceived quality taken from experiments with those taken from surveys.

5. If necessary, experiment with methods to deal with defects in the natural experiment.

6. Draw implications.

Table 2. Surveys Used: Size of Country-of-Origin Effect Estimates and Type

Authors	H, ϕ^2, r	Product Type	Cue Type*
Han and Terpstra (1988)	0.553 0.593	TV Car	M/I M/I
Reierson (1966)	0.5 0.7	Products in general	S/I S/I
Erickson, Johansson, and Chao (1984)	0.150 0.354	Japanese products German products	M/I M/I
Garland and Crawford (1985)	0.310 0.250	Cars Products in general	S/I S/I
Han and Qualls (1985)	0.527 0.516 0.509 0.481 0.436 0.331	TV - Japan TV - Germany TV - South Korea Car - Japan Car - Germany Car - South Korea	M/I M/I M/I M/I M/I M/I
Dickerson (1982)	0.203	Apparel	S/I

* Cue Type: M = Multi-Cue, S = Single Cue / I = Intangible

Results

Single-Cue vs. Multi-Cue Experiment Designs

In the last five years, researchers have argued consistently that country-of-origin studies should use multi-cue designs. The argument is that size of effect estimates in single-cue experiments would be higher than those in multi-cue experiments. This is expected by the logic that if more cues are present to affect consumer evaluations and choices, any one cue should have a smaller effect. In can also be argued that in single-cue experiments, subjects might discern the researcher's interest in country-of-origin. This would create a demand effect in which subjects would provide socially appropriate answers or try to anticipate what the researcher wants to find.

The results, shown in Table 3, reveal that across the experiments, the number of information cues has not significantly affected the size of effect estimates. It should be noted, however, that the mean effect size is lower for multi-cue experiments, which is in the expected direction, but the difference is not large enough to warrant a conclusion that single-cue experiments differentially overestimate country-of-origin effects.

Intangible vs. Tangible Treatment Stimuli

It is commonly asserted that country-of-origin experiments should employ tangible product stimuli rather than intangible product descriptions. The arguments are that: (1) external validity is reduced when intangible stimuli are used; (2) the intrinsic characteristics of products are more important than extrinsic properties to consumers in forming judgments; and (3) the number of cues is reduced when no tangible stimuli are used. Hence the use of intangible stimuli will result in overestimation of country-of-origin effects.

Table 3. Mean Effect Size Estimate & Standard Deviation: Single-Cue vs. Multi-Cue Experiments

	Mean (H, ϕ^2, r)	Standard Deviation
Single-Cue experiments (n = 8)	0.218	0.064
Multi-Cue experiments (n = 14)	0.190	0.075
For HO : Variances are equal,		
F' = 1.37		
df = (13,7) Prob >F' = 0.6957		

The results of the analysis, shown in Table 4, reveal that across the experiments, product stimulus type does not make a difference in the size of effect estimates. Although there is no statistical difference in the means, it should be noted that the mean value for tangible product stimuli is lower, which is in the expected direction. This finding does not support conclusions drawn by Smead, Wilcox, and Wilkes (1981), that it is preferable to use tangible products rather than intangible product descriptions.

Student vs. Consumer Samples

The debate over student vs. consumer samples is found in all areas of the consumer behavior and marketing literature. A common assertion is that, if the researcher's interest is in "effects application" rather than "theory application" of the results, then consumer samples should be employed (Calder, Phillips, and Tybout 1981). The issue revolves around external validity (mundane realism) and the need in effects application to generalize to wider fields of application than the experiment takes into account. Experiments using students as subjects may lead to overestimation of country-of-origin effects because: (1) students may be more likely to "see through" the experiment design, which would lead to positive subject demand effects and bias the results by overestimating country-of-origin effects; and (2) students may be less knowledgeable as consumers and hence rely more than the general population on external cues such as country-of-origin.

The results of this comparison (see Table 5) reveal no statistically significant difference in the estimates of country-of-origin effect size between experiments employing students or consumers as subjects. It should be noted, however, that the mean value of the size of effect estimates is lower for consumer-based experiments, which is in the expected direction.

Table 4. Mean Effect Size Estimate &Standard Deviation: Intangible vs. Tangible Treatment Stimuli

	Mean (H, ϕ^2, r)	Standard Deviation
Intangible descriptions (n = 9)	0.206	0.068
Tangible products (n = 13)	0.196	0.074

For HO : Variances are equal,
   $F' = 1.18$
   df = (12,8) Prob >F' = 0.8372

Country of Subjects and Consumers
vs. Purchasing Agents

The reported results show that consumers rate products made in the country of domicile as high (often highest) in quality. But do consumers in different countries place different importance on country-of-origin as a cue for quality evaluation? The existing experiments allow a test of this question, but only for three countries: the U.S. (n = 8), Canada (n = 13), and Guatemala (n = 1). The one data point for Guatemala was excluded from the one-way ANOVA, but is reported in the table for comparison by judgment.

Additionally, do consumers place different importance than purchasing agents on country-of-origin as a quality evaluation cue? Two experiments reporting purchasing agents' product quality evaluations provide eight data points, sufficient for comparison with the nine U.S. and 13 Canadian data points.

The results of the one-way ANOVA, with planned comparisons of U.S. vs. Canadian and consumer vs. purchasing agent subjects, are shown in Table 6. The F statistic of 17.61 is well beyond chance, indicating that the differences between the three groups are significant. The Duncan's multiple range test shows that the effect size estimates from the two experiments with purchasing agents were much higher than those of the experiments with American or Canadian consumers. Further, the differences between the two consumer groups is not significantly different statistically. Clearly, purchasing agents place more importance on country-of-origin in their product evaluations than consumers. The Guatemalan data point (not included in the statistical analysis) is higher than those of the American or Canadian subjects, suggesting that there may be differences in the

Table 5. Mean Effect Size Estimate & Standard Deviation: Student vs. Consumer Samples

	Mean (H, ϕ^2, r)	Standard Deviation
Student subjects (n = 8)	0.214	0.068
Consumer subjects (n = 14)	0.192	0.074

For HO : Variances are equal,
F' = 1.15
df = (12,7) Prob >F' = 0.8896

Table 6. American vs. Canadian vs. Purchasing Agent Subjects ANOVA Results

Source	df	F	Pr >F
Model	2	17.61	0.0001
Error	27		

Duncan's Multiple Range Test

Duncan Grouping	Mean	N	Group
A	0.4974	8	Industrial
B	0.2014	9	American
B	0.1993	13	Canadian
B	0.380	1	Guatemalan

A and B groups different at the .05 level of confidence.

importance of country-of-origin cues in product evaluations for more culturally disparate groups than Canadians and Americans.

Within-Subject vs. Between-Subject Measurement

Experiments come in many flavors and styles (Campbell and Stanley 1963; Kaplan 1964). One of many important attributes of experiments concerns whether the respondents are exposed to more than one treatment condition. When an experiment uses a "within-subject" design, each subject is exposed to more than one of the experimental treatment conditions. When an experiment has a "between-subject" design, each subject is exposed to only one of the experimental treatment conditions.

Within-subject designs reduce the sample size needed, and simplify the identification of the net effects of a treatment stimulus by analysis of treatment differences within subjects (Han and Terpstra 1988). Several authors have argued that such net effects of stimuli are easily obtained in within-subject designs, but not in between-subject designs (Sloan and Ostrom 1974; Anderson 1982). But if subjects are randomly assigned to treatment conditions, and N is large enough, the net effects of stimuli can be estimated in a between-subjects design. More importantly, however, the within-subject design has been shown to open up the experiment to a number of artifacts generated by subject reactivity which severely threaten external validity (Weber and Cook 1972; Adair et al. 1983; Carlopio et al. 1983). Even more seriously, the within-subject design requires verification of the homogeneity assumption, significance tests for within-subject factors, and taking care not to treat within-subject factors as between-subject factors (LaTour and Miniard 1989). Unfortunately, it is often the case that tests of these threats are not made and these factors are not taken into consideration. Thus the probability of Type 1 error is increased.

Additionally, the theoretical weakness of the within-subject design was well-established prior to evidence documenting its negative impacts on the validity of data. The nature of data collection procedures in a within-subject design, unless carefully controlled, makes the researcher's purpose and the experimental variables known to the subject. This opens up the experiment to two of the four types of threats to external validity elaborated by Campbell and Stanley (1963). These threats are: (1) the "reactive" or "interaction" effect of testing, in which the experiment procedure sensitizes subjects to the experimental variable, thus making the results obtained for a population unrepresentative of the effects of the experimental variable for the universe from which the subjects were selected; and (2) multiple treatment interference (likely to occur whenever multiple treatments are applied to the same respondents). Others have discussed and documented the incidence of subjects' roles and their effects on validity, and these were collected into a single volume (Rosenthal and Rosnow 1969). Finally Weber and Cook (1972, p. 291), in a review of the evidence on subject demand effects in experiments, concluded that

> ... all experiments should be designed so that [their] hypotheses are difficult to learn.

and further,

> The most important implications of the present study concern the validity of inferences that can be made from laboratory experiments about human behavior. As far as valid inference about causal treatments is concerned neither hypothesis learning nor the faithful subject role is likely to lead to false positive, false negative, or false serendipitous findings *if care is taken to camouflage hypotheses.* (p. 293; emphasis added)

The use of within-subject experiment designs, in most cases, effectively converts an experiment into a survey because the transparency of its data collection procedures generates unknown but systematic biases in subject responses.

The comparison of effect sizes made here involves comparing estimates of country-of-origin effects from surveys with those of experiments. It is hypothesized that surveys and experiments using within-subject designs will show larger effect size for country-of-origin and the "home" country in consumer product evaluations. The direction of bias is based on the assumption that subjects recognizing the study's demand characteristics will tend to choose one or both of two roles: (1) the good subject role, and (2) the apprehensive role (Weber and Cook 1972). The good subject tries to guess what answers the researcher is interested in finding and then gives responses designed to provide those assumed answers. Apprehensive subjects try to give off the best personal impression, leading to socially appropriate responses. Thus the expectation is that studies which employ a within-subjects design should have higher effect sizes.

The results of the comparison (see Table 7) support the expectation beyond chance and with a relative large effect size. The mean of within-subject (survey) effect size estimates is more than twice the mean value for the between-subject experiments. It should also be noted that the standard deviation for the within-subject effect size estimates is larger, indicating less stability in survey generated estimates.[9]

This finding supports the expectation that within-subject designs will produce higher effect sizes. However, a caveat is necessary. Referring back to Table 2, it can be noted that surveys tend to use automobiles, TVs, or the generic concept of "products from country X." Cars and TVs are high-value, frequently purchased products. The experiments, on the other hand, have employed low-value, infrequently purchased products. A possibility exists that some of the difference in the average effect size may be attributable to the difference in the nature of the product categories employed.

Conclusions of Meta-Analysis

In this meta-analysis, estimates of the effect size for the impact of country-of-origin cues on consumer evaluations of product quality were

---

9. As this chapter was being finalized a twenty-third experiment was reported in the literature by Hong and Wyer (1990). The effect size estimates for the country-of-origin cue for two conditions were 0.14 and 0.19. It should be noted that these are, respectively, lower than and equal to the mean of the previous experiments reported in Table 7, providing more evidence of the stability of experimentally derived estimates of the effects of country-of-origin cues.

Table 7. Mean Effect Size Estimate & Standard Deviation:
Within-Subject vs. Between-Subject Designs

	Mean (H, ϕ^2, r)	Standard Deviation
Within-Subject Design (n = 15)	0.428	0.169
Between-Subjects (n = 21)	0.198	0.071

For HO : Variances are equal,
F' = 5.65
df = (14,20)   Prob >F' = 0.0005

employed as a dependent variable. The relationship of five independent variables to the dependent variable were examined. It has been argued in the literature, and in some cases empirically assessed (within single experiments), that these independent variables are critical to the validity of empirical evidence.

The results of this meta-analysis suggest that, within the range of studies reported, there is little difference in effect sizes that can be associated with the number of cues, the use of intangible cues, or student samples. A major caveat to this finding, however, derives from the limited bi-variate nature of this meta-analysis made necessary by the limited number of data points. A multivariate analysis of variance would take into account interactions among these three variables. For example, if interaction effects exist between the number of cues and stimulus type, or between stimulus types and subject types, then the exhortations to employ multi-cue designs with tangible product stimuli on consumer subjects may be well founded. As more experimental studies are conducted over the next few years, this important question about interactions will be addressable. Meanwhile, researchers should continue to strive to design experiments with realistic settings, stimuli, and samples.

It is evident that the impact of country-of-origin cues on product quality judgments is different between consumers and industrial purchasing agents, although this conclusion must be tempered because the seven data points for the purchasing agents were taken from only two experiments. Purchasing agents appeared to place much greater importance on the country of manufacture of industrial goods in their product evaluations than consumers placed on the country-of-origin of consumer goods. This finding has major implications for domestic producers and importers of industrial goods, which are discussed in Part III.

With respect to the question of within-subject vs. between-subject measurement, the results are quite clear. The effect size estimates of within-subject designs are much higher than those of between-subject designs. One analysis is insufficient for conclusion but sufficient to demonstrate that this design question needs immediate attention with further research. Possible research approaches are suggested in Part III.

PART III:
IMPLICATIONS AND DISCUSSION

The following discussion has two major sections based on the dichotomy suggested by Calder, Phillips, and Tybout (1981): (1) effects application, with subsections for domestic producers and importers and (2) theory application, subdivided into methodological implications for experiment procedures and implications for theoretical development.

Effects Application

In Canada and the U.S., imports from many countries of the world have gained market share in many consumer goods markets. In industries such as footwear, textiles and apparel, electronics, etc., growth in the sales of imported consumer goods is evidenced not only in the erosion of domestic producers' market shares but also in bankruptcies and plant closings. These marketplace realities raise doubts regarding the validity of research findings that country-of-origin is an important criterion of consumer product evaluations and that the "home" country's products are generally evaluated as being of higher quality than offshore products.

It must be remembered, however, that consumer choice is a multifaceted process. Experimental type country-of-origin research has examined only some of these facets, especially perceived quality, value, likelihood of purchase, and risk in purchase. Zeithaml (1988) also reported that, in general, consumer perceptions of price, quality, and value appear to be poorly related to consumer choice behavior. Thus we should not be too disappointed that the findings of surveys and experiments reported to date do not always fit well with the reality of the marketplace. The importance and role of country-of-origin in consumer choice processes will require examination over a greater number of dimensions of the consumer choice process and over a greater number of product dimensions than quality and value.

It must also be recognized that consumer choice processes and marketplace realities are not, of course, static. While the rate of change of individual phenomena varies, both are dynamic. Research is often not reported until two to five years after the data is gathered. Therefore, studies oriented to describing "current" phenomena (such as the prevailing views of a country's products, as opposed to, for example, researching underlying structures of behaviors or markets) are likely to be explaining reality at the time the data was collected rather than the time of publication.

Also, consumer preferences are affected by available market offerings. Consumers face product selection situations which reflect not only their own preferences but the profit margin expectations of sellers. Offshore clothing suppliers, for example, often provide room for wider margins for retailers, which encourages them to predominantly stock these products. Research must take into account the current characteristics of the marketplace.

Implications for Domestic Producers

Two major implications for domestic manufacturers follow, from the experimental research on country-of-origin cue usage. The reported findings of experimental and survey research, which generally have not used consumer choice as the dependent variable, may inflate the importance/ strength of country-of-origin cues in consumer choice processes. Country-of-origin may well be high in importance in consumer perceptions, but have less strength or importance in actual choice processes. Surveys have difficulty measuring the relative strength of one information cue with respect to others without experiencing yea-saying and other response biases. The experiments conducted to date also have not provided reasonable estimates of the strength of country-of-origin cues in consumer choice processes.

While the assessments of quality taken in research may be reliable and valid, they may not correlate well with consumer choice. One explanation for this failure is the limitation of the number of cues present in the experiment conditions. Thus respondent attention and evaluation are limited to a small number of cues in the experiment, whereas in the marketplace, they face a multitude of cues and conditions. Most importantly, both surveys and experiments have not employed behavioral measures (consumer choice) as dependent variable measures. Questions asking respondents to judge, evaluate, rate, or report their perceptions have dominated both surveys and experiments. Observations of consumer choices have been absent from both surveys and experiments. Whatever the reasons, the bottom line for producers is that marketplace reality reveals that country-of-origin information and home country preference are dominant factors in consumer choice. Other product attributes and marketplace conditions also have strong impact on the choices consumers make. "Ceteris paribus" does not exist in the marketplace. Domestic producers will have to compete vigorously with foreign imports on price, real quality, and other product attributes. They cannot rely on a patriotic preference for the locally produced good over the imported good.

It has been claimed, from time to time, that consumers are affected by country-of-origin cues because they are irrational, but industrial buyers are more logical decision makers and therefore are not so affected by country-of-origin cues. The findings of the meta-analysis do not support this claim. Country-of-origin cues may have more importance in industrial than consumer markets. Only two experiments have been conducted with industrial buyers. Both demonstrated a stronger magnitude of country-of-origin effect with industrial buyers than was found in experiments with consumer samples. Industrial buyers may have more frequent experience with qualities of goods from foreign countries. Moreover, the consequences of poor quality or poor value are magnified in a situation where purchase quantities are large and expensive. In considering the impacts on the production of other products upon which the success of the firm is dependent, industrial buyers may indeed place higher importance on the country-of-origin of goods. This suggests that the competition faced by the domestic producer is even tougher in industrial goods markets than in consumer goods markets if foreign suppliers offer superior quality at better prices.

Implications for Importers

Importers who are experiencing growth in market shares for the goods they import should know intuitively that consumer statements of domestic product preference are unreliable predictors of consumer choice. However, for importers, the bottom line from the experimental research appears to be that country-of-origin cues do affect consumer judgments, even though these effects may not dominate final consumer choices. Should these effects become stronger through patriotic considerations or changed economic conditions within a country, then country-of-origin cues could exert more noticeable effects on consumer choices in the marketplace. If domestic manufacturers provide equal quality and value for money, patriotic marketing appeals may become effective.

Theory Application

Methodological and Procedural Implications

1. *Where is it made? Does it matter?* Do consumers see country-of-origin information and take it into account? In the past, experimental and

survey research concerning the effects of origin information cues has rarely dealt with several important dimensions, including: (1) that materials and labor contained in products today are often from many countries, rather than just one; (2) the visibility, prominence, and readability of country-of-origin information cues on products or labels in stores; and (3) consumers' attention to and use of country-of-origin information on or with the product in the shopping process.

Increasing specialization in production makes the first dimension important. For example, what is the country-of-origin of a Honda Accord assembled in Alliston, Ontario? The streetwise consumer believes firmly that a California or Ontario Honda is poorer in quality than a Honda assembled in Japan. Consumers may, in the face of this confusing state of affairs, find it difficult to execute any notions they have about choosing products which support the local economy.

The second dimension of accessibility of country-of-origin information is easily tested. An afternoon at the supermarket and department store reveals that for many products one has to be an amateur detective to find country-of-origin information. The origin of the product is difficult to find, awkward to expose for reading, difficult to read, and sometimes obscure when read (e.g., "made in the EEC"). Consumers have to be persistent just to discover and attend to information about the product's origin. Even if country-of-origin is an important cue in their perceptions of quality, the difficulty of finding and interpreting country-of-origin information may reduce its role in consumer choice.

If the origin of products is becoming confused and if country-of-origin information is hard to find, then researchers need to continue to examine the degree to which consumers notice and take country-of-origin information into account. In a survey the attention of the respondents to the country-of-origin cue is explicitly requested. In experiments, we limit the number of cues respondents can take into account, and we generally make sure that the country-of-origin information is clearly visible and readable. Thus the assumption that consumers in the marketplace are aware of the country-of-origin information and attend to it has not been tested yet by systematic research.

2. Dependent variables. Jacoby (1978), in examining the state of the art of consumer research, asserted:

> More stupefying than the sheer number of our measures is the ease with which they are proposed and the uncritical manner in which they are accepted. In point of fact, many of our measures are only measures because someone says that they are, not because they have been shown

to satisfy standard measurement criteria (validity, reliability, and sensitivity). (p. 91)

Churchill (1979) criticized marketers who "indeed seem to be choking on their measures . . . . They seem to spend much effort and time operating by the routine which computer operators refer to as GIGO–garbage in, garbage out" (p. 64).
Country-of-origin experiments and surveys often suffer from poorly conceived and unproven dependent variables. Almost universally, the dependent variables employed are consumer evaluations of product attributes such as quality, riskiness in purchase, value, etc., measured with some form of integer rating scale. As Zeithaml (1988) points out, the constructs of price, value, and quality are not only poorly defined but consequently poorly operationalized with unidimensional measurements of what are multidimensional constructs. No discussions were found in the experimental literature concerning attempts to test the validity, reliability, or sensitivity of these dependent variable measures. In only one experiment did the researcher attempt to measure the bottom line of information cues usage–consumer choice (Schellinck 1989b). In future efforts, experimenters will need to pay more attention to the choice, development, and verification of the dependent variable measures employed in country-of-origin and other information cue usage experiments. Where feasible, the dependent variable measures should be choice or simulations of choice. If behavioral measures are not feasible, then constructs such as perceived quality or value, which are theoretically positioned as precursors to choice, will require careful development and testing for validity, reliability, and sensitivity.
   3. Experimental design issues. Many authors have argued that cue usage and decision process experimental designs should employ multiple-cue treatments rather than single-cue treatments. The logic of the argument is that the external validity of the experiment will be higher with multi-cue designs. The results of the meta-analysis do not support this argument. The mean effect size estimates were lower in experiments with multi-cue designs but the difference was not beyond chance. But it must be remembered that to date no experiment has included more than four or five cues in the treatment conditions, while the number of potential cues a consumer takes into account in the marketplace is probably larger. Also, the number of data points available for the meta-analysis was limited. Another possibility is that consumers use inference to "fill in" for the missing information. Huber and McCann (1982) report that consumers do infer from the cues provided to make judgments about the product attributes for which

information is missing. If the experiment designer is at all concerned with mundane realism, then he/she must strive to increase the number of information cues present in the treatment conditions, even though this analysis suggests that the number of cues is not related to the size of effect estimates.

Many authors have argued that experiments should use tangible (products) rather than intangible (descriptions) treatment stimuli. The meta-analysis did not support this argument. Although differences between the means were in the expected direction, they were not statistically significant. The number of data points for the meta-analysis was limited, and this question is further complicated with the issue of intrinsic versus extrinsic levels of product cues. Several researchers have reported that intrinsic cues are important factors in consumer choice processes (Rao and Monroe 1988; Szbillo and Jacoby 1974; Pincus and Waters 1975). In the marketplace, consumers do not make choices from shelves or counters that have only one brand/model/style/color/size/etc. They choose among several alternatives, each of which represents a different bundle of attributes. Consequently, additional research is needed to better understand the interaction of tangible vs. intangible product stimuli, and extrinsic and intrinsic cues.

4. Decision process. A fuller understanding of the effects of country-of-origin cues would necessitate decision process tracing. Characteristically, experimenters carefully control treatment conditions and exposures to information cues. The intervening processes of attention, awareness, cognition, and affect are not measured, the focus being on the consequences of the treatments on the dependent outcome variables. Only Schellinck (1989a, 1989b) reports collecting process information (did consumers notice the cue, access it, etc.). For a complete understanding, we need to know not only whether country-of-origin has an effect on choice, but how, when, where, and why it occurs.

5. Subjects. The use of student samples in consumer research is commonly disparaged and pointed at as reason to doubt the generalizability of research results. The meta-analysis results do not support this view. While the average effect size for consumer samples was lower than for student samples, the difference was not statistically beyond chance. If the products employed in experiments are products which students use and which are part of their consumer realities, then the use of student samples is clearly appropriate. More importantly, the issue is not student vs. consumer samples, but rather buyer vs. non-buyer samples. Few experiments report screening of subjects for prior purchase and/or use of the products under investigation. Yet it is well-established in the consumer literature that information search behaviors differ greatly between consumers with different degrees of prior experience and/or knowledge with the products (Rao and Monroe 1988). It is clearly inappropriate to draw conclusions about the effects of country-of-origin information cues, or indeed any information cues, using subjects who have never purchased or used the product class used in the research. Patterns of cue usage and importance will differ greatly between consumers who do and do not have experience with or knowledge about the product, and require separate study.

6. *Implications for the design of surveys.* The meta-analysis demonstrates a major difference in the effect size estimates between methods employing within-subject vs. between-subject designs. Within-subject designs produce higher estimates of the effects of country-of-origin information cues. This implies that survey methodologies report a relationship between country-of-origin and the dependent variable, which is a consequence of both the demand artifacts of the method and the independent variables. This does not mean that survey methods are inadequate for studying country-of-origin effects. Rather, it suggests that surveys must be designed to take demand effects into account and incorporate devices to reduce them. One approach for removing within-subject demand effects from surveys is to use a between-subject survey sampling design. This can be accomplished by using many versions of the survey instrument, each version being similar to a treatment in an experiment (this implies a need for larger sample sizes).

Theory Development Implications

If better variables, experiment designs and subject selection were achieved, would experiments provide insight and understanding of the processes of product evaluation and choice, and the role of country-of-origin in those processes? This question raises the broader issues about research philosophy and method that are currently receiving extensive debate in the fields of consumer behavior and marketing (Anderson 1986; Arndt 1985; Hirschman 1986; Hudson and Ozanne 1988). Calder and Tybout (1987, p. 136) suggest that understanding can exist at three levels:

> Everyday Knowledge consists of the shared thoughts people have about their own consumer behavior. . . Scientific Knowledge consists of theories that are capable of and have been subjected to rigorous empirical testing. . . Interpretative Knowledge uses a system of ideas developed by a particular group to analyze consumer behavior [i.e., Humanistic, Historical, Psycho-analytical, etc.].

Experiments and surveys are methods of generating scientific knowledge. Literature in which an interpretative approach is used for understanding the role of country-of-origin cues in consumer information choice is almost nonexistent. Clearly, theoretical development is needed at the inquiry level of interpretative knowledge.

But even within a positivistic scientific knowledge approach, theoretical development is sorely needed for country-of-origin cue usage in consumer choice. Obermiller and Spangenberg (1989) argue that "in order to generalize the effects of CO labels, researchers must understand them at the theoretical level, which implies a focus on the construct level of the variable rather than the operational level" (p. 457). Only a few experiments reported in the literature include a theoretical perspective design of the treatment conditions, identifying dependent or independent variables, or for interpreting of results.

Although prior experiments have not explicitly addressed the process of country-of-origin cue usage, the more general information processing and consumer decision process literature provides a starting point for theoretical development in country-of-origin research. Experiments can be a powerful research approach for theory development within the positivistic approach to understanding. A number of authors have begun the process of developing theoretical frameworks and theories of process for the role of country-of-origin cues in consumer choice (Obermiller and Spangenberg 1989; Schellinck 1989a, 1989b; Hong and Wyer 1989; Han 1989; Erickson, Johansson, and Chao 1984; Zeithaml 1988; Johansson, Douglas, and Nonaka 1985). However, theoretical work is needed to significantly advance our understanding of the complex processes by which consumers come to understand and use country-of-origin information.

EPILOGUE

While academic researchers nibble away at understanding country-of-origin cue usage in consumer choice, the reality of the marketplace is undergoing rapid change. Some of these changes render our endeavors obsolete before they are accomplished. Free trade, global marketing, and products with multi-country origin for materials and labor, are rapidly changing the nature of questions asked by marketing practitioners. Practitioners mostly want descriptive information—what do consumers in country X think about my product in order to make marketing strategy decisions? Should we give emphasis to or minimize country-of-origin information about the products we are selling in country Y? What should we do to increase consumer rejection of offshore products? How can we increase acceptance of our products by consumers in other countries? However, descriptive research alone is insufficient to deal with such questions. Effective answers also require understanding of the mechanisms and processes of consumer choice, the role of country-of-origin information in those processes, and its effects. To meet the needs of practitioners better, country-of-origin research must be refocused on explanation and/or prediction.

REFERENCES

Adair, J.G., J. Spinner, J. Carlopio, and R. Lindsay (1983), "Where is the Source of Artifact? Subject Roles or Hypothesis Learning." *Journal of Personality and Social Psychology*, 45, 1129-1131.

Anderson, Norman (1982), *Methods of Information Integration Theory*. Academic Press.

Anderson, Paul (1986), "On Method in Consumer Research: A Critical Relativist Perspective." *Journal of Consumer Research*, 13: (September) 155-73.

Arndt, Johan (1985), "On Making Marketing Science More Scientific: Role of Orientations, Paradigms, Metaphors, and Puzzle Solving." *Journal of Marketing*, 49: (Summer) 11-23.

Calder, Bobby J. and Alice M. Tybout (1987), "What Consumer Research Is." *Journal of Consumer Research*, 14: (June) 136-140.

Calder, Bobby J., Lynn W. Phillips, and Alice M. Tybout (1981), "Designing Research for Application." *Journal of Consumer Research*, 8: (September) 197-207.

Carlopio, J., J.G. Adair, R. Lindsay, and B. Spinner (1983), "Avoiding Artifact in the Search of Bias: The Importance of Assessing Subjects' Perceptions of the Experiment." *Journal of Personality and Social Psychology*, 44: 693-701.

Campbell, Donald T. and Julian C. Stanley (1963), *Experimental and Quasi-Experimental Designs for Research*. Chicago: Rand McNally College Publishing Co.

Churchill, Gilbert A. (1979), "A Paradigm for Developing Better Measures of Marketing Constructs." *Journal of Marketing Research*, XVI: (February) 64-73.

Dickerson, Kitty G. (1982), "Imported Versus U.S.-Produced Apparel: Consumer Views and Buying Patterns." *Home Economics Research Journal*, 10:3 (March) 241-52.

Dickerson, Kitty G. (1987), "Relative Importance of Country-of-Origin as an Attribute in Apparel Choices." *Journal of Consumer Studies and Home Economics*, 11: 333-43.

Erickson, Gary M., Johny K. Johansson, and Paul Chao (1984), "Image Variables in Multi-Attribute Product Evaluations: Country-of-Origin Effects." *Journal of Consumer Research*, 11: (September) 694-699.

Ettenson, Richard, Janet Wagner, and Gary Gaeth (1988), "Evaluating the Effect of Country of Origin and the 'Made in U.S.A.' Campaign: A Conjoint Approach." *Journal of Retailing*, 64(1): 85-100.

Farley, John U. and Donald R. Lehman (1986), *Meta-Analysis in Marketing: Generalization of Response Models*. Lexington, MA: Lexington Books, D.C. Heath and Company.

Fischer, Eileen (1990), "Regularities and Consumer Behaviour: Tangencies Between Positivist and Interpretive Approaches to Research." In M.E. Goldberg, G. Gorn, and R.W. Pollay (eds.), *Advances in Consumer Research*, vol. XVII (New Orleans, Louisiana, Assoc. for Consumer Research) 19-24.

Fishbein, M. and I. Ajzen (1975), *Belief, Attitude, Intention and Behaviour: An Introduction to Theory and Research*. Reading, MA: Addison Wesley Publishing Co.

Gardner, Meryl P. (1988), "Mood States and Consumer Behavior: A Critical Review." *Journal of Consumer Research*, 12: (December) 281-300.

Garland, Barbara C. and John C. Crawford (1985), "Satisfaction With Products of Foreign Origin." In C.T. Tan and J.N. Sheth (eds.), *Historical Perspectives in Consumer Research: National and International Perspectives* (Proceedings, Association of Consumer Research International Meeting, Singapore, July 18-20) 160-161.

Han, Min C. (1989), "Country Image: Halo or Summary Construct?" *Journal of Marketing Research*, XXVI: (May) 222-229.

Han, Min C., and William J. Qualls (1985), "Country-of-Origin Effects and their Impact Upon Consumers' Perception of Quality." In C.T. Tan and J. Sheth (eds.), *Historical Perspectives in Consumer Research: National and International Perspectives* (Association for Consumer Research, School of Management, University of Singapore).

Han, Min C., and Vern Terpstra (1988), "Country-of-Origin Effects for Uni-National and Bi-National Products." *Journal of International Business Studies* (Summer) 235-54.

Hakansson, H. and B. Wootz (1975), "Supplier Selection in an International Environment: An Experimental Study." *Journal of Marketing Research*, XII: (February) 46-51.

Heimbach, Arthur E., Johny K. Johansson, and Douglas L. MacLachlan (1989), "Product Familiarity, Information Processing, and Country-of-Origin Cues." In Thomas K. Srull (ed.), *Advances in Consumer Research* (Association for Consumer Research) 16: 460- 67.

Heslop, Louise A. and John P. Liefeld (1987), "Country of Origin As a Symbol." *Invited Paper* presented at the *John Labatt Symposium "Signs and Symbols in Marketing"* (Montreal).

Heslop, Louise A., John P. Liefeld, and Marjorie Wall (1987), "An Experimental Study of the Impact of Country-of-Origin Information." In R.E. Turner (ed.), *Marketing*, Vol. 8 (Toronto, Ont.: Proceedings, Administrative Sciences Association of Canada–Marketing Division, June) 179-185.

Hirschman, Elizabeth C. (1986), "Humanistic Inquiry in Marketing Research:

Philosophy, Method and Criteria." *Journal of Marketing Research*, XXIII: (August) 237-249.

Holbrook, Morris B. (1990), "The Role of Lyricism in Research on Consumer Emotions: Skylark, Have You Anything to Say to Me?" In M.E. Goldberg, G. Gorn, and R.W. Pollay (eds.), *Advances in Consumer Research* (Association for Consumer Research, New Orleans, Louisiana) XVII: 1-18.

Hong, Sung-Tai and Julie F. Toner (1989), "Are There Gender Differences in the Use of Country-of-Origin in the Evaluations of Products?" In Thomas K. Srull (ed.), *Advances in Consumer Research*, vol. 16 (Provo, UT: Association for Consumer Research) 468-472.

Hong, Sung-Tai and Robert S. Wyer, Jr. (1989), "Effects of Country- of-Origin and Product-Attribute Information on Product Evaluation: An Information Processing Perspective." *Journal of Consumer Research*, 16: (September) 175-187.

Hong, Sung-Tai and Robert S. Wyer, Jr. (1990), "Determinants of Product Evaluation: Effects of the Time Interval Between Knowledge of a Product's Country of Origin and Information About Its Specific Attributes." *Journal of Consumer Research*, 17 (December) 277-288.

Huber, Joel and John McCann (1982), "The Impact of Inferential Beliefs on Product Evaluations." *Journal of Marketing Research*, XIX: (August) 324-32.

Hudson, Laurel A. and Julie L. Ozanne (1988), "Alternative Ways of Seeking Knowledge in Consumer Research." *Journal of Consumer Research*, 14: (March) 508-521.

Jacoby, Jacob (1978), "Consumer Research: A State of the Art Review." *Journal of Marketing*, 42: (April) 87-96.

Johansson, Johny K. and Israel D. Nebenzahl (1986), "Multinational Production: Effect on Brand Value." *Journal of International Business Studies*, 17, 3 (Fall) 101-126.

Johansson, Johny K., Susan P. Douglas, and Ikujiro Nonaka (1985), "Assessing the Impact of Country of Origin on Product Evaluations: A New Methodological Perspective." *Journal of Marketing Research*, XXII: (November) 388-96.

Kaplan, A. (1964), *The Conduct of Inquiry: Methodology for Behavioral Science*. Scranton, PA: Chandler.

Kincaid, W.M. Jr., (1970), *A Study of the Perception of Selected Brands of Products as Foreign or American and Attitudes Towards Such Brands*. Ph.D. Dissertation, University of Texas at Austin.

LaTour, Stephen A. and Paul W. Miniard (1989), "The Misuse of Repeated Measures Analysis in Marketing Research." *Journal of Marketing Research*, XXVI: (February) 45-47.

Levin, Irwin P., Jordan J. Louviere, Albert A. Schepanski, and Kent L. Norman (1983), "External Validity Tests of Laboratory Studies of Information Integration." *Organizational Behaviour and Human Performance*, 31: 173-93.

Mill, J.S., (1930), *A System of Logic*. London: Longmans Green (originally published in 1843).

Nes, Erik B. (1981), *Consumer Perceptions of Product Risk and Quality for*

Goods Manufactured in Developing Versus Industrialized Nations." PhD Dissertation, University of Wisconsin, Madison, WI.

Obermiller, Carl and Eric Spangenberg (1988), "An Information Processing Framework for Predicting the Effects of Country of Origin Labels." *Working Paper,* University of Washington, Seattle, WA.

Obermiller, Carl and Eric Spangenberg (1989), "Exploring the Effects of Country of Origin Labels: An Information Processing Framework." In Thomas K. Srull (ed.), *Advances in Consumer Research,* vol. 16 (Provo, UT: Association for Consumer Research) 454-459.

Olson, Jerry C. (1977), "Price as an Informational Cue: Effects in Product Evaluation." In Arch G. Woodside, Jagdish N. Sheth, and Peter D. Bennet (eds.), *Consumer and Industrial Buying Behaviour.* New York: North Holland. 267-86.

Olson, Jerry C. and Jacob Jacoby (1972), "Cue Utilization in the Quality Perception Process." In M. Venkatesan (ed.), *Proceedings, Third Annual Conference of the Association for Consumer Research,* 167-179.

Papadopoulos, Nicolas, Louise A. Heslop, Françoise Graby, and George Avlonitis (1987), "Does Country-of-Origin Matter? Some Findings from a Cross-Cultural Study of Consumer Views About Foreign Products." *Working Paper #87-104, Marketing Science Institute,* Cambridge, MA.

Peterson, Robert A., Gerald Albaum, and Richard F. Beltramini (1985), "A Meta-Analysis of Effect Sizes in Consumer Behaviour Experiments." *Journal of Consumer Research,* 12: (June) 97-103.

Pincus, Steven and L.K. Waters (1975), "Product Quality Ratings as a Function of Availability of Intrinsic Product Cues and Price Information." *Journal of Applied Psychology,* 60:2, 280-282.

Rao, Akshay R. and Kent B. Monroe (1988), "The Moderating Effect of Prior Knowledge on Cue Utilization in Product Evaluations." *Journal of Consumer Research,* 15: (September) 253-264.

Reierson, Curtis C. (1966), "Are Foreign Products Seen as National Stereotypes." *Journal of Retailing,* 42, 3 (Fall), 33-40.

Reierson, Curtis C. (1967), "Attitude Change Toward Foreign Products." *Journal of Marketing Research,* IV: (November) 385-87.

Rosenberg, M.J. (1956), "Cognitive Structure and Attitudinal Affect." *Journal of Abnormal and Social Psychology,* 53: 367-72.

Rosenthal, Robert and Ralph L. Rosnow, eds. (1969), *Artifact in Behavioral Research.* New York: Academic Press.

Rosenthal, Robert and Ralph L. Rosnow (1984), *Essentials of Behavioral Research: Methods and Data Analysis.* New York: McGraw Hill Book Company.

Schellinck, D.A. (1986), "An Exploratory Study into the Impact of Country of Origin as a Cue in Product Choice." In T.E. Muller (ed.), *Marketing,* vol. 7 (Whistler B.C.: Administrative Sciences Association of Canada–Marketing Division, June) 181- 190.

Schellinck, D.A. (1989a), "Exploring Issues Relevant to the Development of a Theory of Cue Usage." In Alain d'Astous (ed.), *Marketing*, vol. 10 (Montreal, Quebec: Administrative Sciences Association of Canada, June) 276-285.

Schellinck, D.A. (1989b), "Determinants of Country of Origin Cue Usage." In Alain d'Astous (ed.), *Marketing*, vol. 10 (Montreal, Quebec: Administrative Science Association of Canada, June) 268-275.

Schleifer, Stephen and S. Watson Dunn (1968), "Relative Effectiveness of Advertisements of Foreign and Domestic Origin." *Journal of Marketing Research*, V: (August) 296-299.

Schooler, Robert D. (1965), "Product Bias in the Central American Common Market." *Journal of Marketing Research*, II: (November) 394-397.

Schooler, Robert D. (1971), "Bias Phenomena Attendant to the Marketing of Foreign Goods in the U.S." *Journal of International Business Studies*, 2: (Spring) 71-80.

Schooler, Robert D. and Don H. Sunoo (1969), "Consumer Perceptions of International Products: Regional vs. National Labelling." *Social Science Quarterly* (March) 886-890.

Schooler, Robert D. and Albert R. Wildt (1968), "Elasticity of Product Bias." *Journal of Marketing Research*, V: (February) 78- 81.

Sloan, L.R. and T.M. Ostrom (1974), "Amount of Information and Interpersonal Judgment." *Journal of Personality and Social Psychology*, 29: 23-29.

Smead, Raymond J., James B. Wilcox, and Robert E. Wilkes (1981), "How Valid Are Product Descriptions and Protocols in Choice Experiments." *Journal of Consumer Research*, 8: (June) 37-42.

Szbillo, George and Jacob Jacoby (1974), "Intrinsic Versus Extrinsic Cues as Determinants of Perceived Quality." *Journal of Applied Psychology*, 59: (February) 74-78.

Wall, Marjorie and Louise A. Heslop (1986), "Consumer Attitudes Toward Canadian-made versus Imported Products." *Journal of the Academy of Marketing Science*, 14(2): 27-36.

Wall, Marjorie, John P. Liefeld, and Louise A. Heslop (1989), "Impact of Country-of-Origin Cues and Patriotic Appeals on Consumer Judgments: Covariance Analysis." In Alain d'Astous (ed.), *Marketing*, vol. 10 (Montreal: Administrative Sciences Association of Canada–Marketing Division, June) 306-315.

Wall, Marjorie, John P. Liefeld, and Louise A. Heslop (1991), "Impact of Country-of-Origin Cues on Consumer Judgments in Multi-Cue Situations: A Covariance Analysis." *Journal of the Academy of Marketing Science* 19(2):105-113.

Wang, Chih-Kang and Charles W. Lamb (1983), "The Impact of Selected Environmental Forces Upon Consumers' Willingness to Buy Foreign Products." *Journal of the Academy of Marketing Science*, 11(2): (Winter) 71-84.

Weber, S.J. and T.D. Cook (1972), "Subject Effects in Laboratory Research: An Examination of Subject Roles and Demand Characteristics, and Valid Inference." *Psychological Bulletin*, 77: 273-295.

White, Philip D. and E.W. Cundiff (1978), "Assessing the Quality of Industrial Products." *Journal of Marketing,* (January) 80-86.

Zajonc, Robert B. and Hazel Markus (1982), "Affective and Cognitive Factors in Preferences." *Journal of Consumer Research,* 9: (September) 123-31.

Zeithaml, Valerie A. (1988), "Consumer Perceptions of Price, Quality, and Value: A Means-End Model and Synthesis of Evidence." *Journal of Marketing,* 52: (July) 2-22.

PART III.
METHODOLOGICAL
AND BEHAVIORAL PERSPECTIVES

INTRODUCTION

The chapters in this part of the book address a variety of methodological and behavioral perspectives concerning the images of origin countries. Chapter 6 suggests a methodology for estimating demand functions in relation to transnational shifts in the location of production. Building on earlier work by one of the authors, the chapter shows how arc elasticities of price can be estimated and how they can be taken into account in making production location decisions. Chapter 7 explores a related subject through a multi-cue experiment intended to assess perceived risk among consumers with regard to products from less developed countries. Combined, these chapters show, among other things, that it is imperative to take country-of-origin considerations into account when making decisions about a product's place of manufacture.

Chapter 8 also uses a multi-cue experimental design but focuses on personality variables as moderators of the influence of the made-in concept. By indicating that some personality factors are likely to have more and some less impact, and that this impact varies among various types of buyers, the authors make a strong case for taking personality into account in international market segmentation decisions.

Chapters 9 and 10 represent a change of scenery from consumer to industrial products and their buyers. Many have argued that industrial buyers, being more "rational," are not likely to be influenced by product origin decisions. In fact, Chapter 3, as well as Chapter 9 in this part, provide evidence that this simply is not so.

One of the problems of past research in this area has been that researchers focusing on the views of industrial buyers study them with methodologies designed in the context of consumer research. Chapter 10, which is framed as a "research note," argues that industrial product research must take into account the unique decision-making environment in organizations as opposed to end-consumers, and points to ways of how this can be done. Although written independently from one another, Chapter 9 portrays some of the adaptations that are necessary for origin studies in industrial settings, and some of the different results obtained, which are suggested in Chapter 10.

Chapter 6

Estimating Demand Functions
from the Country-of-Origin Effect

Israel D. Nebenzahl
Eugene D. Jaffe

INTRODUCTION

The sourcing of international production for marketing to third countries or back to the investor's country should depend, in part, upon which
alternative location offers the highest return (revenue minus cost), assuming that the risks of each option have been considered. The relative cost of
producing an identical product in one country versus another is a straightforward calculation. So are the shipping, insurance, and customs costs.
This is not so for the revenue side.

Revenue is a function of the price schedule that customers will pay for
the product in the target market. Price, moreover, is partly a function of
country image because that image affects customers' perceptions of product quality and desirability. In this chapter, we set the groundwork for a
more rigorous treatment of the relationship between country image and
perceived acceptable price. Our methodology calls for the development of
preference curves and elasticity analysis of these curves. We then use the
proposed methodology to show that an identical product/brand will have a
differently shaped preference curve depending upon its country-of-origin.
The subject is significant because it has important pricing implications for
multinational companies which have a variety of options for product
sourcing.

OVERVIEW OF RELEVANT RESEARCH

In an early review of country-of-origin literature (Bilkey and Nes 1982)
and a later one (Papadopoulos et al. 1987), it was shown that most studies

---

Both authors contributed equally to this chapter.

in this area employ multiattribute scales using mean ratings. While useful in many ways, the "classical" approach utilized in most country image studies, based on mean ratings, has certain weaknesses. First, the "country image effect" construct assumes that country image affects consumers' perception of product attributes made in the surveyed countries. To the degree that the observed differences result from true mean differences among corresponding products, they reflect reality and not the country image effect. The validity of this assumption was tested in Jaffe and Nebenzahl (1988). In short, using traditional measures of halo errors which have been extensively utilized in the psychology literature over the last three decades, Jaffe and Nebenzahl found little evidence for the presence of a clear country image effect. Therefore, studies utilizing mean ratings alone may provide valid measures of how consumers perceive products made in different countries, but not necessarily country image effects.

Second, traditional analyses do not provide clues as to what would be the image of a brand associated with a certain country when products marketed under this brand name are produced in another country. Would such products retain the original image of the country-of-origin? Will they acquire the image of the made-in label country? Or will they somehow assimilate the two images into a hybrid image which is different from the original two? For example, we later discuss that Japan is perceived as a producer of a large assortment of relatively inexpensive products, while West Germany (before unification) is perceived as a producer of exclusive quality products. Will a Japanese brand produced in Germany be perceived as being of better quality than the same product produced in Japan? Or, will it be perceived as being just more expensive? Will a German brand produced in Japan lose its exclusiveness and become more common? Unless these questions can be answered, the study of country image effect will be of academic interest, but of limited practical value, since it does not provide information which can assist the formulation of marketing strategies.

Johansson and Nebenzahl (1986) addressed these questions and suggested a method for answering them. Their method calls for replication of multiattribute scale questions for each production shift considered. However, applying this method to the present study, for example, would have required replicating 13 scales six more times. Such an expansion of the questionnaire by 78 questions would have made it prohibitively long. This problem can be solved by a factorial design which divides production shifts among subsamples of respondents. This method, while keeping the questionnaire reasonably short, results in a reduction in the sample size per question.

Finally, even when perceived country image differences are extreme, the economic significance of such perceptual differences remains unknown. There remains a need to show how country image affects consumer perception of product prices.

Few researchers have attempted to study the country image effect on product price. Rather, most studies have assumed that a negative country image is synonymous with low perceived product quality, while the opposite is true of a positive country image. Peterson and Jolibert (1975) studied the extent to which price level, brand image, and the consumer's nationality affect product quality. Their conclusion was that price is an indicator of perceived product quality, but that the price-quality cue differs across cultures. Chadraba and O'Keefe (1981) found that consumers in several countries expressed similar value perceptions, but the influence of brand was not tested. Neither study used country-of-origin as an explanatory variable of value or quality perception.

In a study by Heslop, Liefeld, and Wall (1987), country-of-origin information was generally found to be more important in affecting quality assessments than price and brand information. Respondents were asked to judge the overall quality of products made in Canada, the United States, Italy, Taiwan, Hong Kong, and South Korea. Also, respondents were queried as to their intention of buying products made in these countries, the perceived risk associated with purchasing them, the expected price they would have to pay for them (when price was not used as a cue), and the value of the products (when price was given). The authors concluded that well-known brand names and pricing policies cannot improve a negative country-of-origin effect.

Johansson and Thorelli (1985) and Johansson and Nebenzahl (1986) have attempted to determine pricing strategy based on country image affect. Johansson and Nebenzahl (1986) measured in absolute terms how much above or below a base price consumers would be willing to pay for an identical model car manufactured in several countries. The mean price change across respondents was their measure of the relationship between country-of-origin and price. Johansson and Thorelli (1985) measured country-of-origin effect on product value by a term called "benefit-per-dollar."[1] The higher the benefit per dollar, the higher the probability that the consumer would purchase the product.

Using an average dollar amount for product price, as in Johansson and

---

1. Benefit-per-dollar was arrived at by weighing a perceived price against attribute ratings for each product.

Nebenzahl (1986), results in a price-quantity relationship on only one point of a preference curve. The usage of average price tacitly assumes the same price elasticity for all consumers. It fails to recognize that lowering the price may mean that some consumers still will not buy the product because their expected price is even lower. Others might have bought the product at a higher price, resulting in lost revenue. Instead of using one mean price, we propose a method which allows for calculating price elasticities at several points on a preference curve. If different elasticities were to be found at several points on such a preference curve, this would be an indication of different market segments, suggesting a strategy of product differentiation (Smith 1956).

RESEARCH DESIGN

Country-of-origin effect was measured for products familiar to a broad section of consumers. The product class chosen was consumer home electronics and was described to respondents as including such products as television sets, videocassette recorders (VCRs), compact disks, microwave ovens, and stereo systems. Three countries whose manufacturers market these products in Israel were chosen for the study: Japan, South Korea, and West Germany. West Germany and Japan were selected because their products were well-established in the Israeli market. South Korea was selected because its products began to enter the Israeli market just prior to the research and were only selectively distributed. No Korean-made products were promoted in Israel prior to our research. Thus, ownership of Korean-made products was believed to be negligible and familiarity limited because of the absence of an advertising campaign. Therefore, an opportunity existed to study country image stereotype effects for a group of products for which consumer knowledge was nearly nonexistent.

The Research Instrument

The task that respondents were asked to perform included two different assessments of country image. First, respondents gave ratings for a class of electronic products made in each of the three subject countries on a 12-attribute semantic-differential scale and an overall evaluation question. Questions were rotated so that positive attributes were sometimes to the right and sometimes to the left of the scales.

Second, respondents were asked to relate price to specific products (e.g., VCRs), brands (e.g., Sony), and brand-origin (e.g., Japan) in a simulated environment. Combinations of such product-brand origin-price questions were given for studying shifts of production from West Germany to Japan and South Korea and from Japan to West Germany and South Korea.

Using a third-person role-playing technique, respondents were asked to relate to a friend who is shopping in a retail electronics store, planning to buy a VCR. In another scenario, the VCR was replaced by a microwave oven, etc. Each respondent was told that his or her friend had decided to purchase, say, a Sony VCR made in Japan and priced at NIS2,000 ($1,333, at the exchange rate of NIS1.5 = $1).[2] However, the salesperson suggested that the consumer buy instead an identical Sony VCR made in South Korea. The respondent was then asked to estimate how much more or less than the base price of NIS2,000 his or her friend would be willing to pay for the Korean-made VCR. This procedure was repeated eight times as outlined in the construct shown in Table 1.

Role playing and third-person projective techniques are commonly used for revealing consumers' feelings and attitudes (Dillon, Madden, and Firtle 1987, pp. 136-137). We have combined the two methods by asking respondents about their friends' simulated behavior rather than their own for the following reason. In the pretest stage, the simulation was directed to the respondents themselves with the instruction "consider yourself in a store. . . ." It was found that some respondents had difficulty relating to the

Table 1. Research Model: Shift of Brand Production
to New Location

Product	Japan	Country W. Germany	S. Korea
a. VCR			
Initial Location	Sony	Grundig	--
New Location	Grundig	Sony	Sony Grundig
b. Microwave oven			
Initial Location	Sanyo	Grundig	--
New Location	Grundig	Sanyo	Sanyo Grundig

2. NIS: New Israeli Shekels

situation. A typical response of these persons was: "I don't need a micro-wave..." or, "I won't buy a VCR at any price...." Apparently, for some respondents, the simulation required a level of abstraction beyond their capability. However, the same respondents had no difficulty thinking of a friend in the same situation.

Sample Selection

A multistage area sample was drawn from the Tel Aviv metropolitan area which numbers some 500,000 residents out of a total Israeli popula-tion of four million. This area is representative of the entire urban popula-tion. The Tel Aviv metropolitan area includes 12 urban municipalities from Rehovot in the south to Netanya in the north. In the first stage, the sample size from each municipality was determined in proportion to its population, rounded to the nearest tenth. In the second stage, each munici-pality sample size was divided by ten to determine the number of geo-graphical area clusters to be sampled. These geographical areas were selected randomly from the map of each municipality, excluding nonresi-dential zones. In the third stage, a specific block within each geographical area was selected at random. In the final stage, apartments from each block were sampled. In order to minimize the risk of interviewer bias, each interviewer was limited to ten interviews. Interviewers were given the address of the first apartment to be sampled on each block and then selected every tenth residence from the first address, but no more than two respondents from a single multiple dwelling.

Data Collection

The questionnaire used in this study was pretested on a small sample prior to writing the final version. After corrections were made, interview-ers were given specific addresses and requested to interview an adult member of the household. In case an adult was not present or refused to participate, interviewers were instructed to try next door. Since we were interested in interviewing only those people who were unfamiliar with products made in South Korea, respondents were screened on the basis of whether they had seen any advertisement for Korean products. If they answered in the affirmative, the interview was terminated and the inter-viewer tried next door. At the termination of the interview, respondents were asked to give their name and telephone number so that project direc-tors could later verify that the interview took place at the assigned location and ask some confirmatory questions.

In order to reach the required sample size of 420, the interviewers approached 526 adults. Of these, 106 either refused or were rejected due to familiarity with Korean products, giving a response rate of 80 percent. Seven questionnaires were rejected because they were not filled out properly, yielding a net response rate of 78 percent. A total of 413 usable questionnaires were included in the data analysis. A frequency distribution of respondents' socio-economic characteristics is shown in Table 2.

FINDINGS

The first analysis that was conducted resulted in mean ratings on all dimensions for each of the three countries, across all respondents. In order to facilitate interpretation, means were rotated so that low values (1 to 3.49) represent the negative attributes, while high values (3.5 to 6) represent the positive attributes on the bipolar scales. The results are shown in Table 3 and Figure 1, along the lines of the traditional data presentation of most country image studies. In interpreting these results, it should be noted that differences between any two corresponding means of 0.2 or larger are statistically significant at $p < .05$, and differences of 0.3 or larger are significant at $p < .01$.

Table 2. Sample Distribution
(N = 413; non-responses excluded)

Sex

	N	%
Male	245	59.6
Female	166	40.4
Total	411	100.0

Age

	N	%
20-30	97	26.1
31-40	150	40.3
41-54	90	24.2
55-64	20	5.4
>65	15	4.0
Total	372	100.0

Education

	N	%
Grade School	28	6.9
Some High School	99	24.3
High School grad.	102	24.9
Post-High School	46	11.2
Some College	43	10.5
College graduate	91	22.2
Total	409	100.0

Standard of Living*

	N	%
Low	8	2.6
Below avg.	13	4.3
Average	263	86.8
Above avg.	17	5.6
High	2	0.7
Total	303	100.0

* Perceived, self-reported

Table 3. Mean Scale Ratings

			Countries	
Descriptors		S. Korea	W. Germany	Japan
1	Known	2.41	5.54	5.58
2	Reliability	3.15	5.39	5.05
3	Reasonable Price	4.51	3.41	4.22
4	Performance	3.47	5.49	5.19
5	Exclusivity	2.35	4.75	3.03
6	Quality	2.99	5.35	4.82
7	Innovativeness	2.67	5.06	4.78
8	Pride of Ownership	3.13	5.03	4.93
9	Technology	3.58	5.11	5.03
10	Liking	3.29	4.52	4.73
11	Maintenance	3.36	4.96	4.44
12	Assortment	3.47	4.92	5.33
13	Overall	3.31	5.52	5.34

As shown in Figure 1, the mean ratings of South Korea are significantly lower than those of Germany and Japan on all dimensions, with the exception of price, which is above that of Germany (p < .01) and Japan (p < .05). It may be that most respondents have interpreted the price dimension of "reasonably priced" versus "unreasonably priced" as reflecting the purchase price in its absolute monetary value, rather than the intended cost-benefit meaning. Since the overall profile of South Korea is so far below those of Germany and Japan, it can be concluded that the image of South Korea as a producer of home electronic products is perceived by Israeli consumers to be far inferior to those of the other two countries studied.

Turning now to the relative profiles of Japan and West Germany, no statistically significant differences were found between the ratings of these countries on the dimensions "known," "pride of ownership," and "technology." Germany was found to be significantly superior (p < .01) on the dimensions "reliability," "performance," "exclusivity," "quality," "innovativeness," and "maintenance," and on the overall evaluation question number 13 (p < .05).

On the dimensions "reasonable price," "liking," and "assortment," Japan is significantly superior to Germany. It should be noted that most of the observed differences, while being statistically significant as a result of the large sample, are too small to indicate a clear perceptual advantage of one country over another. Notable exceptions are three dimensions: "exclusivity," "quality," and "maintenance." These show that German products are perceived as better in exclusiveness, quality, and maintenance. On the other hand, Japan seems to be clearly superior on the dimensions

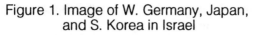

Figure 1. Image of W. Germany, Japan,
and S. Korea in Israel

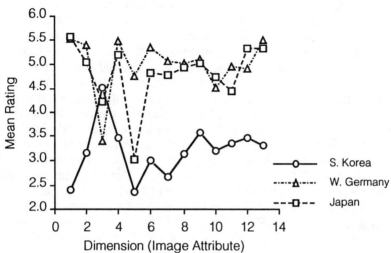

"reasonable price" and "assortment," indicating that it provides a larger assortment of product models at much better prices. Based on these results, we can conclude that while West Germany seems to have a better overall image as a producer of exclusive quality products, Japan has the advantage of being seen to offer consumers more models to select from and at better prices.

As previously noted above, even when perceived country image differences are extreme, as is the case in the observed image of South Korea relative to those of Japan and West Germany, the economic significance of these perceptual differences remains unknown. While our data clearly indicate that Israeli consumers expect products made in South Korea to be least expensive and German products to be most expensive, it is not clear what should be the ratios among these prices. If we were to judge by the observed differences in the price dimension of Figure 1, the prices of products made in South Korea and Japan should be closer to each other than to Germany. On the other hand, the similarity between the profiles of Japan and Germany suggests that the prices of these two countries should be closer to each other than either should be to South Korea. Johansson and Nebenzahl (1986) provide a partial solution to this limitation by asking respondents to assign dollar values to each production shift considered. Combining the price data with the multiattribute scale data provides a clue to the mean economic value of each perceptual map.

In the second step of the analysis, we extend Johansson and Nebenzahl's (1986) approach by deriving preference curves. From responses to the eight simulated research situations, the percent of respondents who would pay more or less than the base price for Japanese- and German-branded products made in Japan, West Germany, and South Korea were tabulated into the frequency distributions that are shown in Tables 4, 5, 6, and 7. These frequency distributions are proxies of preference schedules for each of the products studied. Each preference schedule represents the proportion of people who would buy a given product at a price above or below the base (quoted) price. For example, Table 4 shows that 81 percent of the respondents would purchase a Sony VCR made in South Korea if it was priced at NIS1,200 or less. In other words, this represents a discount of 40 percent or more below the base price of NIS2,000 for the same Sony made in Japan. One-third of respondents demand a discount of 20 percent or more (price of NIS1,600 or less). Only 7 percent of respondents would be willing to pay the same price for a Sony VCR made in South Korea as

Table 4. Estimated Preference Schedules:
Japanese Products Made in S. Korea

Sony VCR Made in South Korea			Sanyo Microwave Made in South Korea		
Price for Equivalent Value (NIS)	% Price Change	% Willing to Pay Price or More	Price for Equivalent Value (NIS)	% Price Change	% Willing to Pay Price or More
700	-65	99.7	400	-60	99.7
800	-60	99.7	500	-50	97.7
1000	-50	99.7	600	-40	76.6
1200	-40	80.7	700	-30	65.8
1400	-30	72.2	800	-20	44.0
1600	-20	33.1	900	-10	18.3
1800	-10	16.8	* 1000	0	8.2
* 2000	0	6.8	1100	10	0.8
2200	10	0.5	1200	20	0.8
2400	20	0.0	1300	30	0.3
2600	30	0.0	1400	40	0.3
			1500	50	0.3
			1600	60	0.0

* Base Price

Table 5. Estimated Preference Schedules:
W. German Products Made in S. Korea

Grundig VCR Made in South Korea			Grundig Microwave Made in South Korea		
Price for Equivalent Value (NIS)	% Price Change	% Willing to Pay Price or More	Price for Equivalent Value (NIS)	% Price Change	% Willing to Pay Price or More
700	-65	100.0	400	-60	100.0
800	-60	98.4	500	-50	96.7
1000	-50	97.9	600	-40	70.8
1200	-40	76.7	700	-30	54.7
1400	-30	64.9	800	-20	30.2
1600	-20	31.3	900	-10	10.2
1800	-10	15.0	* 1000	0	5.5
* 2000	0	3.6	1100	10	0.8
2200	10	0.0	1200	20	0.8
2400	20	0.0	1300	30	0.3
2600	30	0.0	1400	40	0.3
			1500	50	0.3
			1600	60	0.0

* Base Price

for the Japanese-made Sony. Similar results were obtained for a Sanyo microwave oven made in South Korea compared with the Japanese-made version.

In the case of Grundig VCRs made in South Korea (Table 5), only 4 percent of respondents would be willing to pay the base price (NIS2,000 for a Grundig VCR made in Germany). Nearly one-third of respondents would buy the Korean-made VCR at a discount of 20 percent or more (NIS1,600 or less), and two-thirds would buy at a discount of 30 percent or more.

Contrast these findings with Japanese branded products made in Germany and Grundig products made in Japan (Tables 6 and 7). Eighty percent of respondents would purchase a Sony VCR made in West Germany at the base price (NIS2,000) or less, while 19 percent would be willing to pay a premium of 10 percent above the base price. About half of the latter, or 11 percent of the total sample, were willing to pay a 20 percent or higher premium for VCRs. Similar findings resulted for Sanyo microwaves made in West Germany.

In the case of Grundig VCRs made in Japan, 46 percent of respondents

Table 6. Estimated Preference Schedules:
Japanese Products Made in W. Germany

Sony VCR Made in West Germany			Sanyo Microwave Made in West Germany		
Price for Equivalent Value (NIS)	% Price Change	% Willing to Pay Price or More	Price for Equivalent Value (NIS)	% Price Change	% Willing to Pay Price or More
700	-65	100.0	400	-60	100.0
800	-60	100.0	500	-50	100.0
1000	-50	100.0	600	-40	98.8
1200	-40	98.3	700	-30	98.0
1400	-30	97.8	800	-20	95.8
1600	-20	93.6	900	-10	86.8
1800	-10	90.9	* 1000	0	77.9
* 2000	0	80.4	1100	10	22.1
2200	10	19.1	1200	20	10.4
2400	20	8.3	1300	30	3.2
2600	30	2.5	1400	40	2.2
			1500	50	2.0
			1600	60	0.2

* Base Price

would pay the base price (NIS,2000) or less, while 72 percent would purchase at a discount of 10 percent or more below the base price. Few would be willing to pay a premium for either a Grundig VCR or microwave oven made in Japan.

Preference curves for the above data are shown in Figures 2 and 3. In Figure 2, the shape of the curves for Japanese-branded VCRs and microwave ovens made in Germany are almost identical. So are the curves for German-branded VCRs and microwave ovens made in Japan, shown in Figure 3. These similarities are most striking considering the two different products (VCRs and microwave ovens), the brand names (Sony and Sanyo), and the wide dispersion between the two anchor prices (NIS1,000 and NIS2,000). This means that perception of the made-in country-of-origin is a stronger cue in determining the shape of the relative preference schedule than product type, brand name, and price.

Looking at the preference curves for Japanese-branded products made in Germany (Sony VCR and Sanyo microwave) in Figure 2, a very small proportion of respondents would be willing to pay a higher price than for identical Japanese-branded products made in Japan, while most respon-

Table 7. Estimated Preference Schedules:
W. German Products Made in Japan

Grundig VCR Made in Japan			Grundig Microwave Made in Japan		
Price for Equivalent Value (NIS)	% Price Change	% Willing to Pay Price or More	Price for Equivalent Value (NIS)	% Price Change	% Willing to Pay Price or More
800	-65	100.0	400	-60	100.0
900	-60	100.0	500	-50	99.8
1000	-50	100.0	600	-40	97.3
1200	-40	96.1	700	-30	95.1
1400	-30	95.1	800	-20	86.5
1600	-20	81.6	900	-10	64.2
1800	-10	72.1	* 1000	0	47.1
* 2000	0	46.3	1100	10	2.9
2200	10	1.7	1200	20	2.5
2400	20	0.7	1300	30	1.5
2600	30	0.2	1400	40	1.2
			1500	50	1.2
			1600	60	0.7

* Base Price

dents would pay the same price for both products. Another small segment would buy the Japanese brands made in Germany only at a discount, while the majority of respondents would buy at 20 percent less than the base price.

A similar analysis of the preference curves for the Grundig products made in Japan (Figure 3) shows that more than half of the respondents require at least a 10 percent discount. In order to reach 95 percent of the market, a 30 percent discount is required. Thus, substantial discounts are needed for products made in South Korea in order to generate significant demand in Israel.

To summarize, shifting the manufacture of German products to Japan would necessitate some price discounting, while a shift of Japanese brand name products to Germany would allow them to be sold at somewhat higher than the base price. Producing both German and Japanese brand name products in South Korea shifts the preference curves to the left. No matter what the origin of the brand name itself, a substantial price discount would have to be offered if the products have a "Made in South Korea" label.

PRICE ELASTICITIES
AND THE MAXIMIZATION OF REVENUE

Up to this point we have considered the relationships between prices and sales volume in units. The present approach has been extended in this chapter thus far to the estimation of more detailed preference schedules rather than their expected value alone. We now further extend the analysis by recognizing that the estimated preference curves facilitate consideration of elasticities as well as expected revenue in addition to expected unit sales.

In analogy with demand functions, the preference curves provide price-quantity relationships. Accordingly, price elasticities can be computed. Under an assumption of constant costs, we contend that profit maximizing firms should maximize dollar revenue rather than unit sales. Let us recall that in downward sloping demand curves, as price is increased or decreased, sales volume changes in the opposite direction. The combined net effect on revenue may be positive or negative depending upon the price elasticity of demand. If the absolute value of the price elasticity is greater than 1.0, revenue is increased when the price is cut. If it is less than 1.0, revenue increases with an increase in price. Thus, revenue is maximized at the point where absolute elasticity is unitary.

Theoretically, elasticity may vary continuously and should be evaluated accordingly. In empirical studies, however, it is customary to use arc elasticities rather than point elasticities. Arc elasticity may be used to calculate price elasticities for nonlinear demand curves, by drawing an arc between two points and computing the elasticity at the midpoint using the formula (Hughes 1973, pp. 89-90):

$$Eqp = (dQ/Q)/(dP/P)$$

Applying similar elasticity analysis to the preference functions, price elasticities for Japanese- and German-branded products made in Japan, West Germany, and South Korea are given in Tables 8 and 9.

Price elasticity is high for prices above the base price (dP +10 –0%) in the case of both German and Japanese brands made in Japan and West Germany, but relatively higher for Korean-made products. This shows that consumers are highly sensitive to price in the case of Korean-made goods.

Given the price elasticities in Tables 8 and 9, the pricing strategies are evident. To maximize revenue, price should be determined at that point where elasticity is closest to –1.0. Taking as an example the Grundig brand for both VCRs and microwaves made in Japan, the optimum price would be in the range of a 10 to 20 percent discount from the base price. For the

Figure 2. Effect of Shifting Japanese
Brands to S. Korea and W. Germany

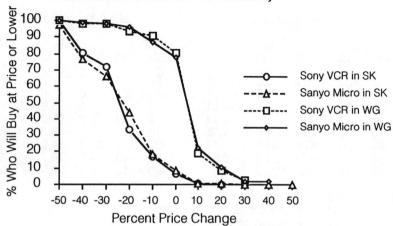

Sony VCR in SK
Sanyo Micro in SK
Sony VCR in WG
Sanyo Micro in WG

Figure 3. Effect of Shifting W. German
Brands to S. Korea and Japan

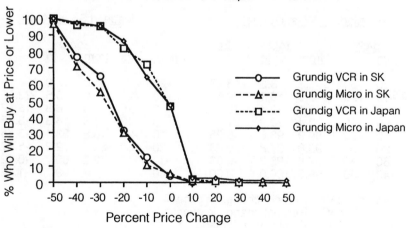

Grundig VCR in SK
Grundig Micro in SK
Grundig VCR in Japan
Grundig Micro in Japan

Table 8. Mean Price Elasticities:
West German Grundig VCRs and Microwave Ovens

Made in Japan					Made in South Korea				
dΔP from	to	dΔQ from	to	Ed	dΔP from	to	dΔQ from	to	Ed
+20	+30	0.2	0.8	-13.89	+20	+30	0	0	--
+10	+20	0.7	1.7	- 9.58	+10	+20	0	0	--
+0	+10	1.7	46.3	-19.51	+ 0	+10	0	3.6	-21.00
0	-10	46.3	72.1	- 4.14	0	-10	3.6	15.0	-11.65
-10	-20	72.1	81.6	- 1.05	-10	-20	15.0	33.3	- 5.98
-20	-30	81.6	95.1	- 1.14	-20	-30	31.3	64.9	- 5.24
-30	-40	95.1	96.1	- 0.07	-30	-40	64.9	76.7	- 1.08
-40	-50	96.1	100.0	- 0.22	-40	-50	76.9	99.9	- 1.34

Legend. dΔP   Percent change in price
dΔQ   Percent change in quantity
Ed   Elasticity of demand

Table 9. Mean Price Elasticities:
Japanese Sony VCRs and Sanyo Microwave Ovens

Made in West Germany					Made in South Korea				
dΔP from	to	dΔQ from	to	Ed	dΔP from	to	dΔQ from	to	Ed
+20	+30	2.3	8.3	-13.43	+20	+30	0	0	--
+10	+20	8.3	19.1	-9.07	+10	+20	0	0.5	-23.00
0	+10	19.1	80.4	-12.94	+ 0	+10	0.5	6.8	-18.12
0	-10	80.4	90.9	-1.16	0	-10	6.8	16.8	-8.05
-10	-20	90.9	93.6	-0.25	-10	-20	16.8	33.1	-5.55
-20	-30	93.6	97.8	-0.33	-20	-30	33.1	72.2	-5.57
-30	-40	97.8	98.3	-0.03	-30	-40	72.2	80.7	-0.72
-40	-50	98.3	100.0	-0.09	-40	-50	80.7	99.7	-1.16

Legend. dΔP   Percent change in price
dΔQ   Percent change in quantity
Ed   Elasticity of demand

Sony and Sanyo brands made in Germany, the optimum price would be the base price up to a discount of 10 percent. Thus, sourcing German-branded products in Japan would require a larger discount from the base price than producing in West Germany either German- or Japanese-branded VCRs and microwave ovens.

The price elasticity for German- and Japanese-branded products made in South Korea is very high. For German-branded products, revenue will be maximized only at a discount of 30 to 40 percent below the base price. In the case of Japanese-branded products, the discount would have to be in the same range.

The value of elasticity analysis is evident when we compare the results for Japanese products made in West Germany. Considering unit sales alone, we previously concluded that such products can be sold at a premium price in Israel. However, revenue is maximized at a lower price, which should be between the base price and a 10 percent discount. In contrast, West German products made in Japan require a price discount in the range of 10 to 20 percent for revenue maximization, rather than the suggested 30 percent cut needed to reach 95 percent of unit sales as compared with original made-in-Germany products. Thus, the elasticity analysis suggests higher prices for German products made in Japan relative to the prices indicated by sales analysis alone. These improvements are due to the analysis of the joint effects of price and changes in sales volume on revenue.

IMPLICATIONS

Several implications are apparent from the findings reported above. For manufacturers seeking to implement a global strategy, our findings have important implications for sourcing. One of the advantages of a multinational company is the flexibility to shift production from one country to another in response to economic imperatives. In theory, dispersed manufacturing plants producing identical components or assembling a finished product provide the opportunity to coordinate production across countries (Kogut 1990). For example, Ford could shift production of cars from a plant in the U.K. to one in Brazil if wage rates escalate in the U.K. However, once consumers realize that the cars they are purchasing are made in Brazil and not the U.K., will they regard them as having the same value? The answer to this question depends on the country-of-origin effect. For manufacturers seeking to implement a multisourcing strategy for finished products, it would be well worth the effort to determine the country-of-origin implications and not only the comparative production costs.

When cost considerations are dominant, as in the case of production in countries such as Mexico, South Korea, or Singapore, a manufacturer must determine a marketing strategy to offset less than favorable image effects. A number of possibilities exist. To compensate for negative image effect, some countervailing strategy should be selected. Alternative tactics include promotion, price discounting, emphasizing a well known brand name rather than country, dealer incentives to push the product, and longer product warranties.

CONCLUSIONS

Up to now, country-of-origin effect has been treated as an exogenous variable in general terms of positive or negative stereotyping. Calculations of preference schedules based on country-of-origin effect give marketers an analytical and strategic tool by which they can make production-location and pricing decisions. Using the methodology presented in this chapter, multinational companies can decide whether it is advisable to source production in various alternative countries. When a sourcing policy is undertaken, pricing strategies for each target market can be determined when all other elements of the marketing strategy are held constant. It should be recognized that the total marketing mix can be used as a strategic tool to neutralize negative stereotyping. On the tactical level, however, little is known about the interaction between price and the other elements of the marketing mix. Research is sorely needed on the interrelationship between price and other mix elements (e.g., advertising, other means of promotion, product, brand policy, and distribution). For example, the fact that a Korean-made product must be discounted for sale in Germany is a relative one–this would hold true unless the manufacturer took other steps (e.g., twice the advertising budget of competitors, better service-warranty package) to counterbalance the negative country-of-origin effect on price.

Attempts to use advertising to improve country image have in fact been used by South Korean manufacturers. The campaign intended to compare Korean-made consumer goods with Japanese quality is a major goal of the "more Korean than the Japanese" theme. Whether or not this attempt has succeeded has not been reported in the literature.

An example of research that studied the effect of promotion on country image is Jaffe and Nebenzahl's chapter in this book, which demonstrates that South Korea's image improved as a result of the Seoul Olympic games. However, their research did not examine other elements of the marketing mix which might contribute to improving country image. Further analysis is necessary to determine how market segments may be derived from elasticities. It may very well be that certain consumer segments (say, those that are highly price elastic) can be appealed to by production in countries with a relatively poorer product image, whereas highly inelastic demand segments would be marketed products made in countries with relatively favorable product images. Segmentation analysis of this sort would complete the pricing strategy described.

The analyses presented in this chapter assume a market with established price and demand for the studied brand(s) when produced in the home country. Under these conditions, total unit sales may be derived as deviations from current sales. The estimation of preference schedules under alternative conditions should be the subject of future research.

REFERENCES

Bilkey, Warren J. and Erik Nes (1982), "Country-of-Origin Effects on Product Evaluations." *Journal of International Business Studies*, 8(1) (Spring/Summer) 89-99.

Chadraba, Petr and Robert O'Keefe (1981), "Cross-National Product Value Perceptions." *Journal of Business Research*, 9: 329-337.

Dillon, William R., Thomas J. Madden, and Neal H. Firtle (1987), *Marketing Research in a Marketing Environment*. St. Louis, MO: Times Mirror/Mosby College Publishing. pp. 136-137.

Heslop, Louise A., John P. Liefeld, and Marjorie Wall (1987), "An Experimental Study of the Impact of Country-of-Origin Information." In R.E. Turner (ed.), *Marketing*, Vol. 8 (Toronto, Ont.: Proceedings, Administrative Sciences Association of Canada–Marketing Division, June) 179-185.

Hughes, G. David (1973), *Demand Analysis for Marketing Decision*. Homewood, IL: Richard D. Irwin. pp. 89-90.

Jaffe, Eugene D. and Israel D. Nebenzahl (1988), "On the Measurement of Halo Effect in Country Image Studies." Paper presented at the Annual Meeting of the *European International Business Association* (West Berlin, December).

Johansson, Johny K. and Israel D. Nebenzahl (1986), "Multinational Production: Effect on Brand Value." *Journal of International Business Studies*, 17, 3 (Fall) 101-126.

Johansson, Johny K. and Hans B. Thorelli (1985), "International Product Positioning." *Journal of International Business Studies*, XVI, 3 (Fall) 57-75.

Kogut, Bruce, (1990), "International Sequential Advantages and Network Flexibility." In C.A. Bartlett, Y. Doz, and G. Hedlund (eds.), *Managing the Global Firm*. London: Routledge. 56.

Papadopoulos, Nicolas, Louise A. Heslop, Françoise Graby, and George Avlonitis (1987), "Does Country-of-Origin Matter? Some Findings from a Cross-Cultural Study of Consumer Views About Foreign Products." *Working Paper #87-104, Marketing Science Institute,* Cambridge, MA.

Peterson, Robert A. and Alain Jolibert (1975), "A Cross- National Investigation of Price and Brand as Determinants of Perceived Product Quality." *Journal of Applied Psychology,* 61: 533-536.

Smith, Wendell (1956), "Product Differentiation and Market Segmentation as Alternative Marketing Strategies." *Journal of Marketing* (July) 3-8.

Chapter 7

A Multi-Cue Test
of Country-of-Origin Theory

Erik Nes
Warren J. Bilkey

BACKGROUND

From an information theoretic perspective, products may be conceived as an array of informational cues. Such cues may be intrinsic (taste, design, fit, etc.), or extrinsic (price, brand name, warranties, etc.). Each cue provides a basis for developing impressions of the product. This chapter reports a study on the impact of one such cue–the extrinsic cue of the country where the product is produced. This cue has generated a large body of international research which has been reviewed by Bilkey and Nes (1982) and other researchers.

Bauer (1967) suggested that it is not the objective risk, but rather the subjective risk, that consumers perceive as being present or absent. The perceived risk concept has generated empirical research on a wide range of consumer behavior problems, such as word of mouth, opinion leadership, new product adoption, brand loyalty, mode of shipping, personality, and risk reducing strategies. Much of this research is summarized and critically reviewed by Ross (1974). Factors which have been found to influence quality perceptions based on country-of-origin considerations include demographic variables (e.g., Schooler 1971), and Tongberg (1972) found that older persons tended to evaluate foreign products more highly than did younger persons. The culture of the source country also is a factor: Tongberg (1972) found that among high dogmatics there was a favorable attitude toward culturally similar countries. Hampton (1977) found that

This chapter is based on the PhD Dissertation by Dr. Nes (The University of Wisconsin-Madison, 1981) under the guidance of Professor Bilkey.

American products made in the U.S. had less perceived risk than the same products made abroad.

A fundamental issue is whether the country-of-origin really is a salient information cue in a multi-cue setting. In Olson's (1977) review of studies concerning price as an information cue, it is clear that a price effect on quality evaluations was consistently found as long as price was the only cue provided. Later studies (e.g., Monroe and Krishnan 1985; Heslop, Liefeld and Wall 1987) found that multiple cues do not necessarily decrease the importance of price as a determinant of perceived quality. Research on the effects of other informational cues suggests that they may influence the country cue through complex interactions among cues (Olson and Jacoby 1972; Rao 1972). White and Cundiff (1978) found that the country-of-origin cue was also important in the quality evaluations of industrial buyers. Logically, a hierarchy of bias may be expected on the part of consumers who perceive an inverse relationship between product risk and a source country's level of economic development.

To the extent that such a hierarchy of bias exists, can various risk-reducing strategies compensate for it? Roselius (1971) tested the relative effectiveness of 11 risk relievers, and found that "brand loyalty" and a "major brand image" evoked the most consistently favorable response. Rao and Monroe (1989), in their integration of previous research on how price and brand names influence buyers' evaluations of products, confirmed that brand name is a salient informational cue for quality evaluations. In line with this, it is expected that well-known brand names cause a lower perceived risk than brand labeling, which does not provide respondents with any salient information. Schooler and Wildt (1968) found that for many consumers the effect of product evaluation bias can be offset by price concessions.

Several analysts (Dornoff, Tankersley, and White 1974; Lillis and Narayana 1974; Hampton 1977; Bannister and Saunders 1978; Yaprak 1978; etc.) have found that attitudes toward products from a given country may vary by product. Concepts in information processing suggest that the country-of-origin cue may be more important for high-risk products than for low-risk products. The apparent reason is the increased search needed for information, and the use of more product attributes for the evaluation process.

Studies dealing with perceived risk and information handling in some cases have supported and in other cases rejected these notions. Swan (1972) found that consumers who perceived high risk also searched for more information, while Jacoby, Chestnut, and Fisher (1978) failed to find such a relationship. Lutz and Reilly (1973) found support for the hypothesis that consumers tend to use sources of information when faced with an increased degree of perceived performance risk.

HYPOTHESES

An integrated model of the country-of-origin cue and perceived risk is presented in Figure 1. This chapter focuses on the following questions relating to that model:

1. Whether, in a multi-cue situation consumer perceptions of risk and quality depend significantly on the economic development of the producing country (which is implied in the studies that were referred to earlier)
2. Whether a well-known brand name can compensate for country-of-origin bias; and
3. Whether, if there is such a bias, it is higher or lower for product types which are inherently more risky to buy.

Also considered in this study are the issues of brand name and product risk–that is, the problems or cost that the buyer may encounter in using the product–and certain internal and external validity problems of previous country-of-origin studies regarding products sourced in LDCs.

The study is structured to address the following hypotheses (stated in the null form):

• H1. There are no differences in perceived risk regarding the products analyzed on the basis of the level of the economic development of the manufacturing country.

• H2. There are no interactions between perceived risk scores for brand name and the source country factors studied. If the null hypothesis is not rejected, the study will support the notion that a well-known brand name cannot compensate for country-of-origin bias.

• H3. There are no interactions between perceived risk scores regarding the experimental factors. If this null hypothesis is not rejected, the study will reject the proposition that the source country's degree of economic development is more important for high-risk products than for low-risk products, and that the concepts of perceived product risk and perceived product quality (reliability, wear, performance, etc.) are strongly related.

• H4. There are no interactions between the perceived risk scores for the source country and product risk-class experimental factors. If this null

Figure 1. An Integrated Model of the Country-of-Origin Cue
and Perceived Risk

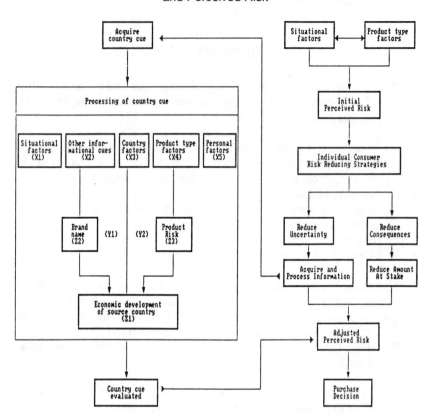

hypothesis is not rejected, the study will reject the proposition that the degree of economic development in the source country is more important for high-risk products than for low-risk products.

The reasoning used to develop the perceived product risk hypotheses also will be used to formulate commensurate product quality hypotheses. The same reasoning can also be used to generate theoretical extensions from this study. Specifically, an inverse relationship between perceived product risk and perceived product quality is expected. For these reasons, H1 to H4 have been repeated with perceived quality (in place of perceived risk) as the dependent variable.

RESEARCH METHODOLOGY

Dependent Variables

Perceived risk is the main dependent variable in the present study. The perceived risk concept has generated a large body of consumer behavior research regarding perceived risk reductions, such as word-of-mouth, opinion leadership, new product adoption, brand loyalty, store loyalty, mode of shipping, personality, and risk reducing strategies. Much of the early research in this field is summarized and critically reviewed by Ross (1974). Perceived product quality was used as an alternative dependent variable for testing. The reason is that measurement validity and reliability are improved when two or more highly correlated alternative dependent variables are used, and both are more or less equally correlated with the independent variables.

Independent Variables

Seven independent variables were used:

1. The risk class of the product, classified into two categories according to whether it is a low-risk product (the possible loss to the buyer is limited to the cost of the product), or a high-risk product (the possible loss to the buyer can greatly exceed the cost of the product).
2. The product's country-of-origin, classified into three categories according to whether the product was made in a low-income country, a middle-income country, or a high-income country.
3. The product's brand name, classified according to whether the brand name is well-known, new/unknown, or not indicated.
4. The interaction between country-of-origin and the product's brand name.
5. The interaction between country-of-origin and the product's risk class.
6. The interaction between the product's brand name and its risk class.
7. The interaction among the product's country-of-origin, its brand name, and its risk class.

The study was based on interviews that were conducted as an experiment having a $2 \times 3 \times 4$ fixed-effects factorial design. The factors were:

1. Two risk-class categories of products. Eight products were used in the test, divided into high-risk and low-risk categories with four products in each.
2. Three brand name categories: "no brand merchandise" (no brand name appearing on the samples shown to the subjects), "unknown brand name" (the brand name presented was not known to the subjects), and a "well-known brand name."
3. Four country-of-origin categories. The product samples were presented to the subjects with no information regarding the country-of-origin nor whether they were made in a low-, medium-, or high-income country.

The elements of each of these three factors are listed in Table 1.

As part of the pretest, four high-risk and four low-risk products were selected by a class of 33 students at The University of Wisconsin-Madison. Their selection was based on the inherent overall perceived risks for the product sample (see Table 2). For example, a tire blow-out at high speed could wreck an automobile, and an improperly insulated drill, radio, or hair dryer could kill. However, a defective flashlight, towel, or toothbrush could only fail to perform well.

When conducting interviews in subjects' homes during the main phase of the experiment, small samples of the products were used to facilitate handling. For example, the automobile tire was a "demonstration sample"–a small slice of a tire provided by a local retailer.

The same items were shown to all of the subjects. The main reason for using tangible products rather than a verbal description of them was to avoid confounding problems (which are possibly associated with many of the earlier country-of-origin studies). For example, the use of intangible products may induce subjects to perceive a variety of intrinsic cues as dependent on experimental manipulations. Such cues could be the softness of a towel, the weight of an electric power drill, the thickness of an automobile tire, and so on. Where these cues are not included in the experimental design, they should be kept constant. Several studies that have been reviewed by Olson and Jacoby (1972) and White and Cundiff (1978) found that intrinsic cues have a more powerful effect on quality judgments than extrinsic cues. This suggests that studies of extrinsic cues (such as the country-of-origin, brand name, etc.) are not expected to exert very strong effects on perceptions unless more potent, intrinsic cues have been omitted from the study. Hence, a second reason for using tangible products was to make the results more meaningful and externally valid.

Thirty-two countries were initially selected according to GNP as a

Table 1. Product and Brand Name Assignment

Product		Brand Name		Country of Origin Income		
Low Risk	High Risk	Unknown	Well Known	Low	Medium	High
Flashlight		Eiser	Ray-O-Vac	Niger	Chile	W. Germany
Towel		Roza	Cannon	India	Panama	France
Glue		Home's	Elmer's	Kenya	Brazil	U.S.A.
Toothbrush		T2	Pepsodent	Tanzania	Colombia	Canada
	Drill	Algot	Black & Decker	Chad	Mexico	U.K.
	Clock radio	Avery	General Electric	Mali	Turkey	Switzerland
	Hair dryer	Tekam	Conair	Malawi	S.Korea	Japan
	Car tire	Elkem	Goodyear	Pakistan	Taiwan	Sweden

Table 2. Pretest Results for Each Product Tested

Risk class	Product	Average Score*
Low	Towel	1.667
risk	Toothbrush	1.727
products	Flashlight	2.303
	Glue	2.455
	Average	2.038
High	Clock radio	3.455
risk	Hair dryer	4.091
products	Electric power drill	4.242
	Car tire	4.578
	Average	4.092

* Average scores calculated by assigning numbers
(1 - 5) to the categories, where 1 = very low risk.

reflection of the country factor. Oil exporting countries with capital-sur-plus economies were excluded as were centrally planned countries, and an attempt was made to get a broad representation of the continents in the final country set. As a pretest, 33 undergraduate students categorized 24 countries into "high-income," "medium-income," and "low-income" groups. Only countries that were nearly unanimously categorized in one of the groups were selected. Approximately equal numbers of countries were in each group.

The original labels that were on the products shown to the subjects were removed. Replacement labels were made up by the researchers to keep the objective quality of the products constant. The labels listed information regarding the product's brand name and the producing country, plus some technical information. Since there were two product risk categories, three categories of brand name, and four of country-of-origin, 12 different labels were made for each product shown to the subjects. Labels having a brand name, a producing country, and technical information were on a fabricated stick-on label, and listed on the questionnaire for each subject as a means for ensuring that the information was being processed. The respondents examined each product before answering the questionnaire, but the interviewer did not mention the labels.

After five pretest interviews it was clear that some subjects had guessed the purpose of the study. Since this could create a demand effect (subjects altering their answers to conform with the purpose of the study), a cover story was fabricated. The remaining pretest interviews did not exhibit this problem.

A sample of 96 subjects was selected by means of a two-stage area sampling procedure in Verona, Wisconsin, a suburb of Madison having about 3,500 inhabitants and its own economic base. Interviews were conducted in the respondents' homes. The subjects also were debriefed after the interviews. This indicated that four subjects had guessed that the country-of-origin was being tested. Their responses were eliminated from tabulation, and replacement interviews were conducted. The research design provided 32 observations for each of 12 cells.

All factors except brand name and country-of-origin were constant for all subjects. For this reason, subjects' statements regarding perceived risk and perceived quality were attributed to only these two experimental factors. Each subject made evaluations for all eight products.

Measurement Validity and Reliability

The questionnaire was developed to measure perceived risk and perceived quality for each of the products. The eight perceived risk products were operationalized as in Jacoby and Kaplan (1972), so as to draw on the measurement validity and reliability demonstrated in their study. Perceived quality was measured by a single question.

Coefficient alpha was calculated for the risk measure; the values for each product are given in Table 3. These reliability estimates are satisfactory according to Nunnally (1967, p. 226). A priori, one might expect that perceived high-quality products create low risk. The Pearson correlation coefficient between judgments of the perceived quality of the products and of the perceived risk was –0.496 at the 0.001 level of significance. Hence, a degree of convergence validity is demonstrated. Previous research has suggested that brand loyalty and brand image are important risk relievers (Arndt 1967; Cunningham 1967; Schooler, Sheth, and Venketesan 1968; Roselius 1971). The risk measure in this study captures a significantly

Table 3. Coefficient Alpha Values for Each Product Used

Flash-light	Towel	Glue	Tooth brush	Power drill	Clock radio	Hair dryer	Car tire
.77	.88	.78	.85	.83	.80	.68	.88

lower risk for the well-known names than for the other two categories (see Table 4), which is evidence of construct validity.

ANALYSIS OF RESULTS

Main factors effects and interaction effects were analyzed by means of a three-way analysis of variance. ANOVA results for perceived risk are given in Table 4. All main factors are significant at the 0.01 level, and all stated null hypotheses were rejected.

In hypothesis H1, a hierarchy of effects is expected, with products made in LDCs being perceived as more risky than products made in

Table 4. Perceived ANOVA Risk Values

Source	s.s.	d.f.	F	P-values
Country	6.050	3	4.622	.003
Brand	20.555	2	23.557	.000
Risk-class	41.642	1	95.447	.000
Country X brand	1.637	6	.625	.710
Country X risk-class	1.168	3	.892	.445
Brand X risk-class	1.480	2	1.696	.184
Country X brand X risk-class	5.857	6	2.238	.038
Explained	78.389	23	7.812	.000
Total	402.983	767		

Multiple Classification Analysis

Grand mean = 2.08

Country	Deviation
Not available	-.08
Low income	+.10
Medium income	+.08
High income	-.10

Brand
Not indicated	+.13
Unknown	+.10
Well known	-.23

Risk-class
Low risk products	-.23
High risk products	+.23

developed countries. The multiple classification analysis in Table 4 shows that countries in the "low-income" and "medium-income" categories gave higher risk scores than the categories "high-income" and "nation not available."

A posteriori contrasts for comparing all possible pairs of categories of source countries' means were tested using the Tukey-HSD procedure at a < .05 level of significance. Products made in low- and medium-income nations were perceived as being significantly more risky than products made in high-income nations. None of the other possible pairs were significant. The Tukey-HSD procedure tests for differences in category means, by treating each category as a separate entity. Further inferences regarding the direction of country effects were provided by combining the low- and medium-income countries and performing T-tests on the differences between this combination and remaining categories. Products made in "high-income" countries and products with "no country information" were both perceived as having a significantly lower risk at the 0.01 level than products from LDCs. Therefore, the direction of effects expected in hypothesis H1 is confirmed.

The Tukey-HSD test at the 0.05 level of significance was also performed on the brand name categories. The "well-known" brand names were perceived as having a significantly lower risk than products with "new unknown" brand names and those where the brand name was not available, while other differences were not significant. The brand name categories behaved as expected, so null hypothesis H2 was rejected.

None of the two-way interactions were significant. For this reason, null hypotheses H3 and H4 were not rejected (see Table 4). The ANOVA results for perceived product quality are given in Table 5. The multiple classification analysis shows that products belonging in the low-risk category were perceived as having a higher quality than high-risk products. No such difference was attempted as an experimental manipulation. The reason for this difference may be that people are more critical of high-risk products, which are more complicated (and, therefore, more can go wrong with them).

The Tukey-HSD test at the 0.05 significance level showed a difference in perceived quality between products from both high-income and medium-income countries. None of the other possible pairs of factor categories were significant.

The "low-income" and "medium-income" country groups were combined, and t-tests were conducted for their differences in relation to "high-income" countries. Products from the latter countries were perceived to be of higher quality than products from "low-income" and "medium-in-

Table 5. Perceived ANOVA Product Quality

Source	s.s.	d.f.	F	P-values
Country	4.797	3	2.954	.032
Brand	40.112	2	37.050	.000
Risk-class	3.255	1	6.013	.014
Country X brand	2.523	6	.777	.588
Country X risk-class	1.943	3	1.196	.310
Brand X risk-class	.159	2	1.146	.864
Country X brand X risk-class	4.206	6	1.295	.257
Explained	46.995	6	1.295	.257
Total	459.744	767		

Multiple Classification Analysis

Grand mean = 3.18

Country	Deviation
Not available	+.07
Low income	-.04
Medium income	-.11
High income	+.09

Brand
Not indicated	-.20
New unknown	-.11
Well known	+.32

Risk-class
Low risk products	+.07
High risk products	-.07

come" countries at the 0.01 significance level. Products with "no source country" labels were perceived to be of higher quality than products from "low-income" and "medium-income" countries at the 0.05 confidence level. Therefore, we conclude that the perceived quality measures, relative to perceived risk, behaved exactly as expected.

Conclusions

This study was concerned with three main issues. First, to obtain evidence as to whether the country-of-origin cue is salient for product evaluations in a multi-cue situation (which is more valid than single-cue situations). Second, to obtain inferences regarding the direction of country-of-origin effects: for example, whether a previously suggested positive relationship between product evaluations and degree of economic development of the source country is present in a multi-cue situation. And third, to introduce and explore how the impact of the country-of-origin cue varies with different levels of brand name and product risk.

In this context, the findings lead to two main conclusions. First, the country-of-origin informational cue is salient for evaluating perceived product quality and risk. Second, the hypothesized positive relationship between product evaluations and degree of economic development of the source country was confirmed–although respondents did not distinguish between "low-income" and "medium-income" countries. This finding suggests that the degree of economic development of the producing country also influences perceptions when other informational cues are present. More specifically, the directions of effects were as follows:

1. Products labeled as made in LDCs were perceived to be more risky and of lower quality than products having "no country-of-origin" labels.
2. Products labeled as made in LDCs were perceived to be more risky and of lower quality than products labeled as made in developed countries.
3. There were no differences in perceived risk and perceived quality between products labeled as made in the very poorest countries and those labeled as made in countries at an intermediate level of economic development.
4. There were no differences in perceived risk and perceived quality between products labeled as made in industrialized countries and products having "no country-of-origin" labels.

None of the two-way interactions were significant. This supports the following two conclusions:

1. The magnitude of bias against products labeled as from LDCs does not depend on whether the product is high-risk or low- risk.
2. A well-known brand name will cause the LDC-made product to be perceived as being of higher quality and lower risk than if the brand name is unknown or not given. However, a well-known brand name does not completely compensate for the country-of-origin bias. In other words, products from LDCs are rated as being lower in quality and higher in risk regardless of brand name.

Limitations

Both the size and representativeness of the sample are limited. This study's contribution to the main effects of country-of-origin bias is its internal and external validity. It also tends to confirm that country-of-origin biases indeed do exist in a multi-cue setting.

A distinction was made between "low-income" and "medium-income" countries. However, this study indicates that it seems likely that neither the sample studied nor consumers in general are able to distinguish between these two types of countries. The products tested in this research were randomly assigned to source countries. The result is that the study does not imply that a bias is actually taking place against specific countries. Rather, it depicts a situation where the source country, either a less- or more-developed nation, has earned a "no product specific" reputation. No problems were encountered in using the two independent variables rather than only one independent variable.

IMPLICATIONS

Implications for Firms Sourcing Abroad

A well-known brand name is an important factor for multinational companies considering sourcing in developing countries, as well as for large retail chains in developed nations that are importing from independent producers in LDCs under retailers' private labels. This study confirms the notion that a well-known brand name is a highly effective risk-reducing remedy. The lack of interaction between the country and brand factors in this study indicates that the country impact also is operational for well-known brand names. Such a bias should be treated as an intangible cost, and weighed against possible price gains.[1] Generally, it would be in the interest for such importers to disguise country-of-origin, labeling their products with more-developed country origins to the extent possible, within, of course, existing legal constraints.

Implications for LDCs

Generally, current laws regarding country-of-origin labeling are decided unilaterally by countries that are attempting to protect their domestic

---

1. Ed. note: See also the chapter by Nebenzahl and Jaffe concerning the value effect from production location shifts.

markets against imports. One solution for LDCs would seem to be to negotiate the greatest possible reduction of country-of-origin labeling requirements by working through international organizations. For instance, label requirements might be fulfilled by using codes. Where country-of-origin labeling is allowed but not required, domestic manufacturers and manufacturers in countries with a specific reputation for their products (e.g., French wines) could still label their products as they wish. LDCs also could refrain from providing country-of-origin information.

No interaction was found between country and product risk. This implies that the magnitude of country-of-origin bias is just as strong for low-risk products as for high-risk products. For this reason, LDCs have nothing to gain by concentrating their exports on low-risk products. This conclusion is valid only for the measures of evaluation used in this study. It is possible that consumers have a wide latitude of acceptance of various source countries for low-risk products and a narrow latitude of acceptance for high-risk products. A change in perceived risk and perceived quality caused by the cue "Made in [developing country] XYZ" may be acceptable when buying a towel, while the same change in perceptions may be intolerable when buying a new automobile or a critical pharmaceutical product. Other studies (Bettman 1973; Hakansson and Wootz 1975) have found that the relative importance of price in the purchasing process is higher for low-risk products than for high-risk products. Exports from LDCs have been found to be lower priced than comparable domestic manufactured products (Cline 1979). Consumers and industrial buyers seem to attribute the highest importance to this price advantage for low-risk products. While the variables used in this study do not suggest any preference between high-risk and low-risk products, other marketing factors suggest that LDCs may benefit from concentrating their exports in products with relatively low perceived risk.

It has been found that U.S. consumers are unwilling to pay as much for products made in a country about which they have negative quality associations, as for the same products made in the U.S. (Schooler and Wildt 1968). This indicates that, for comparable manufactured exports, LDCs tend to receive lower prices for given quantities than do producers from developed countries–or that they export smaller quantities than the latter (assuming that quality and prices are identical between those countries). Unfavorable quality perceptions could be an important barrier for LDC exports to industrialized countries. If changes in labeling requirements lead to changes in consumers' perceived risk and perceived quality of LDC exports, then changes in export prices and/or export quantities may be a very important stimulus to LDC development.

REFERENCES

Arndt, Johan (1967), "Perceived Sociometric Integration and Word-of-Mouth in the Adoption of a New Food Product." In D.F. Cox (ed.), *Risk Taking and Information-Handling in Consumer Behavior.* Boston: Harvard University Press, 290-316.

Bannister, J.P. and J.A. Saunders (1978), "U.K. Consumers' Attitudes Towards Imports: The Measurement of National Stereotype Image." *European Journal of Marketing,* 12, 8, 562- 570.

Bauer, R.A. (1967), *Risk Taking and Information-Handling in Consumer Behavior.* Boston, MA: Harvard University Press.

Bettman, J.R. (1973), "Perceived Risk and Its Components: A Model and Empirical Test." *Journal of Marketing Research,* X: (May) 184-190.

Bilkey, Warren J. and Erik Nes (1982), "Country-of-Origin Effects on Product Evaluations." *Journal of International Business Studies,* 8(1) (Spring/Summer) 89-99.

Cline, W.R. (1979), "Imports and Consumer Prices: A Survey Analysis." *Unpublished Study* prepared for the American Retail Federation and the National Merchants Association.

Cunningham, S.M. (1967), "Perceived Risk and Brand Loyalty." In D.F. Cox (ed.), *Risk-Taking and Information-Handling in Consumer Behavior.* Boston: Harvard University Press, 507-523.

Dornoff, Ronald J., Clint B. Tankersley, and Gregory P. White (1974), "Consumers' Perceptions of Imports." *Akron Business and Economic Review,* 5(2) (Summer) 26-29.

Hakansson, H. and B. Wootz (1975), "Supplier Selection in an International Environment: An Experimental Study." *Journal of Marketing Research,* XII: (February) 46-51.

Hampton, Gerry M. (1977), "Perceived Risk in Buying Products Made Abroad by American Firms." *Baylor Business Studies* (October) 53-64.

Heslop, Louise A., John P. Liefeld, and Marjorie Wall (1987), "An Experimental Study of the Impact of Country-of-Origin Information." In R.E. Turner (ed.), *Marketing,* Vol. 8 (Toronto, Ont.: Proceedings, Administrative Sciences Association of Canada–Marketing Division, June) 179-185.

Jacoby, Jacob and L.B. Kaplan (1972), "The Components of Perceived Risk." In M. Venkatesan (ed.), *Proceedings of the Third Annual Conference of the Association for Consumer Research.*

Jacoby, Jacob, R.W. Chestnut, and A. Fisher (1978), "A Behavioral Approach to Information Acquisition in Non-Durable Purchasing." *Journal of Marketing Research,* XV (November) 532- 543.

Lillis, Charles M. and Chem L. Narayana (1974), "Analysis of 'Made-in' Product Images–An Exploratory Study." *Journal of International Business Studies* (Spring) 119-127.

Lutz, R.J. and P.J. Reilly (1973), "An Exploration of the Effects of Perceived Social and Performance Risk on Consumer Information Acquisition." In S.

Ward and P. Wrights (eds.), *Proceedings of the Fourth Annual Convention of the Association for Consumer Research*, 393-405.

Monroe, K.B. and R. Krishnan (1985), "The Effect of Price on Subjective Product Evaluations." In Jacob Jacoby and Jerry Olson (eds.), *Perceived Quality: How Consumers View Stores and Merchandise* (Boston, MA: Lexington Books) 209-232.

Nunnally, J.C. (1967), *Psychometric Theory.* New York: McGraw-Hill Book Company. 226.

Olson, Jerry C. (1977), "Price as an Informational Cue: Effects in Product Evaluation." In Arch G. Woodside, Jagdish N. Sheth, and Peter D. Bennet (eds.), *Consumer and Industrial Buying Behaviour.* New York: North Holland. 267-86.

Olson, Jerry C. and Jacob Jacoby (1972), "Cue Utilization in the Quality Perception Process." In M. Venkatesan (ed.), *Proceedings, Third Annual Conference of the Association for Consumer Research*, 167-179.

Rao, V.R. (1972), "Marginal Salience of Price in Brand Evaluations." In M. Venkatesan (ed.), *Proceedings of the Third Annual Conference of the Association for Consumer Research.*

Rao, Akshay R. and Kent B. Monroe (1989), "The Effect of Price, Brand, Name, and Store Name on Buyers' Perceptions of Product Quality: An Integrative Review." *Journal of Marketing Research*, XXVI (August) 351-358.

Roselius, T. (1971), "Consumer Rankings of Risk Reduction Methods." *Journal of Marketing*, 35 (January) 55-61.

Ross, I. (1974), "Perceived Risk and Consumer Behavior: A Critical Review." In M.J. Schlinger (ed.), *Advances in Consumer Research*, II (Urbana, IL: Association for Consumer Research).

Schooler, Robert D. (1971), "Bias Phenomena Attendant to the Marketing of Foreign Goods in the U.S." *Journal of International Business Studies*, 2: (Spring) 71-80.

Schooler, Robert D. and Albert R. Wildt (1968), "Elasticity of Product Bias." *Journal of Marketing Research*, V: (February) 78- 81.

Schooler, Robert D., Jagdish N. Sheth, and M. Venketesan (1968), "Risk Reduction Process in Repetitive Consumer Behavior." *Journal of Marketing Research*, V, 307-310.

Swan, J.E. (1972), "Search Behavior Related to Expectations Concerning Brand Performance." *Journal of Applied Psychology*, 56 (August) 332-335.

Tongberg, R.C. (1972), *An Empirical Study of Relationships Between Dogmatism and Consumer Attitudes Towards Foreign Products.* PhD Dissertation, Pennsylvania State University.

White, Philip D. and E.W. Cundiff (1978), "Assessing the Quality of Industrial Products." *Journal of Marketing*, (January) 80-86.

Yaprak, Attila (1978), *Formulating a Multinational Marketing Strategy: A Deductive, Cross-national Consumer Behavior Model.* PhD Dissertation, Georgia State University.

Chapter 8

Personality Variables and the Made-in Concept

Sadrudin A. Ahmed
Alain d'Astous
Saïd Zouiten

BACKGROUND

A substantial body of marketing literature has produced consistent findings regarding the country-of-origin effect in product evaluations (Bilkey and Nes 1982). This effect has been shown to occur at the level of consumer beliefs about specific product attributes (Johansson, Douglas, and Nonaka 1985). The extent of this bias has also been found to correlate with demographic as well as sociopsychological characteristics of consumers (Johansson 1986). It is also possible that the intensity and direction of the country-of-origin effect may vary by product class (Kaynak and Cavusgil 1983). Negative product image seems to be associated with products made in less-developed countries (Gaedeke 1973). In developed countries, there is sometimes a tendency for consumers to show a preference for products made in their own country (Nagashima 1970). Papadopoulos, Heslop, and Bamossy (1990) show, however, that preference for domestic products is not universal.

How such consumer resistance to negatively evaluated products can be overcome successfully is of practical significance to managerial decision makers. Our review of research findings pertaining to the use of marketing mix variables to improve consumer acceptance of products with different country affiliations reveals the need for a multiple-cue approach to the

The authors wish to thank the Social Sciences and Humanities Research Council of Canada for its financial support.

197

study of this subject across a variety of products using psychographic segmentation variables (Bilkey and Nes 1982).

In examining the effects of product promotion, Reierson (1967) notes that consumer attitudes toward products made in countries other than those of North America can be made positive if the products are associated with a quality brand image and high levels of service. It has also been shown that consumers are willing to purchase products manufactured in developing countries if the price is right. Johansson and Nebenzahl (1986) report, for instance, that Japanese and American automobiles made at developing country plant locations may require large price concessions if they are to be sold in North America. In terms of personality variables, Anderson and Cunningham (1972) found an inverse relationship between Status Concern and Dogmatism, on the one hand, and preference for foreign products, on the other. Hampton (1977) indicates that perceived risk has an inverse relationship with the willingness to buy products manufactured in developing countries.

Past research on the country-of-origin effect has concentrated mostly on the study of consumer attitudes toward export and import products (e.g., Anderson and Cunningham 1972). A limited number of studies addressing consumer product evaluations have approached the subject from the point of view of North American multinational companies (e.g., Johansson and Nebanzahl 1986). The basic concern of these companies is a possible negative effect on consumer product perceptions of well-established brands if product manufacturing location is changed. The reduction in demand for the Volkswagen Rabbit when it is made in the United States may be a good case in point (*Business Week* 1984; Seaton and Vogel 1981). Manufacturers in developing countries face a different issue of whether a consumer franchise can be established by manufacturing in a developed country (Chao 1989).

With these issues as background, the main objective of this chapter is to explore in depth the effectiveness of brand, price, and service strategies in the framework of global marketing and production decisions across three countries-of-origin, using psychographics as segmentation variables.

Chao (1989) has studied similar issues using electronic products in a large midwestern United States city, and Heslop, Liefeld, and Wall (1988) have carried out a multi-cue study using consumer products in the Canadian province of Ontario. However, the results of these studies were equivocal. Whereas Chao (1989) found that country-of-origin had a substantial impact on purchase decisions, Heslop, Liefeld, and Wall (1988) found the opposite. Therefore, to provide greater depth, it was decided to obtain data from a different region of North America with a distinct cultural environment, namely, French Canada (Ahmed 1990), and a different but very familiar product category, namely, automobiles.

HYPOTHESES

Our hypotheses represent a logical extension of findings from previous studies. To the extent that consumers are biased in favor of developed countries, the perception of products claimed to be made in developing countries should improve if they are associated with a well-known brand name. A prestigious country may serve as a strong cue in consumer evaluation of products. Therefore, one would expect that perception of purchase appropriateness (defined as whether a purchase decision is good or bad) may be higher if a country is evaluated positively. Similarly, one might expect that consumers' perceptions of purchase appropriateness will be higher if the product brand name is well known. Service quality is an important characteristic of a product, and therefore, it may be used to overcome a negative brand and/or country-of-origin effect. Finally, purchase appropriateness should be affected by price in the reverse direction.

The preceding discussion leads to the following main hypotheses:

• H1. Perceptions of purchase appropriateness will be significantly higher for automobiles made in developed countries than for those imported from developing countries.

• H2. Perceptions of purchase appropriateness will be significantly higher for automobiles with prestigious brand names than for automobiles with poorly regarded brand names.

• H3. Perceptions of purchase appropriateness will be significantly higher for automobiles supported by good service.

• H4. Lower prices will lead to higher perceptions of purchase appropriateness.

The fact that price concessions are necessary to compensate for a poor product image may lead to the prediction of a significant interaction effect of price with brand name and country-of-origin. Similarly, to the extent that consumer attitudes can be made more positive by associating a product with a prestigious brand name, one would expect a significant interaction effect of brand name with country-of-origin. Such interactions between the study variables should be of particular interest to both international marketing researchers and practitioners. Thus, it is hypothesized that:

• H5. The effects of price, brand name, and the product's country-of-origin on perceptions of purchase appropriateness are interactive.

Personality variables may moderate perceptions of purchase appropriateness and may help to discriminate among market segments in country-of-origin perceptions. Four personality variables were used in this study. Jackson, Ahmed, and Heapy (1976) define Excellence as an individual's motivation to aim for perfection. The higher one's score on Excellence, the greater is one's motivation to aim for perfection in decision making. Therefore, one would expect persons scoring high on Excellence to use a larger number of cues in making product evaluations than those who score low. Similarly, individuals who score high on Self-Esteem (Jackson 1967), because they are self-confident, are less likely to be concerned about social risk in purchasing a product with a poorly evaluated brand name and/or country-of-origin. Value Orthodoxy denotes ethnocentrism and conservatism (Jackson 1967). Studies discussed earlier have indicated that conservative people tend to prefer domestic products. Similarly, Harmavoidance denotes risk aversion (Jackson 1974). The higher one's score on Harmavoidance, the less willing one is to take risks. Therefore, risk-taking should be associated with the willingness to try products with a negative country-of-origin and/or brand image if price and/or service is right. Thus, it is hypothesized that:

• H6. The personality variables Harmavoidance, Excellence, Self-Esteem and Value Orthodoxy will moderate the simple and the interaction effects of brand name, country-of-origin, price, and service on consumers' evaluations.

METHOD

Selection of Stimuli

Three brands of automobiles–Toyota, Ford, and Lada–were chosen for the study. All of these automobiles are presently available in Canada. Japan, Canada, and the Philippines were selected as the countries-of-origin. Toyota was chosen as the most prestigious brand and Lada as the least prestigious one. Similarly, Japan was selected as the most desirable country-of-origin and the Philippines as the least desirable one. The price levels were $9,000, $8,000, and $7,000 and the service quality was rated as poor, average, and good.[1]

These brand, country-of-origin, price, and service level sets were established after a pilot study. No difficulty was encountered in the selection of price points, service levels, countries, and brand names. Lada (made in the

---

1. All figures in this chapter are in Canadian dollars.

Soviet Union) turned out to be the only familiar automobile brand with a substantial negative image. However, in 1988, when the study was carried out, location of a developed country branch plant in the Soviet Union for re-export was unimaginable by the pilot sample. Therefore, based on the recommendations of Johansson and Nebenzahl (1986), the Philippines was used to represent the least desirable country-of-origin.

Experimental Design

A nine-point bipolar rating scale measuring whether the automobile is a very good or very bad buy (purchase appropriateness) served as the dependent variable. Combining all attributes results in 81 (3^4) possible profiles. In order to make the profile evaluation task easier for the respondents, a one-ninth fractional factorial plan in three blocks was constructed (Cochran and Cox 1957). Subjects had to evaluate only nine profiles. With this reduced plan it was not possible to estimate all interaction effects, but the fractional design was constructed such that the interaction effects of interest (i.e., those associated with the research hypotheses) would be estimable. Table 1 presents the study design.

Personality Variables

The selection of the four specific scales to measure the personality variables was based on the necessity to maintain consistency in measurement and the robustness of the scales. To measure risk taking, Harmavoidance (Jackson 1974) was chosen. Self-Esteem and Value Orthodoxy were derived from Jackson Personality Inventory (Jackson 1967), and Excellence was derived from a six-dimensional Achievement Scale (Jackson, Ahmed, and Heapy 1976). Each one of these four scales contained sixteen true or false questions. The scale items were dispersed systematically to avoid response bias.

Research Instrument

The questionnaire consisted of two parts. In the first part, the respondents evaluated the nine profiles of automobiles chosen according to the fractional plan. The nine-point rating scale was used to determine if the chosen automobile was a very bad buy or a very good buy. The second part measured the psychological profile of the respondents (94 true-false questions), their age, sex, automobile ownership (with brand), and possession of a driver's license.

Table 1. Design of the Study

1.a. Attributes and Their Levels

Country of Origin	(A)	Japan	(0)
		Canada	(1)
		Philippines	(2)

Brand Name	(B)	Toyota	(0)
		Ford	(1)
		Lada	(2)

Price	(C)	$9,000	(0)
		$8,000	(1)
		$7,000	(2)

Service	(D)	Good	(0)
		Average	(1)
		Bad	(2)

1.b. Factorial Design

BLOCK I	BLOCK 2	BLOCK 3
ABCD	ABCD	ABCD
0000	0021	0012
0122	0110	0101
0211	0202	0220
1022	1010	1001
1111	1102	1120
2011	2002	2020
2100	2121	2112
2222	2210	2201
1200	1221	1212

Source: Cochran and Cox (1957, p. 290)

Data Collection

Ninety undergraduate business students at the University of Sher-brooke, a French-Canadian University in the Province of Quebec, were chosen for this study. They completed the questionnaire in a classroom setting with 30 students answering nine profiles each. The method of data analysis was repeated-measures analysis of variance (d'Astous and Ri-gaux-Bricmont 1987).

As the focus of this study was on exploring the interaction effects of product cues and personality variables, the selection of a student sample would not substantially affect the results. Using a homogeneous student sample allows for the exploration of the interaction effects without being concerned about the confounding effects of such demographic variables as age and level of education. For example, age has been found to be related to Value Orthodoxy and Harmavoidance, and education to Self-Esteem (Jackson 1967).

RESULTS AND DISCUSSION

Sample

The average age of the respondents was 24 years. The sex distribution was 53 percent males and 47 percent females. Ninety-eight percent of the respondents possessed a driver's license and 60 percent owned their own cars. Among these, 57 percent possessed American cars, 26 percent Japanese, and 17 percent European.

Influence of Country, Brand, Price, and Service

Table 2 presents the analysis of variance statistical results. The results support H1, H2, and H3, but not H4. On the basis of mean squares size it

Table 2. ANOVA Table of Main and Interaction Effects

Source of Variation	Sum of Squares	Degrees of Freedom	F Statistic	P-value
Brand Name (A)	1215.75	2	261.02*	0.0001
Country of origin (B)	184.03	2	39.51*	0.0001
Price (C)	0.74	2	0.16*	0.8525
Service (D)	409.60	2	87.94*	0.0001
A X B	33.40	4	3.59*	0.0066
A X C	3.02	4	0.32*	0.8613
B X C	31.65	4	3.40*	0.0091
Block	7.88	2	1.69**	0.1848

*   With 700 degrees of freedom to the denominator
**   With   87 degrees of freedom to the denominator

appears that brand name explains the largest proportion of common variance, followed by service and country-of-origin. The effect of price is negligible. Price interacts statistically significantly with the country-of-origin but not with the brand name cue.

Graphical plotting of the results presented in Figures 1, 2, and 3 indicates that Japan was evaluated as the best manufacturing location for Toyota and Lada brands. The preferred location for the Ford brand was Canada. Respondents associated highest price with the made-in-Japan specification, to be followed by Canada and the Philippines. Ford made in the Philippines was evaluated higher than Lada made in Japan. The Philippines was rated as the worst country-of-origin. These results agree with those found by Erickson, Johansson, and Chao (1984) and Johansson and Nebenzahl (1986).

Our results indicate that both the brand name and country-of-origin are significantly related to the evaluation of a product. In this respect, the results supported the findings reported by Chao (1989) and a stream of findings summarized by Bilkey and Nes (1982). However, unlike Chao (1989), who had found country-of-origin to be the most important cue, brand name was the most important cue in our study.

Similar to Chao (1989), we also found that the two extrinsic cues interact with one another and that there is a significant interaction between country-of-origin and price. Plotting of the results indicates that Toyota and Ford made in the Philippines are evaluated higher than Lada made in Canada or Japan. Ford made in Japan is evaluated almost the same as Ford made in Canada. The Japanese car selling for $9,000 is evaluated much higher than those selling for $7,000 or $8,000. The Canadian car selling for $8,000 is evaluated higher than the ones selling for either $7,000 or $9,000. The highest-rated car made in the Philippines was the one at the $7,000 price level. Thus, there is some indication that for a poor image country, price concessions are needed to sell a product. In this respect, our findings support those of Johansson and Nebenzahl (1986).

Moderating Effect of Personality Variables

To carry out these analyses, we divided the sample into low (median and below) and high (above median) groups, using the median personality scores as a cutoff point. Table 3 presents the analyses of variance results incorporating the four personality variables–Excellence, Harmavoidance, Self-Esteem, and Value Orthodoxy–in the design.

As shown in Table 3, Excellence shows the strongest explanatory effect (three effects: F = 12.9, 9.1, and 2.8), followed by Harmavoidance (two

Table 3. ANOVA with the Four Personality Variables

Source of Variation	Sum of Squares	Degrees of Freedom	F Statistic*	P-value
Brand name (A)	1215.75	2	261.02	0.0001
Country of origin (B)	184.03	2	39.51	0.0001
Price (C)	0.74	2	0.16	0.8525
Service (D)	409.60	2	87.94	0.0001
Value Orthodoxy (E)	0.00	1	0.00	0.9826
A X E	8.88	2	1.37	0.2543
B X E	4.81	2	0.74	0.4756
C X E	3.74	2	0.58	0.5610
D X E	6.66	2	1.03	0.3577
A X B X E	37.51	8	1.45	0.1725
A X C X E	15.97	8	0.62	0.7640
B X C X E	46.51	8	1.80	0.1745
Self Esteem (F)	2.47	1	0.79	0.3759
A X F	11.29	2	1.79	0.1672
B X F	0.82	2	0.13	0.8770
C X F	2.65	2	0.42	0.6562
D X F	1.81	2	0.29	0.7503
A X B X F	44.87	8	1.78	0.0776
A X C X F	23.28	8	0.92	0.4959
B X C X F	102.60	8	4.07	0.0001
Excellence (G)	39.67	1	12.97	0.0003
A X G	2.29	2	0.38	0.6871
B X G	5.67	2	0.93	0.3957
C X G	56.00	2	9.15	0.0001
D X G	17.67	2	2.89	0.0563
A X B X G	53.26	8	2.18	0.0273
A X C X G	16.06	8	0.66	0.7301
B X C X G	69.59	8	2.84	0.0041
Harmavoidance (H)	1.08	1	0.35	0.5558
A X H	0.16	2	0.02	0.9831
B X H	3.43	2	0.55	0.5788
C X H	14.45	2	2.31	0.1004
D X H	1.96	2	0.31	0.7307
A X B X H	62.85	8	2.51	0.0108
A X C X H	18.37	8	0.73	0.6628
B X C X H	100.29	8	12.53	0.0001

* With 768 degrees of freedom to the denominator.

Figure 1: Graph of Main Effects

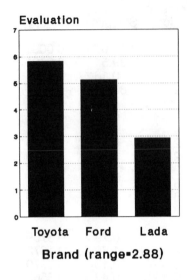

Brand (range=2.88)

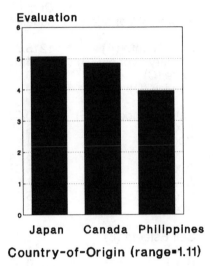

Country-of-Origin (range=1.11)

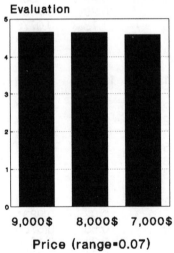

Price (range=0.07)

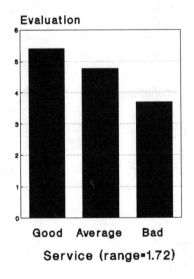

Service (range=1.72)

Figure 2: <u>The Country-of-Origin x</u>
<u>Brand Interaction</u>

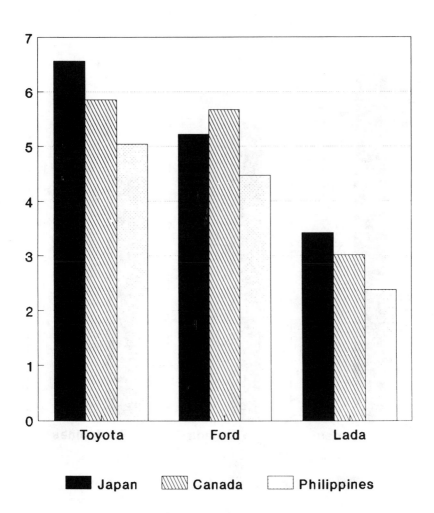

Figure 3: The Country-of-Origin x
Price Interaction

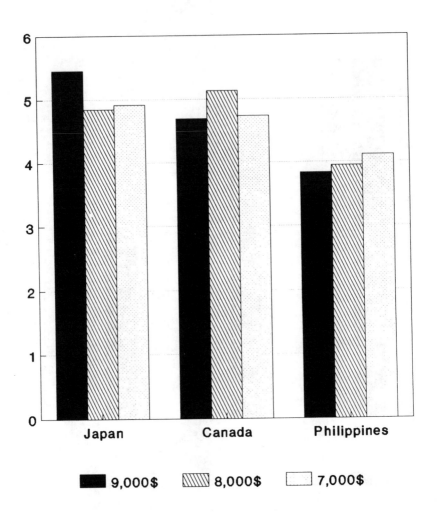

effects: F = 12.5 and 2.5), and Self-Esteem (one effect: F = 4.0). The effect of Value Orthodoxy is quite weak. Neither its main effect nor its interaction effects are statistically significant. On the other hand, in addition to a significant main effect, Excellence interacts significantly with both the price and service cues.

In terms of the second-order interactions, Excellence interacts significantly with [brand name × country-of-origin] and [brand name × price]. The plotting of the interaction effects, shown in Figures 4 and 5, indicates that individuals scoring high in Excellence valued a $9,000 made-in-the-Philippines car the highest, followed by the $8,000 car and the $7,000 car. This was completely opposite of respondents who scored low in Excellence. They valued the $7,000 Philippines car much higher than the $9,000 car. The $7,000 Philippines car was valued almost as high as the $9,000 Canadian-made car. Low Excellence respondents evaluated the $7,000 Japanese car the highest and the $9,000 one the lowest.

Therefore, it appears that with price concessions, perhaps foreign-made cars can be made appealing to low Excellence customers. Low Excellence respondents did not seem to evaluate Japan and Canada differentially as countries-of-origin. High Excellence respondents valued Toyota made in Japan the highest, followed by Ford made in Canada and Toyota made in Canada. It is interesting to note that Toyota made in the Philippines, Ford made in the Philippines, and Ford made in Japan were almost equally rated by low Excellence respondents.

For Lada, Japan was evaluated as the best location and the Philippines as the worst by all respondents. These results indicate that low Excellence respondents perhaps treat all developed origin-countries similarly. There is also some evidence to indicate that the high Excellence group may have a tendency to associate price with quality.

Harmavoidance showed a statistically significant effect in second-order interaction with [brand name × country-of-origin] and [country-of-origin X price]. The plot of these interaction effects, shown in Figures 6 and 7, indicates that risk-averse respondents considered Japan to be the most desirable country-of-origin and Toyota the best brand name. Ford made in Japan is more desirable to them than Ford made in Canada. Thus, risk avoiders are perhaps most likely to stereotype systematically in favor of Japan. Risk takers evaluated a $9,000 Japanese-made car higher than did risk avoiders. On the other hand, risk avoiders evaluated a $9,000 Canadian-made car higher than risk takers. In general, it appears that for risk avoiders, Canada was perhaps the choice country-of-origin for higher-priced cars.

Self-Esteem shows a triple interaction effect with [country-of-origin ×

210

Figure 4: The Brand x Country-of-Origin x Excellence Interaction

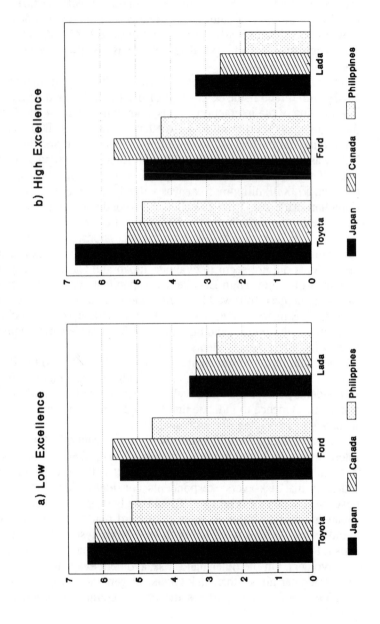

a) Low Excellence

b) High Excellence

Figure 5: The Price x Country-of-Origin x Excellence Interaction

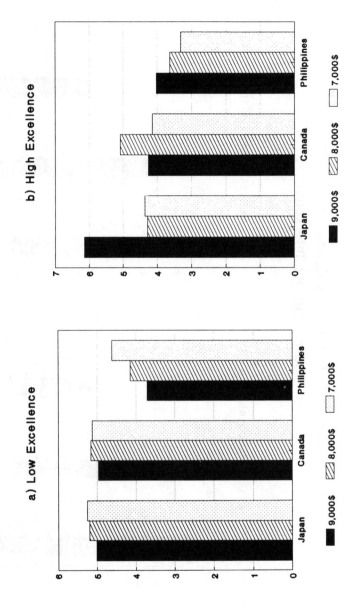

Figure 6: The Brand x Country-of-Origin x
Harmavoidance Interaction

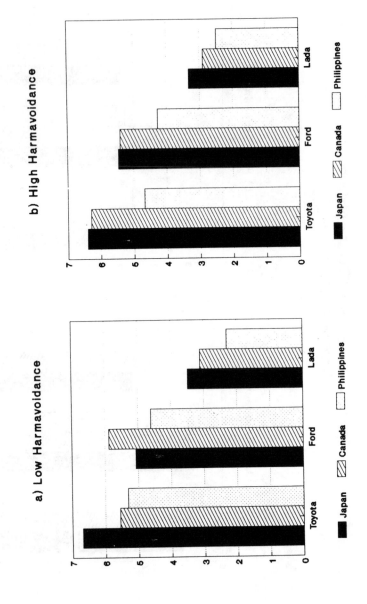

a) Low Harmavoidance

b) High Harmavoidance

Figure 7: The Price x Country-of-Origin x
Harmavoidance Interaction

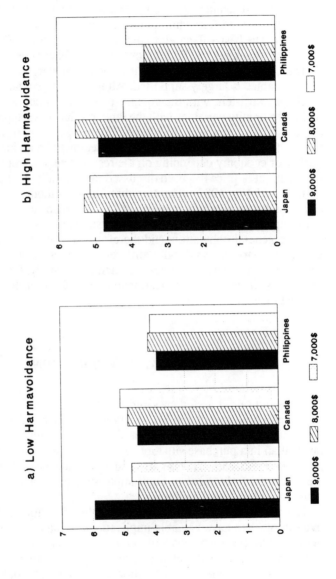

price]. The plot of this interaction effect, in Figures 8 and 9, indicates that high Self-Esteem respondents value a $9,000 Japanese automobile higher than low Self-Esteem respondents. Interestingly, high Self-Esteem respondents value an $8,000 Philippines car similarly to a $9,000 Canadian-made car. The best-valued Philippines car would cost $7,000 for low Self-Esteem respondents and $8,000 for high Self-Esteem respondents.

Thus, it appears that our hypothesis on the moderating effect of personality variables is largely supported. Although the general direction of our results is consistent with the country-of-origin literature, the relationship of the personality variables with the three product cues appears to be rather complex. This becomes particularly evident when one tries to interpret the results dealing with the price cue. Price seems to be an indicator of either quality or economy depending on the respondent's personality. This compound effect of price has been discussed in the quality perception literature (Bilkey and Nes 1982). The fact that Value Orthodoxy did not interact significantly in this study may be attributed perhaps to the homogeneity of our sample. Almost by definition, university students are less conservative than the general population, and therefore our low and high conservative groups perhaps showed only different degrees of low conservatism. Among the moderator variables included in the study, Excellence appears to be the strongest. The low Harmavoidance subgroup seems to show the greatest level of stereotyping.

MANAGERIAL IMPLICATIONS

This study used a student sample with a research design involving a fractional conjoint full profile questionnaire. Respondents were not exposed to a tangible product. Data was collected in a classroom setting rather than in a purchase situation. Therefore, the study results have to be interpreted with care. This is particularly so since the information base and the level of involvement of our sample subjects would tend to be lower than those of potential car buyers.

The findings we have presented, if replicated with a more representative sample, can have valuable implications to international and domestic marketers. Implications concern international sourcing, branding, pricing, and service strategies, and the psychographic segmentation of markets where both domestic and international products are sold. Although our discussion is based principally on the North American market, similar comments could be made with regard to other markets.

Figure 8: The Brand x Country-of-Origin x
Self-Esteem Interaction

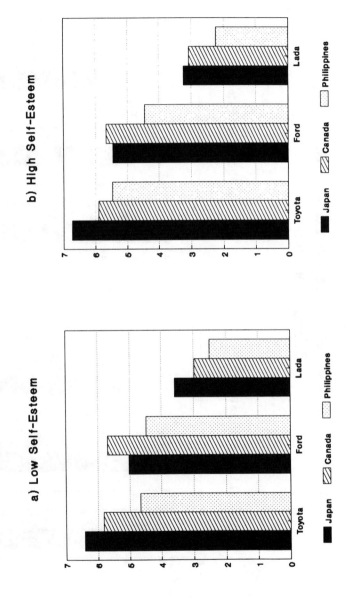

a) Low Self-Esteem

b) High Self-Esteem

Figure 9: The Price x Country-of-Origin x
Self-Esteem Interaction

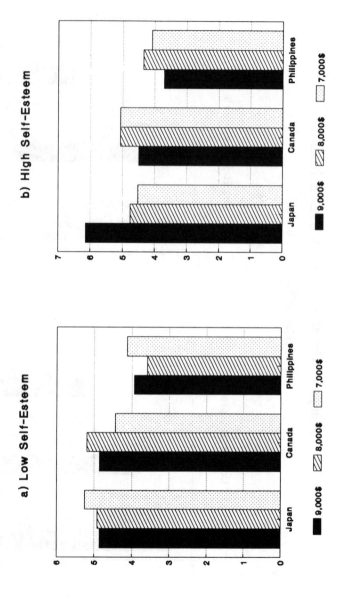

a) Low Self-Esteem

b) High Self-Esteem

North American Domestic Marketers

Producers in North America, as in other industrialized regions, are facing tremendous competition from foreign producers in the domestic market. This competition arises from both imports and North American production of these foreign producers. The car brands and countries that were included in the present research exemplify this tough competitive environment. There are many possible responses to this competition. The four sets of variables that were considered in this study may be part of the competitive response of North American producers. Specific suggestions regarding what brand names to use, whether or not the product should be made locally or imported, what prices to charge, and what level of service to provide can flow from these exploratory research findings if replicated by larger studies of this type.

In sourcing policy, North American sellers may choose North American sourcing for the domestic market. Our exploratory findings suggest that when considering foreign sourcing, the seller must consider not only labor costs in the foreign country but also the sourcing country's overall image, the quality of the product, and the level of service that can be provided to the customers. Specifically, when sourcing from a foreign country, North American sellers may perhaps emphasize or down-play the sourcing country. When sourcing from a country with a favorable image (such as Japan), the seller may choose to target its promotional efforts at highlighting sourcing country information (e.g., emphasize the quality of Japanese cars). If a source country's product quality is high, associating its brand name with high-quality service may help to overcome a negative made-in image.

When sourcing in North America, North American sellers could emphasize those products and product attributes where North America is most favorably viewed. For example, North American sellers whose cars emphasize such features as comfort, style and security (where North American cars are considered to have an advantage over Japanese cars) may mention that their domestic-branded product is locally made. Recall that the Ford brand made domestically enjoyed consumers' favorable perceptions in our exploration, especially in the high Excellence group.

In branding policy, North American sellers normally would have a North American brand. There is, however, some flexibility in choosing brand names for products. When a North American firm is selling a product from a foreign supplier–such as Mitsubishi cars sold by Chrysler–the firm has some choice in deciding which brand name to use (e.g., Chrysler Colt). The decision on brand name should be influenced by brand country image for the product under consideration and the market segment at which it is directed. Our findings suggest that using a Japanese brand name may perhaps enhance consumer perceptions of the product quality for such market segments as the high Harmavoidance group. However, a Japanese brand name with a "made-in-Japan" production location was found to be more valuable than a Japanese brand name manufactured in Canada. These exploratory results seem to corroborate Lee Iacocca's (1990) contention that the Japanese-made Mitsubishi brand outsells the made-in-Japan Chrysler Colt three to one.

Exporters to North American Market

Those who wish to export to North America also have at least two extrinsic image variables to consider when marketing their products: where the product should be manufactured and what brand name to use. To help us understand this situation, various scenarios are examined in the following paragraphs.

In their study, Han and Terpstra (1988) found that the country image of Japan was the highest, followed by the United States and South Korea. Our findings, in which the country ordering was Japan, Canada, and the Philippines, follow the same pattern. As pointed out in a newspaper article (*Globe and Mail* 1988), these perceptions are comparable with the actual record of defects in cars. Based on our results and those of other similar studies, it appears that, by relocating production to a developed country, foreign sellers from countries that have an unfavorable image may see an improvement in the perceived quality of their products by emphasizing "Built in Japan" (or Canada, etc.). However, such an improvement in product image may not be sufficient to offset the higher cost of having to shift the product's manufacturing location to a developed country.

When relocating production to North America from a country with a more favorable image, such as Japan, it may be advisable, if possible, for the foreign seller to down-play its location of production; or the seller may, to some degree, be able to offset the disadvantages of the products made in North America by communicating to consumers the favorable brand image. For example, Honda should perhaps emphasize the Japanese origin of its product design and quality control when advertising its Canadian-made automobiles.

Our exploration indicates that consumers, especially those belonging to quality-conscious segments such as high Excellence, are willing to pay a price that reflects the quality and service offered by a product. Inasmuch as the country-of-origin and/or brand name reflect the above factors, a premium commanded by products with a favorable country image and/or brand name will be paid by the consumers. If the Japanese are able to deliver the quality of made-in-Japan automobiles in their North American manufactured lines, then over the long run they may perhaps be able to maintain and increase their market share by targeting a high Excellence segment.

Personality Segmentation

It would appear from our exploration that those groups who score low on risk taking, such as young males (Jackson 1967), are more willing to adopt a lesser-known brand from an unfavorable-image country. The initial success achieved by Hyundai cars with young Canadian males (and specifically in the province of Quebec) perhaps attests to this fact. Similarly, Japanese cars were launched successfully in California during the 1950s before achieving national recognition. Californians have a greater tendency to take risks compared to the national American norm (Kahle 1986), and therefore, were willing to adopt a product bearing a poorer-image brand from what then was a poor-image country. What was true for Californians in the 1950s was perhaps true in the context of our study.

The message for exporters with unfavorable-image brands from unfavorable-image countries is that perhaps their product should be targeted to risk takers in order to attain market entry. Exporters' promotional messages may emphasize how such risk taking pays off by receiving better value for money. By contrast, domestic marketers of good-image brands manufactured in good-image countries may aim their promotional messages at low-risk-taking groups such as the elderly and women. Competitive messages could perhaps highlight the poor image of the "made-in" of their competitors' products and how the quality of workmanship is tied with where the product is made.

Perfectionists, exemplified in our study by those who score high on Excellence, also appear to be less influenced by the low price cue. These individuals seek out information and therefore are quite likely to be swayed by such product attributes as quality and service. The success achieved by Volkswagen with college-educated Americans in the 1960s perhaps attests to the mediating impact of Excellence. Exporters marketing high-quality products with excellent service may launch them with the high Excellence segment (college graduates, professionals, etc.).

RESEARCH IMPLICATIONS

The tentative exploratory results that were presented here should encourage researchers to pay attention to personality as an important variable in the study of country-of-origin effects. As this study indicates, personality variables may moderate the effect of country-of-origin, brand name, and price cues. Other researchers may replicate our study with a larger sample of consumers who are actually shopping for a car. It is possible that some of the results from our study are region-specific. Therefore, other studies may be aimed at examining the moderating effect of personality variables across several countries or regions in a multi-cue, multi-product context. Thus, it may be possible to isolate the interaction of such factors as level of economic development and product involvement with country-of-origin effects.

Our results indicate that for some respondents, brand name and country-of-origin cues may be too tightly coupled. That is, it is inconceivable for certain types of respondents that Japan can manufacture high-quality Ford automobiles. This bias deserves clarification. Perhaps a post-study debriefing session may be used to probe the respondents to obtain greater clarification.

The treatment of price needs further refinement. Price appeared to be an indicator of quality for respondents in the high Excellence group, and of economy for the high Self-Esteem group. There is also a hint that higher price is associated with quality for prestigious origin countries. This duality of price effects deserves further investigation.

Because the current study was limited to only 90 students in one geographic area, it should be viewed very cautiously as raising significant questions more than providing definitive answers. Hopefully, it will encourage other researchers to try new approaches to examine how personality may be a key moderator of country-of-origin effects.

SUMMARY AND CONCLUSIONS

This chapter explored various brand, price, and service strategies in the framework of global marketing and production decisions across three countries-of-origin, using psychographics as segmentation variables. The results indicate that the effect of price on perceptions of purchase appropriateness is not very high. Also, brand name as a cue is more important than country-of-origin. The "Excellence" personality variable, and to a lesser extent Self-Esteem and Harmavoidance, interact with the evaluation of purchase cues.

This type of tentative findings shows the value of carrying out large-scale studies of this type using representative samples. Producers would be especially interested in running such studies in the context of the specific product category, country, brand, and attribute combinations that are of interest to them before making international expansion and strategy decisions. These studies could indicate to producers whether or not it makes sense to manufacture products in high-image countries, just to be able to use their "made-in" label, as well as which psychographic segments would be most appropriate for launching a new product and what might be the most appropriate pricing and service strategies to be adopted.

REFERENCES

Ahmed, Sadrudin A. (1990), "Impact of Social Change on Job Values–A Longitudinal Study of Quebec Business Students." *Canadian Journal of Business Studies*, 6(2), 12-24.

Anderson, W.T. and W.H. Cunningham (1972), "Gauging Foreign Product Promotion." *Journal of Advertising Research*, 12, 1 (February) 29-34.

Bilkey, Warren J. and Erik Nes (1982), "Country-of-Origin Effects on Product Evaluations." *Journal of International Business Studies*, 8(1) (Spring/Summer) 89-99.

Business Week (1984, August 6), "Can VW Regain its Magic Touch." 50-58.

Chao, Paul (1989), "Export versus Reverse Investment: Strategic Implications for Newly Industrialized Countries." *Journal of International Business Studies* (Spring) 75-91.

Cochran, W.G. and G.M. Cox (1957), *Experimental Designs*. New York: John Wiley and Sons.

d'Astous, Alain and Benny Rigaux-Bricmont (1987), "Functional/Structural Market Segmentation Strategies Using Conjoint Analysis." *Business Journal* (Fall) 28-33.

Erickson, Gary M., Johny K. Johansson, and Paul Chao (1984), "Image Variables in Multi-Attribute Product Evaluations: Country-of-Origin Effects." *Journal of Consumer Research*, 11: (September) 694-699.

Gaedeke, Ralph (1973), "Consumer Attitudes Toward Products 'Made In' Developing Countries." *Journal of Retailing*, 49(2) (Summer) 13-24.

Globe and Mail, The (1988, February 9), "World Car Quality Study Shows Japan Still on Top." B19.

Hampton, Gerry M. (1977), "Perceived Risk in Buying Products Made Abroad by American Firms." *Baylor Business Studies* (October) 53-64.

Han, Min C. and Vern Terpstra (1988), "Country-of-Origin Effects for Uni-National and Bi-National Products." *Journal of International Business Studies* (Summer) 235-54.

Heslop, Louise A., John P. Liefeld, and Marjorie Wall (1988), "Impact of country-of-origin Cues on Consumer Judgements in Multi-Cue Situation: A Covariance Analysis." *Working Paper* no. 88-101, University of Guelph (April) 1-12.

Iacocca, Lee (1990, January 25), *Interview*. On television program *"American Interests,"* Public Broadcasting Service.

Jackson, D.N. (1967), *Jackson Personality Inventory*. London, Ont.: University of Western Ontario.

Jackson, D.N. (1974), *Jackson Personality Research Form Manual*. New York: Research Psychologists Press Inc.

Jackson, D.N., Sadrudin Ahmed, and N.A. Heapy (1976), "Is Achievement a Unitary Construct?" *Journal of Research in Personality*, 10, 1-15.

Johansson, Johny K. (1986), "Japanese Consumers: What Foreign Marketers Should Know." *International Marketing Review* (Summer) 37-43.

Johansson, Johny K. and Israel D. Nebenzahl (1986), "Multinational Production: Effect on Brand Value." *Journal of International Business Studies*, 17, 3 (Fall) 101-126.

Johansson, Johny K., Susan P. Douglas, and Ikujiro Nonaka (1985), "Assessing the Impact of country-of-origin on Product Evaluations: A New Methodological Perspective." *Journal of Marketing Research*, XXII: (November) 388-96.

Kahle, R. (1986), "The Nine Nations of North America and the Value Basis of Geographic Segmentation." *Journal of Marketing*, (April) 37-47.

Kaynak, Erdener and S. Tamer Cavusgil (1983), "Consumer Attitudes Towards Products of Foreign Origin: Do They Vary Across Product Classes?" *International Journal of Advertising*, 2 (April/June) 147-157.

Nagashima, Akira (1970), "A Comparison of Japanese and U.S. Attitudes Towards Foreign Products." *Journal of Marketing*, 34 (January) 68-74.

Papadopoulos, Nicolas, Louise A. Heslop, and Gary J. Bamossy (1990), "A Comparative Analysis of Domestic Versus Imported Products." *International Journal of Research in Marketing*, 7, 4 (December).

Reierson, Curtis C. (1967), "Attitude Change Toward Foreign Products." *Journal of Marketing Research*, IV: (November) 385- 87.

Seaton, Bruce and Robert H. Vogel (1981), "International Dimensions and Price as Factors in Consumer Perceptions of Autos." Paper presented at the *Conference of The Academy of International Business* (Montreal, October).

Chapter 9

Influence of Place-of-Production on Industrial Buyers' Perceptions

Sally Stewart
Edmen Chan

INTRODUCTION

The emergence of multinational production locations catering to a global market has a number of consequences for international firms. One particular problem concerns the impact of brand value on customers' perceptions when well-known products are made outside the manufacturer's home country. As Johansson and Nebenzahl (1986, p. 101) point out: "There are many indications that the firm-specific advantage a company possesses in the form of its brand name is often tied closely to the country where the firm is located."

For this reason, the perceived value of the brands may well change, should manufacturing be carried out in a different place than the manufacturer's original home country. Therefore, to evaluate the feasibility and profitability of a direct foreign investment, ideally a company should attempt to identify and balance the potential loss in brand name value against the economic advantages of producing abroad.

One of the earliest industries to establish multinational production locations was the passenger car industry. There have been various studies on the effect on brand value arising from manufacturing motorcars in different locations (e.g., Agarwal and Ratchford 1980; Johansson and Thorelli 1985; Johansson, Douglas, and Nonaka 1985), but little attempt seems to have been made to assess the attitudes of business buyers, or compare them with those of consumer buyers, to vehicles manufactured in different places.

The study reported in this chapter originated when an opportunity arose to analyze the effects of a move by the Daimler-Benz company to find cheaper overseas production alternatives by locating manufacturing plants outside West Germany (before unification). Daimler-Benz decided in 1987 to start manufacturing tourist buses in Brazil for sale in Hong Kong as well as elsewhere, but little was known about how business buyers would react to the buses' new manufacturing location. There was a need to reconcile this location shift with the fact that brand image often is inseparable, insofar as buyer perceptions are concerned, from the country of manufacture.

The study was an attempt to measure the effect of this location shift on attitudes of Hong Kong industrial users towards the long-established Mercedes-Benz name. The research was extended to compare attitudes towards three brands of vehicles produced in either of four countries (two "home" and two "offshore"). The methodology of the study is based on the approach of Johansson and Nebenzahl (1986), who researched consumer evaluations of passenger cars made in different places. This enables us to also contrast the findings of the two studies in this chapter.

BACKGROUND

Mercedes-Benz cars have long dominated the upper end of the passenger car market in Hong Kong, and in 1987 the brand accounted for 17,000 (14.2 percent) of the 120,000 cars on Hong Kong's roads (Transport Statistics 1987).[1] The name is strongly associated with high-prestige passenger cars. However, it is less well-known to consumers that Daimler-Benz AG, the manufacturer of Mercedes-Benz vehicles, is also the biggest producer in the world of commercial vehicles with gross vehicle weight of six tons and above. The particular type of Mercedes commercial vehicle being considered in this study is the tourist bus or high-quality coach.

The Tourist Bus Market
in Hong Kong

Tourist coaches in Hong Kong are mainly operated by three types of companies: large travel agents, who offer regular tours in Hong Kong and usually use their own coach fleet; other travel agents hiring coaches from the tourist coach companies (in December 1987, there were in all about 50 inbound travel agents and 30 coach operators); and, lastly, bus companies which provide coach services between Hong Kong and various parts of China.

The total number of buses in Hong Kong in 1987 was about 2,200 but only around 300 of these were tourist coaches. The remainder were factory and school buses. In addition, about 100 luxury mini-buses were also used

---

1. Industry and related data are from Statistical Review (1986), Handbook (1987), and Hong Kong Business Annual (1988).

for transporting visitors. There were, on average, more than 35,000 tourists staying in Hong Kong every day during 1986, and 44.4 percent of Hong Kong's visitors during that year took organized tours for which bus tranportation was necessary. This would indicate that the available buses were fully utilized. To maintain and upgrade service, bus companies needed more coaches.

About 70 percent of the tourist coaches in Hong Kong in 1987 were Nissans. This brand has a good reputation for service and wide availability of spare parts. However, Nissan's market share was beginning to be challenged by other suppliers, such as Mitsubishi and Mercedes-Benz. Tourists appear to be much more demanding than in the past, especially Japanese visitors who represent a significant proportion of inbound Hong Kong tourists. On the other hand, while expenditure on tourist buses accounts for only less than 2 percent of the total cost of a tour, it directly affects the overall impression of the tour. As a result, most travel agents are willing to pay more for more luxurious and newer coaches.

Prices of Tourist Coaches

With the global readjustment of major currencies and the corresponding strengthening of the West German mark, original Mercedes-Benz products have become extremely expensive. An original factory-built Mercedes-Benz sightseeing coach made in Germany would cost over HK$2 million, as compared to HK$900,000 for an original factory-built Nissan, HK$700,000 for a Taiwan-bodied Mitsubishi, and HK$490,000 for a Hong Kong-bodied Isuzu (December 1987 prices).[2] In both of the latter cases the chassis is manufactured in the home factory and the body put on at another location. More specifically, in December 1987, the market competitors and their prices in each category were:

Coaches		Price in HK$
Hong Kong-bodied:	Isuzu	490,000
	Mitsubishi Fuso	500,000
Taiwan-bodied:	Mitsubishi Fuso	700,000
	Mercedes-Benz	800,000
Original Factory-built:	Nissan (Old Model)	650,000
	Nissan (New Model)	900,000
	Kassbohrer (W. Germany)	1,300,000

---

2. The exchange rate at that time was HK$7.8 = US$1, and so bus prices ranged from US$63,000 to US$256,000.

In order to try to improve its position, Daimler-Benz decided in 1987 to import less expensive vehicles produced in a less developed country, Brazil, one of its eight production plants located outside Germany. This study was then undertaken to discover the feasibility of marketing a version of this highly regarded brand produced in a country with an inferior national image.

REVIEW OF PREVIOUS STUDIES

Since the general literature on the country-of-origin phenomenon is reviewed in other parts of this book and elsewhere, this discussion focuses on the studies that are especially relevant to the present chapter. Concerning the overall influence of country images on product evaluations, it is sufficient to repeat here Bilkey and Nes's (1982) conclusion to their extensive literature review of made-in research: "all of the studies reviewed indicate that the country-of-origin does indeed influence buyer's perceptions of the products involved."

Studies by Gaedeke (1973), Lillis and Narayana (1974), Erickson, Johansson, and Chao (1984), and other researchers who have investigated "Made-in" product images, generally suggest that there are positive relationships between product evaluations and the source country's culture, political climate, belief system and, most important of all, degree of economic development. Nonetheless, as emphasized by Bilkey and Nes (1982), the degree of influence that this attribute has on product evaluations varies and is difficult to determine. Olson and Jacoby (1972) suggest that intrinsic attributes such as a product's tangible characteristics might have a greater effect, while Andrews and Valenzi (1971) found that other extrinsic attributes, such as a well-known brand name or a product guarantee, can compensate for a negative country image.

One of the most relevant previous studies on the effect of manufacturing location on brand value is the 1986 research by Johansson and Nebenzahl. They examined the brand image of passenger vehicles among consumers in New Jersey, U.S.A., including such factors as reliability, workmanship, durability, quality, performance, price, innovativeness, economy in use, servicing costs, exclusivity, pride of ownership, style, and appeal to young people.

The same attributes were used to measure stereotypes of countries as makers and potential makers of the product. With the various inputs available, the researchers mapped the respondents' perceptions into a joint product/country space, which allowed brand and country position to be matched in the same product space. Their most important findings in the context of the present study were that West Germany was consistently rated as the best country in which to produce cars, and that moving production to West Germany would boost the image of all the brands studied. On the other hand, moving production to any of the three low-wage countries in that study (South Korea, Mexico and the Philippines) would result in a loss of brand attractiveness.

Previous work on the attitudes of Chinese people toward the country-of-origin of products by one of the present authors (Stewart, Sung, and Yeung 1988; Stewart and Sung 1990) has shown the high rating also given by Chinese to European products in the industrial goods field.

Concerning the influence of country images on industrial buyer behavior, Bilkey and Nes (1982) suggested that industrial products from less developed countries are thought to involve the risk of price instability, uncertainty regarding delivery times, quality problems, and so on. White (1979) found that stereotypes do exist for industrial products manufactured in various countries and that West Germany received significantly higher ratings on the product quality dimension, which is relevant to the Mercedes-Benz case. Cattin, Jolibert, and Lohnes (1982) asked Directors of Purchasing in large American and French firms to evaluate products from England, France, West Germany, Japan, and the U.S. on a seven-point semantic differential scale. They also found that the "made in West Germany" concept was the most favorably perceived by both American and French respondents. Lastly, it is also relevant to the present study that White and Cundiff (1978) found that Brazil received a very low rating on product quality.

RESEARCH METHOD

Design

One way of assessing the difference in brand image among different production locations is that employed by Johansson and Nebenzahl (1986). The researchers used measures of the image of products from the manufacturer's home country and then contrasted those with the image of products made in each of the foreign source countries. This makes it possible to evaluate the degree to which brand value would improve or deteriorate with a shift in place of production.

The present study used a modified version of Johansson and Nebenzahl's research design, adapting it to make it suitable for examining tourist coaches as opposed to passenger motorcars. The brand image was specified by a number of attributes derived from Johansson and Nebenzahl's list but altered to fit the case of tourist buses.

Three brands and four countries were chosen, reflecting the market situation in Hong Kong. The brands were Nissan, Mitsubishi and Mercedes-Benz. The two "home" countries were Japan and West Germany, and the two "offshore" countries were Brazil and South Korea.

Sample

In industrial marketing, unlike the situation for most consumer products, the target population in most sectors is limited. According to Wilson (1973), most industry patterns conform to the 80-20 rule: about 80 percent of sector turnover is accounted for by about 20 percent of the firms within the industry.

In this particular case, two categories concerned with tourist bus purchasing were identified. The first was travel agents who organize inbound tour packages. Large agents, who organize a great number of tour packages at one time, usually have a fleet of buses of their own to satisfy a high proportion of their needs, while the demand due to seasonal fluctuations is filled by buses on hire from coach operators. A recent trend in the industry has been for even the smaller travel agents to have at least one or two buses of their own for their core clientele, while other requirements are filled by buses from coach operators. Overall, then, these companies are the originators of the demand for tourist buses and may also be buyers.

The second group selected for the study was coach operators who charter buses to travel agents. The role of the coach operators is still vital despite the fact that many bigger travel agents are also running their own coach fleets, since the majority of smaller travel agents do not have sufficient business volume to justify coverage of their needs through owned vehicles to any significant extent. While small travel agents rely mostly on coach operators, the large travel agents own as much as about 60 percent of the total number of buses they need, leaving the coach operators to fill the rest of their requirements.

There were approximately 30 coach operators and 50 travel agents offering inbound tour packages at the time of the study. A total of 32 companies were selected for sampling and approached with an interview request, and only two refused to participate. Therefore, the sample consisted of 30 companies out of the total population of 80. To generate the sample, the ten companies which owned the largest number of buses were identified first and a further 20 companies were selected from the remainder on a purely random basis. The ten large companies owned a total of 145 buses (from seven to 45 each) and accounted for about 45 percent of the total tourist coach population. The final respondent profile is shown in Table 1.

Data Collection and Research Instrument

The fieldwork was carried out by means of personal interviews. Respondents generally showed little reluctance to perform the task of checking several concepts on a variety of scale items. Specific brand image

Table 1. Sample and Respondent Profile

a. Sample

Co. Size	Selection	Coach Operators	Travel Agents	Total
Large	Exhaustive	6	4	10
Small	Random	6	14*	20
Total		12	18	30

* Of the 32 firms approached in total, only two out of 16 in this category did not agree to participate in the study.

b. Participating Company Profile

Length of operation (years):	0-22 (avg: 13)
Coaches owned (number of units):	0-45 (avg: 7.0)
Coaches used daily (number of units):	2-45 (avg: 9.7)
Passenger origins (in order of importance):	Japan, U.S., SE Asia, Europe, Australia

c. Respondents

Sex	Percent	Position	Percent
Female	30	Director	43
Male	70	General Manager	37
		Manager	20

Age	Percent	Experience with tourist coaches	Percent
Below 25	6		
25-34	22	2-6 years	13
35-44	36	7-10 years	33
45-54	36	11-20 years	47
		over 20 years	7

perceptions were sought in the early part of the questionnaire, allowing assessments without triggering artificial origin country associations. The questionnaire also addressed the issues of multinational production locations and their effect on price perceptions. The same procedures and attributes were used to establish national stereotypes and to measure images of specific brands from different origins.

The attitude part of the research instrument consisted of five-point bipolar scale items (where 1 = poor and 5 = good) derived from earlier studies, and especially the research by Johansson and Nebenzahl. Respondents were asked to rate seven attributes, and also to offer an overall affect rating,[3] for: Nissan, Mitsubishi, and Mercedes-Benz coaches in general, tourist coaches in general, made in Japan, West Germany, Brazil, and South Korea; and each of the three brands made in either of the four countries. Respondents were also asked to indicate the amount above or below a base price which they would be willing to pay for the same model bus made in a different country.

RESULTS

General Brand and Country Evaluations

Figure 1 shows the image profile for the three brands and the mean ratings achieved on the five-point scale items. Perhaps the only surprising finding was that Mercedes-Benz buses did not receive as high an "overall" rating as their high ratings for such attributes as road performance, durability, design, and pride in ownership might have led one to expect. Mercedes-Benz was, however, consistently the highest rated bus. Its biggest advantages over the Japanese buses were in areas such as pride of ownership, road performance, and durability, and it was not perceived as being unreasonably priced nor as uneconomical to use in relation to the Mitsubishi and Nissan products. Nissan was evaluated above Mitsubishi in road performance, durability, pricing, and economy, but had less appeal in terms of design and pride of ownership.

The images of countries as coach producers in general are shown in Figure 2. As can be seen, West Germany was clearly perceived as the best

---

3. Scales: pride of ownership (none-much); design (poor-superior); quality of materials and workmanship (low-high); road performance (poor-high); durability (not-very durable); pricing (over-reasonably priced); economy of usage (costly-economical to run); and overall rating (like-don't like).

Figure 1. Image Profiles of Tourist Coaches

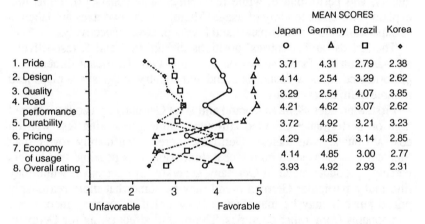

MEAN SCORES

	Mitsubishi ○	Mercedes-Benz △	Nissan □
1. Pride	3.14	3.79	3.00
2. Design	2.64	2.86	2.93
3. Quality	3.57	3.71	3.79
4. Road performance	2.79	4.21	3.21
5. Durability	2.71	4.50	3.00
6. Pricing	2.79	3.00	2.71
7. Economy of usage	2.93	3.86	2.71
8. Overall rating	2.57	4.36	1.86

Figure 2. Image Profiles of Tourist Coaches Made in Selected Countries

MEAN SCORES

	Japan ○	Germany △	Brazil □	Korea ◆
1. Pride	3.71	4.31	2.79	2.38
2. Design	4.14	2.54	3.29	2.62
3. Quality	3.29	2.54	4.07	3.85
4. Road performance	4.21	4.62	3.07	2.62
5. Durability	3.72	4.92	3.21	3.23
6. Pricing	4.29	4.85	3.14	2.85
7. Economy of usage	4.14	4.85	3.00	2.77
8. Overall rating	3.93	4.92	2.93	2.31

country in which to produce these commercial vehicles. It scored highest in all aspects, except pricing and economy where it was perceived as the most unfavorable country-of-origin. Japan had a favorable country image, but still scored consistently behind West Germany except in the areas of price and economy of use. Japanese vehicles were seen as the most economical to run among all four origins, but also as the most expensively priced after German buses. Although Brazil had quite an unfavorable country image, it still scored above South Korea on all the attributes tested

except "road performance," where the two countries received virtually
identical mean ratings. Vehicles from Brazil were seen as the lowest priced
overall. South Korea received the lowest ratings in all cases except in
pricing (second among the four origins) and road performance and economy of use (where its ratings were similar to Brazil's and Germany's,
respectively).

In addition to generating brand and country profiles, the data were analyzed by joint space mapping using the technique described by Johansson
and Nebenzahl. The results are shown on Figures 3, 4, 5, and 6. The
derivation of the reduced space is done via a Principal Components factoring analysis (PA2 in SPSS PC Advanced) with a varimax rotation. The
eigenvalues and percent of variance explained by the factors are in Table 2.

By using a standard cutoff eigenvalue of 1.0, two significant dimensions which explain three-quarters of the original variation in the data can
be identified. The two-dimensional space for product attributes is shown
in Figure 3. From the attributes given, it is possible to generate an interpretation of space. The horizontal axis consists of items that explain pride,
quality, and performance, while the vertical axis consists of items that
explain price and economy of usage. Therefore, the two axes are labelled
as superior/inferior performance and low/high cost, respectively.

The brands' and countries' positions in Figures 4 and 5, respectively,
are based on the factor scores on the same two significant dimensions:
performance and low cost. The brand and country image space maps lead
to three main observations.

First, Mercedes-Benz as a brand and West Germany as a country scored
high on performance-oriented attributes, while performing less well on
cost attributes. Nonetheless, Germany scored significantly lower than
Mercedes buses as such on the cost dimension. It is possible that buyers
perceive products made in Germany generally as expensive, while they
find that a particular German brand may be somewhat more reasonably
priced since it may be manufactured/assembled in, or may incorporate
components from, other countries. The overall affect rating for Germany
and Mercedes-Benz was high.

Second, Japan as a country was viewed favorably on both dimensions
and was rated highly overall on affect. On the other hand, the two Japanese
brands, Nissan and Mitsubishi, scored low on performance. This might be
partly due to the fact that most of the Japanese tourist buses operating in
Hong Kong at the time of the study were old and outdated. As the respondents were all from the tourist industry and, therefore, in one way or
another had come across these old buses, perhaps this affected their overall perception of the Japanese brands.

Figure 3. Attribute Space Mapping

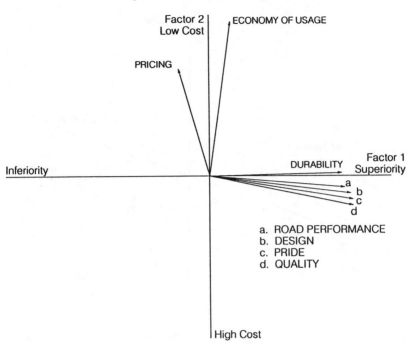

Third, Brazil scored low on performance but high on the cost-oriented attributes, and was perceived more favorably than South Korea on both dimensions.

Shifts in Manufacturing Locations

Figures 7, 8, and 9 show the image profiles and mean attribute ratings of each of the three brands of coaches when made in each of the four countries under consideration. The main finding from this analysis is that in each case, the highest rating was given to the buses made in their "home" country. In other words, Nissan and Mitsubishi buses were rated most favorably when made in Japan, and Mercedes-Benz buses when made in West Germany. Figures 10, 11, and 12 show the image space maps for each brand. Overall, South Korea is rated as the least desirable place in which to produce any of the three brands of tourist coaches.

Figure 4. Brand Image Space Map

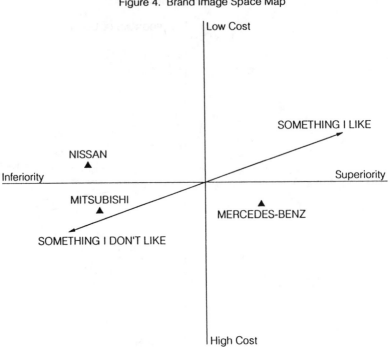

Dollar Preference Analysis

The final part of this study tries to examine the monetary consequences of the contemplated shift in production, following again the method employed by Johansson and Nebenzahl. The joint space mapping, shown earlier, allows the seller to interpret buyers' attitudes in terms of rating scales. For business purposes, however, this preference would be measured better in terms of the difference it would make in the price the product would (or could) command depending on its country of manufacture. Compared to the cost savings from shifting to a less expensive production country, the price difference can help the producer determine where the move would result in a net profit or loss.

As noted, during the interviews respondents were asked to indicate the amount above or below a base price which they would be willing to pay for the same model bus made in a different country. This dollar preference

Figure 5. Country Image Space Map

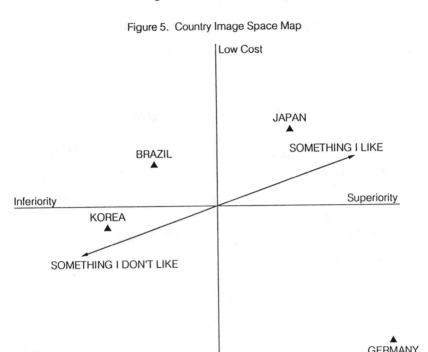

question forced the respondents to translate their choices into monetary terms. The question was open-ended. The base price stated was HK$800,000 for each bus produced in its home country.

The average acceptable prices given by the respondents for a brand made in different countries are shown in Table 3. The results in the table match well with the overall affect findings and thus apparently reinforce the validity of the preference measures. It is worth emphasizing that the figures are compiled with reference to the same baseline of HK$800,000 for each brand produced in its home country. Any variation in prices as a result of a production shift would be relative to this baseline (i.e., horizontally across each line in the table) and no direct comparisons of brands within the *columns* can be made. For example, although the Mercedes-Benz bus made in South Korea is shown to be cheaper than the Mitsubishi bus made in the same country, in actual fact this would not be the case. The actual price of a Mercedes-Benz made in West Germany would be much higher than the actual price of a Mitsubishi made in Japan, and, if the

PRODUCT-COUNTRY IMAGES

Figure 6. Country/Brand Image Space Map

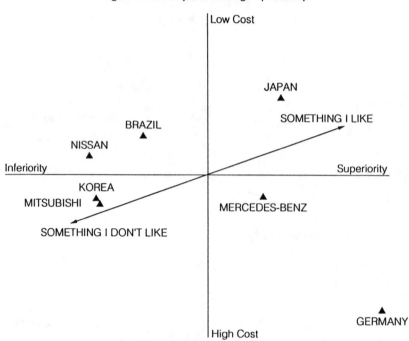

Table 2. Factor Analysis Results for Joint Space Mapping

Factor	Eigen value	Percent of Variance	Cumulative %
1	4.46206	55.8	55.8
2	1.62479	20.3	76.1
3	0.53204	6.7	82.7
4	0.47436	5.9	88.7
5	0.27703	3.5	92.1
6	0.23360	2.9	95.0
7	0.21455	2.7	97.7
8	0.18156	2.3	100.0

Figure 7. Image Profiles of NISSAN Coaches Made in Selected Countries

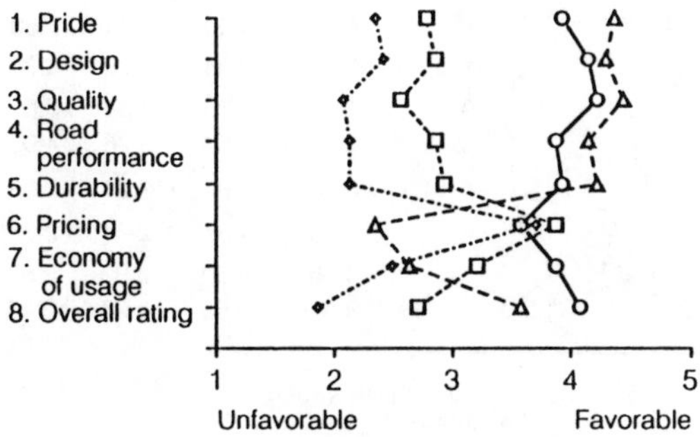

	MEAN SCORES			
	Japan	Germany	Brazil	Korea
	O	Δ	□	◆
1. Pride	4.07	3.57	2.71	1.86
2. Design	3.86	2.64	3.21	2.50
3. Quality	3.57	2.36	3.86	3.71
4. Road performance	3.93	4.21	2.93	2.14
5. Durability	3.86	4.14	2.86	2.14
6. Pricing	4.21	4.43	2.57	2.07
7. Economy of usage	4.14	4.29	2.86	2.43
8. Overall rating	3.93	4.36	2.79	2.35

```
1        2        3        4        5
Unfavorable              Favorable
```

Mercedes-Benz were to be built in South Korea, even though there would be a big drop in monetary terms, the actual price would still be higher than that of the Mitsubishi.

IMPLICATIONS AND CONTRASTS
WITH FINDINGS ON PASSENGER CARS

In the study by Johansson and Nebenzahl, which focused on passenger vehicles, only one factor ("Status") stood out from the rest (eigenvalue of 6.85, explaining almost 50 percent of the variance). A second factor ("Economy") had an eigenvalue greater than 1.0 but explained less than 10 percent of the variance. The remaining three main factors had more or less similar significance explaining 7.0 percent, 4.9 percent and 4.2 percent of the variance. The original image attributes tended to scatter within the vector space between the two dimensions, implying that the consumer buying decision is fairly complex and that the consumers' bases for forming product attitudes may be quite diversified.

In the present study, it was possible to identify two distinct factors, performance and cost, which explain 56 percent and 20 percent of the original variation in the data. In this case, the cost factor explained over twice as much of the variance as in the passenger car study, suggesting the greater importance of this dimension in structuring overall buyer perceptions. The original image attributes tend to cluster around these two main

PRODUCT-COUNTRY IMAGES

Figure 8. Image Profiles of MITSUBISHI Coaches Made in Selected Countries

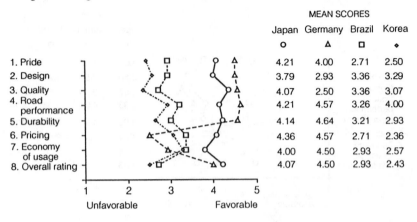

	Japan O	Germany Δ	Brazil □	Korea ♦
1. Pride	4.21	4.00	2.71	2.50
2. Design	3.79	2.93	3.36	3.29
3. Quality	4.07	2.50	3.36	3.07
4. Road performance	4.21	4.57	3.26	4.00
5. Durability	4.14	4.64	3.21	2.93
6. Pricing	4.36	4.57	2.71	2.36
7. Economy of usage	4.00	4.50	2.93	2.57
8. Overall rating	4.07	4.50	2.93	2.43

Figure 9. Image Profiles of MERCEDES Coaches Made in Selected Countries

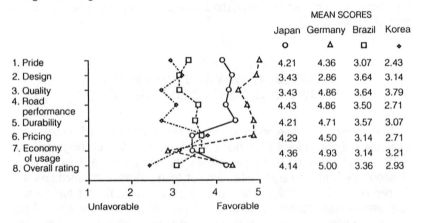

	Japan O	Germany Δ	Brazil □	Korea ♦
1. Pride	4.21	4.36	3.07	2.43
2. Design	3.43	2.86	3.64	3.14
3. Quality	3.43	4.86	3.64	3.79
4. Road performance	4.43	4.86	3.50	2.71
5. Durability	4.21	4.71	3.57	3.07
6. Pricing	4.29	4.50	3.14	2.71
7. Economy of usage	4.36	4.93	3.14	3.21
8. Overall rating	4.14	5.00	3.36	2.93

dimensions, implying that the industrial buying decision may be more straightforward and the bus buyers may have more established and distinct criteria in forming product attitudes.

The orientation of the overall affect scale in both studies suggests that buyers may be biased more towards "Status" or "Superiority" oriented attributes. However, one point worth noting is that in the case of automobiles, Johansson and Nebenzahl found that the positive affect scale falls, surprisingly, into the negative quadrant of "Economy." One explanation

Figure 10. NISSAN Country Image Space Map

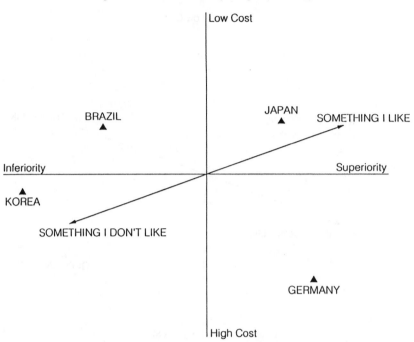

for this is that buyers for a certain product prefer exclusivity and have a positive association between it and price. This often occurs in the case of luxury items, such as jewelry, but seems surprising in the case of automobiles, at least for the practical range of cars (Honda, Mazda, Ford, etc.) under study.

By contrasting the results of the Dollar Preference Analysis with Johansson and Nebenzahl's (1986) findings on passenger cars, it would seem that the effect of moving production to a country with a lower image may be stronger for cars than for buses, in that the drop in brand value may be somewhat more significant in the case of cars. On the other hand, moving production to a country with a higher image may bring about a proportional increase in the brand value perception for cars, but somewhat less so for buses. This may be because the purchasers of buses have more straightforward criteria for their purchasing decisions, namely product superiority and cost.

Johansson and Nebenzahl suggest that the strategy of improving image

Figure 11. MITSUBISHI Country Image Space Map

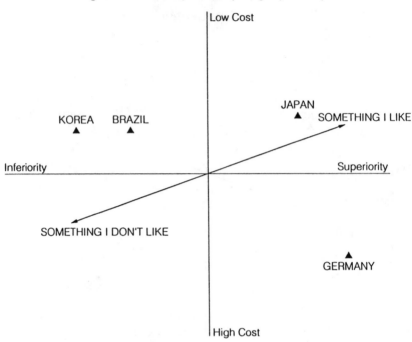

by concentrating production locations in well-regarded countries, and charging a premium price, can work for cars. For buses, due to the somewhat smaller effect of multinational production on brand value, it may be possible to sacrifice some of the image value by locating production in low-cost countries, providing, of course, that the cost benefit is substantial enough to offset the deterioration in the image of the brand name.

Earlier studies, such as the one by Cattin, Jolibert, and Lohnes (1982), showed the strength of the "made in West Germany" label and this was also found to hold true in Hong Kong. But, in contrast to Cattin, Jolibert, and Lohnes' findings, Japan's image in this study was perceived as good, and buses manufactured by Japanese firms in Japan were highly rated by the Hong Kong respondents. This probably reflects the growing worldwide awareness of the high quality of Japanese products that developed throughout the 1980s and is a factor that has considerable implications in markets everywhere. The fact that South Korea scored lowest in all respects, except for price, was interesting and perhaps rather surprising in

Figure 12. MERCEDES-BENZ Country Image Space Map

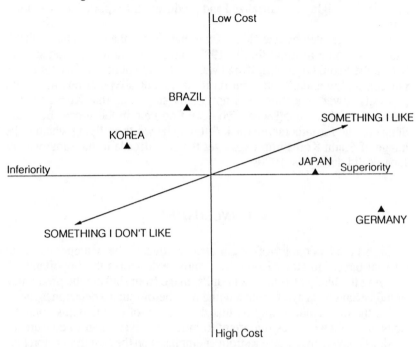

Table 3. Acceptable Prices in thousand HK$
for a Brand Made in Different Countries

Brand	Country of Manufacture			
	W. Germany	Japan	Brazil	S. Korea
Mercedes-Benz	800	748	657	641
Mitsubishi	847	800	691	656
Nissan	863	800	670	638

view of the fact that South Korea, one of the four "Little Dragons" of Asia, is now highly industrialized and produces and exports its own motor cars.

It was suggested by one Hong Kong manager in the bus industry that it should be borne in mind that in 1987 (when this study was conducted), before the Seoul Olympics, Korea was relatively unknown "except for its ginseng and women." He went on to say: "For a typical bus man with generally lower education, it is not totally surprising that Korea appeals less to them than Brazil where you can find Pele in the soccer field and Senna on the formula racing track." It may be worth studying whether the image of South Korea improves over the next decade in the same way as Japan's did during the 1980s.

CONCLUSION

Each brand's country-of-origin clearly affected the perceptions of industrial buyers in Hong Kong. The study underscores the importance of studying the likely effects on a brand's image from shifting the production of industrial goods away from a home base before such a decision is made.

On the one hand, it may be that the country-of-origin status connotations are somewhat less important to business buyers than to consumers. Business buyers may place a stronger emphasis on the cost dimension than consumers when looking at the country-of-origin of the products they buy–or they may be processing origin information differently. While consumer processing of the country-of-origin cue has been given a fair amount of attention in the international marketing literature, the same cannot be said for buyers in the industrial context. Much more research is needed, both within the industrial market and comparatively between industrial and consumer purchase situations, before any conclusions concerning this matter can be drawn safely.

On the other hand, the study clearly shows that industrial buyers prefer products made in the manufacturer's home country, and points to the difficulties which a company must face in trying to establish the middle path between cutting costs by producing overseas and the loss in brand image consequent of such a move. Further, the present study essentially replicated the research of Johansson and Nebenzahl (1986), albeit with some changes and in a different context. The methodology suggested, including the estimation of location effects on product price levels, can help companies to assess the relative value of alternative production locations and thus to develop a sounder basis for international expansion decisions.

REFERENCES

Agarwal, M.K. and B.T. Ratchford (1980), "Estimating Demand Functions for Product Characteristics: The Case of Automobiles." *Journal of Consumer Research* (December).

Andrews, I.R. and E.R. Valenzi (1971) "Combining Price, Brand Name and Store Cues to Form an Impression of Product Quality." *Proceedings of the 79th Annual Convention of the American Psychological Association.*

Bilkey, Warren J. and Erik Nes (1982), "Country-of-Origin Effects on Product Evaluations." *Journal of International Business Studies*, 8(1) (Spring/Summer) 89-99.

Cattin, Philippe, Alain Jolibert, and Colleen Lohnes (1982), "A Cross-Cultural Study of 'Made In' Concepts." *Journal of International Business Studies* (Winter) 131-141.

Erickson, Gary M., Johny K. Johansson, and Paul Chao (1984), "Image Variables in Multi-Attribute Product Evaluations: Country-of-Origin Effects." *Journal of Consumer Research*, 11: (September) 694-699.

Gaedeke, Ralph (1973), "Consumer Attitudes Toward Products 'Made In' Developing Countries." *Journal of Retailing*, 49(2), (Summer) 13-24.

Handbook (1987). Hong Kong Association of Travel Agents.

Hong Kong Business Annual 1988. Communication Management Ltd., Hong Kong.

Johansson, Johny K. and Israel D. Nebenzahl (1986), "Multinational Production: Effect on Brand Value." *Journal of International Business Studies*, 17, 3 (Fall) 101-126.

Johansson, Johny K. and Hans B. Thorelli (1985), "International Product Positioning." *Journal of International Business Studies*, XVI, 3 (Fall) 57-75.

Johansson, Johny K., Susan P. Douglas, and Ikujiro Nonaka (1985), "Assessing the Impact of country-of-origin on Product Evaluations: A New Methodological Perspective." *Journal of Marketing Research*, XXII: (November) 388-96.

Lillis, Charles M. and Chem L. Narayana (1974), "Analysis of 'Made- in' Product Images—An Exploratory Study." *Journal of International Business Studies* (Spring) 119-127.

Olson, Jerry C. and Jacob Jacoby (1972), "Cue Utilization in the Quality Perception Process." In M. Venkatesan (ed.), *Proceedings, Third Annual Conference of the Association for Consumer Research*, 167-179.

Statistical Review of Tourism in Hong Kong (1986). Hong Kong Tourist Association.

Stewart, Sally and Raymond Sung (1990), "Chinese Attitudes to Foreign Goods." In Oliver H.M. Yau (ed.), *Consumer Behavior in Asia*. Addison-Wesley.

Stewart, Sally, Raymond Sung, and Arthur Yeung (1988), "Why American Goods Need to Be Promoted in China: A Look at the Image of US Products in Southern China with Suggestions on How It Could Be Improved." Paper presented at the *Symposium on Export Promotion Services* (Washington, D.C.: U.S. Department of Commerce and Michigan State University, May 26-27).

Transport Statistics (1987). Hong Kong Government.

White, Phillip D. (1979), "Attitudes of U.S. Purchasing Managers Toward Industrial Products Manufactured In Selected Western European Nations." *Journal of International Business Studies*, 20, (Spring-Summer) 81-90.

White, Philip D. and E.W. Cundiff (1978), "Assessing the Quality of Industrial Products." *Journal of Marketing*, (January) 80-86.

Wilson, A. (1973), "The Assessment of Industrial Markets." *Associated Business Programmes Ltd.*

Chapter 10

A Research Note on Country-of-Origin in Industrial Settings

Chwo-Ming Joseph Yu
Cheng-Nan Chen

INTRODUCTION

Buyers evaluate products on the basis of information cues. Country-of-origin has been generally accepted as an important cue for the evaluation of consumer products (Bilkey and Nes 1982). Existing research also indicates that product origins influence the views of industrial buyers (e.g., Cattin, Jolibert, and Lohnes 1982). However, the number of studies that address the impact of country-of-origin on the evaluation of industrial products is very limited in comparison to the considerable work that has been done on consumer products. Since buying behavior for the two types of products is quite different, the empirical findings from consumer research may not be readily applicable to industrial goods. There is a need for more research on the role of origin cues in industrial product evaluations.

The objective of this research note is to augment the managerially-oriented discussion about the country-of-origin phenomenon in industrial buying settings which is found elsewhere in this book.[1] The intent is to summarize existing knowledge regarding the effect of country-of-origin on the evaluation of industrial products, and then combine this summary with existing knowledge about industrial purchasing behavior to propose five generalized hypotheses for future research.

The authors would like to acknowledge the helpful comments of the anonymous referees and the co-editors of this book.

1. Ed. note: See the chapter by Stewart and Chen.

This note should be useful to academic researchers in that it suggests directions for new studies that would help to enhance our understanding of the impact of origin cues in industrial buying decisions. At the same time, it raises some important questions for consideration by industrial marketing practitioners, whose products may be influenced by their target markets' perceptions about the products' origins.

LITERATURE REVIEW

Impact of the Country-of-Origin Cue

Studies generally indicate that country-of-origin does indeed influence buyer perceptions of consumer products (Nagashima 1977; Bilkey and Nes 1982; Papadopoulos et al. 1987). A major criticism of early work, that is, that country-of-origin used to be the only information respondents received about a product, has been tackled by recent studies (e.g., Johansson, Douglas, and Nonaka 1985; Heslop, Liefeld, and Wall 1987; Han 1989). These studies confirm the impact of country-of-origin along with other cues and product characteristics on the subjective evaluation of consumer goods.

In comparison with the research on consumer products, only a few studies have addressed the impact of country-of-origin on product evaluations in industrial settings. These studies show that country-of-origin influences the decision-making process for industrial buyers (Abdel-Malek 1975; Chasin and Jaffe 1979; White 1979; Cattin, Jolibert, and Lohnes 1982). Three studies have also examined the impact of additional information cues, besides country-of-origin, on the evaluation of industrial products (Hakansson and Wootz 1975; White and Cundiff 1978; Kaynak 1989). The findings of these studies enhance our understanding of industrial buying behavior regarding the impact of other information cues, such as previous experience with a product, size of supplier, and product price and quality, and also provide insights about the industrial buyer's education, income, age, and role in the use of various information cues.

Additional Determinants of Industrial
Buying Behavior

The research on the impact of country-of-origin on industrial products tends to overlook the differences between industrial buying and consumer behavior. Since the studies mentioned above adopt the same methodology as the studies of consumer purchasing, their research findings may have some biases and provide an incomplete picture of country-of-origin influences in industrial markets.

There are many differences between industrial buying and consumer behavior (Hutt and Speh 1981). Two of these differences are considered to have a potentially significant effect on the importance of country-of-origin cues on product evaluation. First, most industrial buying decisions are made by groups of people, or Decision Making Units (DMUs) (Buckner 1976; Moriarty 1983), and only a few of them are made by individuals (Patton, Puto, and King 1986). By contrast, consumer buying decisions are frequently made only by the person involved. A DMU involves many people from different departments and different levels of a company, and the size of the DMU varies with the size of the company, the type of industry, and the product being purchased (Moriarty 1983). Therefore, participants in a DMU play different roles in the buying decision and will have different influences on other participants (Silk and Kalwani 1982). For example, Lilien and Wong (1984) found that in the metalworking industry, the influence of participants in DMUs varies in each of the seven phases of the purchasing decision process. Therefore, the technique of surveying a single member of the DMU in institutional purchasing decisions, as has been the case in most made-in research on industrial products to date, is widely considered to give a very incomplete picture (Wind 1978; Anderson, Chu, and Weitz 1987).

Second, there are more determinants involved in industrial than in consumer purchase decisions. The determinants of consumer decisions are mainly individual and environmental variables. The determinants of an industrial buyer's decision also include interpersonal and organizational variables (Webster and Wind 1972). For example, Nicosia and Wind (1977) have classified the determinants of industrial buying behavior into four sets, with emphasis on the organizational variables (including interpersonal variables).

Some of the organizational variables might affect the impact of country-of-origin. For example, Robertson and Wind (1980) found that "resistance to change" is negatively related to the likelihood of acquiring an innovation. By the same reasoning, resistance to change might affect the impact of the country-of-origin cue by discouraging the acquisition of foreign products.

Product-specific variables also have some impact on industrial buying behavior (Sheth 1973). Buyclass (or frequency of buying) and perceived risk, as proposed by Sheth (1973), are two major variables relevant to the impact of the country-of-origin cue. Different buyclasses will have quite different decision processes (Robinson, Faris, and Wind 1967). For example, purchasing agents dominate straight rebuy decisions whereas engineers dominate new purchases (Pingry 1974).

The perceived risk in an industrial buying decision is generally much greater than that in a consumer buying decision (Moriarty 1983). The degree and types of risk perceived are different for DMU members who come from different organizational positions (McMillan 1972). For example, a purchasing representative usually perceives less risk in how a product performs than other members of the DMU. The perceived risk might affect the impact of country-of-origin information. If a manager feels that there is a great risk in the performance of a machine and has an unfavorable attitude toward a particular country's products, he or she might evaluate a machine made in that country unfavorably because of this belief.

Firms from different nations pursue different industrial marketing strategies (Hallen and Johansson 1985) and, as in the case of consumer products, the marketing strategies of industrial goods producers have an impact on industrial buying behavior (Busch and Wilson 1976; Choffray and Lilien 1978). Hence, marketing efforts by firms, such as attending industrial shows and other promotional activities, can influence the evaluation of industrial products.

RESEARCH FRAMEWORK AND HYPOTHESES

The preceding overview of the literature suggests that a wider range of factors must be accounted for when evaluating the impact of the country-of-origin cue on industrial buying behavior. In this section, we outline a research framework and propose directions for new research into the role of origin information in industrial buying decisions. These directions are formulated as five generalized research hypotheses, which, needless to say, would be modified and specified more explicitly depending on the research setting in which they are used.

The considerations that must be taken into account in attempting to understand the country-of-origin phenomenon in industrial markets are summarized in Figure 1. As can be seen in the figure, these considerations include the potential impact of marketing strategies, product-specific attributes, organizational attributes, and attributes of DMUs. The specific attributes listed in Figure 1 under each heading are only for illustrative purposes and do not include all relevant characteristics. This framework is similar to the one proposed by Samli, Grewal, and Mathur (1988). While

Figure 1. The Country-of-Origin Phenomenon
in Industrial Markets

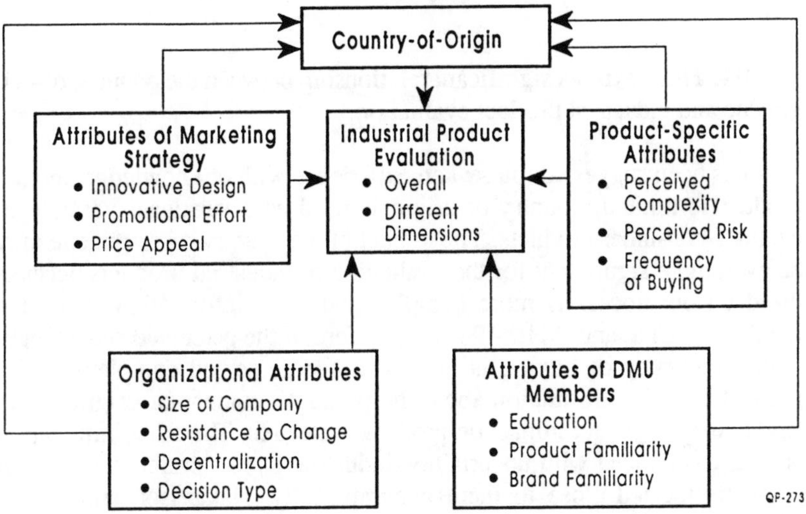

their model emphasizes environmental and governmental factors, ours includes product attributes, marketing strategies, and country-of-origin.

Industrial products can be evaluated by an overall rating or by different dimensions/attributes, as is the case with consumer products. Studies on the effect of country-of-origin have shown that, for consumer products, the ratings among countries differ for different attributes (e.g., Johansson, Douglas, and Nonaka 1985). Because the dimensions are product-specific, we address only the overall rating in our discussion. The hypotheses which follow are derived from the characteristics of industrial buying behavior, as these were discussed briefly in the previous section. Where possible, the tentative supporting evidence, mainly from the area of consumer product evaluations, is cited. Since the focus of this note is to evaluate the impact of the country-of-origin cue, the direct relationship between other attributes in Figure 1 and product evaluation will not be discussed here. While the first hypothesis postulates the *direct* relationship between the country-of-origin cue and industrial product evaluation, hypotheses 2, 3, 4, and 5 deal with the impact of the interaction between this cue and four groups of attributes.

Based on the findings of previous studies on consumer and industrial product evaluations, we postulate the significant impact of country-of-origin. The impact probably will be positive for products from industrialized countries and negative for less developed countries (Kaynak 1989). Therefore:

• H1: There exists a significant relationship between the country-of-origin cue and industrial product evaluation.

It has been suggested that, when experience with or knowledge about a product is limited, country-of-origin is used as a surrogate variable to evaluate consumer products. The impact of the country-of-origin cue may be even more significant for the evaluation of industrial products because the decision process is more complex and more information is needed (Anderson, Chu, and Weitz 1987). Therefore, if the perceived risk is high, if the frequency of buying is low, or if the perceived complexity of a product is high, information about the product's country-of-origin would tend to have a greater impact on product evaluation. The other implication is that, when faced with uncertainty, industrial buyers prefer to deal with suppliers located close to them geographically (Hakansson and Wootz 1975). Therefore:

• H2: The impact of the country-of-origin cue on industrial product evaluation is affected by product-specific attributes.

Since seller familiarity interacts with country image for consumer products (Han 1989), and since marketing strategies can change the perceptions of firms by consumers, we hypothesize that the interaction between the country-of-origin cue and marketing strategies will have a significant impact on the evaluation of industrial products. Hence, when the reputations of suppliers are not too different from each other, when the promotional efforts of suppliers are low, or when suppliers use price appeals (e.g., setting the price significantly higher or lower than average), the country-of-origin cue would tend to have a greater impact on product evaluation. Therefore:

• H3: The impact of the country-of-origin cue on industrial product evaluation is affected by attributes of marketing strategies of suppliers.

Industrial buying behavior is affected by some organizational attributes (Sheth 1973). We postulate that the interaction of these organizational attributes and country-of-origin information will have an impact on purchasing behavior. Examples in support of this view include the following:

1. Since large corporations tend to have decisions made jointly, the impact of the country-or-origin cue will be more diffuse and less significant at the DMU as compared to the individual level;
2. The country-of-origin cue has a greater impact when purchasing decisions in a company are not group decisions or are made by smaller DMUs;
3. The more resistant to change a company is, the more it deals with countries with which it is familiar; and
4. Since the degree of decentralization tends to be positively associated with joint decision making, the impact of the country-of-origin cue will be greater when the degree of centralization of a company is high. Therefore:

• H4: The impact of the country-of-origin cue on industrial product evaluations is affected by organizational attributes of buyers.

We argue that certain attributes of DMU members will affect the extent of the influence of country-of-origin information on industrial product evaluations. Though the relationship between respondents' education and foreign product ratings by consumers is unclear (Han 1988), Kaynak (1989) demonstrated that, because of the knowledge needed to understand product specifications, the evaluation of industrial products from abroad differ for Chinese buyers with different levels of education. While White and Cundiff (1978) found that the perceived quality of industrial products manufactured in different nations does not differ between purchasing managers with and those without previous purchasing experience, Kaynak (1989) found that work experience affects the evaluation of industrial products with different countries of origin. Johansson, Douglas, and Nonaka (1985) also found that familiarity with consumer products of different national origins, and experience with using these products, affect product evaluations (note, however, that some conflicting results are found in Han 1989). Thus, when DMU members have a lower level of education, or are less familiar with a product or brands, their evaluation of products is likely to be affected significantly by country-or-origin information. Therefore:

• H5: The impact of the country-of-origin cue on industrial product evaluation is affected by the attributes of buyers' DMU members.

CONCLUSION

In this note, we propose a theoretical framework to examine the country-of-origin effect for industrial products. Unlike other studies, we suggest the examination of the influence of origin cues in relation to four additional sets of attributes, namely, product-specific characteristics, marketing strategies, organizational elements, and characteristics of DMUs and their members.

The need to study the use of origin information in the context of industrial products based on this expanded framework arises from the greater complexity of industrial buying decisions. Given this, existing studies, which have tended to research industrial decisions based on approaches and frameworks developed by consumer researchers, may be providing an incomplete picture of the country-of-origin phenomenon. Therefore, new research in both the academic and applied environments is needed. Lastly, it should be noted that industrial buying behavior differs greatly across countries, and especially between firms in developing versus industrialized nations (Rao and Krishna 1987; Wortzel 1983). Therefore, the usefulness of empirical testing of the hypotheses we have proposed would be enhanced significantly if new research is carried out in comparative settings.

REFERENCES

Abdel-Malek, Talaat (1975), "Comparative Profiles of Foreign Customers and Intermediaries." *European Journal of Marketing*, 9(3) 198-214.

Anderson E., W. Chu, and B. Weitz (1987), "Industrial Purchasing: An Empirical Explanation of the Buyclass Framework." *Journal of Marketing*, 51 (July) 71-86.

Bilkey, Warren J. and Erik Nes (1982), "Country-of-Origin Effects on Product Evaluations." *Journal of International Business Studies*, 8(1) (Spring/Summer) 89-99.

Buckner, P. (1976), *How British Industry Buys*. London: Hutchinson.

Busch, P. and P.T. Wilson (1976), "An Experimental Analysis of a Salesman's Expert and Referent Bases of Social Power in the Buyer-Seller Dyad." *Journal of Marketing Research*, 13, 3-11.

Cattin, Philippe, Alain Jolibert, and Colleen Lohnes (1982), "A Cross-Cultural Study of 'Made In' Concepts." *Journal of International Business Studies* (Winter) 131-141.

Chasin, J.B. and Eugene D. Jaffe (1979), "Industrial Buyer Attitudes Towards Goods Made in Eastern Europe." *Columbia Journal of World Business* (Summer) 74-81.

Choffray, J.M. and G. Lilien (1978), "Assessing Response to Industrial Marketing Strategy." *Journal of Marketing*, 20-31.

Hakansson, H. and B. Wootz (1975), "Supplier Selection in an International Environment: An Experimental Study." *Journal of Marketing Research*, XII: (February) 46-51.

Hallen, L. and J.K. Johansson (1985), "Industrial Marketing Strategies and Different National Environments." *Journal of Business Research*, 13 (December) 495-509.

Han, Min C. (1988), "The Role of Consumer Patriotism in the Choice of Domestic versus Foreign Products." *Journal of Advertising Research*. 28(3) (June-July) 25-32.

Han, Min C. (1989), "Country Image: Halo or Summary Construct?" *Journal of Marketing Research*, XXVI: (May) 222-229.

Heslop, Louise A., John P. Liefeld, and Marjorie Wall (1987), "An Experimental Study of the Impact of Country-of-Origin Information." In R.E. Turner (ed.), *Marketing*, Vol. 8 (Toronto, Ont.: Proceedings, Administrative Sciences Association of Canada–Marketing Division, June) 179-185.

Hutt, M.D. and T.W. Speh (1981), *Industrial Marketing Management*. New York: Dryden Press. 15-16.

Johansson, Johny K., Susan P. Douglas, and Ikujiro Nonaka (1985), "Assessing the Impact of Country of Origin on Product Evaluations: A New Methodological Perspective." *Journal of Marketing Research*, XXII: (November) 388-96.

Kaynak, E. (1989), "How Chinese Buyers Rate Foreign Suppliers." *Industrial Marketing Management*, 18 (August) 187-198.

Lilien, G.L. and M.A. Wong (1984), "An Exploratory Investigation of the Structure of the Buying Center in the Metalworking Industry." *Journal of Marketing Research* (February) 1-11.

McMillan, J.R. (1972), "The Role of Perceived Risk in Industrial Marketing Decisions." In *Proceedings of the American Marketing Association*, Series #34, 412-417.

Moriarty, R.T. (1983), *Industrial Buying Behavior*. Lexington, MA: Lexington Books.

Nagashima, Akira (1977), "A Comparative 'Made In' Product Image Survey Among Japanese Businessmen." *Journal of Marketing*, 41 (July) 95-100.

Nicosia, F.M. and Y. Wind (1977), "Emerging Models of Organizational Buying Processes." *Industrial Marketing Management*, 6, 353-369.

Papadopoulos, Nicolas, Louise A. Heslop, Françoise Graby, and George Avlonitis (1987), "Does Country-of-Origin Matter? Some Findings from a Cross-Cultural Study of Consumer Views About Foreign Products." *Working Paper #87-104, Marketing Science Institute*, Cambridge, MA.

Patton, W.E., C.P. Puto, and R.H. King (1986), "Which Buying Decisions Are Made by Individuals and Not by Groups." *Industrial Marketing Management*, 129-138.

Pingry, J.R. (1974), "The Engineer and Purchasing Agent Compared," *Journal of Purchasing*, 10 (November) 33-45.

Rao, C.P. and E.M. Krishna (1987), "Dimensions of Industrial Buyer Behavior in a Newly Industrializing Country." Paper presented at the *Conference of The Academy of International Business* (Chicago).

Robertson, T.S. and Y. Wind (1980), "Organizational Psychographics and Innovativeness." *Journal of Consumer Research*, 7 (June) 24- 31.

Robinson, P.J., C.W. Faris, and Y. Wind (1967), *Industrial Buying and Creative Marketing*. Boston: Allyn & Bacon.

Samli, A.C., D. Grewal and S.K. Mathur (1988), "International Industrial Buyer Behavior: An Exploration and a Proposed Model." *Journal of the Academy of Marketing Science*, 16 (Summer) 19-29.

Sheth, J.N. (1973), "A Model of Industrial Buyer Behavior." *Journal of Marketing*, 37 (October) 50-56.

Silk, A.J. and M.U. Kalwani (1982), "Marketing Influence in Organizational Purchase Decisions." *Journal of Marketing Research*, XIX (May) 165-181.

Webster, F.E. and Y. Wind (1972), "A General Model for Understanding Buying Behavior." *Journal of Marketing*, 36 (April) 12-19.

White, Phillip D. (1979), "Attitudes of U.S. Purchasing Managers Toward Industrial Products Manufactured in Selected Western European Nations." *Journal of International Business Studies*, 20, (Spring-Summer) 81-90.

White, Philip D. and E.W. Cundiff (1978), "Assessing the Quality of Industrial Products." *Journal of Marketing* (January) 80-86.

Wind, Y. (1978), "The Organizational Buying Center: A Research Agenda." In G. Zaltman and T.V. Bonoma (eds.), *Organizational Buyer Behavior*. Chicago: American Marketing Association. 14-21.

Wortzel, L.H. (1983), "Marketing to Firms in Developing Asian Countries." *Industrial Marketing Management* (April) 113-123.

PART IV.
COUNTRIES AS "PRODUCTS"
IN THE GLOBAL ARENA

INTRODUCTION

Part IV contains three chapters which focus on the images of countries as corporate entities in the international arena. Since this view has rarely been discussed before in the literature, if at all, these chapters break new ground and offer a glimpse into a new and different facet of product and country images.

Chapter 11 uses France as the context for showing how countries can be seen as "companies" which, in addition to just "having an image" (and doing little about it), can take specific proactive steps to enhance the international position of their manufacturers. (To maintain the analogy, manufacturers are to countries what product lines and brands are to companies.) France serves as an ideal example for this discussion since its government is more aware than most others of the relevant issues and has taken specific steps, such as the establishment of a "French Image Committee," to address them.

Chapter 12 offers another unique view of the country-as-company perspective. Based on a very large scale research undertaking in The Netherlands on behalf of Italy, it couples for the first time country image with the competitive position of various industrial and consumer goods sectors and analyzes the results by drawing on Porter's SWOT approach. The author concludes by recommending that, unlike the undifferentiated approaches that have characterized national promotion efforts in the past, governments need to (1) ascertain their exact position carefully, and (2) use this knowledge as a base for employing one of three differentiated strategies ("information," "balancing," and "reinforcement").

Chapter 13 also discusses country image but from a 180-degree-different perspective: it views countries as "investment products" vying for foreign capital. The chapter uses findings from a study of U.S. decision makers concerning investment in Southeast Asia and analyzes them using multidimensional scaling and other techniques. A number of significant implications are drawn based on the finding that investors have clear, distinct, and different images of "countries," geographic "regions," nations at various levels of development, and national trade groupings such as ASEAN, as potential locations for investment.

Chapter 11

Countries as Corporate Entities in International Markets

Françoise Graby

INTRODUCTION

In industry and government circles in France, the loss of international market share in some areas over the past few years, and difficulties in expanding France's market presence in others, were seen as a function of the comparatively high prices of French products in relation to those of their foreign competitors. This argument was also commonly encountered in other industrialized countries and still finds favor in many quarters in France and elsewhere.

However, contemporary insights into buyer behavior and the functioning of markets show that price competitiveness is a relative concept whose influence is tempered by a variety of intrinsic and extrinsic factors, including the products' country-of-origin. The country-of-origin literature essentially argues that all attributes of all products from a given country, coupled with the characteristics of the country itself and its people, combine to create an overall market position which is perceived subjectively as a total image by buyers and influences their market choices.

France is a particularly interesting case for the study of the country-of-origin phenomenon. It is the fourth-largest exporting nation in the world, with a global share of about 6 percent. French products have been present in foreign markets for centuries and are the market leaders in several sectors. A large part of France's exports is in highly visible product categories where image plays an important role in buyers' awareness and choices (e.g., fashion, perfumes, wine, aerospace). Thus foreign consumer awareness about specific products has been found consistently to be high

I wish to express my sincere appreciation to Dr. Papadopoulos for his contribution in developing this chapter.

and French products in general are likely to be subject to considerable stereotyping.

Because of these and other related factors, many country-of-origin studies have studied the image of French products within single markets or cross-culturally. Further, French decision makers in business and government are highly sensitized today to the importance of country and product images. Many exporters feel that while the quality of French products is not in doubt, stereotyping is having a significant impact on foreign buyers' perceptions about their price competitiveness. As a result, France has more public and industry programs in place than most other countries for researching and promoting the image of its products abroad.

This provides an opportunity to examine the role of government and "country" in general in image formation. As a result, the main thrust of this chapter is the examination of the country-of-origin phenomenon based on the notion that countries can be thought of as companies, whose products are the outputs of such actors as exporters, industry associations, and governments. This is done by drawing on the relevant literature and outlining French programs related to country image promotion. While France provides the context for the study, the underlying concepts in this chapter can be applied to any other country.

The chapter has three main sections. The first examines the notion of countries-as-companies and outlines the impact of country-of-origin perceptions on foreign consumers' behavior. The second examines the image of France and French products abroad based on an overview of past research. And the third outlines and appraises the main image-related programs in France, and discusses how the view of a country as a corporate entity influences public policy and industry actions for promoting its products in foreign markets.

PERSPECTIVES ON COUNTRY IMAGES

Brand, Company, and Country Image

The importance of perceived images is well known in marketing and is especially associated with the concept of the brand. In fact, "brand image" has become almost synonymous with "image" and can be thought of in connection with any offering including products, ideas, organizations, events, or people (Marion 1989). Since "image" comprises both rational and emotional elements, it may be radically different from intrinsic reality. As stated by Breuil (1972), brand image "is a collection of ideas, feelings, emotional reactions and attitudes, which arise from the evocation of the brand, well beyond the objective perception of it."

A significant component of brand image is the image of the brand's producer: "The company's history, style and dynamics are often determining factors in the creation of a brand image" (Serraf 1964). Including company image as part of brand image complicates attempts to understand the latter. Company image encompasses a broader set of actors that contribute to its formation and diffusion (e.g., retailers, shareholders, employees, trade unions), and thus expands considerably the range of rational and emotional elements that are part of brand image, (Cohen and Gschwind 1971).

Since producers, intermediaries, consumers, and other parties take part in the creation of company images, companies are far from having complete control over the images conveyed about them and, by extension, their brands. Thus, to understand the concept of "image," it is necessary to think of it at three different levels (Marion and Michel 1986):

1. "Desired image" refers to the target image that emerges from the strategic planning process of the firm.
2. "Diffused image" concerns the execution of plans by such actors as company employees and associate agents (e.g., advertising agencies, retailers), and almost always varies to a greater or lesser degree from the first.
3. "Registered image" refers to the image actually held by consumers and other publics. It is formed on the basis of actions of the company and the actors it controls, but also of inputs from other actors in the general business environment (e.g., governments, trade unions, the media).

This tri-level view of image can be applied to countries as much as to companies or brands. A country can be likened to a company whose chief executives (government) design strategic plans (national objectives and policies) that are executed by its employees (government agencies, political leaders) and also influence, directly or indirectly, the actions of "associated agents" (e.g., companies, other organizations, the public). The country's total registered image is the result of at least three types of outputs:

1. its own outputs ("products"), which range from exports and foreign investments by its companies to cultural products (e.g., book or movie production) and the statements and actions of its leaders;

2. the effects of external elements, such as association with regional conditions (e.g., "Balkan-style yoghourt") and the outputs of other actors (e.g., competing global brands or actions of neighboring countries); and,

3. the economic, political, and social conditions of the country as these are perceived by foreign "customers" (foreign governments, buyers, the media, foreign publics, etc.), who also serve to diffuse their conception of a country's image to other publics.

Exhibit 1 portrays the main elements of brand, company, and country image for each of the three image levels.

Dimensions of Country and Product Images

Country (as well as company and brand) images can be assessed in terms of clarity (how well they are understood), direction (how positive or negative they are), and strength or rigidity (how difficult they are to change). Most of the developed nations tend to have fairly clear images since substantial information about them is available through education, the media, and other sources. However, clarity does not mean that the country images held also are clear. For instance, the mention of "France"

Exhibit 1. Three Levels of Image

Image level	Brand image	Company image	Country image
Desired	Positioning strategy (brand-product managers)	Institutional corporate strategy (board of directors, top executives)	National strategy (government, political leadership)
Diffused	Brand name, advertising, packaging, end-user prices, distribution, other mix variables	Publicity, public relations, stakeholder relations, institutional advertising	Economic/social programs, industrial subsidies, educ., tourism/investment promotion
Registered	(above plus-) Word-of-mouth, experience from use, competitive actions publicity	(above plus-) Word-of-mouth, media, trade unions, competitive & government actions	(above plus-) History, foreign gov't & competitor actions, consumer experiences from visits, media, word-of-mouth

may evoke images of Paris (e.g., the Eiffel Tower) or of the country's cultural or fashion output–but few people would be able to describe landmarks in Bordeaux or Toulouse, not to mention other, more involved characteristics of the country. Needless to say, the image of less-well-known countries (e.g., Senegal or Borneo) is likely to be far less clear.

The direction of images will of course vary by country, but certain consumers hold fairly uniform views about foreign nations in general. In fact, earlier researchers often conceptualized country images in the context of xenophobia or xenophilia (e.g., Malliaris 1980), and Scott (1965) has stated that there is "substantial evidence of a widespread disposition either to like or dislike foreign countries in general." Further, because of their relatively greater importance to those who hold them, views about countries tend to be stronger and more rigid (i.e., to be less amenable to change) than those of companies or brands.

Most researchers generally agree that the complexity of country images often results in significant emotional influences on the cognitive characteristics attributed to nations. The significance of emotions in forming images about complex objects has been stressed by Kapferer (1988). He suggested that company images can be understood in terms of an "identity prism" comprising six facets, of which only the first can be considered as a largely "technical" matter (although it, too, is subject to emotional interpretation): physical characteristics, cultural characteristics, personality, relations with publics, "reflection" (the ways in which the previous four facets are passed on to buyers), and "internalization" (the relation between the company's image and the buyer's own conception about him/herself). The same concept can be applied to the images of countries as corporate entities. Exhibit 2 compares the elements of the identity prism for companies and countries.

Generally, friendly images of the world tend to be more common among well-informed consumers who use a larger number of attributes in assessing nations. Greater cognitive complexity makes an ethnocentric view of foreign countries less likely. Inevitably, the images of foreign countries may be stereotyped (in most cases they are formed, by necessity, without any contact with the object), but the problem really is not this simple. Rather, the issue is whether or not the individual who simplifies is conscious of the limitations of doing so–in other words, whether or not the stereotype is "open."

Effects of Country Images

The potential effects of country images on consumer behavior have been studied extensively. The presence of an origin bias in product assess-

Exhibit 2. Company and Country "Identity Prism"

Facets	Company	Country
Physical	Skills, products, size, resources, performance, markets	Geography, resources, demographics, economic performance
Cultural	Corporate values & mythology	History, culture, the arts
Personality	Name, logotype, brands, visual symbols	Name, flag, famous people, visual symbols
Relations	With employees, agents, competitors, government, customers, other publics	With domestic & foreign business, governments, & other organizations
Reflection	Controlled image conveyed to customers & various other publics	Controlled image conveyed to foreign customers & others
Internalization	Extent to which company expresses customers' & others' psyche	Extent to which country expresses foreign publics' psyche

ments was established by the first generation of "made in" studies (e.g., Reierson 1966; Anderson and Cunningham 1972; Nagashima 1977). Some of the findings of these studies have been challenged on methodological and other grounds (Bilkey and Nes 1982). However, while subsequent research has stressed the complexity of the country-of-origin phenomenon, it has also reaffirmed its significance and its potential impact on consumer choices (e.g., Johannson, Douglas, and Nonaka 1985; Papadopoulos et al. 1987).

These and other studies are examined in detail elsewhere in this volume, and so a review of empirical research findings is not necessary here. Rather, this discussion focuses on country images from the perspective of the main notion that underlies this chapter–the view of countries as corporate entities.

It seems reasonable to assume that, as the image object becomes more complex (brand, company, country), the audience concerned becomes more diverse (entire nations vs. a company's publics or a brand's customers), control of the registered image becomes more difficult, and it becomes more likely that the emotional components of image may have a greater influence on attitude formation and behavior than rational ones.

Thus the image of a product's origin country, viewed as a corporate entity, can be thought to affect brand image in a way similar to that of the company itself. In fact, since knowledge about foreign companies is generally poor and country images are more rigid, it can be argued that in foreign markets country image may often supplant and override company image.

This argument is supported by earlier studies which suggest that country of manufacture may override the producer's image in consumers' product assessments. For example, Seaton and Vogel (1981) tested perceptions in the U.S. about competing car brands and found that where they are made (Germany vs. the U.S.) had a more significant impact than who makes them (Ford vs. Volkswagen).

Naturally, as with the various brands of a company, not all products of a country have the same image or are influenced to the same extent by the image of the country (or company) itself. Nonetheless, company and country images often convey certain common characteristics which are perceived as such by consumers. For example, Jetta is different from Passat, but both are Volkswagen cars and they, as well as other manufactured products of the same origin, are promoted as "German-engineered."

In this regard, Johansson (1988) posits that origin information will be useful if it has predictive value and can be used to reduce risk by improving consumers' confidence in their judgements. Thus, for example, if a country's products vary greatly in quality, its image would have little influence. Conversely, country images would be more useful to consumers if the differences among various producing countries are more pronounced, or if the cognitive content about specific products is weak. This last point may help explain cases where low-involvement products draw from their origin country's strengths, such as Lowenbraü beer which is also promoted as "German-engineered" (Papadopoulos et al. 1987).

The relationship between product and country images has been supported by Han (1989), who suggests that country image can be viewed in one of two main ways. Where consumers do not have adequate information about a product, the image of its origin country may be used as a halo for assessing it. Conversely, if a foreign country's products are widely available and well known, consumers may abstract the products' collective qualities into a summary construct which affects their view of the products' common origin.

Domestic vs. Foreign Products

It was believed traditionally that consumers would tend to prefer domestic over foreign products. This view was supported by some of the earlier country-of-origin studies (e.g., Darling and Kraft 1977; Baumgartner and Jolibert 1977). A preference for domestic goods could be explained by reference to patriotism, availability, and the fact that consumers are more familiar with home products and companies and would have to incur higher information acquisition costs for foreign ones (e.g., Linder 1961).

However, the evolution of modern markets challenges these assumptions and more recent country-of-origin studies have shown that a preference for domestic goods is far from universal (Papadopoulos, Heslop, and Bamossy 1990). One explanation for this shift can be found in Scott's (1965) distinction between four types of countries' reactions to each other as a result of their respective images: war, national and collective defense, peaceful coexistence, and active peaceful interchange. Peaceful interchanges occur at various levels, and one of these is purchasing other countries' products (other exchanges range from learning about other nations through education or the media to visiting, studying in, or emigrating to them). So, the growth in international trade, availability of foreign products, communication media, and transportation means, has helped to bring about "active peaceful interchange" at the consumer level.

Another explanation for the decrease in a "de facto" preference for domestic goods can be found in the declining cost of information about foreign products (and their producers and origin countries) which is often similar to, if not lower than, the cost of information about domestic goods. The ever-increasing amount of information about foreign goods and countries today reduces, if not eliminates, the advantage that domestic goods might have enjoyed in earlier times insofar as information acquisition is concerned. In fact, at least two studies suggest that information about foreign goods may be easier to acquire and/or retain than information about domestic products:

1. Regulations requiring producers to specify their products' origin usually apply to foreign goods. Domestic producers do not have to, and most do not, specify that their goods are "Made in [home country]." As a result, even those consumers who deliberately seek home products often have difficulty identifying them (Wall and Heslop 1986).

2. By virtue of their foreign-ness, brand names of foreign products tend to "stick out" more and, as a result, tend to be recognized more easily and be remembered than brand names of domestic goods (Niffenegger, White, and Marmet 1982).

The information acquisition and processing cost can also help to explain the differences in behavior between younger and older consumers. Theory suggests that it is more difficult for older people to change their behavior, since this implies a disinvestment of their existing knowledge capital. By contrast, new knowledge is naturally less constricting for younger people, who tend to be won over more readily by new concepts. Recent country-of-origin studies generally support the contention that domestic product preference tends to be greater among older consumers (e.g., Han 1988).

Lastly, the premises of Veblen's and Duesenberry's social theories of consumption also help to explain the relative decline of a domestic bias as a factor in product choice. The logic of social differentiation by means of the goods owned is particularly applicable when it comes to the acquisition of foreign products. This theory considers difference to be the key element when attempting to explain international exchange in general (Lassudrie-Duchesne 1971). Demand for foreign products is demand for something different. It arises from the needs for progress, novelty, and prestige, and can be satisfied by reference, among other attributes (e.g., brand name, physical properties, performance, price), to a product's foreign origin. While the pursuit of difference would have various shades of meaning depending on whether the need for it is independent (demand for difference alone) or linked to other factors (e.g., cost constraints), the possession of certain foreign goods can provide consumers with opportunities to express their autonomy and social personality.

This line of reasoning must be tempered, of course, by Johansson's (1988) linking of the potency of country images with the extent to which they are noticeably different from one another. In other words, if the products from various countries are similar and offer no opportunities for differentiation to consumers, then the products' national images will play a lesser role. In turn, this suggests the potential significance of a favorable and clear country image. Insofar as exporters are concerned, the clearer and more favorable the image of their country is among consumers, the more likely it is that it will have a positive influence on preferences for their products.

Conclusion

The environment of active peaceful interchange among nations (especially industrialized countries) over the past few decades, recognition of the concept of global interdependence, and the growth in international trade have combined to provide consumers with a plethora of product choices from a variety of countries. Countries can be thought of as corporate entities with multifaceted identities which produce a variety of outputs. Their image becomes part of the total registered image of individual brands.

The relative significance of country image within the image of the brand depends on factors ranging from the consumer's familiarity with the brand's other attributes to the clarity of national images and the differences among them. While an element of loyalty to domestic brands may exist, its importance in consumer choices is being eroded as a result of the lower cost of information acquisition for foreign products and the consumer's need for differentiation. We now turn to consider the image of France and French products among foreign consumers.

THE IMAGE OF FRANCE
AND FRENCH PRODUCTS ABROAD

Image of France and the French People

A hastily conjured-up image of France and the French would comprise deep-rooted clichés; the "typical Frenchman," whether wearing a Basque beret, carrying a French baguette under his arm, or picking grapes to make French wine, has been around the world and his image has been strengthened by promotional programs aiming to attract tourism. Inasmuch as it seems to be commonly acknowledged, one might add that France is seen as an inhospitable country, where the welcome leaves something to be desired and where the people are arrogant and self-important.

Clichés perhaps can be found more commonly with regard to a country's inhabitants than to its products, partly because they are historically rooted and partly because of such factors as intercultural contact and the centrality of people in education and media reports. But even if cognitive elements play a smaller part than emotions in forming images about foreign peoples, "there is no smoke without fire." The ground common to stereotypes often has objective foundation.

For example, Frischer (1989) pinpoints certain elements which are better founded and consequently in a better position to explain the potential effects of national characteristics on the image of French products abroad. She states that "France's tragedy is that it works in such a way that since the post-war years, the illusion of grandeur and French glory throughout the world has been kept up at all costs." This megalomania explains erroneous and costly economic and industrial choices (e.g., the Concorde), which rarely prove to be commercially successful (like the TGV).

Concerns about such characteristics and their potential effect on the image of French technology abroad, and more generally of French exporters, were confirmed by a survey of French press officers carried out by the Agency for Technical, Industrial, and Economic Cooperation (Agence pour la Coopération Technique, Industrielle et Économique–ACTIM 1989). Respondents reported that French exporters are criticized for their reluctance to undertake systematic exports, their lack of commercial aggressiveness and business professionalism, and their failure to transfer technological innovation to marketable production, in countries ranging from Holland and Germany to Canada and Venezuela.

The ACTIM study also confirmed the presence of stereotyped views, such as those mentioned previously, about the French in general. For example, (English) Canadians feel that French people do not speak enough English and are unfriendly, arrogant, and indifferent; Spaniards feel that what best characterizes France is its superiority complex, judging it to be a hostile and irritating country; Mexicans report problems with the French "personality and character"; and reputation goes far, since people from Singapore find the French to be both arrogant and poor at English!

Another study that surveyed views about French exporters among the "American elite" (Boy 1986) found similar results in some areas but also fairly strong feelings of affinity towards the French people in general. Its findings are particularly significant because its sample comprised opinion leaders who can have a broad influence on others. It consisted of 791 experts in technology-intensive fields, including purchasing and R&D directors (from companies listed by Dunn and Bradstreet) and government officials in such departments as energy, transportation, and defense (listed in the U.S. Federal Executive Directory). Because it indicates the strong interest in image issues among the "French elite," which is one of the basic notions that underlie this chapter, it should be noted that the research was sponsored by CEVIPOF, the Centre d' études de la vie politique française contemporaine (Center for Studies in Contemporary French Political Life; the Center operates under the aegis of the Fondation Nationale des Sciences Politiques).

The study assessed familiarity with France using as a gauge "behavior" (speaking French, having visited France) and "cultural affinity" (opinions about France as an ally and about the influence of French culture on the U.S.). Given the sample used, familiarity with France was found to be rather high (one-third of the respondents had some comprehension of the French language and more than half had visited France) and so was the perceived affinity level (40 percent of respondents regard France as a U.S. ally and 32 percent believe that French culture has played a major role in American history). Interestingly, Boy (1986) found a correlation between cultural affinity and the respondents' level of education. For example, only 7 percent of respondents with no college degree were measured as having "strong cultural affinity" with France, while 55 percent of the same respondents were found to have no affinity at all. Conversely, the corresponding proportions for respondents with Bachelor degrees were 28 percent and 30 percent, and for respondents with Doctorates, 33 percent and 27 percent.

The study also attempted to relate perceptions about French exporters, along six dimensions, with the amount of information respondents have about French technology, the number of French people met during the last five years, and cultural affinity. The main findings are shown in Table 1.

As a general rule, the table shows that as the amount of information, the number of French people met, and cultural affinity increase, views about French exporters' reliability, efficiency and competence, and ability to deal with technical problems become more favorable. Nevertheless, Boy (1986) qualifies these findings by pointing out that respondents who have had multiple working relationships generally have less positive attitudes than those who have had only infrequent contact. Boy calls this "disturbing" since "prejudices are not necessarily dissipated, beyond a superficial change in attitude, by knowing French colleagues better."

Further, greater familiarity with and affinity toward the French does not seem to influence the last three criteria in Table 1. It would appear that the more Americans know, see of, and feel close toward the French, the more they believe that the latter are not able to conduct business in English, are incapable or unwilling to adapt to the American market, and are late for meetings!

Despite these reservations, the overall attitudes of foreign people toward France and the French tend to be, at the least, "friendly." Maisonrouge (1986) provides evidence of this by citing the findings of two related studies:

1. A 1982 Gallup Institute poll, carried out for the French American Foundation, showed that 22 percent of Americans had a very friendly attitude, and 56 percent a friendly attitude, toward France; and
2. A 1983 poll by the Chicago Council of Foreign Relations asked respondents to rate various foreign countries on a scale from zero (cold) to 100 (warm); France's score (60) placed it in third position together with West Germany (59), below Canada (74) and the U.K. (68), but above Italy (55) and Japan (53).

Overall, while the studies cited above certainly do not provide enough evidence for definitive conclusions, the consistency both among their findings and between them, and the commonly held stereotypes about France provides useful insights that can help us understand consumer views of French products.

Although this chapter focuses on views about France abroad, it is interesting to note that the views of French consumers themselves about their home country are not very different from those of foreign respondents. Table 2 shows partial findings from a study that compared the images of France and four other industrialized countries among French consumers (Papadopoulos, Heslop, and Graby 1990). As can be seen, in line with the traditional images of the peoples concerned, French respondents gave France the highest score, and the U.S. the lowest, on "refined taste." On the other hand, nations such as Japan and the U.S. were rated higher on several key dimensions. More importantly, the difference between France and those countries that are perceived more favorably on such variables as

Table 1. U.S. Views of French Exporters (percent)
(see note for explanation of figures in this table)

	Reliability	Good control over technical problems	Efficiency and competence	Ability to do business in English	Poor efforts to adapt to US market	Late for meetings
Information						
None	20	12	19	37	38	46
Medium	26	26	27	41	42	60
Great	36	41	40	47	53	66
No. of French people met						
None	12	11	14	30	33	33
1 - 5	38	30	36	50	34	71
6 +	29	29	28	42	36	64
Cultural affinity						
None	23	18	20	36	35	51
Medium	26	23	29	40	46	57
Strong	30	30	29	45	44	58

Source. Boy (1986)
Note. Respondents were presented with statements, such as "They have a good control over technical problems", and asked to state whether this was a good, moderately good, or not good description of their French counterparts. Of the six statements, the first four were presented as "positive" and the last two as "negative" (e.g., "good control" vs. "no effort to adjust"). The figures in this table are the percentages of respondents who saw the first four statements as "good descriptions", and the last two as "not good descriptions".

Table 2. French Views About France and Four Other Countries

Variable	France	Origin countries studied U.S.	Japan	Canada	Sweden
Managing their economy successfully	4.9	5.5	6.1	4.7	4.8
Technologically advanced country	5.6	6.5	6.4	4.9	4.9
Industrious people	3.5	5.2	6.7	4.8	4.6
People with refined taste	5.4	2.7	4.8	3.7	4.2
Trustworthy people	5.1	5.4	5.3	5.6	5.1
Likeable people	3.7	5.1	5.0	5.3	4.6

Notes. The origin with the highest mean score is underlined. Scale from 1 (poor) to 7 (good). Differences among means over 0.2 are significant at 0.05 based on paired comparison T-tests.

"likeability," "trustworthiness," and "industriousness" is not only statistically significant, but also large in absolute terms (and French people rated themselves as the least trustworthy and likeable among the origins evaluated!).

Image of French Products

French products abroad are usually seen as distinctive luxury goods. Table 3 compares the findings of three studies (two American and one French) that asked respondents to identify France's main products. As can be seen, notwithstanding the differences in sampling and method, there is general agreement that France's strengths lie in such areas as wine and fashion, and, in the industrial sector, telecommunications and aerospace. The next few paragraphs provide an overview of the findings from academic studies which aimed to research the country-of-origin effect and included France as an origin country.

Darling and Kraft (1977) assessed the impact of "made in" images among Finnish consumers, using 31 five-point Likert-type statements, for eight countries (Finland, France, the U.K., the U.S., West Germany, Sweden, Japan, and the U.S.S.R.). Their results show that French products were rated relatively highly on creativity and design, but lower on performance, quality, reliability, and degree of adaptation to the Finnish market. Furthermore, of the eight countries studied, France was rated the lowest, with the exception of the U.S.S.R., on market practices such as quality of advertising, after-sales service, and price. As a result, France scored relatively low in a summary question asking consumers to rank-order the eight countries, on a 1-8 scale, in terms of preference for a product of equal

Table 3. Principal French Products

Study 1	Study 2	Study 3
In which sector is France a world leader? (Americans - %)	Which products come to mind when you think of France? (Americans - %)	Name the first four products that come to mind when you think of France (French - %)
Fashion 55	Wine/Liqueur 85	Wine 21
Wine 52	Fashion 81	Cars 19
Culture 28	Food/cheese 57	Fashion 9
Arms 11	Cars 52	Cosmetics 8
Nuclear energy 10	Furniture 24	
Medical research 8	Chemicals 17	
Aerospace 4		
Telecom products 4		

Sources. Study 1 - Gallup Institute (1982), and Study 2 - Research and Forecasts Inc. (1983), both in Maisonrouge (1986); Study 3 - Papadopoulos, Heslop, and Graby (1990).

price, quality, and style. The ranking placed France in fifth place and below the midpoint of the scale:

Finland 1.57; Sweden 3.20; West Germany 3.36; U.K. 4.26; France 5.30; U.S. 5.58; Japan 5.66; U.S.S.R. 7.05.

The opinions of Canadian consumers have been studied by Kaynak and Cavusgil (1983), with regard to the overall quality of products from 11 industrialized and 14 less advanced countries, and specifically concerning four product classes (electronics, food, fashion, household goods). French products were placed in the fourth or fifth position behind the U.S., Canada, the U.K., West Germany, and/or Japan, in all cases except in fashion, where they were ranked third (behind the U.S. and Canada). While the fashion ranking, in particular, suggests a certain degree of ethnocentrism on the part of respondents, generally the findings confirm those of Darling and Kraft (1977) and other studies which place France behind some of its major international competitors. These findings were also confirmed in a later Canadian study (Heslop and Wall 1985), which, interestingly, also found that women gave France an overall higher rating than men largely because they use fashion as a more significant indicator of a country's product strengths.

In Britain, Bannister and Saunders (1978) studied the images of seven countries on five dimensions: reliability, value for money, appearance, availability, and workmanship. As with the Finnish and Canadian studies, the findings placed France behind its major competitors in most areas except appearance (although even on this variable French products were ranked behind West Germany and Japan and equal to Italy). An analysis of respondents by age, social class, and sex showed no significant difference among segments with the exception that consumers of higher social classes tend to have more favorable views about French products on availability and workmanship. Hooley, Shipley, and Krieger's (1988) study in the U.K. was limited to cars and fruits and vegetables, but it also confirms the findings of others. French produce was seen as expensive, and cars were found to have a nondistinct image; only 27 percent of respondents could cite a reason (style) why people would buy a French car, compared to German and Japanese cars which scored high on quality (cited by 62 percent of respondents) and reliability (49 percent) respectively.

Three studies have researched the views of American and Japanese businessmen (Nagashima 1970, 1977) and consumers (Lillis and Narayana 1974). Nagashima's studies were based on the battery of 20 semantic differential scales that were adopted for use in later studies by several researchers. Of the five origins studied in Nagashima's (1970) first study, Japanese respondents found French products to be the most expensive and having an overall image of luxury and craftsmanship. While their ratings on technical aspects were generally low, they were regarded as prestigious products aimed especially at well-to-do women and young people. The views of American respondents were somewhat less favorable, agreeing with their Japanese counterparts on the technical evaluation but also seeing French goods as less expensive and luxurious. Nagashima's (1977) second study found some improvement in the global image of French products but no significant change in their specific characteristics.

Lillis and Narayana (1974) used essentially the same scales as Nagashima but found greater differences between the views of Japanese and U.S. respondents. While both groups see French products as expensive, "craftsy," technically not advanced, and primarily for women, Japanese consumers perceive them as more exclusive, inventive, and aimed at higher social classes, and rated them high on pride of ownership. By contrast, American consumers consider French goods to be imitative and poor in workmanship.

In the U.S., three studies examined the views of purchasing agents about domestic and foreign products: White (1979), Cattin and Jolibert (1979), and Cattin, Jolibert, and Lohnes (1982). The first study assessed industrial products based on 12 attributes, while the other two used Nagashima's 20 semantic differential scales. The findings were generally similar, though certainly not identical, concerning the comparative position of French products. White (1979) found that while some countries were rated clearly higher on certain variables (e.g., West Germany on quality and the U.S. on marketing practices), the remaining origins in each case, including France, were not seen as substantially different from each other. On the other hand, in the other two studies, French products had a distinct image as luxuries, and as less reliable, more imitative goods that offer limited choice; and their global score was the lowest among the five countries studied (U.S., France, West Germany, U.K., Japan).

In addition to the research cited above, which aimed to study the country-of-origin phenomenon as such rather than to describe the image of French products in detail, a handful of studies that have been carried out on behalf of French agencies have provided data that are specifically tailored to assessing the image of French products. The main ones are the annual surveys of 50 professionals in each of six countries (West Germany, Belgium, Switzerland, Italy, the U.K., and the U.S.) that have been carried out since 1981 by the Center of Economic Observation (Centre d' observation économique–COE 1986-1989) of the Chamber of Commerce and Industry in Paris. Unfortunately, findings have been published only for the years 1986-1989 (the U.S. sample was added in 1986).

The survey focuses on about 15 products from five main classes and asks respondents to assess the position of French products on eight criteria in comparison to foreign products overall and to selected countries. A combined examination of all products and countries shows some gradual improvement over time, but, while French products are seen as reasonably strong on certain technical dimensions (e.g., quality, innovativeness), there are perceptions of French weakness in commercial practices (e.g., dynamism, quality of advertising, ability to adapt).

Views in specific countries do not vary substantially from the norm. For example, German respondents rate the quality of French products highly but are less positive on innovation and ease of communication (with French exporters); while Italian respondents are somewhat more positive on the questions of commercial dynamism and ability to adapt, their Swiss and American counterparts are particularly critical of French suppliers on such dimensions as reaction time, commercial dynamism, promotion efforts, and ability to adapt products to market needs. The results by product category suggest that French products are seen as competitive in some areas (e.g., hygiene/beauty, agro-foodstuffs), average on others (e.g., clothes), and weak in such sectors as household equipment.

Generally, therefore, these tracking studies tend to confirm the findings of research that were reported earlier in both the "people" (exporters) and "products" sections. Of particular concern are perceptions among industrial buyers about French suppliers. The prevalence of such concerns was confirmed in a France-Telecom study quoted by Maisonrouge (1986), in which respondents were asked the question, "In which countries can you find the companies which provide the best after-sales service?" France was named by 4 percent of the respondents, below its European competitors (e.g., U.K. 8 percent; Sweden 20 percent; West Germany 27 percent) and at a significant distance from Japan (43 percent) and Canada (39 percent), which received the largest number of mentions. These types of findings have been summarized by Perrin (1979), who decried the French firms' inefficiency in exports by referring to their lack of punctuality, lack of capacity to deliver, and an overall failure to comprehend and account for the decision-making process of the buyer.

IMPROVING THE IMAGE OF FRANCE AND FRENCH PRODUCTS

As can be seen from the preceding overview, France certainly remains a major international competitor with a clear and strong image in several sectors, but its national image has several weaknesses.

Overall, France's large share of world exports and its dominant share in some specific product categories, coupled with objective technical assessments, would suggest that French products can certainly be improved but are not poor as such in terms of quality and their technical elements. In fact, many of the weaknesses that are perceived by foreign buyers and were reviewed earlier are related to the characteristics of French suppliers. In France, these are attributed by many largely to the attitudes of French company owners and managers, which are perceived as being far too insular and ethnocentric ("products which sell in France must be perceived as good and sell well abroad").

Nevertheless, the findings of some of the aforementioned studies (particularly those carried out on behalf of French agencies) have been publicized widely and noticed by government as well as industry leaders, giving rise to calls for steps to improve France's image. This section presents and assesses the initiatives that have been undertaken for this purpose. It is particularly noteworthy that, unlike other countries where similar programs are part of broader undertakings for industry development, in France many of these initiatives deal explicitly with image issues.

Government Programs

The main government department that deals with promoting France's image abroad is the Ministry of Foreign Trade, which supports exports through the External Economic Relations Directorate (Direction des Relations Économiques Extérieures–DREE). DREE operates mainly through the Centers of Economic Expansion which have about 2,400 agents in more than 130 countries. They gather intelligence and act as points of reference and support for French companies (especially small and medium-sized firms) with special emphasis on market research and commercial promotion initiatives.

Within the Ministry of Foreign Trade, the Department of Cultural, Scientific, and Technical Relations deals explicitly with diffusing significant components of France's image abroad. Its main purpose is to ensure the transmission of information about French scientific and technological activities through the Scientific Service and the Service of Embassy Cooperation.

A related agency also found within the Ministry of Foreign Trade is the Intermedia Association, created in 1984. Its task is to promote and distribute multimedia documentaries on cultural, scientific, and technical issues concerning France.

The "Superior Board of Patrons," established within the Ministry of Culture, is intended to encourage and coordinate corporate patronage of cultural projects, many of which are addressed to international audiences and thus form an integral part of France's national image.

France's Ministry of Tourism, like similar agencies in other countries, also contributes to the creation of the country's national image through initiatives aimed at attracting foreign tourists. However, the ministry also recognizes the validity of both traditional clichés and research findings such as those that were reported earlier, which suggest that perceptions of arrogance contribute significantly to France's registered national image. As a result it sponsors campaigns addressed to the French people themselves, urging them to be more hospitable toward foreign visitors who can have a significant impact on the formation of national images.

Para-government Organizations

A large number of public organizations whose general purpose is the support of foreign commerce also participate directly or indirectly in improving and promoting France's image.

The Centre Français du Commerce Extérieur (French Center of Foreign Trade–CFCE), aims to promote exports and, among other activities, publishes and markets economic and commercial documentation. The document series "Origine France," produced in collaboration with sectoral associations and the Ministry of Industry, is of particular interest here since its objective is to inform foreign buyers about the range of product offerings that are available on the part of various industrial and technology-intensive sectors. In addition, since 1984 the CFCE has been creating and distributing high-quality short industrial films which highlight the strengths of French technology.

Within the CFCE, the French Committee of Foreign Economic Events (Comité Français des Manifestations Économiques à l'étranger–CFME) accompanies official engagements at trade fairs with a wide range of promotion materials including a catalogue of participating French companies, press releases, direct mail to decision makers in client organizations and other opinion leaders, and audio-visual presentations.

The Agency for Technical, Industrial, and Economic Cooperation (Agence pour la Coopération Technique, Industrielle et Économique–ACTIM) also plays an important role in promoting French technology abroad. Its activities range from sponsoring trips to France by foreign opinion leaders to providing press information about specific technological sectors and innovations.

A number of other organizations provide advice and technical assistance to French exporters but also participate in promoting France's image. These include, for example, the Chambers of Commerce and Industry (Chambres de Commerce et d'Industrie–CCI) and the Chambers of French Commerce and Industry Abroad (Chambres de Commerce et d'Industrie Française à l'étranger–CCIFE). A similar task is performed by sector-specific associations, such as the Society for Sales Promotion of Agricultural and Food Products (Société pour l'Expansion des Ventes des Produits Agricoles et Alimentaires–SOPEXA).

Radio France Internationale (RFI), whose main objective is to diffuse French culture, also contributes to the promotion of France's image. While RFI is similar in many ways to like organizations elsewhere (e.g., Voice of America or Radio Canada), it is more directly involved in the promotion of French industry. For example, RFI accepts commercial advertising and makes available opportunities for French companies to appear in specific "economic magazines." In particular, the "Challenge" program, conceived in collaboration with the Ministry of Industry, presents "Made in France" sections which focus on high-performance French companies or sectors.

The Association for French Science, Industry, and Technology (AFSIT) aims to enhance know-how, innovation, and quality within industrial and technological sectors and promote their products through advisory boards located in specified countries and cities abroad.

Like AFSIT, the "Comité Colbert" is a private organization that must be mentioned, especially because it represents, as stated by Maisonrouge (1986), the "model of an organization which is truly coordinated, effective and high-performance." Founded in 1954 by Guerlain, the perfumer, the committee aims to represent and develop luxury arts in France and abroad, and its 70 members combined have an exports-to-sales ratio of 70 percent.

The French Image Committee

While some of the aforementioned French organizations can be found in other countries as well, many deal more explicitly with image promotion than do their foreign counterparts. Nonetheless, until 1989 the promotion of France's image was fragmented, since it was carried out by a variety of agencies with various different objectives.

A first attempt at establishing a coordinating body in this area was an agency set up by the Ministry of Industry in 1985 to promote the industrial and technological image of France abroad (Incentive Fund for the Promotion of France's Industrial and Technological Image Abroad–Fonds Incitatif pour la promotion de L'Image Industrielle et Technologique de la France à l'étranger). Its main purpose was to raise industry awareness about the need to communicate more effectively with foreign countries, by bringing into play the skills of both private and public actors in collaborative promotion projects.

However, the Fund was abolished in early 1989 for a variety of reasons. In its place, a project was undertaken at about the same time under the aegis of the Ministry of Foreign Trade, establishing a committee with explicit responsibility for the national image of France abroad.

This project was first presented as part of the Ministry's export development plan in January and implemented in May 1989. The rationale for establishing the committee was that

> ... the promotion and defence of France's image abroad [is] not the object of a single and coherent policy. This task is in fact entrusted to a diverse number of administrative or para-administrative organizations which rarely consult one another. Now, as in the case of a company which has a unique world-wide brand, it is necessary to have a global policy to promote it. (Ministère 1989)

This statement clearly shows the strong government support for the concept with which we opened this chapter–that in foreign markets, the image of a country can contribute significantly to the export penetration of its products, and that promoting this image necessitates the adoption of the view that countries, insofar as export markets are concerned, essentially are corporate entities.

The committee, titled "Comité Image France" (CIF), is chaired by Jacques Maisonrouge, the noted business executive and C.E.O. of IBM France. The approach of the committee places more emphasis on complementing, augmenting, and coordinating existing programs than on launching new initiatives. Its projects begin in France itself, aiming essentially to raise awareness about the importance of France's image and its consequences, primarily among export managers but also other groups, including university students (whose significant role as future managers is explicitly recognized).

While it is still early to assess the effectiveness of its programs, the CIF's objectives cover a broad spectrum which in itself suggests the complexity of the image issue. For example, the committee aims to:

1. work with the CFME to promote greater participation of French firms at foreign trade fairs and to include special sessions about France and French technology at international conventions and symposia;
2. establish CIF sections abroad (the first of these was established in Sweden soon after the committee was convened);
3. coordinate and enhance the distribution of French films, both generally and specifically corporate productions that are presented by French firms at the annual Biarritz festival of company films;
4. expand the use of French materials among French organizations, especially where they may have a broader influence on foreign audiences–including the screening of French films on Air France flights; and
5. establish and distribute a periodic publication that will review French science and technology issues; the intent is to develop an "objective" rather than a propaganda instrument, which would have a greater probability of gaining respectability among its intended audience.

CONCLUSION AND DIRECTIONS FOR ACTION

As can be seen in the previous section, French decision makers are highly sensitized to the issue of France's image abroad, and the French government has formally adopted the view of countries as corporate entities in global markets.

Of course, as suggested in Kapferer's (1988) identity prism, the registered images of a country, its companies, and its products are complex and multifaceted. These images depend both on the image objects' intrinsic characteristics and on perceptions about them, which are influenced by a multitude of additional variables. Further, the images of brands, companies, and countries are interrelated, and so their creation can be influenced both by government action as well as (and more importantly so) by the promotional activities of the brands' producers.

Notwithstanding their complexity, national images evolve over time and, as shown by researchers that have dealt with the images of such countries as Japan and South Korea (e.g., Nagashima 1977; Khera and Wise 1986), change can occur rather rapidly. In this light, French interest in France's national image seems to be well placed. While the nature of relationships between industry and government varies from country to country, it is possible that the example of the CIF, with modifications, can be emulated elsewhere.

The findings of research into the country-of-origin phenomenon suggest that collaborative industry-government programs for the promotion of national image essentially need to address three basic marketing questions:

1. What do we need to convey? At the most basic level, what needs to be marketed is the corporate image of a country. However, this image has many components. Which ones will be emphasized depends on many factors, including the country's real strengths and the existing registered image about them among foreign publics. For example, the fact that cultural affinity was correlated with American views about French products would suggest that image promotion might be more effective if it focused more on affective than cognitive elements. Other research points to the importance of familiarity in image formation, and studies about France show greater dissatisfaction with the practices of exporters than with their products. Respectively, then, providing more product information, and/or improving the image (and actual behavior) of French exporters, could help to improve France's image. Lastly, research findings from specific studies can be used to refine the content of messages aimed at improving national images (e.g., Heslop and Wall, 1985, have shown that men and women base their national stereotypes on different products).

2. To whom do we need to convey it? Country-of-origin research, as well as the concept of brand image itself, clearly show that image promotion must be addressed at several different targets. While programs aimed exclusively at customers may bear fruit over the longer term, simultaneous programs directed at opinion leaders (e.g., the media, foreign governments) and enhancing many of the diverse elements of image (e.g., culture, views about a country's people) would certainly speed up the process.

Concerning specific segments within the population of customers of a country's products, the studies of country-of-origin effects offer many insights that can help to identify suitable targets. For example, it is clear that not only end consumers but also industrial buyers hold stereotyped images of various countries. Further, as pointed out previously, some people (e.g., younger and/or better educated consumers) seek to differentiate themselves through purchases of foreign products, and those who feel greater affinity toward the origin country are more likely to have favorable views about its products. On the other hand, others (especially older consumers) may be less likely to adjust their views and more likely to prefer domestic goods.

3. How do we convey it? National stereotypes about France as well as other countries usually are too firmly rooted to contemplate changing them by confronting them directly. With reference to research findings that were cited earlier, for example, convincing foreign consumers that not every French man or woman is swimming (lazily) in a sea of luxury products cannot be accomplished simply by saying so.

Improving a country's image is akin, albeit on a much larger scale, to attempting to reposition the market image of a well-established brand. It necessitates a coordinated effort that includes all relevant facets, ranging from its intrinsic characteristics and the behavior of the main actors involved, to promotion addressed at current and potential users as well as opinion leaders and other influencers.

A large part of such efforts would have the objective of associating the country's image with its true strengths at the cognitive level. As suggested by Dunn (1976), stressing the origin of a product would be appropriate only if consumers would consider it helpful in recognizing the product's value. Therefore, government, sector-wide, and company-specific image promotion programs need to be coordinated so as to stress those areas where country characteristics can be related to industry strengths. In this way, country characteristics are incorporated into, and enhance, the images of brands–while the images of individual products help to reinforce the national image of their origin country.

REFERENCES

ACTIM (Agence pour la Coopération Technique, Industrielle et Économique; 1989), *Résultats de l' enquête menée auprès de 16 bureaux de presse.* Unpublished report (Paris).

Anderson, W.T. and W.H. Cunningham (1972), "Gauging Foreign Product Promotion." *Journal of Advertising Research,* 12, 1 (February) 29-34.

Bannister, J.P. and J.A. Saunders (1978), "U.K. Consumers' Attitudes Towards Imports: The Measurement of National Stereotype Image." *European Journal of Marketing,* 12, 8, 562- 570.

Baumgartner, Gary and Alain Jolibert (1977), "The Perception of Foreign Products in France." In H.K. Hunt, ed., *Advances in Consumer Research,* vol. V (Ann Arbor, MI: Association for Consumer Research) 603-605.

Bilkey, Warren J. and Erik Nes (1982), "Country-of-Origin Effects on Product Evaluations." *Journal of International Business Studies,* 8(1) (Spring/Summer) 89-99.

Boy, D. (1986), *La Technologie Française vue par les Elites Americaines.* Paris: CEVIPOF–Centre d'études de la vie politique française contemporaine.

Breuil, L. (1972), *Image de marque et notoriete.* Paris: Dunod.

Cattin, Philippe and Alain Jolibert (1979), "An American vs. French Cross-Cultural Study of Five 'made-in' Concepts." *Proceedings, 1979 Educators' Conference* (Chicago, IL: American Marketing Association) 450-454.

Cattin, Philippe, Alain Jolibert, and Colleen Lohnes (1982), "A Cross-Cultural Study of 'Made In' Concepts." *Journal of International Business Studies* (Winter) 131-141.

COE (Centre d' observation économique, 1986-1989), *La Compétitivité des Produits Français de Grande Consommation.* Paris: Chambre de Commerce et d' Industrie.

Cohen, M. and P. Gschwind (1971), *L' image de Marque de l' Entreprise.* Paris: Ed. d' Organisation.

Darling, John R. and Frederic B. Kraft (1977), "A Competitive Profile of Products and Associated Marketing Practices of Selected European and non-European Countries." *European Journal of Marketing,* 11, 7, 519-531.

Dunn, S. Watson (1976), "Effect of National Identity on Multinational Promotional Strategy in Europe." *Journal of Marketing* (October) 50-57.

Frischer, D. (1989), *La France vue d' en face.* Paris: Laffont.

Han, Min C. (1988), "The Role of Consumer Patriotism in the Choice of Domestic versus Foreign Products." *Journal of Advertising Research.* 28(3) (June-July) 25-32.

Han, Min C. (1989), "Country Image: Halo or Summary Construct?" *Journal of Marketing Research,* XXVI: (May) 222-229.

Heslop, Louise A. and Marjorie Wall (1985), "Differences Between Men and Women in the Formation of Country-of-Origin Product Images." In J.C. Chebat (ed.), *Marketing,* Vol. 6 (Montreal: Administrative Sciences Association of Canada–Marketing Division, May) 148-157.

Hooley, G.J., D. Shipley, and N. Krieger (1988), "A Method for Modelling Consumer Perceptions of Country of Origin." *International Marketing Review,* 6, 1 (Autumn) 67-76.

Johansson, Johnny K. (1988), "Determinants and Effects of the Use of 'Made-in' Labels." *International Marketing Review,* 6, 1, 47-58.

Johansson, Johny K., Susan P. Douglas, and Ikujiro Nonaka (1985), "Assessing the Impact of Country of Origin on Product Evaluations: A New Methodological Perspective." *Journal of Marketing Research,* XXII: (November) 388-96.

Kapferer, J.N. (1988), "Publicité: une revolution des méthodes de travail." *Revue Française de Gestion* (September-December) 102- 111.

Kaynak, Erdener and S. Tamer Cavusgil (1983), "Consumer Attitudes Towards Products of Foreign Origin: Do They Vary Across Product Classes?" *International Journal of Advertising,* 2 (April/June) 147-157.

Khera, Inder and Gordon Wise (1986), "U.S. Consumers' Perceptions of South Korean Products." In M.F. Bradley and Nicolas Papadopoulos (eds.), *Workshop on International Marketing Strategy* (Brussels: European Institute for Advanced Studies in Management) 57-67.

Lassudrie-Duchesne, B. (1971), "La Demande de Différence et l' Echange International." *Cahiers de l' ISEA,* Série P, No. 6 (June).

Lillis, Charles M. and Chem L. Narayana (1974), "Analysis of 'Made- in' Product Images–An Exploratory Study." *Journal of International Business Studies* (Spring) 119-127.

Linder, S.B. (1961), *An Essay on Trade and Transformation.* New York: John Wiley & Sons.

Maisonrouge, J. (1986), *L' image de la France aux Etats-Unis et un plan d' action pour l' améliorer.* Unpublished report, Paris.

Malliaris, Petros (1980), *Xenophilic Consumer Behaviour: Theoretical Dimensions and Measurement.* PhD Dissertation, University of Oklahoma.

Marion, G. (1989), *Les images de l'entreprise.* Paris: Ed. d' Organisation.

Marion, G. and D. Michel (1986), *Marketing Mode d' emploi.* Paris: Ed. d' Organisation.

Ministère du Commerce Extérieur (1989), décret no. 89-344, Comité pour l'image de la France à l'étranger (29 mai).

Nagashima, Akira (1970), "A Comparison of Japanese and U.S. Attitudes Towards Foreign Products." *Journal of Marketing,* 34 (January) 68-74.

Nagashima, Akira (1977), "A Comparative 'Made In' Product Image Survey Among Japanese Businessmen." *Journal of Marketing,* 41 (July) 95-100.

Niffenegger, P., J. White, and G. Marmet (1982), "How European Retailers View American Imported Products: Results of a Product Image Survey." *Journal of the Academy of Marketing Science* (Summer) 281-291.

Papadopoulos, Nicolas, Louise A. Heslop, and Gary J. Bamossy (1990), "A Comparative Analysis of Domestic Versus Imported Products." *International Journal of Research in Marketing,* 7, 4 (December).

Papadopoulos, Nicolas, Louise A. Heslop, and Françoise Graby (1990), "Relative Competitiveness of International Products: A French Consumers' View." *Unpublished paper,* Carleton University, Ottawa, Canada.

Papadopoulos, Nicolas, Louise A. Heslop, Françoise Graby, and George Avlonitis (1987), "Does Country-of-Origin Matter? Some Findings from a Cross-Cultural Study of Consumer Views About Foreign Products." *Working Paper #87-104, Marketing Science Institute,* Cambridge, MA.

Perrin, M. (1979), *Mieux exporter les produits industriels: l'industrie européenne juge les enterprises françaises*. Paris: CFCE Ed.

Reierson, Curtis C. (1966), "Are Foreign Products Seen as National Stereotypes?" *Journal of Retailing*, 42, 3 (Fall), 33-40.

Scott, William A. (1965), "Psychological and Social Correlates of International Images." In Herbert C. Kelman (ed.), *International Behavior.* New York: Holt, Rinehart and Winston, 70-103.

Seaton, Bruce and Robert H. Vogel (1981), "International Dimensions and Price as Factors in Consumer Perceptions of Autos." Paper presented at the *Conference of The Academy of International Business* (Montreal, October).

Serraf, G. (1964), "Réflexions sur l'image de marque," *Revue Française du Marketing,* trim. 2, no. 11.

Wall, Marjorie and Louise A. Heslop (1986), "Consumer Attitudes toward Canadian-made versus Imported Products." *Journal of the Academy of Marketing Science,* 14(2): 27-36.

White, Phillip D. (1979), "Attitudes of U.S. Purchasing Managers Toward Industrial Products Manufactured In Selected Western European Nations." *Journal of International Business Studies,* 20 (Spring-Summer) 81-90.

Chapter 12

International Product Competitiveness and the "Made in" Concept

Gabriele Morello

INTRODUCTION

This chapter focuses on integrating the images of countries and their products with the competitive positions of these products, and examining how these elements may influence the communication strategies of nations and individual companies wanting to promote their products abroad.[1]

The study on which the chapter is based was undertaken on behalf of the Italian Institute of Foreign Trade (ICE) and concerned the image of Italian products in the Netherlands.[2] However, the actual context and findings of this specific study are presented here for illustrative purposes only. The research provided an opportunity to apply an interesting practical approach which differs from most studies in the country-of-origin area,

---

1. This chapter was invited and rewritten especially for this book based on a paper by Morello and Boerema (1989) which won the Best Paper Award at the Seminar "How to Increase the Efficiency of Marketing Communication in a Changing Europe" (European Society for Opinion and Marketing Research, Turin, Italy, October 1989).

2. The study on which this chapter is based was commissioned by the Istituto Italiano per il Commercio Estero (ICE). It was carried out by the Netherlands Institute for Public Opinion and Marketing Research (NIPO) and the Free University, under the direction of Dr. Elzo Boerema (former research director of NIPO), and by the author. The author wishes to thank Dr. Cesare Gentile, Italy's Trade Commissioner in Holland at the time of the study; Dr. Boerma, co-author of the original paper; Dr. Papadopoulos, who took an active part in the revision; and the following Free University students who carried out the sector studies: G. van Bentum, M. Dijk, E. van El, A. Holtzappel, P. Kaag, W. Neerincx, J. van Rekon, D. Zwaan, and J. Zweegman.

in that it combines quantitative and qualitative data and examines country images within the SWOT framework and Porter's models of competitive analysis. The approach used can be applied to any combination of origin and destination countries, and the overall findings can be useful to international marketing managers and market researchers with more general interests in product and country image issues.

Italy presents an interesting case for image-related studies. It has a long history of exporting and a strong positive image in various sectors, and its position in the international arena has improved noticeably in recent years. For example, its share in world exports grew from 4.3 percent to 4.7 percent between 1982 and 1988 (IMF 1989), and it registered the second-highest rate of growth between 1980 and 1986 among OECD members, behind Japan, in outward foreign investment (from $750 million to $2.7 billion, respectively; *Fortune* 1988). Coupled with growing international competition, these developments have prompted Italian business and the government to take measures to protect, consolidate, and further enhance the position of Italian products abroad. It was this thinking that led ICE to commission the present study, and that provided a unique opportunity to research product images in the practical context of generating input for a national communication program aimed at promoting them.

The study combined economic indicators and professional buyers' assessments of competitiveness for eight product sectors with findings from image surveys concerning Italian products in Holland. The chapter deals with such questions as: What is the role of the "Made in" label? Would a product's competitive image be helped or hindered if its origin was known to or noticed by prospective buyers? In other words, does it matter if cameras come from Japan or shoes from Italy? And what can, or should, governments and business do about it?

Discussion is divided into five main sections. The first examines the main principles of the country-of-origin concept; the next two present the study's research framework and main findings; and the last two examine managerial implications and the development and implementation of related communication strategies in practice.

THE "MADE IN" CONCEPT

A Hundred Years of "Made in"

In an earlier paper (Morello 1984), I refered to the significance of "made in" labels after the First World War, indicating how the "Made in

Germany" label was imposed by the victors as a means of helping consumers identify and *avoid* products of the former enemy. In that instance, Germany's reputation for good engineering in fact made consumers use the label to identify and *purchase* German products. The "made in" theme, however, has a longer history. Archival research may identify earlier manifestations, but, as one example, Great Britain's Merchandise Marks Act of August 23, 1887, made it a punishable offense to apply "any false trade description to goods." This was specified, among other things, as "any description, statement, or other indication, direct or indirect . . . as to place a country in which any goods were made or produced."

The act was essentially a protectionist measure. Its main objective was to make it illegal to sell an article made abroad, and to prevent the use of words or marks that might lead the purchaser to believe that it was made in Great Britain. Interestingly, in that time the Germans were prime culprits in using fraudulent markings (e.g., "German cutlery adorned with suggestions of the best Sheffields marks"; Williams 1986). Whether used by governments as a measure of market protection, or by companies to enhance their products' image, the "made in" label itself has been in use for a long time.

Importance and Use of Country Images

The relative importance of the designation of origin as a selling point is discussed in other chapters of this book.[3] For this discussion, suffice to say that in contemporary markets, the use of origin identifiers (whether on labels or in brand names, advertising, etc.) has established itself as a distinct strategy that is employed widely by companies of various nationalities in domestic and international marketing.

Communication strategies, in particular, have used and are using the origin connection extensively to enhance product appeal. The common element in using "made in" appeals is stereotyping: British moustaches are white and patrician while Italian ones are thinner, carefully manicured, and black–and while Britons wear bowler hats and hold perfectly rolled umbrellas, Italians sling camel hair coats casually over their shoulders and wear fashionable shoes.

Why do people use these and many other stereotypes? The answer is simple: because they serve as symbols for instant communication. They immediately trigger all kinds of associations, and, insofar as marketers are concerned, they can enrich (or harm) a brand's perceived image. Given the

---

3. Ed. note: See, for example, the chapters by Heslop and Papadopoulos; Johansson; and Liefeld.

increasing number of branded goods in the market and the growing difficulty for consumers of evaluating their quality "objectively," the made-in label is one means that enables producers to position their brands simply, strongly, and quickly.

The country-of-origin notion fits within perceptual, attitudinal, and belief constructs, which are commonly accepted as determinants of choice and buying behavior. In fact, once the influence of the country-of-origin on consumer feelings toward goods and services is accepted, it may well be considered one of the specific elements which, together with other intangible features, make up the very concept of "product" as marketing understands it (that is, as more than just a collection of tangible ingredients or parts).

In addition to leading to extensive use of origin images in business marketing, this acceptance has led to considerable research into the country-of-origin phenomenon among academic researchers. Some of the main findings from this research have been summarized by Bamossy and Papadopoulos (1987) as follows:

- consumers hold stereotyped images of both foreign countries and their own;
- these images are used as information cues in judging products of various origins;
- the relative importance of origin cues differs according to buying situations and product categories;
- buyers are not always aware of products' true origins but are able to express preferences for production locations;
- "made in" images can act as a halo (e.g., evaluation of one product or sector of activity in a given country may influence the judgement of other products or sectors from that country);
- the extent of consumer preference for domestic vs. foreign goods varies by origin and destination country; and
- like price, brand name, and other intangible extrinsic attributes, country-of-origin may serve as a surrogate of product quality (especially when other information is lacking and/or in the case of complex market conditions).

These findings, coupled with the growing complexity of products and the difficulties in establishing unique selling propositions (USPs) as a result of product standardization, are likely to result in greater use of country-of-origin cues by marketers in the future.

In fact, the growth of multinational production presents a wider and more subtle set of possibilities for using origin cues in marketing strategy. Furthermore, the range of actors using origin information is likely to expand as national governments (and, increasingly, industry associations) around the world undertake origin-related campaigns to protect their home markets ("buy domestic") and/or to enhance their exports and their companies' competitiveness abroad.

"Made in" and the Frontierless Market in Europe

Of particular interest to this study, and to marketers and researchers with interests in European (and global) integration, is the potential impact of "Europe '92" on country images and their role in influencing consumer choices. Will integration diminish the usefulness of "made in" approaches? Will the age of "Made in Germany" soon be a thing of the past?

Attitudes are long-lasting and national images can be "sticky."[4] National or regional stereotypes are likely to continue to exist in the minds of consumers, and therefore to play an important role in influencing their preferences. Paradoxically, the more European Community (EC) trade liberalization policies come into effect, the more likely it is that the origin of products may need to be stressed for effective communication strategies.

This apparent paradox can be explained by reference to the basic tenets of consumer information processing and the corporate need for brand differentiation. Consumers will always need symbols to help them sort out the complexities of daily life. The beliefs and impressions that make up the images of nations are long-lasting and strong, and often serve as useful symbols for differentiating among products. Even globally-oriented companies are still perceptually bound to their origins in spite of their efforts to convince consumers otherwise (e.g., Coca Cola is American, Nestlé is Swiss, and Toyota is Japanese). In fact, "global" or regional images can be thought of as variants of national ones that may appeal to special target markets (e.g., "Europroducts" appealing to eclectic "Euroconsumers"; Papadopoulos 1982).

On the other hand, in an era of product standardization and multinational production, business marketers also need to use symbols in order to establish differentiated positions in highly competitive markets. Whether a company chooses to use national, regional, or global identifiers, references

---

4. Ed. note: See also the discussion in the chapter by Graby, who points out that country images can be more "rigid" than, for example, brand images.

to its "origin" can serve as a distinct symbol that can enhance its position in consumers' minds.

Thus a crucial managerial task for competing effectively in the 1990s involves developing valid and reliable insights into target markets' perceptions of the origin of goods and services from multiple sources. Exporting countries and companies will need to know more about their strong and weak points in various markets in order to assess their opportunities and threats and to develop their own marketing strategies.

"Made in Italy"

While the image of Italy has been assessed as part of some country-of-origin studies by academic researchers, it was not of central interest to those studies and was discussed only while addressing related, but different, issues. Furthermore, most of the comparable research is concentrated on the consumer behavior aspects of the made-in phenomenon.

As previously mentioned, this chapter is based on a study commissioned by ICE but its approach and findings can be useful in a variety of country contexts. The Institute's belief in the influence of national image on international competitiveness provided the opportunity to add another dimension to the study of the problem: combining the psychological aspects of consumer behavior with the economic dimensions of competitiveness. The Italian strategic objective is to design international communication strategies systematically based on factual research in selected markets. As international competitive pressures grow, other governments are likely to also begin considering systematic approaches to promoting their image in their principal foreign markets.

The study centered on developing an analytical understanding of how Italy as a country, the Italian people, and Italian products are perceived by different people in relation to their competitors. The study was guided by the following three questions:

1. To what extent is the origin of Italian products–the "Made in Italy" label–relevant in the decision-making process of consumers and professional buyers?
2. Under what circumstances does the "Made in Italy" label strengthen or weaken brand perceptions?
3. Could some guidelines be provided concerning the international branding and promotion of Italian products?

RESEARCH FRAMEWORK

To help structure the study, a model was developed with the purpose of combining the competitive image and country image aspects of the problem and providing guidance about the different parts that should be included in the research.

The model, shown in Figure 1, is very simple but also effective in outlining the dimensions of the issue and showing the necessary frame-

Figure 1. Competitive Image and Country Image Inputs to Communication Strategy

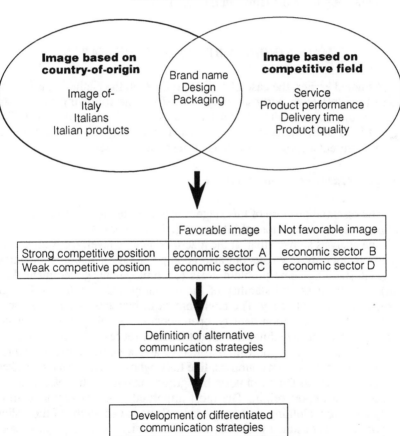

work for the development of a differentiated communication strategy for Italian products.

The research was focused on the upper two circles of the model and consisted of three sequential stages:

1. A macro-economic description of Dutch society;
2. An assessment of the competitiveness of Italian products in the Netherlands; and
3. An assessment of the image of Italy, Italian people and Italian products in the Netherlands.

The rationale for this research framework and the approach used in implementing it are explained in Exhibit 1.

MAIN FINDINGS BY STAGE OF RESEARCH

As noted earlier, the case of Italian products in the Netherlands is used here for illustrative purposes only. Therefore, the following paragraphs outline the main results and present samples of the data obtained. The intent is to show the types of inputs used in strategy development rather than to present a complete analysis of the entire data set.

Stage I. Macro-economic Analysis

The essential purpose of this stage was to outline the "terrain" in terms of business-related factors of interest to Italian exporters.

The analysis showed that, at the macro-economic level, the Netherlands presents not only few risks but also good potential for Italian companies. Notwithstanding some problem areas (unemployment, government deficit), the openness and stability of the economy makes entry by foreign producers relatively easy. The environment in fact acts as a motivator to imports: high population density, open economy, stable political climate, strong consumer spending, no import barriers (at least for companies in other EC countries), good infrastructure, and a strong currency which attracts companies from countries, like Italy, whose currencies are weaker.

Italy's share in Dutch imports has grown, making it the Netherlands' sixth largest import origin. The most important products imported from Italy are shoes, clothing, and cars. This reflects the strengths of the Italian export mix in consumer products, where the design element plays a major role.

Exhibit 1. The Research Framework

Stage I. Macro-economic Analysis

Purpose. To provide insights into the risks and potentials involved in doing business in the Netherlands; to establish a frame of reference for interpreting Dutch thinking and behavior.

Methodology. 1. Desk research on trends in the economy (trade, domestic production and consumption), culture (leisure activities, religion, way of life, consumption patterns), population demographics, business (main production sectors, employment), finance (inflation, budgets), and regulation (trade barriers, role of government, legislation). Examples of sources used: Central Bureau of Statistics, existing research studies, international press, Chambers of Commerce, and Dutch Ministries of Economic and Domestic Affairs.

    2. Ten expert interviews.

Stage II. Competitive Position of Italian Products

Purpose. 1. To assess the economic situation and competitive position of Italy and Italian products in eight sectors (four consumer, four industrial) which (a) are representative of typical Italian exports to the Netherlands in the past five years, and (b) represent related clusters of economic activity in Italy.

    2. To provide information that, when related to the image findings, would make it possible to differentiate among needed communication approaches in the strategy development stage.

Methodology. 1. Desk research on trends in domestic consumption (domestic production plus imports less exports) in the eight sectors (last five years). Same sources as Stage I.

    2. Pilot interviews to determine relevant buying criteria in each sector.

    3. In-depth personal interviews with 15 professional buyers and trade experts in each sector (total 120). Semi-structured questionnaires used to obtain (a) information for carrying out SWOT and competitive forces' analyses (Kotler 1988; Porter 1980), and (b) input for calculating weighted competitiveness scores for selected competing countries by sector.

Stage III. 'Made-in' Image

Purpose. To determine the image of Italy, Italians, and Italian products, and its influence on brand perception and consumer choice.

Methodology. 1. Review of previous "made in" studies.

    2. Pilot interviews to determine suitable semantic differential and Likert-type statements for inclusion.

    3. Structured personal interviews, based mostly on scaled questions and aiming to gather information on (a) cognitive, affective, and conative aspects of attitude with regards to Italy's image; and, (b) associative networks which influence future information processing and behavior. Three samples were used:

    a. 1,000 consumers (random representative sampling of Dutch adults, conducted by NIPO, Holland's largest research bureau);

    b. 200 business professionals (disproportionate stratified sample of higher level managers, favoring larger companies, drawn from the NIPO monitor of 20,000 executives. The original data is collected by the Dutch Institute of Statistics from a list of companies provided by the Dutch Chamber of Commerce); and,

    c. 50 students (convenience sample included as a point of reference viz. future business people; please see text).

On the other hand, cultural differences between Italy and the Netherlands are substantial and include the role of women, the functioning of the family, the way people do business, language, and the role of religion (especially the pervasive influence of Calvinism on Dutch society), etc. Dawson and Bamossy (1990) have discussed these and other elements of Dutch culture in the context of consumption behavior.

As will be discussed, Italian-Dutch cultural dissimilarities are many and are noticed by opinion leaders and buyers, suggesting the need for significant adjustments to marketing strategy and adaptation to the Dutch ways of doing business.

Stage II. Competitiveness

For practical reasons (time and money), the study was limited to eight sectors. Four consumer sectors (shoes, women's fashion, pasta, and office furniture) and four industrial sectors (packaging machinery, medical equipment, food processing machinery, and machinery for the graphics industry) were selected on the basis of the two criteria shown in Exhibit 1.

With the help of the interviews, an inventory of the most important external and internal influences on the position of Italian products could be made. Two techniques were considered very helpful for framing this stage: SWOT analysis and Porter's model for analyzing competitive forces (Kotler 1988; Porter 1980). The first was used to outline the strengths and weaknesses of "Made in Italy" and opportunities and threats from the external environment. The second provided the framework for describing competitive forces (bargaining power of buyers and sellers, threats from substitute products and new entries, entry and exit barriers, rivalry among existing competitors).

Exhibit 2 shows the most important findings from the first part of this stage. The principal strength of Italy is in design, which is an important factor in the buying process of many consumer products. The major threat is "me-too-ism," the imitation of Italian styles by other foreign businesses. Important opportunities are presented by the prominent and continuous showcasing of Italian products by intermediaries (from trade fairs to store windows and advertising) and strong and noticeable product differentiation. On the other hand, Italy does not have a strong image as an industrial goods producer. Nonetheless, better targeting and product adaptation to Dutch market needs could open the way for improved opportunities.

Next, Stage II involved the development of a comparative competitiveness index. This involved four main steps:

1. A list of buying criteria was generated from the pilot interviews.
2. In the in-depth interviews that followed, 15 respondents in each sector were asked to rate the buying variables on a 1-5 importance scale (5 = most important).
3. Respondents were also asked to rate a short list of some of Italy's main competitors for each variable and each sector (where relevant) on a 0-200 scale. In addition to Italy, the countries included were the

Netherlands, Germany (West, before unification), France, the U.K., the U.S., and Japan.
4. The mean ratings of importance from each variable (step 2.) were multiplied by each country's mean rating (step 3.) and the weighted scores were added into total country scores.

Overall, based on this method, Italy was found to hold quite strong positions in the consumer sectors. Among the seven countries that were assessed by professional buyers, it was placed first in shoes, first in pasta (of course!), third in office furniture, and fourth in women's fashion. On the other hand, its position in industrial sectors (where the higher complexity of decision making is indicated by the larger number of purchase criteria used) is weaker: fourth in packaging machinery, fifth in machines for the food processing and graphics industries, and seventh (last) in medical equipment.

Exhibit 2. SWOT and Competitive Forces' Analysis

I. INDUSTRIAL PRODUCTS

External factors		Internal factors	
Opportunities	Threats	Strengths	Weaknesses
- Smart design appreciated	- Cost pressures require economies of scale	- Price	- Lack of industrial image
- Italian skills not widely known		- Design	- Lack of punctuality
- Cost leadership in simpler products	- Perception of outdated production facilities	- User-friendly	- Communication difficulty (language)
- Niche marketing in complex products		- Italian people very friendly	
- Differentiated marketing approach effective	- Currency instability		- Not enough (good) agents in Holland
- Exporter interest in Holland	- Business customs		
- Strengths in relation to France			

II. CONSUMER PRODUCTS

External factors		Internal factors	
Opportunities	Threats	Strengths	Weaknesses
- Smart design	- Me-too-ism from SE Asia	- Design	- Lack of punctuality
- No entry barriers		- Assortment (breadth/depth)	- Poor adaptation to Dutch conditions
- Large market	- Saturated market	- Brand awareness	
- Supply & demand fragmentation	- Concentration of power in retail	- Customized, uniquely designed, hand-crafted products	
- Product differentiation			
- Showcasing	- Strength of Germany		
- Improvement of distribution approach	- Difficult to defend 'Made in'		

As an illustration of the method used, Tables 1 and 2 show the results obtained for one consumer and one industrial sector, respectively (shoes and packaging machinery). The approach is useful in that it identifies relevant criteria and their importance, the mean score of each country for each variable (not shown in the tables), the weighted score for each variable and overall, and an index of the extent to which the products of each competing country appear to meet buyer expectations.

As shown in Table 1, Italy's total score in the shoe sector (6,849) is considerably higher than the second-highest country's (the Netherlands, 6,054) and translates to a "buyer satisfaction" index of 80 percent (vs. the Netherlands, 70 percent). Considering the weighted scores by variable, this is mainly due to the strong competitive position of Italian shoe manufacturers in product reliability and appearance/design. By contrast, Italy's total score in packaging machinery (9,191; Table 2) is considerably lower than the industry leader's (Germany, 10,707) and so is its index (63 percent vs. 73 percent).

It is interesting to note the last position of the "origin" variable, in terms of relative importance, in both the consumer and industrial products' lists of purchase criteria (although, in the consumer sectors, the mean importance score is considerably above the midpoint of the 1-5 scale). One likely explanation for this is that the professional buyers who took part in this stage of the research, like consumers, tend to underemphasize "non-rational" elements in buying decisions. Further, it seems reasonable for buyers to state that a product's origin would be less important than, say, the "noise" level of a packaging machine or the appearance and reliability of a pair of shoes (no one would want a poorly-designed pair that falls apart quickly, regardless of where it was made!).

This, however, does not in any way suggest that origin is not taken into account in decision making. For example, considering the mean scores for each variable *before* weighting (not shown in the tables), Italian-made shoes received the fourth-highest absolute score on "origin" (165, after appearance/design, product range, and reliability, which received, respectively, scores of 175, 173, and 168). This score is higher, for example, than the score for product quality (160), and considerably higher than price (150).

Similarly, in the case of packaging machinery, "origin" was the fourth-highest absolute score (162) received by Germany (the market leader), preceded only by the scores for "durability" (168), "supplier reliability" (166), and "brand name" (165), and above or about equal to the scores for "price" (156) and "product quality" (160). Clearly, buyers distinguish among origins and are fully aware of the meaning of a country's designa-

Table 1. Sample Competitive Position - Consumer Sector: Shoes

Buying Criteria	Relative Importance	Weighted Scores Italy	Holland	France	U.K.	West Germany	U.S.
Product reliability	5.0	840	875	585	625	725	250
Appearance/design	4.8	840	600	562	475	624	422
Supplier reliability	4.7	719	785	470	588	682	296
Supplier services	4.7	696	691	503	494	696	235
Product quality	4.6	736	805	612	598	727	690
Delivery time	4.5	743	563	405	441	531	225
Price	3.9	585	390	390	339	339	195
Responsiveness	3.8	505	380	304	323	418	190
Product range	3.5	607	555	274	326	348	233
Brand origin	3.5	578	410	291	308	350	439
Total weighted score	-	6,849	6,054	4,396	4,517	5,440	3,438
Rank	-	1	2	5	4	3	6
Index to max. score	(8,600)	80	70	51	53	63	40

Notes. The weighted scores are the product of [relative importance of each variable X each country's mean score for it]. For example, first cell for Italy: 5.0 X 168 (not shown) = 840. "Total weighted score" is the sum of weighted scores of all variables. "Maximum score" is the sum of [relative importance X 200] for all variables (i.e., the highest possible score a country could achieve if it were rated "perfect" on the 0-200 scale on each variable, given each variable's relative importance). The "Index" is each country's total weighted score as a proportion of the maximum (e.g., Italy 6,849 : 8,600 = 80).

Table 2. Sample Competitive Position - Industrial Sector: Packaging Machinery

Buying Criteria	Relative Importance	Weighted Scores Italy	Holland	France	U.K.	West Germany	U.S.	Japan
Product reliability	4.7	630	667	616	700	663	555	545
Product quality	4.7	606	705	536	597	752	653	569
Supplier service	4.6	492	695	478	566	704	543	534
Punctuality	4.6	658	593	593	594	630	547	676
Supplier reliability	4.5	527	725	432	621	747	603	626
Noise	4.4	598	563	568	524	598	462	554
Training/documentation	4.4	466	616	862	541	651	532	510
Supplier know-how	4.4	378	422	378	422	444	422	444
Product durability	4.3	546	619	486	589	722	628	542
Supplier cooperation	4.2	550	634	466	542	626	496	424
Price	3.8	605	596	550	626	592	496	487
Delivery time	3.7	418	503	359	440	470	370	440
Size	3.7	518	529	470	496	507	366	500
Delivery reliability	3.5	476	452	448	473	469	438	469
Availability	3.5	375	501	382	483	525	312	399
Brand name	3.0	330	384	282	366	495	357	393
Appearance/design	3.0	438	420	384	378	426	291	381
Line assortment	2.7	386	340	299	332	394	400	381
Brand origin	1.8	194	274	180	248	292	221	248
Total weighted score	-	9,191	10,238	8,769	9,538	10,707	8,692	9,122
Rank	-	4	2	6	3	1	7	5
Index to max. score	(14,700)	63	70	60	65	73	59	62

Notes. Same as Table 1. Example: first cell for Italy, mean score (134, not shown) X importance (4.7) = weighted product reliability score (630); the Index for Italy is 63, obtained by dividing its total weighted score (9,191) by the maximum score (14,700).

tion as the producer of various consumer or industrial products. The high origin scores of Italy and Germany on these two sectors support the view that country image may act as a halo, whether summarizing views about individual product attributes or influencing perceptions about them.

Stage III. Image and Attitudes

The third stage of the study used mainly semantic differential and Likert-type scales, selected by reference to past research (see Bamossy and Papadopoulos 1987) and pilot-tested before the actual fieldwork, and also requested respondents to state words, images, companies, products, and brands they associate with the same seven countries as in Stage II. The main objective was to assess attitudes (overall and in terms of their cognitive, affective, and conative components) towards Italy, Italians, and their products.

Overall attitudes are the result of interactions between cognitive, affective, and conative elements. Associative networks (what do people think of when they hear, for example, the words "Italy" or "Italians") provide insights into prevailing attitudes and can help in determining what information will be accepted or rejected and what behaviors might be expected to occur. Exhibit 3 shows examples of words, terms, and names that were mentioned most frequently by respondents in relation to each of the object countries. As can be seen in Exhibit 3, stereotyped views prevail for Italy as much as for the other countries studied. Simply put, Italy is not associated with chewing gum or saké any more than the U.S. is associated with espresso coffee or Japan with pizza. Stereotypical views cover the entire range of objects from products to geographic characteristics and religion.

Naturally, these views do not necessarily reflect contemporary reality but are, rather, rooted in the traditional understandings which characterize various countries and peoples. Italy has changed over time as much as other countries. It could be argued that today, hot dogs made in Italy may taste as good as pizza made in the U.S. An examination of the findings concerning the components of attitude provides some explanation for the differences between perceived and objective characteristics of countries.

Cognitive Elements (Knowledge)

Stereotyped beliefs prevail mainly among people who have partial knowledge about the object being judged. In this study, consumers reported knowing about Italy mainly from holidays, media reports, and word

Exhibit 3. Sensorial, Emotional, and Rational Associative Networks

Associations	Italy	Holland	France	U.K.	W. Germany	U.S.A.	Japan
Sensorial	Pizza Pasta Parmesan Espresso Fashion Art, Design Ferrari Culture Music Wine Ice cream Shoes	Wooden shoes Cheese Windmills Flower bulbs Diamonds Eggs Potatoes Coffee	Fashion Perfume Wine Haute couture Baguettes Cognac Garlic Champagne Cheese Cars	Rain Tea Sandwiches Bowler hats 3-piece suits Whiskey Bacon & eggs	Beer Bratwurst Sauerkraut Cars	Corn-on-cob Hamburgers Coca-Cola Large cars Dollar Peanuts Donuts Popcorn Hot dogs Chewing gum Ketchup T-Bone steak	Raw fish Kimono Rice Sake Cars Audio/video Cameras Copiers
Emotional	Holidays Nice weather Nice food Beautiful Not punctual Friendly Mafia Sicily Corruption Political instability The Pope	Amsterdam Merchants Discontented Calvinistic Narrow-minded Grocers Sober/down- to-earth Common	Jean-Paul Belmond Holidays Riviera Chauvinistic Paris Arrogant Elegant	Correct Reliable Traditions Royal family Tasteless London Thatcher Arrogant Old fashioned Decay, Chaotic Civil servants Gentlemen Rolls Royce	OktoberFest Berlin Wall Reliable Politics Not friendly	Reagan Naive Power Conservative Hollywood New York Statue of Liberty Not fashionable	Busy people Friendly Hard working Ruthless Inventive Reliable Overcrowded Not commun- icative
Rational	Language Long history Cheap	Solid Functional Traffic jams Bridges High taxes Multinationals	Concorde TGV Famous designers	Labour unions Coal mines Backward technology Furniture Cutlery	Grundig Perfection Solidness Quality Volkswagen Heavy industry Autobahn Ruhr area	Movie stars Democratic Gen. Motors McDonald's Silicon Valley	Industry Econ. power Precision

of mouth. Business executives gave similar responses, but some also mentioned business contacts in Italy itself and/or with Dutch colleagues who have business interests there. Generally, the more respondents knew about Italy, the closer their views were to reality. In fact, several business respondents made references to the biased views that tend to exist in the absence of information and/or that are transmitted by impersonal means, and suggested that the best way to learn about a country (in this case, Italy) is by dealing with colleagues from, and/or visiting, there.

Affective Elements (Likes/Dislikes)

A predominant view of Italy still relates it to La Dolce Vita, "the sweet life," an association that has remained strong since the 1950s' motion picture by the same title (and one which is as different from reality today as it was then). Italy is viewed as a beautiful, artistic country with high cultural standards, but also as one that is plagued by strikes and a high crime rate–whereas such countries as Japan, the U.S., and Germany are viewed as more pragmatic and economically successful. And Italians are viewed as friendly, artistic, and elegant, but less punctual than others and as not particularly good at business–whereas Japanese and Americans are viewed as more hard-working and entrepreneurial, and the Germans as the most "solid" and thorough, but not friendly, people. The U.K. is viewed mostly as a weak, old-fashioned, and outdated country, and, among the countries studied, France was seen as the most similar to Italy. Views about Italy are significantly less uniform and more differentiated, as well as closer to reality, on the part of those who know more about the country, whether through personal visits, business relationships, or other means.

Conative Elements (Behavioral Predisposition)

Given a choice of origins for product purchases, respondents placed the countries studied in this order, from most to least preferred: the Netherlands, Germany, Japan, the U.K., the U.S., Italy, and France. This preference for domestic goods is also portrayed in Tables 1 and 2 above, where, although the professional buyers acknowledge the superiority of Italian shoes and German printing machinery, they rank Holland as second to the market leader in each case. This finding is confirmed by reference to another study which also researched the views of Dutch consumers (Bamossy et al. 1988). In that study, U.S., Canadian, British, Greek, and Hungarian respondents ranked their domestic products in second place (or lower) behind Japanese goods (and, in some cases, below products from other origins as well)–while German, French, and Dutch respondents ranked their domestic products first (in the case of the Netherlands, tied with Japan).

COMMUNICATION STRATEGY

Previous Studies on "Made in" Communication

The main objective of this study was to promote the Italian position in the Netherlands, by means of a communication strategy based on the competitiveness of economic sectors that are of particular interest to Italian industry.

As noted earlier, the country-of-origin literature has focused on analyses from the consumer behavior perspective and offers hardly any information on related communication strategies, especially strategies that go beyond advertising. The literature essentially refers to four main approaches to advertising in relation to the made-in theme (Morello 1986):

1. Appeals to patriotism and national pride by domestic firms, industry associations, and governments (e.g., Dutch companies advertising with "Buy Dutch," "Fly Dutch," etc., slogans).
2. Appeals to national pride but on the part of foreign companies, aiming to clarify that while their brands may be foreign, they are made "at home" or contain significant domestic content (e.g., "The only bus with British wings" (Lufthansa); and "Every Peugeot bought in Britain is being built in Britain").
3. Presenting stereotyped characteristics of a foreign country (e.g., Renault's European advertising, aimed at placing its luxury sports model, the Renault GTA, on the same level as Ferrari and Porsche: "Pizza, bratwurst or nouvelle cuisine"; likewise, the Dutch are often symbolized by portrayals of wooden shoes, windmills and tulips, and so on).
4. Linking a product's image with specific, and presumably recognizable, points of expertise of a country (e.g., German engineering, Japanese electronics, or French elegance).

While these approaches may work under certain circumstances, they do not cover the entire range of conditions that may confront producers from a given country, and they are limited to considering only one of several means that are available for promotion. As a result, in this study the

emphasis is on identifying conditions for differentiating among communication strategies, and on expanding the tools being considered beyond
advertising.

Image Associations and Communication

Deeply-rooted positive and negative associations with a country, its
people, and its products are important since they may influence the attitudes and future behavior of both consumers and professional buyers.
Associations are formed *in,* not *by,* people over long periods of time. They
are the result of the conscious or subconscious processing of countless bits
of information and often are rigid and difficult to change. Although
associative networks exist at the purely individual level, more often than
not they contain views that are shared among large numbers of individuals.

Advertising and other forms of promotion can influence, change, enrich, and build associative networks. If positive image elements predominate (as is the case in the Netherlands, for example, with regards to Made-
in-Italy pasta and shoes), ignoring them in communication strategy can be
counter-productive. It would make sense, and would be relatively easy, to
undertake strategies that reinforce country images and use them to a greater or lesser extent as one of several elements (e.g., brand name, design,
workmanship) that can be incorporated in promotional programs and are
likely to help enhance sales.

Conversely, ignoring existing negative associations involves the risk of
misinterpretation or rejection of the advertiser's message by consumers. If
in a certain economic field the negative elements of image are strong,
shared by many people, and rigid, producers must start by accepting these
feelings. Assessing, recognizing, and addressing their existence is as difficult as it is necessary, especially if they are germane to the brand's attributes and the advertiser's goals (e.g., "punctuality" when one thinks of
Italian medical equipment).

Differentiating Among Communication Strategies

The preceding discussion leads to the conclusion that existing networks
must be the starting point in developing communication strategies, and
that these strategies may differ depending on the direction, strength, and
rigidity of prevailing attitudes.

Following this logic, Figure 2 combines the findings from the various
stages of this study and shows the four combinations of two principal

dimensions–competitiveness and image: (1) weak positions in both image and competitiveness (food processing machinery, machines for the graphics industry, and medical equipment); (2) strong positions in both dimensions (pasta, shoes, and women's fashion); and (3 & 4) intermediate positions, where one of the two dimensions is weak while the other is strong, or where both occupy midpoints in the quadrant (office furniture, packaging machinery).

Weak Competitiveness and Weak Image

When weak competitiveness is coupled with a low image profile (lower-left part in Figure 2), the sector is in the worst possible position. Considerable investment is needed in several areas simultaneously, including product development, overall organizational adjustments (e.g., business customs), and intensive communication efforts. In the industrial goods sectors that we studied, neither product performance nor the "Made in Italy" image are strong in themselves, nor can they strengthen each other. There is a dissonance akin to saying, for example, "cheese from Japan" or "pizza from the U.K."

Turning such perceptions around is not easy. Messages by other actors (e.g., competitors, the media) can reinforce existing negative perceptions and strengthen the negative associative network. Especially in the case of industrial products, and even if one assumes material improvements to product performance, messages reinforcing the buyers' negative attitudes can be (and are) communicated easily and in person by competitive sales forces when they perceive the need to fend off "intruders" from "unlikely" countries. New information by the producer itself, on the other hand, is not in line with customers' existing views and may be rejected or accepted only partly.

Therefore, long-term strategies focused on building new attitudes will work better than strategies which attempt to change traditional beliefs. Since knowledge, feelings, and behavioral intents go hand in hand, and since a lot of the stereotyped beliefs about products and their origins are due to lack of information, the most suitable strategy for products that find themselves in this situation would appear to be an information-based, knowledge-building approach focused on the "rational" aspects of purchase decisions. Product advertising, at least by itself, is not particularly suitable in such cases (e.g., for turning around deeply-rooted beliefs). The principles of sales management (systematic, step-wise approaches tailored to customers' needs and personally executed), public relations, institutional advertising (where the country is the "institution" being promoted), and

Figure 2. Differentiated Communication Strategy

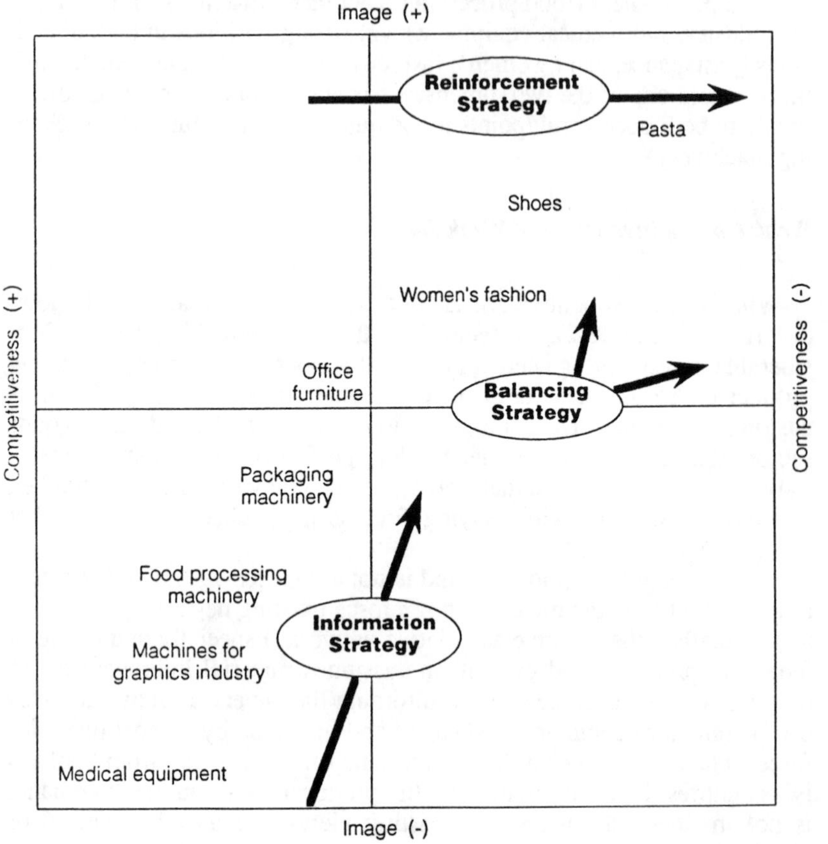

opinion leadership are more likely to be effective. In this context, one of the outcomes of the Italian project was a recommendation for a systematic program of visits to Italy by present and/or future opinion leaders and business professionals. Exhibit 4 outlines the basic strategic elements for sectors in the weak/weak position.

Strong Competitiveness and Strong Image

The positive combination of both competitiveness and image (upper-right part of Figure 2) calls for a strategy of reinforcement. The good features of the products and services are well known and accepted by the target audience and the managerial task is to reassure the market and reinforce the positive aspects of the products' images. In the case of Italy, brand and country perceptions for consumer products (pasta, shoes, women's fashion) are in line with each other, and consumers, business executives, and professional buyers agree on the products' positive elements. Advertising is very suitable for reminding consumers of, and reinforcing, the positive elements of brands, and can be most effective here. In these sectors, the position of Italian products is similar to that of, say, Dutch tulips or Scotch whisky. Exhibit 5 outlines the basic strategic elements for sectors in the strong/strong position.

Intermediate Positions

In the case of Italy, in this position (mid-part in Figure 2) we find products like office furniture and printing machinery. Many of the products in this situation combine some of the positive elements that characterize consumer goods (e.g., design) and some of the negative ones that are often associated with industrial products (e.g., technical advancement). The sectors found in this as in other parts of the position/strategy quadrant will of course differ by country (and their position may be in the middle, or in upper-left or lower-right parts). Other Italian products that are commonly assumed to be in a similar situation include computers, kitchen equipment, and cars.

Exhibit 4. Position/Strategy of Weak Sectors

POSITION	COMMUNICATION
Most important feature Weak image, weak competitiveness	Most important strategy Information
'Made in' does not strengthen and/or may weaken brand image	Public relations, institutional advertising, knowledge-building among opinion leaders, company sales forces

Other features
- Strong competitors
- Limited knowledge
- Poor fit between country/
  people image and product
	Other possibilities
	- Make no use of 'Made in' label
	- Use international or regional branding and
	  promotion (e.g., "Olivetti: the European computer")
	- Strategy of no-denial; e.g., "You know us from
	  (mafia, design, the Pope, dolce vita)... But did
	  you know that we make the most advanced (XYZ)?"
	- High visibility strategy capitalizing on respected
	  individuals (e.g., Agnelli, De Benedetti) or firms
	  (e.g., Fiat, Olivetti)
	- Enhance image by exporting know-how (e.g., design:
	  "The New Volkswagen-Designed by Ferrari.")

Exhibit 5. Position/Strategy of Strong Sectors

POSITION	COMMUNICATION
Most important feature Strong competitive and country image	Most important strategy Reinforcement
'Made in' image strengthens product perceptions	Advertising, showcasing of product, public relations
Other features - Historically strong positions - A lot of well known brands - Imitators from other countries	Other possibilities - Sector-wide promotions (e.g., "Wear 　Italian", "Cook Italian") - Reinforce specific known attributes (e.g., 　design, durability) - Cooperative programs with intermediaries - Cooperative industry-government programs

This intermediate location calls for balancing strategies that may or may not emphasize a product's origin depending on its position along the competitiveness/image dimensions. For instance, an earlier advertisement in Europe by Fiat referred to its "Uno" model as "temperamental," in an apparent attempt to link it to dynamism and aggressiveness. This reference to an aspect of the Italian character, which generally is not considered positive as such, may in fact weaken the brand's appeal. Furthermore, it contributes to strengthening and perpetuating the stereotype in general (which, regardless of its potential validity, does not need to be emphasized), with potential effects on other products as well. Exhibit 6 outlines the basic strategic elements for sectors in intermediate positions.

CONCLUSION:
THE FINDINGS PUT INTO PRACTICE

This type of study makes it possible to develop differentiated strategies at all levels of marketing activity. Producers, distributors, and consumers can be approached with appropriate communication messages and, overall, the assessment of strengths and weaknesses based on both competitive position and country image allows for a better overall deployment of a firm's and country's communication mix. The findings of the specific ICE study were put to use in a variety of ways. Notwithstanding their specific merits and potential eventual outcome, these show how a systematic approach to promoting a country's products abroad can be put to practice. A brief sample of steps taken to implement the ICE study recommendations is provided below.

Exhibit 6. Position/Strategy of Intermediate Sectors

POSITION	COMMUNICATION
Most important feature Dissonance between competitive/ country image, or mid-point position on either/both dimensions	**Most important strategy** Balancing
'Made in' image may strengthen or weaken brand depending on its position	Information if country image weak, reinforcement if strong; product improvement if competitiveness weak, information if strong
Other features - Products at intermediate points have "grey" images - Susceptible to competitive actions - Unclear image can be seen as both opportunity (for improvement) and threat (by better-focused competitors)	**Other possibilities** - Link up with other countries' strengths if possible ("German engineering, Italian design") - Cooperative promotion with intermediaries - Information campaign to emphasize strengths, dispel perceived and downplay significance of real weaknesses - Parallel cross-section association where possible/relevant, such as historical roots (construction of Appian Way) with contemp. products (road-building equip.) or leather apparel with leather office furniture

Showcasing. Steps were taken to enhance the image of Italian products through exhibits, fairs, and demonstration activities, both to reinforce sectors with a positive image and to improve target market knowledge about weaker ones. For example, Italian authorities undertook programs aimed at tying high-tech products with strengths in Italian culture and positive historical images. The exhibits "Italian Technological Renaissance," "Compasso d' Oro," and "Habitat" are cases in point.

Information. ICE published a book based on the study that was discussed in this chapter, titled "La Posizione Competitiva e l'Immagine del Prodotti Italiani–Paesi Bassi" (The Competitive Position and Image of Italian Products–The Netherlands), which acts as a helpful guide for Italian producers and distributors who want to develop foreign communication campaigns. The information in the book is valuable since, in addition to providing data on the Italian image abroad, it also contains comparisons between the competitive and country images of Italy and its major international competitors. In fact, the book is also considered as an "instrument of good will" and circulated among actual and potential buyers and users of Italian products.

Public Relations. Another practical way in which the study's findings were used by ICE involves the sponsoring of visits to Italy for Dutch present and potential opinion leaders, especially in relation to industrial sectors that were found to have weaker images. This program was based on the finding that existing views often differ from reality and that increased first-hand knowledge reduces the discrepancy between the two.

ICE felt that it would be good to show Italian industry for what it is, and to create opportunities for presenting and discussing Italian technological developments. In budget allocation terms, this means a partial shift from mass media advertising to public relations. In a way, this represents a return to the more genuine marketing concept of making friends with, and providing information to, customers, rather than "attacking the competition" based on the military-type strategies that were fashionable in marketing during the 1980s.

In particular, the findings from the student sample of the study (not discussed above–see Morello 1990), coupled with the belief that today's students are tomorrow's business people and potential opinion leaders, led to the sponsoring of student visits to Italy. Selected students from four Dutch universities (Free University of Amsterdam, State University of Groningen, Erasmus University of Rotterdam, and the University of Technical Engineering of Delft) have already taken part in such visits.

The ICE approach of emphasizing, among others, relations with individuals at the pre-professional stage, reflects the belief that national images develop over such long periods of time, are so deeply rooted, and can have such a significant influence, that they warrant an equally long-term and systematic approach to addressing them.

REFERENCES

Bamossy, Gary J. and Nicolas Papadopoulos (1987), "An Assessment of Reliability for Product Evaluation Scales Used in Country of Origin Research." In K. Bahn and M. Sirgy (eds.), *Third World Marketing Congress* (Barcelona, Spain: Academy of Marketing Science, vol. III) 135-142.

Bamossy, G.J., J. Berács, L.A. Heslop, and N. Papadopoulos (1988), "East Meets West: A Country of Origin Analysis of Western Products by Hungarian and Dutch Consumers." *Second International Marketing Development Conference* (Budapest: Assoc. of Consumer Research; July) 149-152.

Dawson, S. and G.J. Bamossy (1990), "A Comparison of the Culture of Consumption Between Two Western Cultures: A Study of Materialism in the Netherlands and United States." *Dimensions of International Business*, 3 (Ottawa: International Business Study Group, Carleton Univ., January) 39-58.

Fortune (1988, March 14), "Entering a New Age of Boundless Competition." 40-48.

IMF (Int. Monetary Fund, 1989), *Direction of Trade Statistics*.

Kotler, P. (1988), *Marketing Management*. Englewood Cliffs, NJ: Prentice Hall.

Morello, Gabriele (1984), "The 'Made-In' Issue–A Comparative Research on the Image of Domestic and Foreign Products." *European Research* (July) 95-100.

Morello, Gabriele (1986), "The Consumer in World Trade." In H. Visser and E. Schoorl (eds.), *Trade in Transit*. Dordrecht: Martinus Nijhoff. 303-313.

Morello, Gabriele (1990), "'Made in Italy' and in Other Countries: A Study of Competitivity and Images." In *Yearbook of European Studies*, 3 (vol. Italy-Europe) 119-132.

Morello, Gabriele and Elzo Boerema (1989), "'Made in' and Communication: A Case History of 'Made in Italy' in the Netherlands." In *How to Increase the Efficiency of Marketing Communication in a Changing Europe* (Seminar, European Soc. for Opinion and Marketing Research, Turin, October) 177-209.

Papadopoulos, Nicolas (1982), "The European Economic Community: One Market, Ten Markets, or Twelve?" In V. Kothari (ed.), *Developments in Marketing Science*, V (Las Vegas: Academy of Marketing Science) 215-220.

Porter, M.E. (1980), *Competitive Strategy: Techniques for Analyzing Industries and Competitors*. New York: Free Press.

Williams, E.E. (1986), *Made in Germany*. London: Heinemann.

Chapter 13

The Image of Countries as Locations for Investment

Chow Hou Wee
David T.E. Lim
Gilbert Y.W. Tan

INTRODUCTION

The importance of foreign direct investment (FDI) in stimulating the economic development and growth of less developed countries (LDCs) is now widely acknowledged and accepted. In fact, with the collapse of the Berlin Wall in December 1989 and having openly admitted the collapse of their central planning systems, socialist bloc countries have now begun to embark on aggressive polices to attract FDI so as to speed up their economic growth. Nothwithstanding the hiatus created by the events of June 1989, China now realizes that it can no longer operate on a closed-door policy and has begun to actively try to attract inward FDI.

Without doubt, multinational corporations (MNCs) bring with them capital, technology, employment, management expertise, and market development. Therefore, it is no surprise that many countries have begun to advertise and market themselves to potential investors. Besides offering economic and investment incentives, these countries also try to position themselves as favorable locations for investment in the eyes of the investors. In other words, they try to create good images of themselves. Such efforts are not surprising considering that FDI is a major and risky decision for any MNC, and no firm will make such a move unless it is impressed by the various aspects of a country's image.

In this light, it is necessary to develop a better understanding of the role of the image of countries as locations for investment, and of the potential influence of this image on investors' decisions. The subject is significant for countries interested in enhancing the effectiveness of FDI promotion programs, investors who want to improve their decision-making process about investment locations, and researchers with interests in the role of country images in buyer choices. From the FDI perspective, countries are "products" whose image may affect the choices of investors, as "buyers," among alternative locations. This chapter studies the images of countries-as-products in the context of U.S. investors' views of Singapore in relation to other Asia Pacific markets. While the research on which this chapter is based focuses on the U.S./Asia Pacific dyad, its findings should be useful to readers with interests in other but similar country contexts.

Among other countries, Singapore is one nation which is very concerned about its image as a location for FDI. Critical changes have occurred in recent years which pose challenges to Singapore in its efforts to attract foreign investment. Developing countries' attitudes towards FDI are generally changing toward the positive direction (Hauser 1986). This would imply stiffer competition for foreign investments. With rapid growth for the past 25 years, and its graduation from the General Agreement on Tariffs and Trade (GATT) framework, Singapore's competitiveness as a location for investment is now challenged in relation to other developing countries.

This concern is even more valid in view of the fact that Singapore had reached a per capita income of about US$11,000 as of 1990. To maintain momentum and ensure future prosperity, Singapore needs to push ahead, possibly even to the league of the developed countries by the end of this century. There are several other countries "hot on its heels" within the Asia Pacific region, including, for example, Taiwan and South Korea. In addition, with the collapse of the Berlin Wall, and the liberalization of the economic systems of Eastern European nations, it is important to point out that many of these countries are in a similar category as Singapore in terms of per capita GNP. They are direct competitors (as alternative locations for FDI) to Singapore, especially for MNCs from Western Europe and the U.S. Thus, there are strong reasons why Singapore needs to know how it is perceived by foreign investors. As a further input to policy makers, it is also necessary to know how its competitors are perceived.

FOREIGN DIRECT INVESTMENT ENVIRONMENT IN SINGAPORE

When Singapore first started to industrialize its economy, it did not have the capacity to produce for export and had to look aggressively for foreign investors to provide the needed capital, technology, management know-how, and markets. Since then, Singapore has grown rapidly to attain its current status as a newly industrialized country (NIC). Singapore's economic success is largely due to its effective export-oriented industrialization programs and open-door policies which attracted much foreign investment into the country. Today, the manufacturing sector is a key component of the economy. In 1989, it contributed 28.7 percent to the Gross Domestic Product (Economic Survey of Singapore, 1989). Owing to its lack of large local industries, foreign investment is still very important and much sought-after today. In fact, Singapore's policy on foreign investment has not changed despite some bad experiences encountered during the 1985/1986 recession when several MNCs pulled out their operations. After the recession, although the government identified the need to nurture local companies to provide a capable and reliable complement of supporting industries to MNCs, it officially acknowledged that Singapore still needed foreign investment. This was reflected in *The Report of the Economic Committee* (1986, p. 19; Ministry of Trade and Industry):

. . . EDB (Economic Development Board) should aggressively increase its efforts to bring home new manufacturing investments. While existing plants have to upgrade their operations, manufacturing productivity is increased even more by the introduction of new high quality investments.

The economic significance of FDI in Singapore is supported by available statistics. In 1987, wholly- and majority-foreign-owned enterprises accounted for only 22.4 percent of all manufacturing establishments in Singapore. However, their contributions to the economy in terms of employment, output, value added, and direct exports were 57.6 percent, 74.9 percent, 72.4 percent, and 86.4 percent respectively. Indeed, in the case of Singapore, FDI contributes highly to the economic development of the nation. As shown in Table 1, since 1985 foreign capital has accounted for at least 80 percent of the total annual investments in Singapore.

While no single nationality dominates foreign investment in Singapore's manufacturing sector, the relative importance of U.S. investment is quite significant. U.S. firms were among the earliest to invest in Singapore and have remained as major foreign investors (Table 1). Although by 1989 they were superseded by Europe and Japan, in that year U.S. companies accounted for 26.6 percent of all investments and 32 percent of total foreign investment. Their cumulative share for 1985-1989 was 30.4 percent of total investment and 37 percent of FDI.

Table 1. Investment in Singapore by Country of Origin (1985-1989)
(million U.S.$)

Origin Country	1985	1986	1987	1988	1989	Total	Percent
U.S.	427.3	443.4	543.5	586.6	520.2	2,520.8	30.4
Japan	244.1	493.8	601.1	691.3	541.2	2,571.5	31.1
Europe	201.0	218.8	285.8	358.1	544.2	1,607.9	19.4
Others	15.6	34.6	17.6	21.7	19.8	109.3	1.3
Foreign	888.0	1,190.6	1,448.0	1,657.8	1,625.4	6,809.5	82.2
Local	232.4	259.4	295.0	349.6	333.3	1,469.7	17.8
Total	1,120.4	1,450.0	1,743.0	2,007.4	1,958.7	8,279.2	100.0

Source: Economic Survey of Singapore, 1989

The contribution of U.S. investments to Singapore's economy is also demonstrated by the fact that in 1987, while U.S. firms constituted only 4.7 percent of all manufacturing companies (164 out of 3,513), they employed 22.4 percent of the workers in manufacturing. In addition, they produced 36.3 percent of total output, and contributed 44.9 percent to direct manufacturing exports.

LITERATURE REVIEW

The impact of country-of-origin has been studied widely in association with consumer buying preferences, and to some extent in relation to industrial purchasing (see Greer and Greer 1986 for an excellent summary). For example, studies by Cattin, Jolibert, and Lohnes (1982) and Wall and Heslop (1986), and the review by Bilkey and Nes (1982), have shown that both industrial and consumer buyers develop images of countries which affect their purchase behavior. Many studies have shown that country image stereotyping is common (e.g., Reierson 1966; Darling and Kraft 1977; Morello 1984), and others have shown that country-of-origin images can change over time (e.g., Nagashima 1970 and 1977).

Studies have also shown that a company may derive an additional advantage in foreign markets from the positive attributes possessed by its home nation (e.g., Nagashima 1970; Bannister and Saunders 1978). Conversely, a poor country image may create a severe obstacle for a company doing business abroad, as was shown in Khanna's (1986) recent study on Asian exports.

Extending this line of analysis, Johansson and Nebenzahl (1986) showed that in the case of multinational production, the brand value of a product (car) was affected by the location of production site. In addition, the studies of Nagashima (1970), Greer and Greer (1986), and Rucker, Sembach, and Cuicci (1986) have all shown that there is a tendency for consumers in developed countries to rate their domestic products more favorably than those from foreign, and especially less developed, countries. Without doubt, patriotism plays an important part here, as evidenced by findings from other studies as well (e.g., Reierson 1966; Nagashima 1970; Gaedeke 1973; Narayana 1981; and Han 1988). On the other hand, the influence of marketing activities should not be discounted (e.g., Reierson 1966 and 1967), and a more recent multination study showed that a preference for domestic goods is not universal (Papadopoulos, Heslop, and Berács 1990).

However, thus far most of the marketing research on the country-of-origin phenomenon has been confined to the micro level of products, although efforts have been made to extend its scope (e.g., Han and Terpstra 1988). Few studies have attempted to study country image at a more macro level. Yet origin images occur at two levels (Hooley, Shipley, and Krieger 1988). At the micro level, they refer to the specific image of a product, while at the macro level, they refer to the general image of a country. For example, studies by Wang and Lamb (1980 and 1983) showed that the willingness of U.S. consumers to buy foreign products was partially determined by the economic, political, and cultural environments of the country-of-origin. Papadopoulos, Marshall, and Heslop (1988), and Papadopoulos, Heslop, and Berács (1990), have shown that such factors as economic development of a country and consumers' affective feelings towards its people influence product evaluations. And Wall and Heslop (1986) found that country images were closely related to the level of political development.

In another study, Wee and Paloheimo (1989) examined Chinese managers' perceptions of foreign investors from the United States, Japan, Singapore, and West Germany, and argued that selecting a joint venture (investment) partner could be influenced by the managers' perceptions of the other party's country image.

Given the rich literature on country-of-origin image, there is no reason why such studies could not be extended at the macro level. To begin with, in recent years, there have been attempts by many countries to market their nations for foreign investments. One of the common approaches taken is the use of aggressive advertising campaigns through the various media. In doing so, such countries are inevitably trying to market their images as potential investment sites to foreign companies and governments. Yet, few studies to date have examined the issue of "countries as products".[1] The importance of FDI to LDCs (e.g., Hennart 1986) and developed countries (e.g., Arpan and Ricks 1986) is well documented. For example, Tallman (1988) investigated the proposition that home country political risk factors influence outward FDI. The importance of FDI to companies has also been studied. Ehrman and Hamburg (1986) developed a model using two-stage country selection procedures to assist firms to decide how to select countries for FDI. Luqmani, Habib, and Kassem (1988) proposed a managerial framework on how to market to the governments of LDCs.

Earlier research has also examined the role of perceptions in making FDI-related decisions. Nigh (1985) examined the effects of political events on the manufacturing foreign direct investment decisions of U.S. MNCs, using regression analysis through pooled time-series and cross-sectional data. They found that for LDCs, both inter-nation and intra-nation conflict and cooperation affect FDI in manufacturing. In contrast, U.S. manufacturing investment in developed countries appeared to be affected only by inter-nation conflict and cooperation. Sabi (1988) developed a model to assess the determinants of multinational banks' FDI and expansion into LDCs. Their results showed that market size, the presence of MNCs from the home country, the extent of economic development, and the balance of payments were all significant determinants of the growth of multinational banks in the LDCs.

Many of the studies cited reveal that FDI decisions are affected to a large extent by how companies perceive the prevailing conditions in both the home and host countries. In particular, for the country wanting to receive FDI, the perception of it by the investing company is very important. The chances of attracting FDI will be better if a country can project a more favorable image in the eyes of foreign investors. Some studies have, in fact, begun to address such issues.

Prasad (1986) studied the perception of U.S. executives toward foreign state enterprises, the threats they posed, and how U.S. companies ought to

---

1. Ed. note: Most of the handful of studies of this type have been carried out by or on behalf of government or para-government agencies. In those cases where the results have been published, it is apparent that methodological difficulties were encountered. For example, in two studies about the image of Canada as a place for investment (1980s), The Conference Board of Canada obtained response rates of only 7 and 12 percent from broadly defined samples of, respectively, 5,500 and 7,500 "potential investors" worldwide. Similar limitations can be noted in *some* of the government studies concerning the image of France abroad, which are reviewed in the chapter by Graby.

factor the existence of such enterprises into their decision-making process. Lee and Lo (1988), in a follow-up study on Brunner and Taoka (1977), examined American businesspersons' perceptions of marketing and negotiating in the People's Republic of China. Their findings showed that among other factors, increased business opportunities between the U.S. and China depended a lot on how accurate Americans' perceptions were in relation to conditions in the target country.

Leong and Tan (1990) reported that, among 170 senior executives from the U.S., Europe, and Japan surveyed at a meeting in Singapore, North America would remain the single most important geographic region for corporate activity to the year 2000. Within Asia, the study reported that the executives expected Singapore would be the country of highest investment attractiveness, followed by China and Thailand. However, Leong and Tan's (1990) study did not dwell in depth on why companies invest overseas. In addition, its description of the area and national images was rather rudimentary.

In conclusion, while past research has addressed some of the relevant issues, there is a need for a more in-depth understanding of the image of countries as products and its role in investors' decisions. This chapter is based on a study that was undertaken to enhance our knowledge in this area.

METHODOLOGY

Conceptualization

In recent years, it has been commonly acknowledged that the Asia Pacific region will become an increasingly important area for trade and investment. It is thus not surprising that more and more U.S. firms are interested in the Asia Pacific region. In fact, it is widely accepted that the region offers vast potential in terms of lower costs of operations and higher profit/market opportunities. In view of this development, there are strategic reasons for Singapore to find out how U.S. firms view the various countries/markets in the Asia Pacific region. Such knowledge will provide useful input for policymakers in their efforts to devise strategies to attract U.S. investments, as well as to differentiate Singapore from the other countries/markets. Thus far, there has been no published large-scale study on how U.S. investors perceive the various markets in the Asia Pacific region.

U.S. firms were chosen because of their importance to Singapore and their keen interest in the growing Asia Pacific markets. The expanding economies of ASEAN (which includes Indonesia, Thailand, the Philippines, Malaysia, Singapore, and Brunei), "nouveau riches" newly industrialized countries (NICs), and the vast potential of China are each acting as economic magnets drawing investments into the region.

Sample

The study was conducted through the U.S. office of the Singapore Economic Development Board (SEDB), and was part of a larger study on how U.S. investors perceived Singapore as a market for investment. The companies that were approached for this study represented corporations which the SEDB had contacted previously with the intention of marketing Singapore as an offshore manufacturing location. The executives that were targeted to respond to a structured questionnaire were thus familiar with Singapore, and were most likely to be interested in the survey subject. These companies also represented a broad spectrum of industries (e.g., aerospace, chemicals, electronics, and machinery), size (from less than US$10 million to more than US$1 billion in total sales), and geographical regions (a total of 35 states classified into the Northeast, Midwest, Southern, and Western regions).

Of the 507 questionnaires sent, a total of 176 usable responses were received. This represented a 35 percent response rate, and also reflected the approximate return rates by region. The characteristics of the final sample are shown in Table 2. Note that there is a good spread of companies in terms of size, industries, and extent of export orientation. The only exception is that of regional representation where there were more companies in the Northeast region. However, this reflected more the characteristics of the population that was surveyed rather than the sample response received.

It is also important to note that over 70 percent of the respondents indicated that their companies had made an overseas manufacturing investment in the last three years. In addition, about 50 percent of the responding companies indicated at the time of the survey that they would be considering making a manufacturing investment decision in the Asia Pacific region within the next two years.

Questionnaire

The survey instrument was designed for a larger study which aimed to determine why U.S. companies want to manufacture abroad, what they look for in selecting a site for offshore manufacturing, and how they go

Table 2. Sample Characteristics

Region	N	Percent	Size (turnover)	N	Percent
Mid West	48	27.3	< or = US$50 million	43	24.4
North East	72	40.9	US$ 51-100 million	68	38.6
Southern	28	15.9	> or = US$101 million	61	34.7
Western	28	15.9	Missing value	4	2.3
Industries			**Exports/Total Sales**		
Aerospace	23	13.1	< or = 10 %	57	32.4
Chemicals	28	15.9	11% to 40%	70	39.8
Electronics	46	26.1	> 40%	37	21.0
Machinery	41	23.3	Missing value	12	6.8
Others	38	21.6			

about making offshore manufacturing decisions. The focus of the study was on the Asia Pacific region, and thus questions were asked about how U.S. companies perceived the various markets within that region. For this research, "Asia Pacific" was defined to include Japan, the four Asian NICs, ASEAN, Australasia (Australia and New Zealand), China, and India. Singapore was considered both independently and as a member of ASEAN and the four NICs.

The questionnaire was designed to be completed within 20 to 30 minutes. This was essential as the respondents included many corporate chairpersons, chief executive officers, and other senior executives. All questions were structured and close-ended, using four- or five-point Likert-type scales, rankings, or multiple-choice items. Some allowances were also made for open-ended questions. Some questions were reversed-scored to minimize response sequence bias.

Each questionnaire was mailed out with a covering note addressed personally to the respondent. It basically emphasized the direct value of the study to the respondent in terms of receiving a copy of the survey results, and the indirect value in that the results could have an impact on future policy formulation by SEDB. For this chapter, only the data pertaining to the investment objectives (the "why"), and the perceived importance of the various Asia Pacific markets were extracted for analysis from the larger data set of the complete study.

INVESTMENT OBJECTIVES

To capture information on why U.S. companies want to invest in the Asia Pacific region, respondents were asked to respond to a list of 20 investment objectives along a five-point Likert-type scale (where 1 = most important). Owing to the nature of the data, factor analysis, the multivariate technique that is concerned with the identification of data structure, was deemed to be the most appropriate tool for understanding the underlying constructs or factors relating to the 20 investment objectives. R-factoring with varimax rotation was used.

Cattell's (1966) Scree test procedure was used to determine the number of factors that should be obtained. An examination of the plot of eigenvalues against the number of factors suggested that three or four factors should be extracted. A further examination of the grouping of statements after the varimax solutions indicated that extraction of three factors yielded the most consistency in terms of interpretation.

Gorsuch (1983) recommended that only statements with loadings of at least 0.30 and loading on one factor should be included in the factor. If the loadings of the statements in the different factors are very close, the statements should be excluded from all the factors. All the 20 statements met these criteria and were included in the final analysis.

Table 3 shows the results of the factor analysis. From the statements grouped under each factor, three factors could be interpreted as market objectives (Factor A), resource and risk hedging objectives (Factor B), and cost and profit objectives (Factor C). The mean scores, standard deviations, and Cronbach's alpha coefficients for all three factors were also calculated and shown. All alpha coefficients were over 0.70, indicating that the psychometric properties of the three factors were not violated. The three factors also explained more than 73 percent of the total variance.

Among the factors, cost and profitability objectives are ranked as most important (mean score of 1.97), followed by market objectives (2.39), and resource and risk hedging objectives (3.37), respectively. It is not surprising that U.S. firms are motivated to invest in the Asia Pacific region by cost and profitability considerations since labor rates in the U.S. are about four times higher than those in the Asian NICs. The importance attached to costs and profits reflects the drive by U.S. firms to regain competitiveness by tackling the cost side of the equation. Clearly, U.S. firms see opportunities in the Asia Pacific region for cost reductions from lower labor and overhead costs, and good tax incentives. Subgroup analysis (by sample characteristics of region, size, industries, and export orientation) revealed some significant variations according to the location and export orientation of the U.S. firms, but not with respect to the other firm characteristics.

Table 3. Factor Analytic Solution of Investment Objectives

Factor
Loadings*

Factor A: MARKET OBJECTIVES
Overcome protectionism	0.32
Closer to existing customers	0.81
Closer to potential customers	0.83
Develop knowledge of the Asia-Pacific markets	0.61
Follow an existing customer overseas	0.52
Establish a global operations	0.67
Establish a regional presence	0.84
Establish strategic alliances with regional companies	0.72

Cronbach's Alpha Coefficient (8 items) = 0.8313
Mean = 2.39   Standard Deviation = 0.7600

Factor B: RESOURCE & RISK HEDGING OBJECTIVES
Tap raw materials from Asia-Pacific region	0.54
Tap scarce design, engineering & other skills	0.66
Take advantage of less stringent environmental regulations	0.52
Follow competitors who have invested in the region	0.49
Meet offset obligations	0.56
Hedge against currency exchange rates	0.66
Hedge against production outages in any single location	0.68
Reduce risk generally	0.59

Cronbach's Alpha Coefficient (8 items) = 0.7441
Mean = 3.37   Standard Deviation = 0.6200

Factor C: COST & PROFITABILITY OBJECTIVES
Lower manufacturing costs	0.77
Seek tax advantages	0.65
Seek higher profits	0.74
Tap lower labor cost	0.74

Cronbach's Alpha Coefficient (4 items) = 0.7280
Mean = 1.97   Standard Deviation = 0.6500

* Varimax Rotation

Relatively, the Southern and Western firms were more concerned with costs and profits (mean scores of 1.81 and 1.67, respectively; see Table 4). This reflected, in part, the predominance of electronics and machinery companies in these two regions of the U.S. Such companies are more sensitive to costs because of their relatively higher labor content (compared to, say, process industries like chemicals).

Table 4. Mean Scores of Subgroup Analysis
of Investment Objectives

U.S. Region	Cost & Profit Objectives
North East	2.11 *
MidWest	2.06 #
Southern	1.81
Western	1.67 * #

Exports/Total Sales	Market Objectives
< or = 10%	2.24 *
11% to 40%	2.60 *
> 40%	2.37

* and # : Groups with significant differences
(Scheffe Method)

In the case of electronics companies which are located mainly in the Western region of the U.S., there are additional concerns for costs. Product life cycles in electronics are relatively short as compared to, for example, chemicals. Companies making electronics products therefore have shorter periods during which to break even and show profits. The electronics industry (especially consumer products) caters to mass markets and is relatively low-cost to enter, as it does not require expensive tooling or machinery. Competition is therefore more dependent on the ability to source/produce low-cost components and use low-cost labor for assembly. This results in generally low margins, as compared to proprietary product and niche market businesses such as software, health-care equipment, or patented pharmaceutical products.

The finding that market objectives were the next most important suggests that there has been a shift away from the traditional focus on overseas manufacturing as feeder plants for the U.S. market. What is almost as important is the establishment of manufacturing facilities in Asia Pacific to serve the regional markets. It appears that U.S. firms are also concerned with the revenue side of the equation, and the need to secure and increase market share in the Asia Pacific region, rather than only re-exporting the manufactured goods back into the U.S. market. Interestingly, subgroup analysis revealed that firms that were least export-oriented (with less than 10 percent of their products exported overseas) were most concerned with the market objectives (mean score of 2.24). They were followed by firms with the highest export-orientation (companies with more than 40 percent of their sales abroad) which had a mean score of 2.37 (see Table 4). In contrast, those companies which exported 11 percent to 40 percent of their total sales (medium export-orientation) were least concerned with market objectives (mean score of 2.60).

This pattern of results (Table 4) could be because when a firm's exports are small, it needs to increase its market share to be viable. In other words, it needs to achieve critical mass in export sales. This in turn creates a heightened awareness of wanting to increase market share and exert market presence. When exports become a large percentage of a firm's total sales, their importance would definitely be high in that they affect a substantial part of the company's total business. However, when export volume is neither very small nor very large, the firm can be caught in the "export complacency trap" in that having overcome the critical mass problem, it may simply be too content to be especially interested in pushing its volume of international sales any further.

Compared to the other two objectives, resource and risk hedging objectives were regarded as least important by the respondents (see Table 3). There were no significant differences in the ratings among subgroups according to the profile variables of region, size, type of industry, and extent of export orientation. This is an interesting finding in that, in earlier times, access to resources was often seen as a more important motivator for undertaking FDI.

PERCEIVED IMPORTANCE
OF ASIA PACIFIC MARKETS

Respondents were asked to rate the various geographic areas in the Asia Pacific region in terms of the degree of importance they attached to them as markets for their companies' products over the next three years. A four-point Likert-type scale was used (where 4 = most important).

As noted earlier, Singapore was treated both as a separate entity and as part of ASEAN and the NICs. While this was a shortcoming of the research, it was done deliberately. This is because the study was concerned with considering Singapore as a site for FDI versus the other countries and regional groupings in the area. As Singapore belongs to ASEAN and is also classified with the NICs, it is important to establish how both Singapore and these two groups as separate entities are perceived. This issue is important as Singapore is a very small nation with a total land area of only 626.4 square kilometers and a population of 2.7 million people. Whether or not Singapore could exist as a single market is often debated among the country's policy makers. Essentially, any country which is comparatively small in terms of market size and part of a regional grouping with a strong identity (for example, Canada in North America; Luxembourg, Belgium, and Ireland in the European Community; and New Zealand in Australasia) would be interested in assessing its image both independently and as part of its region.

To obtain an overall idea of the extent of perceived importance of the various Asia Pacific markets, individual mean scores were calculated. These are shown in Table 5. Japan and the Asia NICs were regarded as the most important markets in Asia Pacific. This result was expected since these countries include both the largest and richest per capita economies in the region. In fact, 47.9 percent of the respondents rated Japan as the market that is of greatest importance as compared to 39.3 percent for the NICs.

ASEAN was considered to be the next most important after Japan and the Asian NICs. Australasia (Australia and New Zealand) and Singapore were given equal importance. These results were not surprising. Although the per capita incomes of Australia and New Zealand are much higher than those of ASEAN as a whole, the population of ASEAN is more than 10 times larger than that of Australia and New Zealand combined. In addition, in terms of economic growth rates, the ASEAN countries are growing faster than Australasia. Thus, ASEAN as a group was perceived as a more important market.

It is interesting to note that Singapore, while recognized as both an NIC and a member of ASEAN, was ranked lower in importance than either one of the two groupings. In fact, only 24.7 percent of the total respondents ranked Singapore as the market of greatest importance to them, in contrast to 29.5 percent for ASEAN and 39.3 percent for the NICs. Again, this result should be expected. This is because although it has the second highest per capita income in Asia after Japan (Brunei is a special case because of its oil wealth), its market is small. The finding suggests how important it is for Singapore to "plug in" and be counted together with the NICs and ASEAN to enhance its ability to attract foreign investments.

China and India, despite their large populations, were not rated highly by the U.S. firms in this study. In the case of China, this could be attributed to its small per capita income and its relatively unstable political direction. The finding suggests that China's emergence as a major market is not expected in the near future despite its proclaimed "open-door" policy. It is important to point out that the survey was conducted before the political upheavals in China in June 1989. If the survey had been done after the June 1989 Tiananmen Square event, the results might have been even more adverse against China.

In the case of India (ranked last in this study with a mean score of

2.22–see Table 5), although it is politically more aligned with the developed Western countries, it is still regarded as a poor market prospect possibly because of its protectionistic trade and investment policies and its low per capita income. Moreover, India has never been active in recent years in promoting itself as a site for FDI. This could be partly a result of the bad "hangover" effects of the Bhopal disaster (which affects foreign investors' confidence in India as well).

When the 176 U.S. firms were analyzed by subgroupings of region, industry, export orientation, and size, there were only a few instances of significant differences in their perceptions of the various Asia Pacific markets. These involved their perceptions of Japan, ASEAN, and Singapore. In the case of Japan (see Table 6), firms located in the Northeast and Midwest regions tended to rate it as more important than those from the Southern region (mean score of 2.52). This could be due to the nature of the industries concerned. In addition, medium-size companies (sales between US$51 million and US$100 million) tended to attach less importance to the Japanese market as compared to the small and large compa-

Table 5. Perceived Importance of Asia Pacific Markets

Market	Rank	Mean
Japan	1	3.22
Asia NICs	2	3.17
ASEAN	3	2.94
Australasia	4	2.81
Singapore	5	2.81
China	6	2.69
India	7	2.22

Table 6. Perceived Importance of Japan
by Profile of U.S. Firms

U.S. Region	Mean Score	Size (turnover)	Mean Score
North East	3.45 *	< or = US$50 million	3.03
Mid West	3.28 #	US$51-100 million	2.98 *
Southern	2.52 * #	> or = US$101 million	3.61 *
Western	3.11		

* and # : Groups with significant differences
(Scheffe Method)

nies (see Table 6). This could be explained by the "export complacency trap" highlighted earlier.

There were also significant variations in the perceived importance of ASEAN. U.S. firms from the Southern region tended to regard ASEAN as a more important market (mean score of 3.37) than those from the Midwest and Western regions (see Table 7). This contrasted interestingly with their perception of Japan (see Table 6). Japan was ranked as the least important by firms in the Southern region (mean score of 2.52). One possible explanation for this difference in perception could be due to the nature of the industries concerned.

Significant differences were also found in the case of Singapore when the perception was profiled by size of company. The smaller firms (those with less than US$51 million sales) were more likely to regard Singapore as an important market compared to the mid-size firms. Note that there was no significant difference in perception between the small and large firms. The "export complacency" phenomenon for mid-size firms may be at work here as well. Also, smaller firms may perceive Singapore as more approachable because of its small size, while large firms may be in a better position to recognize its strategic regional significance. Besides the points highlighted in this discussion, no other differences were found among the U.S. firms in their perception of the other Asia Pacific markets in terms of corporate profile.

MULTIDIMENSIONAL SCALING OF ASIA PACIFIC MARKETS

In order to get a clearer picture of how U.S. firms perceived the various Asia Pacific markets in this study, a multidimensional scaling (MDS) approach was adopted to analyze the results further. MDS has been widely

Table 7. Perceived Importance of ASEAN and Singapore by Profile of U.S. Firms

U.S. Region	ASEAN	Size (turnover)	Singapore
North East	3.03	< or = US$50 million	3.18 *
Mid West	2.67 *	US$51-100 million	2.59 *
Southern	3.37 * #	> or = US$101 million	2.78
Western	2.71 #		

    * and # : Groups with significant differences
              (Scheffe Method)

used in marketing research since its introduction more than two decades ago (Cooper 1983). Essentially, it is a set of statistical techniques that attempt to identify the dimensions upon which consumers perceive or evaluate objects, and how the objects are positioned with respect to these dimensions. There are several approaches to MDS (Green, Carmone, and Smith, 1989, p. 11-136, provide a good description).

The approach adopted in this study involved the use of nonattribute data. This was preferred over the attribute-based approach for two main reasons. First, it was very difficult to generate a comprehensive list of attributes that the U.S. firms would use to evaluate markets in the Asia Pacific region. Second, the respondents might not evaluate the markets in terms of individual attributes. Instead, they might just evaluate the markets as a total whole.

The inputs for the analyses were the derived measures of similarities based on the correlation coefficients (see Table 8). Respondents' evaluations of the importance of the various markets in the Asia Pacific region were correlated. The correlation coefficients were then ranked in ascending order (see Table 9). The rank "1" represents the most similar (highest correlated) pair (in this case, between India and China), while the rank "21" represents the least similar pair (in this case, between Japan and ASEAN).

The program used to obtain the perceptual map was that of Kruskal, Young, Shepard, and Torgerson (Kruskal, Young, and Seery 1973; Young 1968; and Kruskal 1964), or the KYST method for short. This method essentially orients the configuration to principal components axes, as opposed to other methods which orient it to simple structure by means of a varimax subroutine (Young 1968).

The results of the analysis are illustrated in Figure 1. Interpretation of the two dimensions requires additional information which is external to the technique. According to Green, Carmone, and Smith (1989, p. 67),

Table 8. Correlation Matrix of Perceived Importance
of Asia Pacific Markets

	Singapore	ASEAN	Asia NICs	Japan	China	India	Austral-asia
Singapore	-						
ASEAN	.472	-					
Asia NICs	.517	.448	-				
Japan	.195	.089	.472	-			
China	.285	.396	.236	.127	-		
India	.210	.377	.134	.093	.580	-	
Australasia	.247	.336	.234	.227	.373	.455	-

there are several methods that could be used to assist the researcher to identify the two axes. These include research expertise, property fitting procedures, and experimental design methods.

For this study, researcher expertise was used as it is probably the most common approach to axis interpretation (Green, Carmone, and Smith 1989, p. 67). The judgments were formed by examining the configuration itself. After the labeling was done by one researcher, it was confirmed by another researcher to obtain consistency of interpretation. Several other colleagues were also consulted to confirm the interpretation. While this procedure involved some element of subjectivity, it was considered appropriate given that it was not possible to use the other two methods as suggested by Green, Carmone, and Smith (1989).

Based on common agreement using the researcher expertise method, the Y axis in Figure 1 was interpreted as *country versus regional market,* with Australasia towards the country end. The X axis was labeled as *high economic growth versus low economic growth* with Japan towards the high-growth end.

Figure 1 shows that Singapore, the Asian NICs, and ASEAN form a cluster. This, to some extent, supports the earlier argument that Singapore belongs more to a regional group rather than existing as a single market in the minds of investors. Note that in contrast to Singapore, Japan is clearly a distinct market by itself. The same is true of Australasia.

Within the cluster, it is interesting to note that Singapore is positioned closer to the Asian NICs than ASEAN in the perceptual map. In essence, this means that in the respondents' minds, Singapore is more closely associated with being an Asian NIC than being a member of ASEAN. Although this would be an expected finding if factual data were taken into account (since in terms of economic performance, Singapore is closer to Hong Kong, Taiwan, and South Korea than to the other ASEAN countries), it is nevertheless a useful confirmation that the situation is also perceived this way and understood by the executives sampled. This finding should help to alleviate the common fears among other ASEAN countries that Singapore is "pinching" valuable FDI from them. In reality, Singapore is competing for FDI in a different league. It is more likely that other ASEAN countries like Malaysia, Indonesia, and Thailand are competing among themselves for the same pool of FDI, which differs from that which may have an interest in Singapore.

China and India are placed together in the perceptual map. This finding can be explained in view of the many common characteristics that both countries share. Both countries have a large population and land area, and are relatively less developed in terms of infrastructure (generally and

Table 9. Similarities Matrix of the Asia Pacific Markets

	Singapore	ASEAN	Asia NICs	Japan	China	India	Austral-asia
Singapore	-						
ASEAN	3	-					
Asia NICs	2	6	-				
Japan	17	21	4	-			
China	11	7	13	19	-		
India	16	8	18	20	1	-	
Australasia	12	10	14	15	9	5	-

Figure 1. Perceptual Map of Asia Pacific Markets

```
          .*....*....*....*....*....*....*....*....*....*....*....*....*
  3.000**                          COUNTRY                        ** 3.000
  2.769**                             |                           ** 2.769
  2.538**                             |                           ** 2.538
  2.308**                             |                           ** 2.308
  2.077**                             |                           ** 2.077
  1.846**                             |                           ** 1.846
  1.615**                             |                           ** 1.615
  1.385**                             |                           ** 1.385
  1.154**                             |                           ** 1.154
   .923**                             |● Australasia              **  .923
   .692**                             |                           **  .692
   .462**                Japan        |●India                     **  .462
   .231**                 ●           | China                     **  .231
   .000**--HIGH----------------------0---------------------LOW----**  .000
  -.231** GROWTH                      |                     GROWTH **  -.231
  -.462**              Asian NICs     |                           **  -.462
          -.462**                 ●   |                           ** -.462
  -.692**                         ●   |●ASEAN                     **  -.692
  -.923**                  Singapore  |                           **  -.923
 -1.154**                            |                            **-1.154
 -1.385**                            |                            **-1.385
 -1.615**                            |                            **-1.615
 -1.846**                            |                            **-1.846
 -2.077**                            |                            **-2.077
 -2.308**                            |                            **-2.308
 -2.538**                            |                            **-2.538
 -2.769**                            |                            **-2.769
 -3.000**                          REGION                         **-3.000
          .*....*....*....*....*....*....*....*....*....*....*....*....*
          .  -3.3333. -2.0000.  -.6667.  .6667.  2.0000.  3.3333.
          -4.0000   -2.6667  -1.3333   .0000  1.3333  2.6667  4.0000
```

related to FDI). In addition, owing to their low labor skills and wages, they are currently attracting more labor-intensive industries at a level even lower than those in Malaysia and Thailand. For example, over the last five years, Hong Kong has moved out almost all its labor-intensive industries like toys, clothing, and textiles to China. Interestingly, Taiwan has also begun to do likewise although politically it is still at odds with China.

DISCUSSION AND STRATEGIC IMPLICATIONS

The findings of this study have practical relevance to Singapore as well as to other nations faced with similar conditions (e.g., countries with small domestic markets but which are part of a regional grouping). Knowing the underlying reasons why U.S. firms invest in the Asia Pacific region would help Singapore better understand the needs of present and potential investors. For example, the factor analysis results showed that U.S. firms were motivated to seek manufacturing investments in the Asia Pacific region for two main reasons: to lower costs and increase profitability, and to pursue market objectives. They placed somewhat less emphasis on resource and risk-hedging objectives.

Singapore must maintain its price competitiveness in relation to its competitors in order to attract FDI. This does not mean that it should offer the lowest labor cost, however, because Singapore cannot outbid its ASEAN neighbors like Thailand, Malaysia, and Indonesia in providing cheaper labor. These countries had per capita incomes of below US$3,000 as of 1989 (compared to Singapore's US$11,000). Thus, the type of U.S. investments that would be attracted to other ASEAN countries would be very different from those seeking to invest in Singapore. For the former, U.S. firms are likely to be seeking cost reduction, especially in the area of labor. This is something that Singapore cannot offer. More significantly, if Singapore were to use low labor costs as an investment incentive, it may also risk attracting the wrong type of FDI. This would jeopardize its efforts to progress further as a developed nation.

To develop better strategies, an understanding of how U.S. investors position Singapore vis-à-vis the other Asia Pacific countries/markets will provide valuable insights. For example, close examination of the perceptual map in Figure 1 shows that Singapore's immediate competitors are the other Asian NICs–Hong Kong, South Korea, and Taiwan–rather than the ASEAN countries, which tended to compete more indirectly. Thus, the incentives that have to be offered to U.S. investors by Singapore have to be very different from those offered by the other Asian NICs and ASEAN members. Different targeting strategies have to be developed for different audiences. In this case, the target audience of U.S. investors for Singapore is likely to be the same as those of Hong Kong, South Korea, and Taiwan (these three Asian NICs have per capita incomes ranging from a low of US$4,000 for South Korea to US$9,500 for Hong Kong).

It is interesting to note that among the four NICs, Singapore has the highest per capita income. Thus, even among the NICs, Singapore does not have a competitive advantage in the area of lower labor cost. A more realistic approach to maintain its price competitiveness is to offer value for money. This means that Singapore should strive to provide better services to foreign investors by offering highly skilled and productive workers, providing an efficient business infrastructure, and building up a good complement of supporting industries. In other words, Singapore should offer a total investment incentive package which will help foreign investors improve productivity, quality, and return on investment (ROI). Here, it is important to point out that according to a U.S. Department of Commerce survey, Singapore was rated as the most profitable investment site in Asia for U.S. firms in 1988 (see Table 10). In fact, Singapore was rated the third most profitable site worldwide for U.S. firms. Only Norway (ROI of 86.2 percent) and Spain (ROI of 46.3 percent) were rated higher. The favorable ROI of Singapore should be used more extensively and effectively by policy makers, as an added advantage over its direct competitors, to market the country to U.S. firms as a place for investment.

The felt interests by U.S. firms in the Asia Pacific region are reflected by the significance attached by the respondents to Japan and Asian NICs as important markets. This is a positive finding for Singapore because those U.S. firms which want to be closer to Asia Pacific markets will likely consider Singapore as a possible candidate. Given that Singapore is perceived favorably to be part of two regional markets (Asian NICs and

Table 10. Rates of Return on
U.S. Investments in Asia (1988)

Country	ROI (%)
Singapore	40.5
Malaysia	35.4
South Korea	29.8
Hong Kong	27.1
Taiwan	24.8
Thailand	22.6
Japan	19.9

Source: U.S. Dept. of Commerce

ASEAN) with high growth potential, it must capitalize on its unique strategic location as a viable alternative to its direct competitors–Hong Kong, South Korea, and Taiwan–and as a "gateway" to the Asia Pacific markets, especially ASEAN. This is a pull factor for Singapore, although it has to compete with the other countries in the region. Moreover, being considered as part of a regional market (see Figure 1), Singapore's fate is very much affected by the social, political, and economic stability of its neighbors, and must be sensitive to developments there.

One way to ensure its future attractiveness as a place for U.S. investors is for Singapore to play a more proactive role in the economic development of the region. This is because economic development often brings about economic stability, and social and political order. When the region is able to grow economically, it also becomes more attractive to foreign investors. It must be remembered that Singapore is too small to justify large foreign investments by itself for market purposes. Insofar as market access is concerned, the attraction has to be the region. Singapore should play up its distinctive advantage of being part of both ASEAN and the Asian NICs. This allows it to play a "gateway" and "catalyst" role to ASEAN's large markets, and to have access to Asian NICs' industrialization level and sophistication. Therefore, Singapore should embark on an ambitious effort to forge business links in the region. In doing so, there will be greater incentives to invest in Singapore, as it can provide the necessary linkages and support services. In addition, such an approach will also enable Singapore to help fulfill the foreign investors' pursuits of market objectives.

Business links can be established through government initiatives in the form of government-to-government agreement, or through private sector efforts. Singapore's local entrepreneurs should be encouraged to invest in the region to establish such business links. Singapore-based businesses can also invest in markets that are not in their cluster so as to foster stronger business ties. For example, the recent creation of the Singapore-Johore-Riau Growth Triangle represents the coming together of the three governments of Singapore, Malaysia, and Indonesia on economic development that will be of mutual benefit. It also represents a unique combination of abundant land and natural resources (the Riau Islands of Indonesia), plentiful labor supply (Johore state of Malaysia), and advanced infrastructure and other support facilities (Singapore). Thus far, this growth triangle has received very good private sector support as well.

Strategically, Singapore must "plug" itself into growth areas or regions. For example, it could play a more active role as a member of the Asia Pacific Economic Cooperation (APEC) process. APEC membership currently includes the ASEAN countries, Japan, South Korea, Australia, New Zealand, the United States, and Canada, with possible extension to China, Hong Kong, and Taiwan. The need to belong to a grouping is important in view of the increasing trend toward regionalization on a continental scale–the Australia-New Zealand common market, the Canada-U.S. Free Trade Agreement, and the economic integration of Western Europe by 1992, with possible "associate" membership extended to the East European countries.

On the trend toward creating economic groupings, it is interesting to note that they are not confined to affiliation only on a land-based basis (that is, proximity along common borders). In fact, a prominent Japanese, Mr. Hisao Kanamori, Chairman of the Japan Centre for Economic Research, commented recently about the possibility of strategic economic alliances along a sea-based orientation (*Singapore Straits Times*, November 13, 1990):

If the natural resources of the Soviet Far East, Japanese money and technology, Chinese and North Korean labor, and South Korea's low-priced capital and consumer goods are combined, this will bring considerable development to the Japan Sea Rim.

Such remarks should not be taken lightly. In fact, some other scholars have also recently been arguing the case for a resurgence of European economic power as a result of the collapse of the Berlin Wall. This economic power is premised on alliances of Russian scientific research, German technology and capital, and East European semi-skilled labor. A small nation like Singapore cannot afford to ignore such developments. More importantly, it should attempt to develop strategic economic alliances with various economic groupings, either directly or indirectly. It is a truism that it cannot afford to do it alone anymore in the future.

FUTURE RESEARCH AND CONCLUSION

Research on how the image of countries affects consumer and industrial buying behavior has been well developed. This chapter basically extends that stream of research to FDI, by treating countries as products and investors as potential buyers. Just like consumers do with regards to product origin, companies form different images of countries concerning their

potential as places for investment. Such images would affect their decisions on whether to invest in those countries. This study shows that images
of countries can be measured, and that investors do hold different impressions of various countries as potential investment locations.

While the research has been focused on Singapore and U.S. investors,
there is no reason why it could not be applied to other settings. To begin
with, the methodology and statistical techniques employed in this study
can be replicated easily in other studies. When different countries are
competing for FDI, it is important to find out how they are being perceived
and clustered by investors. The use of MDS in this research, for example,
shows that it is possible to segregate the direct from the indirect competing
nations which are going after the same pool of FDI. It also allows a
country to know more precisely its competitive position relative to other
nations. In this way, appropriate packages of investment incentives can be
developed, and more effective marketing strategies can be designed to
attract FDI.

This study also shows that for a small country (like Singapore) which
belongs to a larger regional grouping that has a strong identity, it is important to find out its image both individually and as a part of its region. Thus,
the relevance of this study would apply to countries like Canada, Belgium,
and New Zealand. These countries are easily overshadowed by their respective regions of North America, Western Europe, and Australasia. In
fact, the measurement of image at a macro level of a country or region
need not be confined to what has been just described. It can also be studied
in situations where a country has a strong identity within a regional grouping (e.g. Great Britain and Germany in the context of the European Community), or when it is even stronger than the grouping itself (e.g., the U.S.
in the context of the North American continent).

One immediate application of this research would be to replicate it in
the context of the East European countries. With the collapse of the Berlin
Wall, and the scramble for FDI, the East European countries provide a rich
opportunity for researchers to embark on country image studies. To begin
with, do these countries have favorable images in the eyes of Western
investors? It was originally thought that by embracing Western democra-
cy, FDI would pour in without much difficulty. However, this has not
happened (following the initial excitement after the events of 1988-1989,
many investors are delaying their decisions and it is widely reported that
only about 10 percent of approved investments are in fact operationalized). Studies on country image may provide useful answers to help policy
makers in these countries to do better in attracting FDI.

With the emergence of economic groupings like Australia-New Zealand, U.S.-Canada, the European Community, and other loose groupings like the Asian NICs and ASEAN, it may even be timely to examine not only the images of countries within each of these groupings, but also the images of the different groupings. Do these groups compete with each other? For example, after the collapse of the Berlin Wall, it was argued that the East European bloc (previously Warsaw Pact members) would pose a serious threat to countries in the Asian NICs and ASEAN as an alternative site for U.S., Japanese, and West European investments. But do these investors perceive the East European bloc as being similar to Asian NICs and ASEAN? Do they consider these three regions as substitutes of one another? Are they different, and if so, in what ways in the eyes of the investors? These are questions that could be answered by studies along the same lines as this research.

Finally, it is important to note that country or region image is a complex construct. It needs to be studied more through a detailed operationalization of its underlying variables. This study has attempted to view it on an aggregate basis. Perhaps future studies should try to probe deeper into the various dimensions of a country/region image from the investment standpoint.

REFERENCES

Arpan, J.S. and D.A. Ricks (1986), "Foreign Direct Investment in the U.S., 1974-1984." *Journal of International Business Studies,*17, 3 (Fall) 149-153.

Bannister, J.P. and J.A. Saunders (1978), "U.K. Consumers' Attitudes Towards Imports: The Measurement of National Stereotype Image." *European Journal of Marketing,* 12, 8, 562- 570.

Bilkey, Warren J. and Erik Nes (1982), "Country-of-Origin Effects on Product Evaluations." *Journal of International Business Studies,* 8(1) (Spring/Summer) 89-99.

Brunner, James A. and George M. Taoka (1977), "Marketing and Negotiating in the People's Republic of China: Perceptions of American Businessmen Who Attended the 1975 Canton Fair." *Journal of International Business Studies,* 8, 3 (Fall/Winter) 69-82.

Cattell, R.B. (1966), "The Scree Test for the Number of Factors." *Multivariate Behavioural Research,* 1, 245-276.

Cattin, Philippe, Alain Jolibert, and Colleen Lohnes (1982), "A Cross-Cultural Study of 'Made In' Concepts." *Journal of International Business Studies* (Winter) 131-141.

Cooper, L.G. (1983), "A Review of Multidimensional Scaling in Marketing Research." *Applied Psychological Measurement,* 7, 4, 427-450.

Darling, John R. and Frederic B. Kraft (1977), "A Competitive Profile of Products and Associated Marketing Practices of Selected European and non-European Countries." *European Journal of Marketing,* 11, 7, 519-531.

Economic Survey of Singapore 1989. Ministry of Trade and Industry, Singapore.

Ehrman, C.M. and M. Hamburg (1986), "Information Search for Foreign Direct Investment Using Two-Stage Country Selection Procedures: A New Procedure." *Journal of International Business Studies,* 17, 2 (Summer) 93-116.

Gaedeke, Ralph (1973), "Consumer Attitudes Toward Products 'Made In' Developing Countries." *Journal of Retailing,* 49(2), (Summer) 13-24.

Gorsuch, R.L. (1983), *Factor Analysis.* 2nd ed. Hillsdale, NJ: Lawrence Erlbaum Associates.

Green, P.E., F.J. Carmone, Jr., and S.M. Smith (1989), *Multidimensional Scaling: Concepts and Application.* Boston: Allyn and Bacon. 11-36.

Greer, T.V. and J.G. Greer (1986), "National Image: The Concept and Its Measurement." In C.T. Tan, W. Lazer, and V.H. Kirpalani (eds.), *Proceedings of the American Marketing Association's International Marketing Conference* (Singapore, June) 16-18.

Han, Min C. (1988), "The Role of Consumer Patriotism in the Choice of Domestic versus Foreign Products." *Journal of Advertising Research* 28(3) (June-July) 25-32.

Han, Min C. and Vern Terpstra (1988), "Country-of-Origin Effects for Uni-National and Bi-National Products." *Journal of International Business Studies* (Summer) 235-54.

Hauser, H. (1986), "Promotion of Foreign Direct Investment to Developing Countries: An Exercise in Cooperation." In H. Hauser (ed.), *Promotion of Direct Investment in Developing Countries* (Swiss Institute for Research into International Economic Relations, Economic Structures and Regional Science) 9-18.

Hennart, J.F. (1986), "Internationization in Practice: Early Foreign Direct Investments in Malaysian Tin Mining." *Journal of International Business Studies,* 17, 2 (Summer) 131-143.

Hooley, G.J., D. Shipley, and N. Krieger (1988), "A Method for Modelling Consumer Perceptions of Country of Origin." *International Marketing Review,* 6, 1 (Autumn) 67-76.

Johansson, Johny K. and Israel D. Nebenzahl (1986), "Multinational Production: Effect on Brand Value." *Journal of International Business Studies,* 17, 3 (Fall) 101-126.

Khanna, S. (1986), "Asian Companies and the Country Stereotype Paradox: An Empirical Study." *Columbia Journal of World Business* (Summer) 29-38.

Kruskal, J.B. (1964), "Multidimensional Scaling by Optimizing Goodness of Fit to a Nonmetric Hypothesis." *Psychometrika,* 29, 1-27.

Kruskal, J.B., F.W. Young, and J.B. Seery (1973), "How to Use KYST: A Very Flexible Program to Do Multidimensional Scaling and Unfolding." *Multidimensional Scaling Program Package of Bell Laboratories.* Murray Hill, NJ: Bell Laboratories.

Lee, K.H. and T.W.C. Lo (1988), "American Businesspeople's Perceptions of

Marketing and Negotiation in the People's Republic of China." *International Marketing Review*, 5, 2 (Summer) 41-51.

Leong, S.M. and C.T. Tan (1990), "A Comparative Study of Investment Attractiveness of Nations and Regions." In K.C. Mun (ed.), *Proceedings of the Academy of International Business Southeast Asia Regional Conference* (Hong Kong, June) 306-310.

Luqmani, M., G.M. Habib, and S. Kassem (1988), "Marketing to LDC Governments." *International Marketing Review*, 5, 1 (Spring) 56- 67.

Morello, Gabriele (1984), "The 'Made-In' Issue–A Comparative Research on the Image of Domestic and Foreign Products." *European Research* (July) 95-100.

Nagashima, Akira (1970), "A Comparison of Japanese and U.S. Attitudes Towards Foreign Products." *Journal of Marketing*, 34 (January) 68-74.

Nagashima, Akira (1977), "A Comparative 'Made In' Product Image Survey Among Japanese Businessmen." *Journal of Marketing*, 41 (July) 95-100.

Narayana, Chem L. (1981), "Aggregate Images of American and Japanese Products: Implications on International Marketing." *Columbia Journal of World Business*, 16 (Summer) 31-35.

Nigh, D. (1985), "The Effects of Political Events on United States Direct Foreign Investment: A Pooled Time-Series and Cross- Sectional Analysis." *Journal of International Business Studies*, 16, 1 (Spring) 1-17.

Papadopoulos, Nicolas, Judith J. Marshall, and Louise A. Heslop (1988), "Strategic Implications of Product and Country Images: A Modelling Approach." *Marketing Productivity* (European Society for Opinion and Marketing Research, 41st Research Congress, Lisbon, September) 69-90.

Papadopoulos, Nicolas, Louise A. Heslop, and József Berács (1990), "National Stereotyping and Product Evaluations: An Empirical Investigation of Consumers in a Socialist Country." *International Marketing Review*, 7, 1 (Spring) 32-47.

Prasad, S.B. (1986), "American Executives' Perception of Foreign State Enterprises." *Journal of International Business Studies*, 17, 2 (Summer) 145-152.

Reierson, Curtis C. (1966), "Are Foreign Products Seen as National Stereotypes." *Journal of Retailing*, 42, 3 (Fall), 33-40.

Reierson, Curtis C. (1967), "Attitude Change Toward Foreign Products." *Journal of Marketing Research*, IV: (November) 385- 87.

Report of the Economic Committee (1986), *The Singapore Economy: New Directions*. Ministry of Trade and Industry, Singapore. 19.

Rucker, M.H., S. A. Sembach, and C. Cuicci (1986), "Consumer's Evaluation of Foreign versus Domestic Apparel: The Relationship of Style to Consumer Preference." In C.T. Tan, W. Lazer, and V.H. Kirpalani (eds.), *Proceedings of the American Marketing Association's International Marketing Conference* (Singapore, June) 11-15.

Sabi, M. (1988), "An Application of the Theory of Foreign Direct Investment to Multinational Banking in LDCs." *Journal of International Business Studies*, 19, 3 (Fall) 433-448.

Tallman, S.B. (1988), "Home Country Political Risk and Foreign Direct Investment in the United States." *Journal of International Business Studies,* 19, 2 (Summer) 219-235.

Wall, Marjorie and Louise A. Heslop (1986), "Consumer Attitudes toward Canadian-made versus Imported Products." *Journal of the Academy of Marketing Science,* 14(2): 27-36.

Wang, Chih-Kang and Charles W. Lamb (1980), "Foreign Environmental Factors Influencing American Consumers' Predispositions Toward European Products." *Journal of the Academy of Marketing Science,* 8, 4, 345-356.

Wang, Chih-Kang and Charles W. Lamb (1983), "The Impact of Selected Environmental Forces Upon Consumers' Willingness to Buy Foreign Products." *Journal of the Academy of Marketing Science,* 11(2): (Winter) 71-84.

Wee, Chow-Hou and Annukka Paloheimo (1989), "Perceptions of Foreign Investors by Chinese Top Management." In William Lazer, Eric H. Shaw, and Chow-Hou Wee (eds.), *World Marketing Congress International Conference Series,* IV (Boca Raton, FL: Academy of Marketing Science) 271-277.

Young, F.W. (1968), "Torsca: An IBM Program for Nonmetric Multidimensional Scaling." *Journal of Marketing Research,* V (August) 319-321.

PART V.
INFLUENCES ON PRODUCT
AND COUNTRY IMAGES

INTRODUCTION

As with its predecessor, Part V breaks considerable new ground. The five chapters that comprise it examine various external influences on the formation and impact of country images, the evolution of these images over time, and the potential ways in which they can have a "reverse" influence on the behavior of nations toward each other.

The first three chapters draw from studies of U.S. consumers. Of these, Chapter 14 expands existing knowledge by considering "political realm" and "culture realm" and their influence on consumer views about a variety of countries. The conclusion is that both of these factors as well as perceptions of a country's economic development affect the consumers' willingness to buy products from it.

The next two chapters provide longitudinal perspectives on country images. They both draw from multiple studies conducted by their authors over long periods of time to track the evolution of consumer views. Chapter 15 focuses on consumers' views about products from industrialized countries, while Chapter 16 discusses views about the People's Republic of China. In light of the timing of the studies, the latter chapter also provides an interesting glimpse on the potential influence of an event of major international significance, the Tiananmen Square tragedy, on consumers' future willingness to buy Chinese products.

Following along similar lines, but in a different context, Chapter 17 also considers the potential influence of a major international event. The setting this time is Israeli consumer perceptions about South Korean products in relation to the 1988 Summer Olympic Games in Seoul. Drawing from two studies carried out just before and just after the games, the chapter shows a clear change in perceptions of South Korean products and draws implications for researchers, the private sector, and national governments.

The last chapter in the book rounds out the event-related analyses of the previous two. Chapter 18 poses the question, what may be the significance of the views of people from different countries about each other and their products, if the countries' governments want to expand their economic ties? The context for this chapter is provided by the Canada-U.S. Free Trade Agreement, which came into effect on January 1, 1989. The chapter is able to trace the views of Americans and Canadians about each other in considerable detail since the amount of country-of-origin research that has been carried out in both of these countries is extensive. A number of important implications for business strategy, public policy, and research are drawn and can be useful not only from the North American perspective but also from that of other countries that are interested in closer economic ties (e.g., Australia and New Zealand, ASEAN, and the European Community).

Chapter 14

Environmental Influences on Country-of-Origin Bias

John C. Crawford
James R. Lumpkin

INTRODUCTION

A recent article in *Fortune* (Faltermayer, 1990), titled "Is 'Made in U.S.A.' Fading Away?" made the very valid point that much of U.S. industry has lost ground to imports over the last decade. The loss of market share to foreign companies is most evident in high-tech industries where, according to the article, imports now account for 34 percent of computers, 37 percent of semi-conductors, and 46 percent of machine tools. In other industries the impact of imports is not quite so dramatic but is nonetheless severe (color TV sets 26 percent, apparel 26 percent, tires 19 percent). This loss of market share reduces employment as domestic manufacturers either go out of business or move their manufacturing operations offshore to low wage-rate countries. In the automobile industry, assembly line employment has fallen by 21 percent (a loss of 70,000 jobs) in ten years, and in steel over 50 percent of workers have been laid off in the same period. The $70 billion a year apparel industry lost over 200,000 jobs from 1979-1989.

This loss of market share to often cheaper, sometimes superior, imported products has manufacturers fighting back both in terms of improved products and through advertising campaigns urging consumers to "buy American" in preference to foreign products. For example, "The Pride Is Back" campaign of the 1980s and the 1990 "Advantage: Chrysler," both by Chrysler Corp., show how one automobile manufacturer is trying to overcome the quality perception of imported cars while at the same time appealing to the patriotism of consumers. Obviously, some manufacturers see a need to improve the image of the U.S. as a country-of-origin.

This "country-of-origin" issue has been receiving increased attention in the marketing literature in recent years. That it has commercial as well as academic interest has added to its legitimacy as a research topic. The present study focuses on studying the country-of-origin phenomenon in the context of the apparel sector, for two reasons. First, apparel is a major import category involving many developed and developing countries and, as mentioned, imports have made heavy inroads on a wide front. Second, like automobiles, apparel has been the subject of major advertising campaigns stressing either the superiority of the U.S. product or patriotic appeals on behalf of the product or of U.S. workers in the apparel trade. Retailers such as Wal-Mart, K-mart, J.C. Penney, and Sears Roebuck have all joined the manufacturers and unions in highlighting products "Made in the U.S.A." (*Business Week*, October 27, 1986), although several other major retailers have yet to show their support (Sternquist and Tolbert 1986).

While this study focuses on a specific sector of economic activity in the U.S., the findings are relevant to exporters and importers in other country settings and sectors that are faced with similar conditions (e.g., growing imports affecting the economic performance of domestic industrial sectors). The methodology used, in particular, can be applied in virtually any setting, and its ability to group countries based on consumers' "willingness to buy" products from them should be of interest to both practitioners and researchers.

LITERATURE REVIEW

It seems well-established that knowledge of country-of-origin does influence consumers' evaluations of products (Schooler 1965; Reierson 1966; Nagashima 1970; Chasin and Jaffe 1979; Lumpkin, Crawford, and Kim 1985; Nigh 1985; Han and Terpstra 1988; Hong and Wyer 1989). For certain products, such as automobiles and apparel, American consumers have expressed a bias in favor of products of domestic production (Johansson and Nebenzahl 1986). Canadians, on the other hand, while generally supportive of Canadian products, have been reported to prefer the imported versions of many products to domestic goods (Kaynak and Cavusgil 1983; Wall and Heslop 1986). Several U.S. studies (Dornoff, Tankersley, and White 1974; Czepiec 1984; Lumpkin, Crawford, and Kim 1985) report that the U.S. consumer does make distinctions based on the origin of the product. Like the Canadians, U.S. consumers often regard the foreign-made version as a good substitute for the domestic product. Nevertheless, for apparel there is a reduction in perceived risk when the consumer is made aware that the country-of-origin is the United States (Lumpkin, Crawford, and Kim 1985). So, for this product category, country-of-origin is an important factor in the decision to buy.

The country-of-origin of the product is *one* important factor influencing consumer attitudes (Erickson, Johansson, and Chao 1984; Johansson, Douglas, and Nonaka 1985; Johansson and Thorelli 1985; Han and Terpstra 1988; Hong and Wyer 1989). Investigations of the antecedents of country-of-origin bias reveal that it is multifaceted and there is a hierarchy of biases (see, for example, Bilkey and Nes 1982). Furthermore, one evaluative criterion of the country-of-origin is whether or not it is a developed country. Dickerson (1982, 1986) reported that domestic apparel was perceived to be of higher quality by a majority (61 percent) of U.S. consumers. She speculated that this was due to the poor quality of products from developing countries but did not specifically test this hypothesis. Thus, there is a need to study the effect of an origin country's level of development and the perception it engenders in the consumer's mind.

Wang and Lamb (1980, 1983) reported on research that included two other environmental factors–culture and political climate–in addition to development. The notion of their research was that:

> . . . consumers generalize their knowledge or perceptions of environmental conditions in foreign countries to the quality of products produced. . . using environmental conditions as a surrogate for a great many other pieces of unknown information. (1983, p. 72)

U.S. consumers were found to be willing to buy products from developing countries that were considered to be politically free, but not from Latin American and Asian developing countries. While providing a useful first step in understanding the country-of-origin effect, this research has several shortcomings. First, the sample of 273 respondents represented only one community, which limits the generalization of the findings. Second, the research used the "general product concept" rather than relating bias to a specific product category. As noted, earlier research has found that country-of-origin bias varies by product (although the direction of bias tends to be similar for most product categories). Third, and most important, they concluded that if consumers were more willing to buy from a developed country than a developing one, for example, then that willingness would apply across *all* developed countries. However, it is unlikely that all developed countries, all free countries, or all countries from a given culture realm would be perceived to be the same by consumers. Furthermore, if bias is indeed multifaceted, consumers would use a *combination* of environmental dimensions in their evaluations. Countries with similar environmental profiles should elicit similar "willingness to buy" tendencies. There is support for this approach in a Canadian study by Hung (1989).

Our purpose here is to determine if there is country-of-origin bias based on level of development, political climate, and culture realm and, if so, whether this bias is consistent across countries. Based on the work of Wang and Lamb (1983), our research was designed to test three hypotheses:

- H1: A country's level of development has no impact on U.S. consumers' willingness to buy apparel.
- H2: A country's culture realm has no impact on U.S. consumers' willingness to buy apparel.
- H3: A country's political climate has no impact on U.S. consumers' willingness to buy apparel.

The results will aid merchants in choosing products with a greater likelihood of success, as well as producers interested in penetrating foreign markets. Because perceptions of, and attitudes toward, the country-of-origin can be transferred to the product, the country must be evaluated along with the product. This research should help in that evaluation.

METHODOLOGY

Sample

A self-administered questionnaire was mailed to a nationally distributed random sample of 1,800 U.S. households participating in the Market Facts Consumer Mail Panel. The panel consists of 200,000 households and is representative of the U.S. population. A total of 1,462 (81.2 percent) responses were received. Compared to the U.S. population, the sample was much older than average. It was higher in education and contained slightly more married respondents. Table 1 details the socio-demographic characteristics of the sample compared to national population statistics. The general application of these findings, of course, needs to be considered with caution. However, the sample represents an important segment—the "upscale" consumer–that should be of interest to retailers and producers alike.

Table 1. Socio-Demographic Comparison:
Sample and U.S. Population

Characteristics	Sample (percent)	U.S.* (percent)
Sex		
Male	31	49
Female	69	51
Age		
65 years and older	20	11
(Median in years:		
sample 51, U.S. 30)		
Marital Status		
Married Respondents	82	71
Income		
Household income < $ 6,000	10	11
Household income > $20,000	55	53
Occupation		
Professional/Managerial	52	53
Unskilled	9	28
Education		
High School Graduates	33	37
University Graduates	34	17

* *Source.* U.S. Bureau of the Census (1984, May),
Current Population Reports, Ser. P-25, No. 952.

Questionnaire

The survey measured the willingness to buy apparel from each of 45 countries. Apparel was chosen because it is an important imported good and because of the need to investigate consumer behavior related to a specific product category. Further, it has been found that apparel from the U.S. ranked highest in quality when compared to imported goods (Dickerson 1982). In addition, Hugstad and Darr (1986) found that for two apparel categories (shoes and shirts), 75 percent of consumers placed medium to high importance on knowing the country-of-origin. The fact that a wide range of apparel products from a wide range of countries are imported into the U.S. supports further study of this product category and of consumers' attitudes toward the products' country-of-origin. Country-of-origin is one of the salient factors used in the purchase decision.

Since not all countries export apparel to the U.S., consumer purchasing behavior does not reflect perceptions toward all countries. Also, since few consumers actually would have purchased apparel from each country in any given period, the more general attitude measure of "willingness to buy" was used. Using a broad attitudinal measure rather than a behavioral measure is not an ideal approach. In the marketplace, consumers will have more than just country-of-origin information. However, by not providing other information when asking about willingness to purchase, the baseline effect of country-of-origin can be determined. This method can obtain perceptions about apparel from a given country assuming all other cues are equal. Of course, they never are. In practice, such tactics as using price concessions to overcome negative bias can be implemented (Johansson and Thorelli 1985). This research tries to identify perceptions of countries regardless of whether they currently sell apparel in the U.S. This can provide retailers and producers with guidelines for decisions on current and future sources of supply, and help to determine whether any concessions might be required to counter biases.

There is a limitation to this approach. Familiarity with apparel from a given country may affect the evaluation. The respondent may be processing other cues when completing the questionnaire, even when no other cues were given. Dickerson (1986) suggests domestic products are thought of more favorably. However, other research has found that domestic products (which should be more familiar to consumers) are not *necessarily* evaluated more positively than "foreign" products (Dornoff, Tankersley, and White 1974; Bannister and Saunders 1978; Kaynak and Cavusgil 1983; Czepiec 1984; Lumpkin, Crawford, and Kim 1985; Johansson, Douglas, and Nonaka 1985). This was found across products (including apparel) and with consumers from various countries. Consequently, the familiarity respondents might have with apparel from some of the countries is not thought to bias unduly the perception of apparel from those countries or the "willingness to buy" rating.

The 45 countries selected for study represent a cross-section of political climates and stages of economic development from the world's culture realms. They include both major and minor suppliers of U.S. apparel imports as well as countries that have yet to enter the U.S. market.

The level of economic development variable was based on Howe's (1974) classification. This divides the world's economies into poorest developing, developing, and developed categories.

The variable "political climate" was taken from Gastil (1988) and reflects the performance of the countries on civil and political rights. Each country was classified as free, partly free, or not free. Five culture realms were created based on Preston James' (1976) schema: Latin America, Africa, North America/Europe, Asia, and Middle East/North Africa. Table

3, later in this chapter, presents the classification of each country based on these environmental factors.

Data Analysis

To address the central objective of this research, factor analysis of the consumer's willingness to buy from a named country was employed. If attitude toward foreign countries is related consistently to the countries' environment, then countries similar on these measures should elicit highly correlated "willingness to buy" scores. Thus, they should load together. The data set was judged to be appropriate for factor analysis[1] and the principal axis factor procedure with Oblimin (oblique) rotation was employed.[2]

RESULTS

Using the latent root criterion and the Scree test,[3] five factors were extracted from the factor analysis. As measures of internal consistency,

---

1. In evaluating whether factor analysis could be applied to the data, several criteria were considered. The correlations were "high" (79 percent are above 0.60 and only 2 percent are between 0.40 and 0.50) and all are significantly greater than zero (at the 0.0001 level). In addition, the communalities are "moderately large" (Stewart 1981, p. 57). Finally, the Kaiser-Meyer-Olkin Measure of Sampling Adequacy (MSA) (Kaiser 1970) of 0.977 would be considered "marvelous" based on Kaiser and Rice's (1974) valuative criteria. The MSA measures the extent to which the variables belong together and are thus appropriate for factor analysis.

2. Both the principal axis (common) and principal components factor procedures provided the same factor pattern, as would be expected with this relatively large problem (Gorsuch 1974). However, the principal axis results are reported, as the principal components factor model tends to give inflated loadings and may be misinterpreted (Green and Tull 1987; Acito and Anderson 1980).

The Oblimin (oblique) rotation method was chosen over an orthogonal method because the requirement of uncorrelated factors is unrealistic for this problem. Further, in evaluating both methods, the oblique solution gave a more simple structure as 108 loadings were 0.10 or less (the hyperplane count). The orthogonal (Varimax) rotation has only 35 loadings this low.

3. The latent root criterion (minimum eigenvalue of one) and the Scree test (Cattell and Vogelman 1977) both indicated that the five factors which explain 72.5 percent of the variance give the minimum number of factors that account for the maximum amount of variance.

inter-item correlations of the significant factor loadings and Cronbach's alpha coefficients for groups of factors were calculated. Both of these indicators are high with all alpha coefficients being 0.8 or above. The factor grouping of the 45 countries, the loadings (those of 0.30 and above are highlighted as significant), communalities, eigenvalues, inter-item correlations and alphas are shown in Table 2.

The objective of the study was to determine if there was a bias among U.S. consumers based on the environmental conditions of foreign countries. If so, it was hypothesized that countries with similar characteristics would express similar willingness to buy from those countries. Table 3 shows the environmental characteristics for each country. Presented also are the mean willingness to buy for both the individual countries and for each group of countries, developed from the factor analysis.

In only one of the factor-derived country groups (Group 1) do all the countries have development (high), political climate (free), and culture realm (European) in common. Thus, the three null hypotheses that were posited earlier are rejected only for countries in Group 1. With this exception, the environmental variables did not line up completely by groups, although some support exists for rejecting the hypotheses in other cases. For example, of the five countries in Group 2, all but Japan are "developing" and "partly free" politically, and all but Mexico are in the "Asia" cultural realm. Further, all four countries in Group 5 are classified as "not free." The main findings are discussed in some more detail below.

Overall, the results do *not* support the findings of Wang and Lamb (1980, 1983). In other words, all countries in Group 1 had the same level of development (developed), culture realm (North America/Europe), and political climate (free)—but none of the other groups of countries had all of the environmental variables in common. It should be noted that the U.S., while loading in Group 1, represents a very special case. Consumers do not perceive domestic apparel as being in the same category as imported apparel and somehow discriminate on this basis. That is, for all intents and purposes, the U.S. is perceived as a "country group" of itself (see Table 2).

The "willingness to buy" measure *does* discriminate among the country groups. The group means range from 1.95 to 3.37 (where 5 is "extremely willing"). Based on the Scheffe test for differences in means, there is a significant difference (at the 0.05 level) in mean willingness to buy for each group of countries. Nevertheless, as Table 3 shows, there is some overlap in the individual country means. For instance, the mean willingness to buy from Japan exceeds the means for several of the countries in Group 1.

Table 2. Factor Analysis Results*
With Interitem Correlation and Communalities

Countries	1	2	3	4	5	Inter-item corr.	Communalities
France	.78	.06	-.23	-.04	.04	.75	.77
Italy	.77	.02	-.15	.00	.03	.75	.77
Canada	.77	-.04	.07	.04	-.09	.65	.72
Sweden	.73	-.06	.02	.11	.06	.67	.79
U. K.	.68	-.16	.13	.05	.00	.64	.72
Australia	.63	-.17	-.19	-.11	.03	.78	.79
West Germany	.60	-.23	-.06	-.05	.14	.64	.73
Spain	.55	.05	-.11	.36	.02	.69	.72
New Zealand	.51	-.30	-.01	.11	.08	.78	.76
Israel	.37	-.20	-.14	.19	.06	.65	.65
U.S.A.	.30	.02	.08	.02	-.29	.29	.18
Taiwan	.04	-.70	-.12	.09	.03	.75	.82
Hong Kong	.15	-.69	-.08	-.02	.12	.73	.79
South Korea	.04	-.53	-.05	.35	.03	.75	.78
Japan	.32	-.50	-.04	.05	.07	.69	.74
Mexico	.18	-.30	-.26	.23	-.04	.67	.69
India	.11	-.16	-.62	.13	.03	.86	.84
Thailand	-.07	.31	-.60	.08	.05	.86	.85
Argentina	.19	-.07	-.59	.14	.07	.79	.85
Libya	-.02	.05	-.53	.25	.23	.71	.72
Brazil	.30	-.05	-.38	.27	.02	.74	.74
Honduras	-.05	-.02	-.00	.92	-.00	.89	.87
Nigeria	-.04	.01	-.10	.88	-.06	.92	.86
Ethiopia	-.02	.00	-.10	.86	-.05	.92	.87
Turkey	.03	-.07	.04	.81	.04	.79	.85
El Salvador	-.04	.03	-.05	.79	.14	.89	.85
Papua-New Guinea	-.02	-.23	-.00	.75	-.02	.79	.86
South Africa	.02	-.12	.07	.72	.03	.72	.76
Egypt	.16	.01	-.11	.68	-.00	.75	.82
Haiti	.08	-.05	-.06	.67	-.03	.70	.75
Sudan	-.08	-.03	-.17	.66	.16	.94	.86
Venezuela	.20	-.02	-.07	.66	.07	.81	.85
Hungary	.21	.04	.00	.61	.18	.79	.82
Ghana	-.01	-.01	-.17	.64	.18	.94	.84
Rumania	.20	.05	-.00	.62	.23	.81	.82
Poland	.30	-.00	.04	.53	.17	.74	.73
Ivory Coast	-.01	-.25	-.32	.49	-.04	.86	.84
Saudi Arabia	-.05	-.20	-.21	.48	.09	.73	.78
Singapore	.05	-.45	.02	.46	.03	.79	.77
Indonesia	-.02	-.34	-.30	.42	-.00	.86	.83
Vietnam	-.08	.04	-.10	.41	.42	.74.	.74
U.S.S.R..	.15	.01	-.02	.02	.80	.72	.77
China	.03	-.16	.07	.10	.72	.72	.74
Cuba	-.06	.02	-.13	.25	.63	.73	.79
North Korea	.01	-.07	-.31	.15	.42	.74	.66
Eigenvalues	24.8	4.2	1.3	1.2	1.0		
% of total variance	55.3	9.3	2.9	2.7	2.3		
Cronbach's alpha	.97	.92	.90	.88	.92		

* Based on Principal Axis approach with Oblimin (oblique) rotation.
** Factor loadings of ± .30 are significant, ± .40 are more important, ± .50 are very significant.

PRODUCT-COUNTRY IMAGES

Table 3. Comparison of Country Groups
on Willingness to Buy and Environmental Factors

Country Groups	Mean Willing-ness To Buy (a)	Standard Deviation (b)	Environmental Factors (c)	(d)
Group 1	3.37	.78		
U.S.A.	4.65	.80	3 EU	F
Canada	3.69	1.03	3 EU	F
United Kingdom	3.48	1.12	3 EU	F
Italy	3.47	1.04	3 EU	F
France	3.44	1.06	3 EU	F
Sweden	3.21	1.06	3 EU	F
West Germany	3.18	1.06	3 EU	F
Australia	3.13	1.05	3 EU	F
Spain	3.03	1.05	3 EU	F
New Zealand	2.95	1.04	3 EU	F
Israel	2.82	1.08	3 EU	F
Group 2	2.85	.91		
Japan	3.07	1.08	3 AS	F
Hong Kong	2.89	1.07	2 AS	PF
Mexico	2.85	1.08	2 LA	PF
Taiwan	2.80	1.09	2 AS	PF
South Korea	2.61	1.02	2 AS	PF
Group 3	2.52	.89		
Brazil	2.74	1.03	2 LA	PF
Thailand	2.58	1.03	1 AS	PF
India	2.57	1.04	1 AS	F
Argentina	2.55	1.01	2 LA	PF
Libya	2.23	1.03	2 ME	NF
Group 4	2.41	.85		
Ivory Coast	2.82	.99	1 AF	PF
Singapore	2.63	1.04	2 AS	PF
Poland	2.61	1.06	3 EU	NF
Haiti	2.56	1.05	1 LA	NF
Egypt	2.55	1.05	2 ME	PF
Venezuela	2.55	.98	2 LA	F
Indonesia	2.49	.98	1 AS	PF
Hungary	2.48	1.02	3 EU	NF
Papua-New Guinea	2.45	.98	2 AS	F
Rumania	2.45	1.01	3 EU	NF
Ethiopia	2.44	1.01	1 AF	F
Nigeria	2.41	1.01	2 AF	F
Turkey	2.41	1.01	2 EU	PF
South Africa	2.39	1.04	3 AF	NF
Saudi Arabia	2.38	1.02	2 ME	NF
Honduras	2.37	.99	1 LA	PF
El Salvador	2.26	1.00	1 LA	PF
Sudan	2.23	1.01	1 ME	PF
Ghana	2.21	1.02	1 AF	NF
Group 5	1.95	.86		
North Korea	2.22	1.04	2 AS	NF
Vietnam	1.99	1.01	2 AS	NF
USSR	1.92	1.02	3 EU	NF
Cuba	1.90	1.00	2 LA	NF
China	1.08	1.02	1 AS	NF

(a) Scale from 1=Extremely Unwilling to 5=Extremely Willing
(b) 1=Poorest Developing, 2=Developing, 3=Developed
(c) EU=Europe, LA=Latin America, AF=Africa, ME=Mid.East/N.Africa, AS=Asia
(d) F=Free, PF=Partly Free, NF=Not Free

The most preferred source of apparel for this sample of U.S. consumers is the United States. The overall mean willingness to buy for Group 1 countries exceeded that of every other group. These countries have the highest levels of economic development and political freedom. They are all in the European culture realm (either North American, European, or populated largely by those of European extraction, e.g., Australia).

Group 2 countries provided the second highest overall mean willingness to buy. Japan, the only developed and free country in this group, generated the highest willingness to buy within the group. Generally, as the level of development falls and the degree of freedom is constrained, the respondents' willingness to buy from a country declines.

We also see a cultural pattern becoming evident. Group 1 countries are European and North American in orientation–and the most favored group of nations. Group 2 is mainly Asian but only partly developed and free in character–Mexico being the exception. Less developed Asian countries are *not* perceived the same way, given that they combined on Group 3. Group 3 was split between Latin American, Asian, and Middle Eastern cultures with less development and a variety of political climates. Group 4 is the most heterogeneous. It contains three (previously) "Iron-Curtain" countries–Poland, Rumania, and Hungary (all European)–and one other developed country, South Africa. In addition, this group includes a variety of developing countries, including all the African nations. Group 5–the least popular source of supply–represents all other Communist bloc countries (including the now-defunct U.S.S.R.), regardless of level of development or cultural history. Vietnam was included in this group although it could have been placed easily among the other developing countries in Group 4.

Summing up, U.S. consumers are most willing to buy U.S.-made apparel. They are very willing to "buy European" (or from countries that are culturally European). Apparel exporters in the developing countries of the Far East have apparently made a good impression on the U.S. consumer, as have those of Japan and Mexico. A large bloc of countries, those in Groups 3 and 4, appear not to have established a favorable image either as existing suppliers or as potential ones. However, their image is not always negative. Therefore, some of them do have the potential to enter the apparel market if they develop the necessary expertise in apparel manufacture and design.

Except for those in Europe (this study took place before the Berlin Wall came down), no communist country is a favored source of supply for the U.S. consumer. Obviously, the cultural ties or geographic proximity between the U.S. and these countries (e.g., Cuba) are not sufficient to overcome the negative attitude the average consumer has about their form of government.

CONCLUSIONS

The results of the study show that for apparel at least, in general, consumers' willingness to buy reflects the level of economic development of the producing country. U.S. consumers are most willing to buy from North America, the developed countries of Europe, and Japan. As level of development decreases, so, with some exceptions, does willingness to buy.

Political freedom (or lack of it) was also an important variable in the consumer's decision making. A possible explanation is that while prepared to tolerate some restrictions on freedom in the less developed countries in the sample, the consumer was more reluctant to deal with those developed countries such as South Africa and the European ex-socialist states. The least preferred sources were those countries of the communist bloc whose history displayed overt hostility to the U.S.–the U.S.S.R., Vietnam, Cuba, and China.

The more similar a country is to the U.S. in cultural terms, the more likely it is to be a preferred source of apparel. The European countries, overall, have a distinct advantage over countries not perceived as European in origin. However, not being European obviously does not exclude a country from the U.S. marketplace. Countries such as Japan, Taiwan, and South Korea as well as Hong Kong rank quite highly as sources of supply despite the absence of strong cultural ties. It is interesting to note that Japan is no longer a major exporter of apparel to the U.S., so this high willingness to buy Japanese apparel cannot be based upon recent consumer experience. It would seem that the favorable reputation that Japan has established in other product areas continues to "spill over" to the apparel area.

IMPLICATIONS

Before discussing the implications of this research, it might be useful to point out that retailers are usually the first to know which items customers accept with enthusiasm and which they reject. Reorders of the former and clearances of the latter are the conventional strategies used by merchants. This is the way they adapt to their customers' responses to the merchandise assortments carried by the store. Experience and intuition enable the successful merchant to minimize the volume of clearance merchandise and to determine the timing and appropriateness for both reorder and clearance strategy. The additive knowledge provided by this study will aid retailers and other channel members in exercising better control over inventories.

Importers, as members of the distribution channel, facilitate the flow of merchandise to U.S. wholesalers and retailers. They provide prescreening functions to identify and select goods which the final consumer is most likely to find suitable. This prescreening involves not only the merchandise itself but also the country from which that merchandise originates. Benefits from such activity can be expected to accrue to the importers themselves by recognized merchandise expertise and therefore long-term profitability. Other downstream channel members will be beneficiaries of the importer's acumen in that their merchandise selection functions will reflect more accurately the desires of their customers.

Retailers themselves have at their disposal means of determining the appropriate country-of-origin source of merchandise. Those retailers who are members of large buying groups have the advantage of the prescreening function performed by the buying offices. Nonetheless, based on this study's findings, there are several implications that appear to be significant for those engaged in buying, distributing, and selling foreign-made goods in the U.S. market and should, therefore, be emphasized.

First, unless a low-price strategy is employed, it will require greater effort and expense to sell apparel products of the developing countries, given the obvious bias held by U.S. customers in favor of U.S., European, and Japanese products. In addition, biases in favor of products from Canada, Australia, and New Zealand appear to be very strong in the United States. Hence, market potential for apparel from those countries appears to be good. This suggests that retailers' promotional efforts might best be focused on the traditional sources of supply or on those countries whose images are positive with domestic customers but who are not now major apparel exporters to United States merchants. Further, retail buyers should be supporting the "Buy American" campaigns, since U.S. apparel is viewed by consumers with the *most* willingness to buy.

Second, very few developing countries have the potential to displace the Europeans as apparel suppliers in the short term, and not without considerable effort. This effort is likely to continue to be focused at the low-price end of the market. Those inroads which have been made by countries such as Taiwan, South Korea, China, and Hong Kong are with merchandise in the low-priced categories. Continued success at the low-priced end of the market has enabled some developing countries to achieve familiarity with the consumer. This may act as a base for incursion into the higher-priced market segments. Retailers may very well find that a select few of the developing countries will, in the future, emulate the Japanese in the automobile and electronics markets and may become a major source of apparel products. It will be interesting to see whether their quality reputations in this product category will transfer to other products, as has happened with Japan.

Finally, to keep abreast of likely changes in customers' perceptions of country-of-origin biases, it makes good sense to monitor perceptual changes. The findings of this study point to the fact that customers do have biases, favorable and unfavorable, which affect their perceptions of the apparel produced in various countries. With markets becoming ever more globalized, their biases are sure to change over time. Being aware of the changes can contribute to more effective inventory management by all channel members, thereby improving economic efficiency and enhancing customer satisfaction.

REFERENCES

Acito, Franklin and Ronald D. Anderson (1980), "A Monte Carlo Comparison of Factor Analytic Methods." *Journal of Marketing* Research, VII (May) 228-236.

Bannister, J.P. and J.A. Saunders (1978), "U.K. Consumers' Attitudes Towards Imports: The Measurement of National Stereotype Image." *European Journal of Marketing*, 12, 8, 562- 570.

Bilkey, Warren J. and Erik Nes (1982), "Country-of-Origin Effects on Product Evaluations." *Journal of International Business Studies*, 8(1) (Spring/Summer) 89-99.

Business Week (1986, October 27), "Draping Old Glory Around Just About Everything." 66-67.

Cattell, Raymond B. and S. Vogelman (1977), "A Comparison Trial of Scree and KG Criteria for Determining the Number of Factors." *The Journal of Multivariate Behavioral Research*, 12 (July) 289-325.

Chasin, J.B. and Eugene D. Jaffe (1979), "Industrial Buyer Attitudes Towards Goods Made in Eastern Europe." *Columbia Journal of World Business* (Summer) 74-81.

Czepiec, Helena (1984), "Are Foreign Products Still Seen as National Stereotypes?" *Proceedings of the American Marketing Association* (Chicago).

Dickerson, Kitty G. (1982), "Imported Versus U.S.-Produced Apparel: Consumer Views and Buying Patterns." *Home Economics Research Journal*, 10:3 (March) 241-52.

Dickerson, Kitty G. (1986, November 7), "Consumers Rate U.S. Clothes Higher than Imports." *Marketing News*, 30.

Dornoff, Ronald J., Clint B. Tankersley, and Gregory P. White (1974), "Consumers' Perceptions of Imports." *Akron Business and Economic Review*, 5(2) (Summer) 26-29.

Erickson, Gary M., Johny K. Johansson, and Paul Chao (1984), "Image Variables in Multi-Attribute Product Evaluations: Country-of-Origin Effects." *Journal of Consumer Research*, 11: (September) 694-699.

Faltermayer, Edmund (1990) "Is 'Made in the U.S.A.' Fading Away?" *Fortune* (September 24), 62-73.

Gastil, Raymond D. (1988), "The Comparative Survey of Freedom." *Freedom at Issue* (January-February).

Gorsuch, Richard L. (1974), *Factor Analysis*. Philadelphia: W.B. Saunders Company.

Green, Paul E. and Donald S. Tull (1987), *Research for Marketing Decisions*. Englewood Cliffs, NJ: Prentice-Hall.

Han, Min C. and Vern Terpstra (1988), "Country-of-Origin Effects for Uni-National and Bi-National Products." *Journal of International Business Studies* (Summer) 235-54.

Hong, Sung-Tai and Robert S. Wyer, Jr. (1989), "Effects of Country-of-Origin and Product-Attribute Information on Product Evaluation: An Information Processing Perspective." *Journal of Consumer Research*, 16: (September), 175-187.

Howe, James W. (1974), *The U.S. and Developing World: Agenda for Action*. New York: Praeger.

Hugstad, Paul S. and Michael Darr (1986), "A Study of Country of Manufacturer Impact on Consumer Perceptions." *Developments in Marketing Science* (Anaheim, CA, Academy of Marketing Science).

Hung, C.L. (1989), "A Country-of-Origin Product Image Study: The Canadian Perception and Nationality Biases." *Journal of International Consumer Marketing*, 1, 3, 5-26.

James, Preston E. (1976), "World View of Major Culture Regions." In Fred E. Dohis and Lawrence M. Sommers (eds.), *World Regional Geography: A Problem Approach*. New York: West Publishing Company.

Johansson, Johny K. and Israel D. Nebenzahl (1986), "Multinational Production: Effect on Brand Value." *Journal of International Business Studies*, 17, 3 (Fall) 101-126.

Johansson, Johny K. and Hans B. Thorelli (1985), "International Product Positioning." *Journal of International Business Studies*, XVI, 3 (Fall) 57-75.

Johansson, Johny K., Susan P. Douglas, and Ikujiro Nonaka (1985), "Assessing the Impact of country-of-origin on Product Evaluations: A New Methodological Perspective." *Journal of Marketing Research*, XXII: (November) 388-96.

Kaiser, H.F. (1970), "A Second Generation of Little Jiffy." *Psychometrika*, 35 (December) 401-415.

Kaiser, H.F. and J. Rice, (1974), "Little Jiffy Mark IV." *Educational and Psychological Measurement*, 34 (Spring) 111-117.

Kaynak, Erdener and S. Tamer Cavusgil (1983), "Consumer Attitudes Towards

Products of Foreign Origin: Do They Vary Across Product Classes?" *International Journal of Advertising,* 2 (April/June) 147-157.

Lumpkin, James R., John C. Crawford, and Gap Kim (1985), "Perceived Risk as a Factor in Buying Foreign Clothes." *International Journal of Advertising,* 157-169.

Nagashima, Akira (1970), "A Comparison of Japanese and U.S. Attitudes Towards Foreign Products." *Journal of Marketing,* 34 (January) 68-74.

Nigh, Douglas (1985), "The Effect of Political Events on United States Direct Foreign Investment: A Pooled Time-Series Cross- Sectional Analysis." *Journal of International Business Studies,* 16 (Spring) 1-17.

Reierson, Curtis C. (1966), "Are Foreign Products Seen as National Stereotypes." *Journal of Retailing,* 42, 3 (Fall), 33-40.

Schooler, Robert D. (1965), "Product Bias in the Central American Common Market." *Journal of Marketing Research,* II: (November) 394-397.

Sternquist, Brenda and Sheila Tolbert (1986, May 23), "Retailers Shun Apparel Industry's Buy American Program." *Marketing News,* 8.

Stewart, David W. (1981), "The Application and Misapplication of Factor Analysis in Marketing Research." *Journal of Marketing Research,* XVIII (February) 51-62.

U.S. Bureau of the Census (1984, May), *Current Population Reports,* Ser. P-25, No. 952.

Wall, Marjorie and Louise A. Heslop (1986), "Consumer Attitudes Toward Canadian-made versus Imported Products." *Journal of the Academy of Marketing Science,* 14(2): 27-36.

Wang, Chih-Kang and Charles W. Lamb (1980), "Foreign Environmental Factors Influencing American Consumers' Predispositions Toward European Products." *Journal of the Academy of Marketing Science,* 8, 4, 345-356.

Wang, Chih-Kang and Charles W. Lamb (1983), "The Impact of Selected Environmental Forces Upon Consumers' Willingness to Buy Foreign Products." *Journal of the Academy of Marketing Science,* 11(2): (Winter) 71-84.

Chapter 15

Temporal Shifts
of Developed Country Images:
A 20-Year View

Faramarz Damanpour

INTRODUCTION

The success or failure of a firm is conditional to a large degree on the attitudes of those who are in a position to make purchasing decisions, either as consumers or as agents representing the interest of their countries or institutions. Historically, multinational firms used sales-oriented approaches, via advertising and public relation exercises, to differentiate their products in international marketplaces. Thus, they assigned a limited role to the study of market segmentation in conjunction with the study of demographic factors and consumer behavior. The recent U.S. domestic market success of the late 1970s and early 1980s, especially with the young–as demonstrated by computer games, fast foods, soft drinks, and toys–opened a new approach and attitude toward international consumption. Japanese producers took the first step in pioneering internationalization of consumer-oriented sales and the market segmentation approach in the U.S., by manufacturing their products for special segments of market users.

U.S. producers in the 1970s implemented short-term solutions to long-term problems. They neglected the changes in consumer preferences, failed to foresee weakening economic conditions, and miscalculated the ability of other nations to respond innovatively to international markets as demanded over this period of time. Therefore, the U.S. market became increasingly sensitive to the invasion of foreign exports and the inability of the U.S. government to cope with these changes internally. The overvalued U.S. dollar, high interest rates, and the inflationary environment of the early 1980s further damaged the ability of U.S. manufacturers to change their course to efficient, export-oriented marketing. As a result, the U.S.

further lost its industrial base, and manufacturers curtailed their operations and became marketing organizations for other producers, mostly foreign. This set the stage for more comprehensive internationalization of the industrial base and more careful attention to market demand and consumer behaviors.

Today, more than 200,000 Americans work for Japanese firms in the United States, with an investment portfolio exceeding $18 billion. As a result, consumer knowledge of international products is improving and, to an extent, bias against foreign imports is diminishing. A new era has begun in this rapidly changing world environment.

A recent market study by the Chrysler Corporation regarding the automobile industry revealed that the Japanese have succeeded in persuading the American consumer that Japan provides better quality cars at a relatively lower price. To counter the shift in consumer preferences, a series of advertisements was developed to challenge consumer judgment and provide better information about Chrysler cars. In one advertisement, the Chrysler Chairman and CEO reveals the results of several tests that provide a higher performance record for their car in all the areas of price, quality, accessories, and performance. The advertisement directly states that the American consumer has been fed the wrong information about Japanese cars, and therefore, has overlooked American cars' quality and performance. He also challenges American consumers to further test and compare the U.S.-made labels versus those of the competitors.

This chapter emphasizes the importance of studying demographic factors and consumer behavior, and warns U.S. producers of the danger of further losing their market share if they fail to improve quality and ignore market segmentation. The chapter draws from a survey which was conducted to evaluate the shift in perceptions of American consumers toward foreign products, specifically the U.S.'s main trading partners. The aim of the chapter is not the extension of consumer behavior concepts into the stream of "Made in _____" research, but rather to describe the shifts in consumer attitudes toward "Made in" labels over time. This is an important issue that could determine the future course of action of both U.S. manufacturers as well as foreign competitors who produce for the highly sensitive U.S. import market.

REVIEW OF THE LITERATURE

The literature is rich with various studies of consumer behavior. International marketers have analyzed the relationship between the concept of "country-of-origin" and the product mix beyond the elements of marketing principles. The concept of the "Made in" label was recognized as an element of the marketing mix and its importance was emphasized in a study of imported products by Dichter (1962). A few studies have indicated that there are reasons to believe that the quality and image of foreign products are stereotyped negatively (Reierson 1966; Gaedeke 1973; Bannister and Saunders 1978). The "made in" image concept was further popularized by Schooler and Wildt (1968), Worthing and Venkatesan (1971), and Nagashima (1970 and 1977), in attempts to base consumer perceptions of imported products on the attitudes toward the people of the producing country and the perceived cultural similarities between it and the consumer's home country (Lillis, Narayana, and Hallaq 1974). The early literature in this area was reviewed by Bilkey and Nes (1982).

These preconceptions were claimed to be especially valid against developing countries (Wang and Lamb 1980, 1983). However, the suggestion that consumer behavior and product image are determined by economic development, cultural realm, or political system has been challenged (Lumpkin and Crawford 1985). Along the same lines, other studies suggest that product preferences are directly correlated with the level of like or dislike associated with a country, and that this results in various forms of bias (Damanpour and Hallaq 1983; Barker 1984). At least two of the earlier studies have used socioeconomic characteristics and psychological factors to explain consumer behavior (Schooler 1965; Anderson and Cunningham 1972).

Another topic of concern for international marketers has been the perception and treatment of "specific" products versus "general or combined" products, based on the country-of-origin. Etzel and Walker (1974) recommended that each individual product class be studied separately to evaluate its image, instead of assessing all products globally. This idea was further developed to suggest that product images and perceptions are usually more clearly formed than country images, as a result of direct experience with brands (Bradley 1981), and that perceptions tend to be more product-specific than country-specific (Niffeneger, White, and Marmet 1980; Kaynak and Cavusgil 1983); therefore, generalizations can be misleading and must be made cautiously. The issue has raised such other important questions as familiarity with products and the factors influencing product choice (Lumpkin and Crawford 1985; Stephens, Fox, and Leonard 1985), and how gender influences the perception of products from the same country (Heslop and Wall 1985) and across time (Cattin, Jolibert, and Lohnes 1982).

Other relevant studies include an evaluation of doctrine of consumer behaviors in connection with the marketing mix and marketing promotional considerations (Assael 1984; Damanpour and Hallaq 1979), the impact of women's employment on consumer behavior (Bartos 1977), shopping behavior and market segmentation (Dixon and McLaughlin 1971; Frank, Massy, and Wind 1972), marketing perception and generalization (Leone and Schultz 1980) and brand loyalty and behavioral trends (McConnell 1967). A recent study by Barker (1987) examined how New Zealanders perceive Australian products, and found a bias toward Australian products, primarily due to the country-of-origin. This suggests very strongly that tradition, history, and other factors not related to the product itself may be creating a bias. This finding again supports the claim of other studies that bias is a factor in the development of product image and consumer counterbehavior (Damanpour and Hallaq 1979; Worthing and Venkatesan 1971).

OBJECTIVES OF THE STUDY

A survey of college students in 1984 revealed that American consumers have become less biased and more knowledgeable about foreign products (Damanpour 1985). This prompted the need for a study to measure the preferences of American consumers of various ages and income levels toward the tangible and intangible elements of foreign products. This concept was researched by examining consumers' attitudinal preferences toward aggregate images of the indicative factors influencing their choices. The outcome should be of interest to academics and business managers dealing with the study of market behavior, sales, advertising, marketing strategy, and the international business environment.

The study addressed the following questions:

1. How do U.S. consumers perceive the products of the major industrialized countries?
2. Which country would consumers select to purchase from if the countries in question had an item equal or comparable in price, quality, and styling?
3. Which country is identified as the one which produces the product of the greatest value when considering price, quality, design, and service?
4. To what extent is there consistency among consumers' images of foreign products over a period of time?
5. What products come to mind when seeing the "Made in _____ " label?

6. Do demographic characteristics tend to influence consumers' preferences for foreign products?
7. Do consumers correlate product characteristics with the producing country's level of technological development?

METHOD

To measure consumer attitudes, a profile was constructed of the images of the products of various nations. A survey was conducted in the State of Virginia in 1986. The three locations of Harrisonburg (population 30,000), Richmond (population 300,000), and Northern Virginia (population 700,000) were selected as sites of the survey, due to their cultural diversity, income level, and environmental composition. Harrisonburg is a conservative university town with a few small industrial firms. The population is uniform without much cultural diversity. On the opposite side, Northern Virginia, a suburb of Washington, D.C., consists of many cultural and racial subgroups, with a large proportion of middle- and upper-management residents and a large group of government employees. The level of income far exceeds the other two localities. Richmond, Virginia, despite its capital status, has remained a blue-collar city with very distinct racial and income diversity.

A questionnaire was mailed to 600 households in these areas, followed four weeks later by a second request to those who did not respond to the first mailing. In total, 400 usable questionnaires (a 66.6 percent response rate) were obtained for analysis. The survey aimed at establishing a benchmark parallel to the 1967 and 1975 Nagashima (1970, 1977) studies, the 1973 study by Lillis, Narayana, and Hallaq (1974), and two surveys by this author in 1979 and 1984 (Damanpour and Hallaq 1983; Damanpour 1985). The 1979 survey was conducted among the general public to evaluate consumers' attitudes toward products of selected industrial nations. The 1984 survey measured the same perceptions, using college students. All surveys mentioned used the same methodology and techniques, but differed slightly in their sample sizes (these ranged from 250 to 400).

In this most recent survey, conducted in 1986 and which forms the basis of this chapter, 20 attitudinal variables were selected, similar to the other comparable surveys, employing seven-point semantic differential scales (where 1 = high/good and 7 = low/bad; the scales used are shown in Table 1). These variables addressed themselves to questions relevant to the areas of price and value, service and engineering, advertising and reputation, design and style, and consumer profile (Nagashima 1970, 1977).

Table 1. "Made in-" Product Images as Perceived by U.S. Consumers

Attributes	Gr. Britain	France	Germany	Japan	U.S.
Price and Value					
1. Inexpensive-Expensive	5.08	6.10	3.90	3.30	3.90
2. Reasonably-Unreasonably Priced	5.04	5.25	4.08	3.42	4.05
3. Reliable-Unreliable	4.80	4.53	3.25	3.85	4.10
4. Luxury-Necessary Items	2.80	3.25	4.75	4.70	4.60
5. Exclusive-Common	3.88	2.90	4.63	4.25	5.90
6. Heavy-Light Industry Prod.	3.90	4.20	3.05	3.66	3.80
Engineering and Service					
7. Good-Poor Workmanship	3.92	3.50	2.90	3.80	3.65
8. Technologically Advanced-Backward	4.10	4.00	3.26	2.60	3.10
9. Mass Produced-Hand Made	5.70	4.15	3.87	2.50	3.05
10. Worldwide-Domestic	3.40	4.00	3.10	2.45	4.90
11. Inventive-Imitative	3.90	4.00	2.94	3.83	2.95
Advertising and Reputation					
12. Pride-Lack of Pride of Ownership	3.60	2.90	2.80	3.60	3.94
13. Much-Little Advertising	4.80	3.85	4.10	2.40	2.00
14. Recognizable-Unrecognizable Brand Names	4.10	3.60	3.00	2.50	2.42
Design and Style					
15. Variety-Lack of Variety	5.12	4.20	3.60	2.85	2.60
16. Outward Appearance-Performance	4.10	3.94	5.17	4.80	3.55
17. Clever-Not Clever Use of Color	3.90	3.80	4.05	3.84	4.25
Consumer Profile					
18. Geared Toward Young-Old People	4.85	4.09	4.03	2.70	3.42
19. More for Men-Women	3.20	3.50	3.15	3.60	3.65
20. Geared Toward Upper-Lower Class	3.10	2.85	3.90	4.05	4.00

Mean Ratings*

* Scale from 1=good to 7=bad; lower scores represent left variable values, higher scores represent right variable values.

Forty-eight percent of the respondents indicated that they had a high school diploma or the equivalent and a few held two-year technical degrees. Fifty percent held college degrees, and 2 percent had less than a high school education. The income distribution was approximately 22 percent below $25,000, 68 percent between $25,000 and $60,000, and 10 percent above $60,000. Nearly one-third were housewives with no outside jobs and 10 percent were college students. In age groups, one-fourth were younger than 25 years, one-third were between 26 and 47, one-fourth between 48 and 62, and the remainder were above 62 years of age. An attempt was made to keep the demographic factors similar to other comparable surveys, to permit actual comparisons.

RESULTS AND ANALYSIS

Results are presented separately for each of the seven questions that were previously stated.

1. How do the U.S. consumers perceive the products of the major industrial countries?

The mean ratings on the 20 attributes for each of five countries are shown in Table 1. The attributes in questions 1-6 reflect price and value, 7-11 service and engineering, 12-14 advertising and reputation, 15-17 design and style, and 18-20 consumer profile.

Made in Great Britain. American consumers perceive "Made in Great Britain" products as being expensive, luxury items, but reliable. These products are considered to be exclusive and the country is perceived to be a manufacturer of both heavy and light machinery. The British products are also perceived to be marginally above average on good workmanship, technically advanced, handmade, and, like U.S. products, produced for internal consumption; however, they lack strong innovative features. Similarly, these products scored average in the question concerning pride of ownership and recognizability of brand names. This could be attributed to the relatively limited advertising that British manufacturers have conducted in the United States. Overall, these products were perceived as being traditional, with limited variety and use of colors, but fair in outward appearance and designed for the older population, the upper class, and males.

Made in France. French products are considered to be very expensive, luxury items. They are perceived as being exclusive and technically advanced, with good workmanship. Despite this, American consumers gave French products an average score for innovation and considered them below average in mass production and worldwide distribution. However, consumers recognize the pride of ownership of French products and apparently know little about the variety of products exported abroad, due to the lack of mass advertisement and the limited variety of recognizable brand names. French exports seem clever in use of color and packaging, and are considered to be more for the young and the upper class, but equally for men and women.

Made in Germany. (West Germany before unification) The "Made in Germany" product image in the United States is strong and well-received. German products are not viewed as being too expensive, and are seen as reliable and mostly as products of heavy industry. They scored highest in workmanship, and were considered to be very innovative and technically advanced with mass production for worldwide use. Similarly, they scored high in regard to recognizable brand names, variety, and good outward appearance. American consumers also perceived German products to be made more for the young, the middle class, and males. Overall, these scores were very positive and indicate strong competition with U.S.- and Japanese-made products.

Made in Japan. Japan has made great strides toward becoming a global marketer since its recovery after World War II. It has enjoyed a large trade surplus with the United States, and its products are as recognizable as U.S. products. In this survey, respondents assigned greater confidence to Japanese products than to those of any other major industrial country. American consumers consider Japanese products to be inexpensive, reliable, necessary items which exhibit good workmanship and are technologically advanced. Japan is also credited as producing for worldwide consumption and being innovative. Certainly, the massive Japanese advertisement campaigns have captured the attention of consumers with their recognizable brand names and variety of production for different segments of the market. The U.S. consumer considers Japanese-made items to be more for the young, the lower and middle classes, and men as well as women. Very recently, Japan has made strides to further expand into the upper-income level by introducing a new generation of luxury cars. The major aim is to compete with European car manufacturers who have enjoyed very little competition in this segment of the market for the past two decades.

Made in the U.S.A. American products, despite recent setbacks and the growth of foreign imports, have a special place in the minds of consumers. In the area of price and value, the U.S. ranked second to Japan. In other words, consumers considered U.S.-made products to be relatively inexpensive, relatively reasonably-priced, common, and necessary, but not as reliable as Japanese- and German-made products. The U.S. specialty is considered to be more in heavy industry products that are very technically advanced, with good workmanship. Consumers perceived U.S. products as being inventive and mass produced, with brand name recognition, but made more for domestic consumption. Furthermore, U.S. products received the highest score in advertisement, variety, and recognizability of brand names. They are also perceived to be made more for young, lower- and middle-class people of both genders. This is good news for American manufacturers to be aware of their potential room for rebounding into the hearts of the U.S. purchasers. The key to their success is the recognition of a need for better quality and durability.

Product similarity and correlation. To evaluate product similarity and correlation, a Spearman test was conducted from a question in which respondents were asked to list three products which come first to their minds when they see the "Made in" label from the five major industrialized countries. This information was tabulated according to the frequencies with which each product was associated with a particular country. Correlation analysis was performed to calculate the correlation coefficient, as presented in Table 2.

The results indicated that similarities and high competition existed between German, Japanese, and U.S. products. While the degree of correlation is stronger between U.S. and Japanese products, German products present formidable competition. The strongest correlation was observed between the U.S. and Japan, with a coefficient of 0.68, and Japan and Germany with a coefficient of 0.54. Third was the coefficient of 0.51 between the U.S. and Germany. This finding is another indicator of the Japanese success in the U.S. markets. Among this respondent group, the major competition is from Japan, with Germany as a close second. French and British products did not provide formidable competition.

> 2. *Which country would consumers select to purchase from if the countries in question had an item equal or comparable in price, quality and styling?*

In the 1973 study (Lillis, Narayana, and Hallaq 1974) and the present study (conducted in 1986), respondents were asked to indicate their first and second choices without specifying products, whereas in the 1979 study (Damanpour and Hallaq 1983), they were asked to indicate their first and last choices. The results are illustrated in Table 3.

The first column in each study, compared on a longitudinal basis, indicates the magnitude of popularity of foreign products in the U.S. market. Assuming equal price, quality, and styling, one would conclude, based on a comparison of the three surveys over time, that any U.S. consumer bias that might have existed against Japanese-manufactured products is diminishing fast. Japan's success has been accomplished by the fact that U.S. consumers perceive that they are obtaining a higher quality product for the same or lower price, particularly in the case of automobiles, stereos, televi-

Table 2. Product Similarity and Correlation
Among Five Major Industrialized Countries

	Gr. Britain	France	Germany	Japan	USA
Great Britain	1.0000				
France	.3775	1.0000			
Germany	.2598	.3992	1.0000		
Japan	.2494	.1010	.5442	1.0000	
U.S.	.2101	.3988	.5142	.6760	1.0000

Note. Spearman Rho test was used to tabulate the correlation coefficients.

Table 3. Purchase Preferences by Country

Country	1973 Study		1979 Study		1986 Study	
	1st Choice	2nd Choice	1st Choice	Last Choice	1st Choice	2nd Choice
	(percent of responses)					
Great Britain	4	13	2	14	5	4
France	1	4	6	29	8	5
Germany	24	26	23	8	17	18
Japan	3	6	4	32	33	28
U.S.A.	54	20	62	5	28	32
Others	14	31	13	12	22	13

sions, cameras, and computers in recent years. In the most recent survey 33 percent of the respondents selected as their first choice Japanese products, versus 28 percent for American and 17 percent for German products. Other countries' product scores were low and in the distance when compared to the first three.

This finding was supported by consumers' responses to the question asking them to list the products which come first to their minds when they see the "Made in" label. It also is in line with the findings of the 1984 study (Damanpour 1985) in which young, college-educated, middle-class American consumers showed more interest and respect toward quality and support for foreign products in the United States. That group selected Japanese products over U.S. products by a margin of 38 percent to 31 percent. Concerning German products, one may hypothesize that while they have maintained quality recognition and support in the United States, their North American domination is weakening in relation to Japan. However, this is not a reflection of Germany's overall export market, since its strengths are global in scope and often in sectors different from those where Japan predominates. Germany, for the first time in recent years, bypassed the United States to become the largest world exporter in 1987.

The second column in the 1979 study (Damanpour and Hallaq 1983) presents the least favored source and indicates that there was still a sizable segment of U.S. households that remained reluctant to purchase Japanese products. France was next in line, mainly because U.S. respondents indicated a lack of sufficient familiarity with French products (except for wine and perfume) when asked to identify at least five products made in the specified country. As a result, they tended to associate French products with high risk (expensive, different, and hard to fix). Attitudes towards Japanese products certainly changed by 1986 as, apparently, the bias softened and knowledge of international products increased. More Americans Vare now convinced of the better quality and lower prices of foreign products, and have learned to use the overvalued dollar to their best advantage. France also narrowly improved its position in 1986 over 1979, mostly in regard to automobiles, clothing, and the garment industry. Other nations frequently mentioned by respondents were South Korea, Hong Kong, Taiwan, Brazil, and Italy.

3. Which country produces the product of the greatest value when considering price, quality, design, and service?

The six products specified here were: automobiles, appliances, textiles, cosmetics, food, and drugs. Table 4 illustrates the outcome. The 1973 study (Lillis, Narayana, and Hallaq 1974; not shown in the table) had revealed that U.S. consumers ranked the United States as the leading manufacturer of all products listed in the survey, with Germany in automobiles and Great Britain in textiles as a "competing second." In the 1979 survey, we observed a dramatic loss of U.S. leadership relative to its 1973 position. It continued to lead in food, drugs and the manufacture of appliances but lost its leadership in automobiles to Germany, in textiles to Great Britain, and in cosmetics to France. Surprisingly, Germany, instead of Japan, replaced the U.S. leadership in automobiles. While Japan became a mass marketer in the United States in the 1970s, the Germans' well-known automobile manufacturing quality earned the admiration of U.S. consumers.

However, the situation changed in the 1980s. As expected, Japan captured the automobile market, and scored high in small or non-major appliances. Germany stayed a distant third with regards to automobiles and second in drugs, but scored very low in other categories. Great Britain kept its competitive edge in textiles, and France improved its position in automobiles and textiles. Overall, with the exception of automobiles, the United States ranked first and showed a strong competitive position. While American consumers acknowledge a Japanese stronghold in auto-

Table 4. Selected Countries - Products of Greatest Value

Products	Countries	1979 Study R	F	% R	1986 Study R	F	% R	Coefficient of Correlation 1979*	1986**
	Gr. Britain	4	7	4	5	10	3		
	France	5	1	1	4	35	10		
Automobiles	Germany	1	81	51	3	55	16	.90	.89
	Japan	3	26	16	1	129	37		
	U.S.	2	45	28	2	118	34		
	Gr. Britain	4	0	0	4	5	2		
	France	4	0	0	5	4	1		
Appliances	Germany	3	3	2	3	30	10	.98	.96
	Japan	2	70	44	2	90	28		
	U.S.	1	86	54	1	174	57		
	Gr. Britain	1	71	45	2	75	34		
	France	4	7	4	3	40	18		
Textiles	Germany	5	5	3	5	10	5	.88	.86
	Japan	3	11	7	4	14	6		
	U.S.	1	65	41	1	80	36		
	Gr. Britain	3	5	3	3	49	25		
	France	1	92	60	2	70	36		
Cosmetics	Germany	5	0	0	5	1	1	.70	.74
	Japan	4	1	1	4	3	2		
	U.S.	2	56	38	1	73	37		
	Gr. Britain	4	3	2	3	14	6		
	France	2	22	14	2	29	13		
Foods	Germany	3	4	3	3	14	6	.80	.82
	Japan	5	1	1	4	10	5		
	U.S.	1	130	81	1	150	69		
	Gr. Britain	3	6	4	3	10	4		
	France	4	2	1	4	8	3		
Drugs	Germany	2	13	9	2	74	29	.95	.90
	Japan	4	2	1	5	5	2		
	U.S.	1	132	85	1	161	62		

* Correlation 1973 to 1979; ** Correlation 1979 to 1986
Legend. R = Rank; F = Frequency; % R = percent of Respondents;
Note. Percentages may not add to 100 due to rounding. The Spearman test was used for correlation tabulation.

mobiles, computers, televisions, and stereos, they still apparently believe that the United States can produce competitive products.

4. To what extent is there consistency among consumers' images of foreign products over a period of time?

The Spearman test was used to calculate the correlation coefficient of the rankings of countries across products during the survey periods, to evaluate the stability of a country's ranking over time. As shown in Table 4, although the coefficients were relatively high for all products, they weakened marginally overall, with the exception of cosmetics and foods, reflecting a jockeying in the ranking of the positions of the countries over the time span. Appliances recorded the highest correlation and cosmetics the lowest. Japan is not known for major appliances in the U.S., and the surprising, continuous consumer perception of Japanese appliances indicates that respondents consider the electric can opener, coffee maker, and other small kitchen devices as appliances when responding to this question. This evidence was confirmed when the survey provided the respondents with 40 different product items for country identification and asked them to add any more products that came to mind in association with a specific country. Respondents identified Japanese light kitchen appliances in association with country brand recognition.

5. What products come to mind when seeing the "Made in" label?

The answers have been interpreted as an indication of the popularity, expertise, or esteem given to the country in the area of manufacturing activity. Three to 20 products were named by respondents for the different countries in question. The eight most frequently mentioned products for each country were selected for comparative analysis, as illustrated in Table 5.

The respondents demonstrated a great deal of knowledge about products of various nations. In summary:

- All countries scored high with regard to the automobile industry, with the United States, Japan, and Germany receiving the highest consumer recognition, in this order.
- The United States, France, and Great Britain were more often cited for clothing. France and the United States scored high with regard to food products. Germany and Japan were mentioned more than others with regard to toys and watches.
- France dominated wine products, jewelry, perfume, cosmetics, antiques and ski equipment. Great Britain captured the traditional goods: wool, whiskey, tea, china, and bicycles, with a strong showing in aircraft. Germany, Japan, and the U.S. led in high-technology products. Japan shared leadership with the U.S. in electronic products and televisions, outscored it in stereo and motorcycle products, but showed no competition for the U.S. in gun production, appliances, and aircraft.
- Other products frequently mentioned were: shoes from Italy[1] and Brazil, weaponry from Israel, Scandinavian ski equipment and furniture, Swiss candy, clothing from Taiwan and South Korea, and automobiles

---

1. Ed. note: See also Chapter 12 (Morello); the transnational similarity in consumer perceptions suggests how strongly certain sectors are identified with the image of various countries.

from Italy and Sweden.

6. Do demographic characteristics tend to influence consumers' preferences for foreign products?

Apparently yes. To evaluate demographic connections, the first five most-mentioned products for each country from the 1986 survey were arbitrarily selected and cross-classified by the demographic characteristics of the respondents, to determine whether or not the demographic variables of age, sex, income, and education tended to influence the respondents. The main findings, by country and demographic variables, are shown in Table 6 and highlighted below.

Great Britain. Younger people (30 years or less) emphasized textiles, whereas older people (over 30 years) emphasized wool products. A similar phenomenon was observed when comparing responses of lower- versus higher-income groups ($30,000 or less vs. over $30,000), respectively. Those with college or graduate education associated china, automobiles, and wool products with Great Britain more than those with less education. Gender showed the most pronounced difference. Males associated auto-

Table 5. Degree of Diversification of the Product Mix (ranked)

Great Britain		France		Japan	
Products	Frequency	Products	Frequency	Products	Frequency
Textiles	85	Cosmetics	101	Cars	272
Cars	61	Liquor	93	Cameras	147
China	42	Cars	41	Motorcycles	91
Aircraft	39	Clothing	40	Stereos	87
Tea	27	Food	27	Computers	54
Shipbuilding	26	Jewelry	22	Toys/Watches	54
Bikes	25	Ski Equipment	12	TV/Steel	39
Liquor	25	Antiques	6	Electronics	29

Germany		U.S.		Others	
Products	Frequency	Products	Frequency	Products	Frequency
Cars	102	Cars	284	Ind. Machin.	23
Beer/Wine	99	Guns	116	Candy	19
Cameras	67	Appliances	114	Radios	19
Watches	63	Food/Clothing	110	Musical Instr.	17
Drugs	37	Liquor	96	Sports Equip.	17
Food	31	Steel/TV	63	Tools	14
Steel/Toys	22	Computer	61	Chemicals	9
Musical Instr.	10	Aircraft	47	Furniture/Shoes	8

Note. The following classification was observed:
"Textiles" included textiles, clothing, wool; "Liquor" included liquor, wine, whiskey, beer; "Cosmetics" included cosmetics, perfumes; "Guns" included all military weapons.

mobiles, clothing and textiles with Great Britain but females reported china and wool products.

France. The major difference based on age was that younger groups associated France more with clothing than did older ones. No major differences based on income or education were observed, and the largest differences were on the basis of sex, wherein males tended to associate France with automobiles, food, and wine more than females.

Germany. A significant number of younger respondents differed from older ones in associating Germany with automobiles. Those with a college degree or higher made a similar association, and added cameras and watches as well. Males included beer in addition to both automobiles and cameras.

Japan. Younger respondents associated Japan with toys and stereos, higher-income respondents with cameras. Not surprisingly, lower-income respondents associated Japan with automobiles; higher-income and educated ones included cameras, steel, and toys in the products mentioned.

U.S. No differences were observed based on age. The higher-income and higher-educated groups, and males, associated the United States more with automobiles than the other groups. Males also associated the United States with industrial machinery, liquor, aircraft, and computers more than females.

7. Do consumers correlate product characteristics with the producing country's level of technological development?

Respondents were also asked to rank the countries on six major product attributes. The score received by each country on these characteristics is shown in Table 7.

A number of interesting observations can be made here in comparison to other surveys. The United States and Japan outperformed German products in the areas of price, style, and technology. American products ranked very high in the technology and style characteristics, but Japan offered the best price. Japanese products were also the most consistently highly-rated of all seven countries. The results, based on ranking, question the belief that price and quality were equally important considerations in the formation of a positive and lasting impression of a product. Instead, other factors and their correlates, such as price and style or price and technology, appear to show a positive effect on purchasing decisions.

Despite the progress that France has made in the area of automobiles in the United States via more aggressive advertisements and better service, its products left the impression of low quality, high price, and luxury in the

Table 6. Rank of Consumer Preferences by Demographic Characteristics (1986)

Demographics	England	France	Germany	Japan	U.S.
Age					
Under 30	Automobiles	Cosmetics/Perfume	Automobiles	Automobiles	Automobiles
	Textiles	Clothing	Beer/Wine	Toys	Guns
	Aircraft	Liquor	Cameras	Stereos	Liquor
	China	Automobiles	Watches	Cameras	Food/Clothing
	Liquor	Food	Food	Computers	Steel
Over 30	Wool	Cosmetics	Beer/Wine	Automobiles	Automobiles
	Automobiles	Liquor	Watches	Cameras	Guns
	China	Automobiles	Automobiles	Motorcycles	Appliances
	Bikes	Food	Cameras	Computers	Clothing
	Aircraft	Clothing	Drugs	Toys	Liquor
Education					
College degree	Automobiles	Cosmetics/Perfume	Automobiles	Automobiles	Automobiles
& above	Wools/Clothing	Liquor	Cameras	Cameras	Steel
	China	Automobiles	Watches	Computers	Computers
	Tea	Clothing	Beer	Stereos	Guns
	Aircraft	Food	Drugs	Televisions	Aircraft
High School	Automobiles	Cosmetics	Beer	Automobiles	Guns
diploma or less	Wool	Automobiles	Drugs	Motorcycles	Steel
	Tea	Liquor	Watches	Stereos	Automobiles
	China	Clothing	Food	Toys	Televisions
	Shipbuilding	Food	Cameras	Computers	Food

Table 6. (continued)

Demographics	England	France	Germany	Japan	U.S.
Income					
< $30,000	Textiles/Clothing	Cosmetics	Automobiles	Automobiles	Food
	Automobiles	Automobiles	Beer	Motorcycles	Guns
	China	Liquor	Cameras	Watches	Automobiles
	Tea	Food	Watches	Toys	Liquor
	Aircraft	Clothing	Steel/Toys	Electronics	Computers
> $30,000	Automobiles	Cosmetics/Perfume	Automobiles	Automobiles	Automobiles
	Wools/Clothing	Liquor	Beer/Wines	Cameras	Appliances
	China	Automobiles	Cameras	Toys	Clothing
	Aircraft	Food/Cheese	Watches	Steel	Food
	Liquor	Clothing	Musical Instr.	Computers/TV	Guns
Gender					
Males	Automobiles	Automobiles	Automobiles	Automobiles	Automobiles
	Textiles/Clothing	Liquor	Beer	Cameras	Guns
	Aircraft	Food	Cameras	Motorcycles	Liquor
	China	Clothing	Watches	Stereos	Steel
	Shipbuilding	Cosmetics	Drugs	Electronics/Toys	Computers
Females	China	Cosmetics	Automobiles	Automobiles	Food
	Wools	Clothing	Drugs	Toys	Clothing
	Tea	Liquor/Food	Steel	Cameras	Appliances
	Automobiles	Jewelry	Beer	Stereos	Automobiles
	Bikes	Automobiles	Food	TV/Watches	Liquor

Table 7. Attribute Means and Standard Deviations

	Quality			Durability			Technology		
	R	X	SD	R	X	SD	R	X	SD
England	4	3.45	1.46	4	3.40	1.46	4	3.32	1.42
Germany	1	5.85	1.22	1	5.90	1.41	3	5.25	1.22
France	5	3.30	1.62	5	3.11	1.76	5	3.12	1.64
U.S.A.	3	5.31	1.12	3	4.81	1.68	1	5.90	1.09
Japan	2	5.45	1.50	2	4.94	1.61	2	5.76	1.11

	Price			Style			Prestige		
	R	X	SD	R	X	SD	R	X	SD
England	4	3.14	1.64	5	2.26	1.45	5	2.85	1.30
Germany	3	5.25	1.54	4	2.55	0.90	1	5.49	1.30
France	5	2.95	2.00	3	4.95	1.16	4	2.67	1.06
U.S.A.	2	5.50	1.42	1	5.44	1.34	2	4.85	1.30
Japan	1	5.92	1.38	2	5.35	1.00	2	4.82	1.03

Ranking: 1 2 3 4 5 6 7
Weights: 7 6 5 4 3 2 1

R: Rank
X: Mean
SD: Standard Deviation

minds of consumers. British producers lacked recognition in the U.S. market and were perceived as having failed to approach international markets by manufacturing their products for general mass distribution and with a competitive price, as demonstrated by Japanese manufacturers. One main reason is due to the British style of manufacturing and distribution, which is narrowly designed for special segments of users, mostly for domestic consumers or very high-income international purchasers.

IMPLICATIONS AND CONCLUSION

Several interesting points have emerged from the studies. While they do not strongly contradict the findings of previous research, they show that U.S. consumers have developed specific, but also dynamic, images of products manufactured in different countries, as well as for the product categories that are thought to represent individual countries most closely. The findings suggest several summary implications:

- First, a single promotional theme such as product quality or price cannot be used for a broad spectrum of products and markets because each product within a market has its own peculiar characteristics and consumer image. There is a consistency in product familiarity among the respondents to this survey and the respondents to several other surveys conducted in the past.
- Second, American consumers are becoming less biased against and more knowledgeable about foreign products, suggesting, other things being equal, a greater propensity to accept them.
- Third, the findings portray the perceptual base behind the well-known import statistics, which show the inroads that Japanese products have achieved among American consumers (while, on the other hand, German products are losing perceptual ground partly due to their limited interest in U.S. markets and concentration on European markets). U.S. products are considered innovative with technology and style characteristics, but Japan offers the best price.
- Fourth, the price factor is losing its dominant effect on consumer decisions in the U.S.; instead, consumers have focused attention on other product characteristics such as quality, style, durability, and technology. And,
- Fifth, the demographic characteristics showed a mixed bag of preferences between lower/higher income, educated/less educated, and male/female consumers, but not strong enough to present a significant

gap. The differences observed were based more on consumer familiarity, style, technology, price, and quality than other characteristics.

It is important that multinational corporations, especially U.S.-owned firms, pay more attention to the area of consumer behavior and the study of demographic factors by manufacturing their products for special segments of the market. A geocentric and global market attitude should prevail. The domestic market alone cannot sufficiently respond to the mass production environment of the industrial countries. The rapidly changing status of developed as well as developing countries' economies, from government production systems to the private-enterprise, free market system, more than ever reconfirms the importance of evaluating consumer demands and producing for consumer needs. The recent and unexpected sudden changes in the East European bloc are further evidence of the significance of needs in a consumer-oriented market. This is a strong signal to multinational producers that there are new opportunities developing around the world, in areas which were once considered untouchable. Naturally, considerations of market segmentation are the key to success as needs vary with the different economic stages of production and consumption of each country.

REFERENCES

Anderson, W.T. and W.H. Cunningham (1972), "Gauging Foreign Product Promotion." *Journal of Advertising Research*, 12, 1 (February) 29-34.

Assael, Henry (1984), *Consumer Behavior and Marketing Action*. Boston, MA: Kent Publishing Company.

Bannister, J.P. and J.A. Saunders (1978), "U.K. Consumers' Attitudes Towards Imports: The Measurement of National Stereotype Image." *European Journal of Marketing*, 12, 8, 562- 570.

Barker, Tansu A. (1984), "A Comparative Survey of the Image of Australian Products." *Australian Marketing Researcher*, vol. 8 (December) 81-87.

Barker, Tansu A. (1987), "A Study of Attitudes Towards Products Made in Australia." *Journal of Global Marketing*, vol. 1 (Fall/Winter) 131-144.

Bartos, Rena (1977), "The Moving Target: The Impact of Women's Employment on Consumer Behavior." *Journal of Marketing* (July) 31-37.

Bilkey, Warren J. and Erik Nes (1982), "Country-of-Origin Effects on Product Evaluations." *Journal of International Business Studies*, 8(1) (Spring/Summer) 89-99.

Bradley, M. Frank (1981), "National and Corporate Images." In *Proceedings of the European Academy for Advanced Research in Marketing*, vol. 2, 1172-1189.

Cattin, Philippe, Alain Jolibert, and Colleen Lohnes (1982), "A Cross-Cultural Study of 'Made In' Concepts." *Journal of International Business Studies* (Winter) 131-141.

Damanpour, Faramarz (1985), "Consumers' Attitudes Towards Products of Multinational Firms: A Survey Result." Paper presented to the *Conference of The Academy of International Business.*

Damanpour, Faramarz and John H. Hallaq (1979), "Promotional Considerations for the Multinational Firm." *Proceedings, The American Academy of Advertising* (April) 73-78.

Damanpour, Faramarz and John H. Hallaq (1983), "A Survey to Evaluate 'Made In' Product Images of Industrial Countries: A Comparison of U.S. and Danish Consumers' Perceptions." *Virginia Social Science Journal*, 18, 1 (April) 22-31.

Dichter, Ernest (1962), "The World Customer." *Harvard Business Review,* 40 (July-August) 113- 122.

Dixon, Donald F. and Daniel J. McLaughlin, Jr. (1971), "Shopping Behavior, Expenditure Patterns and Inner City Food Prices." *Journal of Marketing Research,* vol. VIII (February) 960-999.

Etzel, Michael J. and Bruce J. Walker (1974), "Advertising Strategy for Foreign Products." *Journal of Advertising Research,* 14(3) 41-44.

Frank, Ronald E., W.F. Massy, and Yoram Wind (1972), *Market Segmentation.* Englewood Cliffs, NJ: Prentice Hall.

Gaedeke, Ralph (1973), "Consumer Attitudes Toward Products 'Made In' Developing Countries." *Journal of Retailing,* 49(2) (Summer) 13-24.

Heslop, Louise A. and Marjorie Wall (1985), "Differences Between Men and Women in the Formation of Country-of-Origin Product Images." In J.C. Chebat (ed.), *Marketing,* Vol. 6 (Montreal: Administrative Sciences Association of Canada–Marketing Division, May) 148-157.

Kaynak, Erdener and S. Tamer Cavusgil (1983), "Consumer Attitudes Towards Products of Foreign Origin: Do They Vary Across Product Classes?" *International Journal of Advertising,* 2 (April/June) 147-157.

Leone, Robert P. and Randall L. Schultz (1980), "A Study of Marketing Generalization." *Journal of Marketing* (Winter) 10- 18.

Lillis, Charles M., Chem L. Narayana, and John H. Hallaq (1974), "'Made In' Product Images." *Proceedings of the Southeast American Institute for Decision Science Conference,* March, 251- 54.

Lumpkin, James R. and John C. Crawford (1985), "Consumer Perceptions of Developing Countries." In N.K. Malhotra (ed.), *Developments in Marketing Science,* VIII (Miami, FL: Academy of Marketing Science) 95-99.

McConnell, J. Douglas (1967), *A Behavior Study of the Development and Persistence of Brand Loyalty for a Consumer Product.* PhD Dissertation, Stanford University, Palo Alto, CA.

Nagashima, Akira (1970), "A Comparison of Japanese and U.S. Attitudes Towards Foreign Products." *Journal of Marketing,* 34 (January) 68-74.

Nagashima, Akira (1977), "A Comparative 'Made In' Product Image Survey Among Japanese Businessmen." *Journal of Marketing,* 41, (July) 95-100.

Niffenegger, P., J. White, and G. Marmet (1980), "How British Retail Managers View French and American Products." *European Journal of Marketing,* 14, 8, 493-498.

Reierson, Curtis C. (1966), "Are Foreign Products Seen as National Stereotypes." *Journal of Retailing,* 42, 3 (Fall), 33-40.

Schooler, Robert D. (1965), "Product Bias in the Central American Common Market." *Journal of Marketing Research,* II: (November) 394-397.

Schooler, Robert D. and Albert R. Wildt (1968), "Elasticity of Product Bias." *Journal of Marketing Research,* V: (February) 78- 81.

Stephens, K.T., H.W. Fox, and J.J. Leonard (1985), "A Comparison of Preferences Concerning the Purchase of Domestic Products vs. Imports." In N.K. Malhotra (ed.), *Developments in Marketing Science,* vol. 8 (Academy of Marketing Science, Miami) 100-104.

Wang, Chih-Kang and Charles W. Lamb (1980), "Foreign Environmental Factors Influencing American Consumers' Predispositions Toward European Products." *Journal of the Academy of Marketing Science,* 8, 4, 345-356.

Wang, Chih-Kang and Charles W. Lamb (1983), "The Impact of Selected Environmental Forces Upon Consumers' Willingness to Buy Foreign Products." *Journal of the Academy of Marketing Science,* 11(2): (Winter) 71-84.

Worthing, P.M. and M.M Venkatesan (1971), "American Consumers' Perceptions of Imported Products: An Analysis of 'Made In' Images." *Markets Kommunikasion,* 3, 47-59.

Chapter 16

Images and Events:
China Before and After Tiananmen Square

James A. Brunner
Alan B. Flaschner
Xiaogang Lou

INTRODUCTION

Since 1974, the People's Republic of China (China) has placed a high priority on exports in order to build foreign currency reserves for the modernization of its economy. As a signatory of the General Agreement on Tariffs and Trade (GATT), the United States has contributed to the economic development of China by providing liberal trade terms and promoting more liberalized trade. As a consequence, American imports of "Made-in-China" goods in 1989 rose to $12 billion, a 42 percent increase over 1988 (Pear 1990). Apparel was the leading U.S. import from China, followed by miscellaneous manufactured articles such as toys, and then by telecommunication products, footwear, and textiles (see Table 1).

The People's Republic of China represents an interesting case for study in the context of the country image phenomenon because of several reasons. These include: its relative isolation from the international community over a long period of time; its export mix, in which lower-technology and inexpensive products predominate; the significant difference between its ideological and political system and that of Western countries; and the recent swings in its political direction, which served first to attract the interest of Western business as a result of moves toward a more open economy, and then to make the country the focus of international attention as a result of the events that surrounded what is now commonly referred to as the "Tiananmen Square" event.

Table 1. U.S. Chinese Imports by Major Product Class (1989)

Product Class	Amount (billion U.S.$)
Apparel	2.0
Miscellaneous manufactured articles (toys etc.)	2.5
Telecommunications	1.1
Footwear	.7
Textile yard and fabrics	.6
Travel goods, handbags, etc.	.5
Electrical machinery and appliances	.5
Other	4.1
Total	$12.0

Source: U.S. Department of Commerce

The objective of this chapter is to examine how the image of a country and its products evolves over time, based on a longitudinal view that was made possible by four studies of Chinese products conducted over a period of ten years. The most recent study was carried out a few months after the Tiananmen Square event.

In June 1989, the suppression of the pro-democracy demonstrations by the Chinese government aroused strong worldwide opposition. It is conceivable that this oppressive action by Beijing's leaders has affected negatively the acceptance of Chinese goods. If so, have the benefits of the marketing strategies of the past decade been so severely eroded that sales of products "Made in China" will suffer? Did this tragic event and the factors leading to it affect the propensity of American consumers to purchase Chinese products? Will it make it more difficult to market in the future "Made-in-China" merchandise in the U.S., which was done so successfully in the 1980s? While some earlier research has addressed the question of the environmental influences on country-of-origin perceptions (Wang and Lamb 1983), the literature in marketing has not dealt specifically with the effect of events on country images. In addition to the longitudinal analysis, this chapter analyzes the short-term effect of this significant event and addresses questions such as these.

BACKGROUND AND LITERATURE REVIEW

Pertinent Views on the "Country-of-Origin" Phenomenon

Research on the "country-of-origin" effects on the acceptance of foreign products has been conducted for over three decades. One of the earliest studies was by Dichter (1962), who maintained that a product's origin label has a significant influence on its success in foreign markets. He asserted that it should be recognized as an element of the marketing mix and of the images of products. Reierson (1967) observed that there is sufficient justification to believe that the quality images of foreign products are stereotyped, and suggested that product preferences are directly correlated with the level of like or dislike associated with a country.

Schooler (1971) analyzed the effects of socioeconomic characteristics on the acceptance of foreign products, and Lumpkin, Kim, and Crawford (1984) found that the willingness by consumers to purchase foreign products is correlated closely with the perceived risks associated with the countries involved.

A number of researchers have made useful observations about the relationship between product images and consumers' socioeconomic characteristics. Anderson and Cunningham (1972) and subsequent researchers have observed that better educated persons tend to rate foreign products more highly than those with less education. Brunner and Flaschner (1985) noted that higher-income consumers tend to accept foreign products to a greater degree than those with lower incomes. Along the same lines, Johansson, Douglas, and Nonaka (1985) observed that interactive variables such as income, age, and sex influence ratings of automobiles made in selected countries. Lastly, Koh and Brunner (1988) noted that the overall perceptions of Chinese products vary with the age, income, and education of consumers, and also observed that those who had purchased "Made-in-China" products had more favorable attitudes toward Chinese goods than non-purchasers.

Some debate exists about whether product images are global or product-specific. Kaynak and Cavusgil (1983) have suggested that bias toward a product from a foreign country is product-specific, and Etzel and Walker (1974) reasoned that measuring the images of products at the country level may be misleading and too general. On the other hand, Garland and Crawford (1985) have noted that U.S. consumers have a global view of foreign products, which is a function of past experiences with the products and of perceptions about their quality. Similarly, Papadopoulos, Heslop, and Bamossy (1989) point out that while substantial variations among product categories are natural, a country's overall image is likely to influence the image of all its products in the same direction.

Ofir and Lehman (1986) maintain that if consumers are familiar with products from a foreign country, the product images they hold are influenced by their perceptions of the nation's products in general. These perceptions are modified with the addition of new product information, and thus the images of a country's products are crucial in developing marketing and advertising strategies at the product category level. For example, when foreign product categories are in the early stages of their global market development and there is a low level of awareness, consumers would possess only general attitudes toward them. These findings are relevant to the case of China, since its products are in the early stages of global acceptance, and product category images (e.g., textiles, ceramics, clothing, and handicrafts) would tend to predominate over brand images.

Event Analysis

Event history analysis has a wide range of applications in consumer research. Illustrative of a major event affecting attitudes is the Iraqi invasion of Kuwait in August 1990: the subsequent increases in the price of oil caught American car producers leaning toward the manufacture of more powerful vehicles and, at least temporarily, served to refocus consumer attention on fuel efficiency (Templin 1990).[1]

The Tiananmen Square event is an example of an exogenous influence involving a change in a psychological condition which might influence consumer attitudes (Blossfield, Hamerle, and Mayer 1989). One cognitive dimension of a nation's image is the benevolence or malevolence attributed to it (Scott 1965). The event in Tiananmen Square exemplifies an external occurrence described as "spectacular" and a significant shift in the policy of a government, both of which are considered types of significant events (Deutsch and Merritt 1965). This event may effectuate an image which differs from that which existed prior to its occurrence, and may be associated with a lessening of consumer willingness in the U.S. (and other countries) to purchase Chinese products.

OBJECTIVES AND APPROACH TO THE STUDY

The primary objective of this chapter is to add to the literature on the longitudinal evolution of product and country images, based on a pilot study of the image of Chinese products by Brunner and Taoka (1979) and the subsequent studies on the same subject by Brunner and Flaschner

---

1. Notwithstanding Templin's (1990) and others' predictions, by the time of this writing developments in the Gulf War had brought oil prices down again. This, of course, does not alter the base condition that fears of price escalation may result from an event of this type.

(1985) and Koh and Brunner (1988; study carried out in 1987). The findings from this earlier research will be presented as background for a more recent study that was undertaken in 1989, in an attempt to determine the pattern of acceptance of Chinese products over the past decade.

As noted, the focus on Chinese products, and the timing of the four studies (and, in particular, the most recent one) makes it possible to also examine the potential influence of major events on product and country images. The Tiananmen Square event of 1989 in China, and its potential effect upon the willingness of American consumers to purchase "Made-in-China" merchandise, provides the context for the discussion.

The research methodology for all studies was essentially identical: telephone interviews were conducted, using a structured questionnaire, with heads of households or their spouses in the city of Toledo, Ohio. The number of attitudinal statements used differed somewhat among the various studies as the questionnaires were adjusted over time, but a majority were used in all of the studies. To obtain a representative sample, in the 1979 study interviewers were instructed to make two call-backs before substituting the name adjacent in the telephone directory to the initial household selected. In the subsequent studies, substitutes were selected systematically after three call-backs. The sample sizes were 380 in 1979, 389 in 1985, 381 in 1987, and 337 in 1989.

The research centers on specific attitudinal statements concerning Chinese products in general but also assesses "Top of Mind" awareness and specific product purchases, thus also being product category oriented. (As consumers in general have limited experience with "Made-in-China" goods and are unable to associate attitudinal statements with specific products, in designing the questionnaires attention was given to product categories rather than brands.)

In our analysis, based on observations by Koh and Brunner (1988), we hypothesize that consumers with prior purchase experience of "Made-in-China" products will perceive these goods more favorably than non-purchasers. It is further hypothesized that the recent turmoil in China will affect more adversely the willingness of *prior* purchasers of Chinese products to purchase *additional* Chinese goods, than the willingness of *non-purchasers* to *try* such products *for the first time.*

Based on the findings of the earlier studies that were previously mentioned, the expectation was that more favorable attitudes toward "Made-in-China" products would be held by consumers with higher incomes and who are better educated and younger than their demographic counterparts. These consumers presumably are less risk-averse and less provincial, and have fewer prejudices against foreign goods in general.

Limitations

While we took the usual precautions in designing the most recent study and its predecessors (e.g., in sampling and questionnaire design), the unique nature of the research context presents some noteworthy limitations. Opinion surveys are dependent upon the willingness of respondents to express their attitudes and activities accurately. In particular, examining the effect of a significant event such as Tiananmen Square is largely dependent upon the reactions of respondents and their plans for future purchases of Chinese products, which may or may not affect the actions they take in the marketplace. Further, the analysis must be based, by necessity, on the assumption that the respondents' expressions of future purchase plans in response to Tiananmen Square were based on their actual feelings rather than being socially acceptable responses. Significant (and potentially limiting) as it may be, this assumption is inherent to any opinion survey of this type and tends to be supported by the findings. Generally, the findings are a measure of plans that are externalized in reaction to an event, rather than of specific buying behavior.

The ability of respondents to recall past events can also be a limiting factor in a survey of this type. To overcome this limitation at least to some degree, the time span for recalling purchases of Chinese goods was limited to 12 months.

Lastly, a comment is necessary on the location of the studies. In 1979, when the first of this series of studies was undertaken, it was assumed that because Toledo is a major Great Lakes port, its population would be more accepting of foreign products than those in other Midwestern cities. Over time, however, consumers nationwide have tended to become more globally-minded as a partial result of increased exposure to foreign products. Thus, while our respondents would not be the same as consumers in other parts of the United States, there is little reason to believe that they are significantly different from average national norms. Furthermore, the tremendous publicity surrounding the Tiananmen Square event, and its near-unanimous condemnation among consumers in North America, would suggest that the responses of the samples in the most recent study may be fairly representative of the views of U.S. consumers in general.

OVERVIEW OF EARLIER STUDIES

Purchase of Chinese Products Over Time

Before reviewing the four investigations of the attitudes of consumers toward "Made-in-China" goods, it is useful to outline the historical pattern of acceptance for Chinese goods in the Toledo area. In 1979, less than 1 percent of the respondents reported having purchased "Made-in-China" goods in the previous 12 months. The number steadily increased to 24 percent in 1985, 27 percent in 1987, and 31 percent in 1989. This pattern augurs well for the future acceptance of Chinese products.

The 1979 Study

In the 1979 study, the perceptions of Chinese products were compared to those of goods from Japan, Hong Kong, and Taiwan. The findings of this pilot study are presented in Table 2. It is evident that consumers at that time held negative images of "Made-in-China" products: they were not perceived as items of real craftsmanship, but as cheap imitations of better products, to be avoided, lacking high grade style, and usually being unsatisfactory. Products from Hong Kong and Taiwan were viewed in a similar negative vein, while "Made-in-Japan" products were perceived far more favorably. Thus, Far Eastern products with the exception of those from

Table 2. Perceptions of Far Eastern Products by Nation, 1979

	Attitude Statement	Percent Who Strongly Agree or Agree*			
		China	Japan	Hong Kong	Taiwan
1.	Typically meet high quality control standards	39	64	38	38
2.	Are items of real craftsmanship	34	55	34	32
3.	Are very durable	28	54	28	29
4.	(Country-) clothing has high grade style	34	58	34	36
5.	Are among the world's best	17	45	19	16
6.	Are superior in most respects	14	38	14	16
7.	Are of questionable material & workmanship	62	39	62	62
8.	Are to be bought only if you are willing to gamble on quality	54	36	54	57
9.	Are to be avoided if possible	51	39	51	57
10.	Are typically shoddy	49	30	49	49
11.	Low prestige, so I don't tell others I buy them	46	29	46	46
12.	Are usually unsatisfactory	54	29	51	51
13.	Lack polish and detail found in really fine merchandise	56	41	56	58
14.	Are cheap imitations of better products	61	41	63	62
15.	Are made with cheap materials	64	43	68	61

* Excluding non-responses
Scale: 1 = Strongly agree to 5 = Strongly disagree

Japan were perceived negatively. At that time, Japanese products were experiencing a positive change in consumer perceptions from their earlier "cheap" image.

In that first study, 40 percent of the respondents did not express opinions concerning Chinese goods as compared to only 22 percent for Hong Kong, 22 percent for Taiwan, and 10 percent for Japan. Thus, while those familiar with Chinese products held negative perceptions, a large number of respondents had not formulated any perceptions (which, from the viewpoint of Chinese producers, would represent an obstacle since they would have to be modified in order to increase the willingness to buy their products).

Respondents in 1979 perceived "Made-in-China" products to be labor-intensive rather than capital/technology-intensive, as may be noted from Table 3. When asked from which country they would buy a selected list of products assuming equal price and quality, handicrafts and clothing were the most frequently mentioned classes of Chinese products. Yet only about 10 percent of the respondents indicated they would buy products from China, compared to larger percentages of consumers who would buy these goods from the other four countries. In brief, Chinese products were virtually unknown in 1979–and those who knew of them did not think highly of them.

The 1985 Study

In the period from 1979 to 1985, there was a significant improvement in the perceptions of consumers for "Made-in-China" products and the shift was even more notable than the perceptual changes regarding Japanese products (see Table 4). Attitudes toward Chinese products were more favorable on all of the perceptions observed in 1979. More respondents thought positively about "Made-in-China" goods and fewer held negative perceptions concerning their quality. For example, significantly more respondents (44 percent) perceived "Made-in-China" items to be very durable, compared to 28 percent in 1979.

The relative decline in negative perceptions of Chinese products was notable. There was a marked decrease in the proportion of respondents who perceived "Made-in-China" products to be produced with questionable material and workmanship (a decline from 62 to 44 percent); and a decline was observed in the relative number who felt that Chinese products were shoddy (49 to 33 percent). Clearly, over this intervening period, "Made-in-China" products had undergone a very favorable improvement,

Table 3. Origin Preferences*

Product Class	PRC	Percent of Respondents Japan	Hong Kong	Taiwan	Undecided
Handicrafts	12	36	14	17	21
Clothing	7	29	20	27	17
Electronics	2	83	3	2	10
Automobiles	2	74	1	1	22

* Nations from which selected products would most likely be purchased if comparable in price, quality, and styling (1979 study)

Table 4. Perceptions of 'Made-in China' Products for Selected Years

Attitude Statement	Percent Who Strongly Agree or Agree* 1979	1985	1989
1. Typically meet high quality control standards	39	45	42
2. Are items of real craftsmanship	34	45	55
3. Are very durable	28	44	52
4. Chinese clothing has high grade style	34	--	42
5. Are products I tell others about	--	--	42
6. Are among the world's best	17	22	--
7. Are superior in most respects	14	20	42
8. Are of questionable material and workmanship	62	44	42
9. Are to be bought if you are willing to gamble on quality	54	39	40
10. Are to be avoided if possible	51	42	25
11. Are typically shoddy	49	33	25
12. Low prestige, so I don't tell others I buy them	46	37	--
13. Are usually unsatisfactory	54	--	--
14. Lack polish and detail found in really fine merchandise	56	50	--
15. Are cheap imitations of better products	61	--	--
16. Are made with cheap materials	64	--	--
17. Considering both quality and price, Chinese products are a good value	--	--	21
18. Appealing use of design and color	--	--	69

* Excluding non-responses
Scale: 1 = Strongly agree to 5 = Strongly disagree

which was seen as a good omen for the marketing of Chinese goods in the United States.

The 1987 Study

In 1987, the attitudes toward Chinese products continued to improve. As noted earlier, by that time 27 percent of the respondents were reporting having purchased "Made-in-China" products in the previous year. Of these, 48 percent had purchased apparel, 10 percent electronic products, and 7 percent ceramic items. In terms of product features, most purchasers (about 37 percent) rated price as the most important factor influencing their decision to buy Chinese goods. About one-quarter stated that their quality perceptions influenced their decisions to buy "Made-in-China" products, and an equal number indicated that they were influenced by style considerations. Only 9 percent bought because of uniqueness and a negligible number (one-half of 1 percent) were influenced by the "Made-in-China" label.

Further, those who had purchased Chinese products over the previous 12 months held far more favorable perceptions than those who had not. T-tests comparing the means of the purchaser and non-purchaser groups on 10 attitudinal statements showed significant differences at the 0.05 level (see Table 5). This finding supported the observations of Garland and

Table 5. Perceptions of Chinese Products
by Prior Purchase Experience, 1987

Attitude Statement	Group Means (a) Purchaser	Non-Purchaser	t-value
1. Meet high quality control standards	3.11	3.51	-3.92**
2. Items of real craftsmanship	2.71	3.08	-3.65**
3. Very durable	2.90	3.13	-2.62*
4. Among world's best	3.38	3.57	-1.98*
5. Superior in most respects	3.25	3.53	-3.08**
6. Of questionable material and workmanship	3.38	3.13	2.39*
7. Lack polish and detail	3.35	3.11	2.42*
8. Typically shoddy	3.64	3.21	4.31**
9. Lack prestige so I don't tell others I buy them	3.60	3.21	3.75**
10. To be avoided if possible	3.62	3.11	4.38**

* $p < .05$
** $p < .001$
(a) Scale: 1 = Strongly agree to 5 = Strongly disagree.

Crawford (1985), that quality perceptions of foreign-made goods are influenced by the respondents' previous purchase experiences.

In addition, Chi-square analysis of the findings indicated that better educated persons were significantly more likely (at 0.02) to purchase "Made-in-China" products than those with lower educational attainment. Purchasers also tended to be younger (although the level of significance was 0.07), presumably because they are exposed more frequently to foreign goods and therefore are more willing to accept them. Also, many older consumers had previous experiences with low-quality products from the Far East in the period prior to and after World War II. Purchasers of Chinese goods typically had higher incomes, and compared to lower-income consumers, perceived lower financial risks in purchasing "Made-in-China" merchandise (at 0.002).

It was also observed that less educated persons tended to avoid Chinese products, perceived them as typically shoddy, and felt that they were made of questionable materials and inferior workmanship. By age, senior citizens (aged 65 or older) felt that Chinese products should be avoided. Those above 45 perceived "Made-in-China" items to be shoddy; and in contrast to the younger consumers, older ones felt that Chinese products lacked prestige. Lower-income consumers (earning less than $20,000) tended to avoid Chinese products and viewed them as being typically shoddy.

In 1987, while these consumers generally held negative attitudes toward Chinese products, they did view them as possessing several favorable features. Thus, while Chinese goods were perceived as not meeting high quality control standards and lacking durability and inferior in most respects, they were also generally perceived as exhibiting polish and detail and being examples of superior workmanship. An explanation of these conflicting findings is that these respondents held favorable attitudes toward "Made-in-China" merchandise involving craftsmanship, such as ceramics and handicrafts, but held negative perceptions of goods which require advanced technology and skills typical of capital-intensive goods, such as telecommunication items. This supported an earlier finding by Brunner and Flaschner (1985) and suggests the presence of product-specific attitudes.

As a result of the 1987 study, it was concluded that marketers of Chinese products needed to emphasize price, quality, and style, and appeal to younger consumers with high incomes and higher education levels. There was a need to change the negative perceptions held by significant proportions of consumers, and the turnaround in attitudes toward Japanese products provides evidence that this can be accomplished. Based on the findings from the first three surveys, it would be reasonable to expect that, over time, Chinese manufacturers could become effective competitors in technology-intensive industries as they are in such labor-intensive sectors as handicrafts and apparel.

THE 1989 STUDY

Method

In November 1989, or about five months after Tiananmen Square, a systematic probability sample of 337 households was drawn from the Toledo and Vicinity 1989 Telephone Directory. Telephone interviews were conducted with the male or female head of household, using a structured questionnaire that drew from earlier research and was similar to those employed in our previous studies on "Made-in-China" goods. Three callbacks were made before substituting another systematically selected number for absent householders.

Perceptions of these consumers regarding products from China were elicited concerning 12 product attribute statements. A five-point rating scale was used, anchored by (1) "Strongly Agree" and (5) "Strongly Disagree." Selected demographic data were obtained as well as information concerning purchases of "Made-in-China" products. Data were also gathered concerning the categories of products purchased and the effects of the political events of June 1989 upon the respondents' willingness to buy Chinese products in the future.

The Sample

The age, sex, education, and income characteristics of the sample are shown in Table 6. The table also includes the same data for the Toledo metropolitan area and the United States overall. As can be seen, the sample was representative on these demographics.

Findings

Top-of-mind Chinese products. In this study, before ascertaining which Chinese products the consumers had purchased, they were asked to recall what products came to mind when given the phrase "Made-in-China." This top-of-mind awareness would indicate whether Chinese products are

Table 6. 1989 Survey - Sample and Population
Demographics

	Sample (%)	Toledo MSA (%)	U.S. (%)
Age			
18-24	15	19	15
25-34	20	22	24
35-49	30	25	26
50-64	19	18	18
65 and over	14	15	16
Unreported	2	--	--
Sex			
Male	47	46	48
Female	53	54	52
Education			
11th grade or less	6	11	14
Vocational/High school grad.	38	47	39
Some college	26	20	17
College graduate or higher	30	21	20
Income (1988 household income before taxes)			
Under $10,000	10	14	11
$10,000-$19,999	14	16	19
$20,000-$34,999	24	27	26
$35,000-$49,999	20	12	17
$50,000 and over	15	9	21
Unreported	17	22	69

thought to be primarily labor-intensive or capital/technology-intensive. The findings from this question are shown in Table 7. As can be seen, of those who had purchased at least one Chinese product in the previous year, the largest proportions reported having bought porcelain items such as vases (41 percent), women's or men's clothing (37 and 28 percent, respectively), and figurines and handicrafts, including tablecloths and embroidery (21 and 18 percent, respectively). Interestingly, the top-of-mind order rankings for purchasers and non-purchasers were very similar (see Table 7). Chinese products continue to be perceived to be labor-intensive rather than capital-intensive.

Products purchased. As noted earlier, by 1989, 31 percent of the respondents had purchased "Made-in-China" products during the previous 12 months. Within the "purchasers" group, the product pattern is similar, though not identical, to that which emerged from the top-of-mind question. The most frequently mentioned product categories among purchasers

Table 7. Top of Mind Chinese Product Mentions
and Products Purchased, 1989

Product Class	Top of Mind Mentions				Products Purchased	
	Non-Purchasers		Purchasers			
	%	Rank	%	Rank	%	Rank
	(N=234)		(N=103)		(N=103)	
Porcelain items	34	1	41	1	16	3
Women's clothing	21	2	37	2	26	1
Men's clothing	18	3	28	3	21	2
Handicrafts	15	4	18	5	14	4
Figurines	13	5	21	4	11	5
Party Novelties	8	6	10	6	3	6
Bedding	4	7	5	8	2	7
Furniture	3	8	7	7	--	8
Other Products	39	-	39	-	30	-

Note. Columns do not add up to 100 percent because some
respondents mentioned more than one product class.

were women's and men's clothing (26 and 21 percent, respectively), porcelain items (16 percent), and handicrafts and figurines (14 and 11 percent,
respectively). The remaining respondents mentioned a broad range of
other products including party novelties, jewelry, fireworks, toys, etc. As
with the top-of-mind results, the products purchased are labor-intensive
rather than capital/technology-intensive. This finding is consistent with
the product class preference pattern reported previously by Brunner and
Flaschner (1985).

Propensity to purchase. Chinese products were well perceived by these
purchasers. Of those who had bought Chinese products in the previous
year, 72 and 11 percent stated, respectively, that they definitely or probably would buy "Made-in-China" products again. Only 11 percent indicated they probably would not, and no one stated they definitely would not
do so (an additional 6 percent were undecided). This suggests a highly
favorable level of acceptance and supports the trends observed in the
earlier studies (Koh and Brunner 1988).

Perceptions of Chinese products by purchase experience. As noted
previously, in 1979, Chinese products were typically perceived negatively
but, over the intervening period to 1989, these perceptions improved
markedly. Moreover, as is shown in Table 8, respondents who had purchased "Made-in-China" products in the previous year held significantly
more favorable images of Chinese goods than did non-purchasers. Only
on perceptions concerning the overall superiority of Chinese products and
the styling of Chinese apparel merchandise did the two groups not differ
significantly. This overall pattern supports the congruency among attitude

Table 8. Perceptions of Chinese Products by Purchase Experience, 1989

Attitude Statement	1989 Group Means (a)			
	Purchaser	Non-Purchaser	t-value	p
1. Typically meet high quality control standards*	2.70	3.13	3.90	.0001
2. Items of real craftsmanship*	2.73	3.00	2.34	.02
3. Appealing use of design and color*	2.76	2.45	2.98	.003
4. Are very durable*	2.79	3.10	2.92	.004
5. Chinese products are a good value*	2.85	2.40	4.37	.0000
6. Clothing has high style*	2.98	3.15	1.61	.11
7. Products I tell others about*	3.32	2.83	4.07	.0001
8. Are superior in most respects*	3.34	3.41	0.58	.56
9. Are of questionable material and workmanship**	3.36	3.02	2.95	.003
10. To be bought if willing to gamble on quality*	3.39	3.08	2.60	.001
11. To be avoided**	3.79	3.32	4.02	.0001
12. Typically shoddy**	3.82	3.26	5.35	.0000

* Positive attitudinal statements
** Negative attitudinal statements
(a) Scale: 1 = Strongly agree to 5 = Strongly disagree

components reported by Garland and Crawford (1985) and Koh and Brunner (1988): positive perceptions in quality of foreign-made products are related to the purchase pattern of the evaluator.

Demographic influences. As hypothesized, and as supported by Chi-square analysis, consumers who had purchased "Made-in-China" products were, on average, better educated and younger (see Table 9). However, as can be seen in Table 9, a positive association between household income and purchase pattern was not substantiated. The greater willingness to purchase foreign (and largely unfamiliar) products among younger and better educated consumers was noted previously when reviewing the 1985 study. These findings, with the exception of income, are in line with those of Dornoff, Tankersley, and White (1974), Anderson and Cunningham (1972), and Koh and Brunner (1988).

Tiananmen Square and propensity to purchase. As can be seen from the preceding discussion, the trend in perceptions of Chinese products has generally been favorable. Will this pattern continue after the political developments of June 1989 in China? This question is of course difficult to answer, but the timing of this study enabled us to augment the questionnaire with one direct question on this subject. Respondents were asked at the end of the interview: "Finally, what effect, if any, have the recent political events in China had upon your willingness to buy goods made in

Table 9. Prior Purchase Experience
by Selected Demographics, 1989

Demographic Factor	Number in Segment Purchasers (N = 103)	Non-Purchasers (N = 232)
Education		
11th grade or less	1	14
High school graduate	36	94
Some college/College grad.	66	124
No response	--	2

[X^2 = 9.00 with 2 DF.   Significance = .01]

Age		
18-34	46	74
35-49	29	73
50 and over	25	84
No response	3	3

[X^2 = 6.44 with 2 DF.   Significance = .036]

Income		
Under $20,000	27	52
$20,000-$34,999	27	53
$35,000-$49,000	20	48
$50,000 and over	18	34
No response	11	46

[X^2= .527 with 3 DF.   Not significant]

China? Are you more willing, less willing, or haven't these events influenced your willingness to buy Chinese products?"

While 20 percent of the purchasers stated their willingness to purchase
Chinese products had declined as a consequence of Tiananmen Square, 72
percent of the purchasers indicated there would be no such influence (see
Table 10). Conversely, 8 percent of the respondents stated that in spite of
the Tiananmen Square incident, they would be more likely to buy Chinese
goods—presumably because they either favored the actions of the government or felt that their purchases would benefit the Chinese people in this
period of adversity. Conceivably, most consumers will continue to purchase Chinese products as they anticipate the quality enhancement and
price/quality trends to continue, and therefore they were not influenced by
these political developments.

On balance, this lack of a detrimental effect of this event is a positive
finding for marketers of Chinese products: only a fifth of the consumers of
"Made in China" goods expressed dismay to the degree that they would

Table 10. Willingness to Buy Chinese Products
After 1989 Event

Effect	Purchasers (N=103)	Non-purchasers (N=234)
Less willing to buy	20	24
No effect	72	66
More willing to buy	8	10

[X^2 = 1.092 with 2 D.F.   Not significant]

be disinclined to purchase Chinese products in the future. While this proportion is fairly substantial, in light of the overall responses to this question, it does not appear to represent a significant or irreversible loss of purchase interest. The potential adverse effect does not necessarily mean that these consumers will refrain from buying Chinese products in the future, and it may mean that strong motivating factors may be able to offset it. For example, the price advantage of Chinese products, better styling, quality improvements, and selling through recognized retailers could be sufficient motivators to overcome the potential event-inspired reluctance to buy "Made-in-China" products.

Interestingly, the willingness to buy Chinese goods does not seem to be associated with the prior purchase patterns of respondents. As is shown in Table 10, there was no significant relationship (at 0.05 level) between the propensity to purchase Chinese products after the event and whether respondents had or had not purchased Chinese goods in the past 12 months. Purchasers' views about the quality of the goods, price, uniqueness, and other factors appear to have outweighed politically-motivated biases that might have been aroused by this event. In a marketing sense, this would appear to be a "non-event," as was also indicated by the fact that Chinese exports to the United States continued to increase after the turmoil in Tiananmen Square (Pear 1990).

MARKETING IMPLICATIONS AND CONCLUSIONS

This longitudinal study supports the evidence provided by some other researchers (e.g., Nagashima 1977) that country images can change rather swiftly, especially in today's dynamic international environment. Implications for marketing are discussed in this section with a focus on the image of Chinese products, but the discussion essentially is relevant to any country, and its producers, that find themselves in a position partly or largely similar to that of China.

This study and previous research on "Made-in-China" products provide significant implications for the development of marketing strategies for Chinese goods. Lumpkin, Crawford, and Kim (1985) observed that the willingness to purchase products from a country is primarily the result of consumers being exposed to the products. They noted that the negative attitudes of U.S. consumers concerning foreign-made apparel is the result of ignorance of these goods, and that with increased information and familiarity, product biases tend to diminish.

In that regard, in this research, women's and men's apparel were also high in top-of-mind awareness by these respondents and were high on the list of most frequently purchased "Made-in-China" products. It is notable that apparel products from developing countries such as Korea are not perceived well, and the perceived risk across apparel categories is about the same for Chinese goods (Lumpkin, Crawford, and Kim 1985). In spite of this, apparel was the leading Chinese export to the United States in 1989. Further, a political bias may exist toward a country with a halo effect reflected in the attitudes toward its products. There is a potential negative bias toward Chinese products which may have more influence than perceived risk (Lumpkin, Crawford, and Kim 1985). Manufacturers may use China as a production source but de-emphasize the country-of-origin factor to overcome this bias.

Increased familiarity with a product category from a communist country may offset political bias. Also, bias is not a permanent condition and it can be overcome with price concessions and other marketing strategies and tactics. Further, while Chinese products may be identified as "Made-in-China," few Chinese brand names are used. Domestic brand names are substituted as a tactical risk-reduction action. Chinese brands, while easy to remember, pronounce, and recognize, do not suggest product qualities or reflect the products' benefits; and, they lack distinction. Illustrative of these limitations are Pigeon bicycles, Panda radios, Great Wall fans, Great Wall Hotel, and Five Goat raincoats and bicycles produced in Guangzhou.

Foreign trade associations, government agencies, as well as marketers of Chinese goods need to coordinate their marketing strategies to create positive attitudes toward "Made-in-China" products. Since, in the U.S., Chinese product category images rather than brand images predominate, marketing strategies need to be formulated at the product category level until brand awareness is created and consumer brand loyalties develop.

Contributing to this lack of brand awareness is the fact that, as previously noted, Chinese goods are typically not being sold in the U.S. with Chinese brand names, but rather, are merchandised under the labels of leading retailers such as The Limited, Wal-Mart, and K-mart, or by marketers who subcontract the manufacture of their brands. These organizations use China as a manufacturing source for product categories including apparel, toys, shoes, and electronic goods such as radio/cassette players and TVs, in order to benefit from lower labor costs, and from the quality, prices, and terms of delivery which are competitive with those of other foreign and domestic producers.

This research indicates that consumers associate China with labor-intensive goods and not capital/technology-intensive products. Therefore, Chinese products such as apparel and porcelain, which incorporate craftsmanship and are labor-intensive, should be primarily promoted.[2] This reasoning would suggest that Chinese producers would benefit more by focusing first on improving the quality of products which consumers already buy; and then, perhaps they could make the transition to exports of technology-intensive items such as cameras, electronics, and stereo equipment along the lines of the Japanese and South Korean models (market share building with low-priced and good-quality merchandise).[3] If these goods are found to be of higher quality than expected, there is ample evidence from other countries' experiences that the preconceptions noted in our studies can be altered (Bilkey and Nes 1982).

Although Chinese products generally are not as well known as those from some other countries, it should be noted that they are more prominent than is commonly assumed. This provides a base that China can use as a springboard when moving to new product categories for export. For example, several Chinese products are currently being sold through mail order catalogs of leading museums such as the Henry Francis Dupont Winterthur Museum and Gardens, which prominently displays Chinese figurines and other products such as textiles and handcrafted goods with emphasis upon their quality, uniqueness, as well as economic value. Upscale retailers such as Neiman Marcus, I. Magnin, Bloomingdale's, Saks Fifth Avenue, Bonwit Teller, Marshall Fields, and Lord and Taylor have all featured Chinese goods. A significant share of the apparel for The Limited (a store specializing in apparel for women) is manufactured in China. Appealing to a price/value-conscious market, K-mart prominently displays women's apparel manufactured in China. Both The Limited and K-mart have highly effective delivery systems which enable merchandise that is "in style" to

---

2. Ed. note: This is in line with the thinking supported by Morello (see Chapter 12), that it is probably easier to change stereotypes indirectly rather than by "attacking" them head-on.

3. Ed. note: This view is also supported by Jaffe and Nebenzahl (see Chapter 18) concerning the image of South Korean products in relation to the 1988 Seoul Olympics.

be displayed in their retail stores within one week after being received in their U.S. distribution centers.

A significant and interesting finding of the 1989 study was that the events in Tiananmen Square, while shocking to some American consumers, adversely affected only one-fifth of the respondents. Even assuming that a loss of this magnitude is translated into marketplace terms, it does not appear to present an insurmountable obstacle. The findings from other parts of the 1989 study are in line with the trends that were observed in the previous studies since 1979. One possible explanation for this somewhat unexpected finding could be that, for most consumers, the events of June 1989 may not represent a departure from their traditional beliefs and impressions about the Chinese political system. In other words, the period preceding Tiananmen Square– during which some openness was observed in China, and during which relations with the U.S. (and other Western countries) had been improving– may well have been too brief to have affected consumers' views about China's political climate. If that were the case, Tiananmen Square may have been seen as "the rule" rather than as a surprising event, and consumers' views about Chinese products would be similar to those that prevailed under similar political conditions in earlier years.

In this light, it seems reasonable to prognosticate that efforts by the Chinese government to alleviate any negative feelings that might persist, by restoring a modicum of normalcy, will influence the future acceptance of Chinese goods by American consumers. Evidence of the transition to a calmer atmosphere has been the cancellation of martial law in Beijing, and the release of some of the pro-democracy demonstrators. More generally, over the past decade there has been a growing acceptance of Chinese products, and the impact of the recent political events on the propensity to purchase Chinese products appears to be limited. Assuming no major new upheavals occur and although the political environment in China remains strongly under communist control, this portends a promising future for Chinese products in the U.S.

A primary objective of the government is the modernization of the country. A compelling need exists for foreign exchange to service China's $40 billion in foreign debt, and exporting is a logical means of earning foreign funds in order to purchase capital goods and services to support the country's modernization program. Continuing to provide most-favored nation status to China, as the U.S. has done, should not only enable global consumers to have access to Chinese goods but should also support China's economic development and the social, political, and economic changes that are certain to follow. Less oppressive actions on the part of the Chinese government, coupled with continuing international contact through product exports and imports (and, the passage of time), will hopefully allow a return to normalcy and a continuing improvement in attitudes toward Chinese goods.

This research has centered on the longitudinal evolution of the image of China and Chinese products, and has examined the short-term influence of the Tiananmen Square incident upon consumers. China's political climate, coupled with its size and potential, on the one hand, and its present low degree of development on the other, make it a particularly interesting case for long-term study. New research can continue to monitor developments and the evolution of attitudes toward Chinese products over time. A further objective of such research could be to ascertain the rate of change (if any) of stereotyped perceptions in relation to the effect of such factors as price and quality on consumer decisions.

REFERENCES

Anderson, W.T. and W.H. Cunningham (1972), "Gauging Foreign Product Promotion." *Journal of Advertising Research,* 12, 1 (February) 29-34.

Bilkey, Warren J. and Erik Nes (1982), "Country-of-Origin Effects on Product Evaluations." *Journal of International Business Studies,* 8(1) (Spring/Summer) 89-99.

Blossfield, H.P., A. Hamerle, and K.U. Mayer (1989), *Event History Analysis.* Hillsdale, NJ: L. Erlbaum Associates.

Brunner, James A. and Alan B. Flaschner (1985), "Country-of-Origin Marketing Strategy for The People's Republic of China." In C.T. Tan, W. Lazer, and V.H. Kirpalani (eds.), *Emerging International Strategic Frontiers,* Proceedings, International Marketing Conference (Singapore: School of Management, National University of Singapore) 292-295.

Brunner, James A. and George M. Taoka (1979), "Consumer Attitudes Towards Products from the People's Republic of China and other Far Eastern Countries." *Proceedings, Asia-Pacific Dimensions of International Business* (Academy of International Business, Honolulu, Hawaii; December) 464-469.

Deutsch, Karl W. and Richard L. Merritt (1965), "Effects of Events on National and International Images." In Herbert C. Kalman (ed.), *International Behavior.* New York: Holt Rinehart and Winston. 132-187.

Dichter, Ernest (1962), "The World Customer." *Harvard Business Review,* 40 (July-August) 113- 122.

Dornoff, Ronald J., Clint B. Tankersley, and Gregory P. White (1974), "Consumers' Perceptions of Imports." *Akron Business and Economic Review,* 5(2) (Summer) 26-29.

Etzel, Michael J. and Bruce J. Walker (1974), "Advertising Strategy for Foreign Products." *Journal of Advertising Research,* 14(3) 41-44.

Garland, Barbara C. and John C. Crawford (1985), "Satisfaction with Products of

Foreign Origin." In C.T. Tan and J.N. Sheth (eds.), *Historical Perspectives in Consumer Research* (Proceedings, Association of Consumer Research International Meeting, Singapore, July 18-20) 160-161.

Johansson, Johny K., Susan P. Douglas, and Ikujiro Nonaka (1985), "Assessing the Impact of Country of Origin on Product Evaluations: A New Methodological Perspective." *Journal of Marketing Research*, XXII: (November) 388-96.

Kaynak, Erdener and S. Tamer Cavusgil (1983), "Consumer Attitudes Towards Products of Foreign Origin: Do They Vary Across Product Classes?" *International Journal of Advertising*, 2 (April/June) 147-157.

Koh, Anthony and James A. Brunner (1988), "Consumer Perceptions Towards Products Made in the People's Republic of China: Implications for Marketing Strategy in Development." In *Developments in Marketing Science*, Academy of Marketing Science, vol. X, 122-126.

Lumpkin, James R., Gap Kim, and John C. Crawford (1984), "Perceived Risk in Apparel Due to Country of Origin: A Study of Inherent vs. Handled Risk." In J.R. Lumpkin and J.C. Crawford (eds.), *Proceedings, Southwestern Marketing Association Conference* (San Antonio) 119-122.

Lumpkin, James R., John C. Crawford, and Gap Kim (1985), "Perceived Risk as a Factor in Buying Foreign Clothes." *International Journal of Advertising*, 157-169.

Nagashima, Akira (1977), "A Comparative 'Made In' Product Image Survey Among Japanese Businessmen." *Journal of Marketing*, 41 (July) 95-100.

Ofir, Chezy and Donald R. Lehman (1986), "Measuring Images of Foreign Products," *Columbia Journal of World Business*, XXI, 2, 105-108.

Papadopoulos, Nicolas, Louise A. Heslop, and Gary J. Bamossy (1989), "International Competitiveness of American and Japanese Products." *Dimensions of International Business*, 2 (Ottawa, Canada: International Business Study Group, Carleton University).

Pear, Robert (1990, March 11), "Bush Distressed as Policy Fails to Move China." *The New York Times*, 11.

Reierson, Curtis C. (1967), "Attitude Change Toward Foreign Products." *Journal of Marketing Research*, IV: (November) 385- 87.

Schooler, Robert D. (1971), "Bias Phenomena Attendant to the Marketing of Foreign Goods in the U.S." *Journal of International Business Studies*, 2: (Spring) 71-80.

Scott, William A. (1965), "Psychological and Social Correlates of International Images." In H.C. Kelman (ed.), *International Behavior*. NY: Holt-Rinehart, 70-103.

Templin, Neal (1990, August 7), "Gulf Crisis Catches Car Makers Pushing Larger Models." *Wall Street Journal*, B1.

Wang, Chih-Kang and Charles W. Lamb (1983), "The Impact of Selected Environmental Forces Upon Consumers' Willingness to Buy Foreign Products." *Journal of the Academy of Marketing Science*, 11(2): (Winter) 71-84.

Chapter 17

Through the Looking Glass: Product-Country Images and International Trade Agreements

Louise A. Heslop
Marjorie Wall

INTRODUCTION

The United States and Canada share the longest undefended border in the world. This symbol of their unique relationship signifies the close association of the two countries, their openness to mutual influence, their trust in each other, and the confidence of each in their ability to maintain their distinctive identities. But they are not indifferent neighbors. Particularly in the last ten years, the political, economic, and cultural involvement of the two countries has intensified. In many respects they are closer together and more intertwined than ever before.

What are the manifestations and implications of this greater closeness? In this chapter, a partial answer to this question will be sought through examining the views of Canadians and Americans about themselves and each other, in terms of the products they produce and their countries and peoples. Perhaps because of the intensive and extensive trade between them, there is a substantial body of literature about product-country images (PCIs) of the two countries concerning each other. Such a set of comparable bilateral information developed over time is unique in the product-country image literature.

On the international trade side, the greater closeness is most clearly manifested in the recent implementation of the Canada-U.S. Free Trade Agreement (FTA). Information on reciprocal attitudes toward products made domestically and in the other country can provide insights of relevance in predicting the likely impact of the agreement. So, this chapter will center on that agreement as a focus for application of the PCI information.

On a broader scale, the format used in this investigation has relevance beyond the two countries which are studied here. In many other areas of the world, extensive bilateral or multilateral trade agreements are being considered, coming into effect, or being enhanced (e.g., in Western Europe in 1992). Similar questions can be posited about the effects of such agreements on domestic markets and international trade flows, and information on product-country images and international shopping behavior can help to answer them.

Through the Looking Glass

When Americans and Canadians are asked about each other–what they think the other is like, how they live, what kinds of products they produce–it reminds one of Lewis Carroll's famous book, *Through the Looking Glass*. In the story, Alice is fascinated by the mirror image of her own drawing-room. She notes that the drawing-room in the Looking Glass World is "just the same as our drawing-room, only the things go the other way" (Carroll 1946 edition, p. 166). What she could see from her own room she found "quite common and uninteresting." However, she was extremely curious to know about what she could not see, what was on the wall on which the mirror hung, and what was down the hallway–"it's very like our passage as far as you can see, only you know it may be quite different on beyond" (Carroll p. 167). To her delight, Alice is able to pass through the looking glass and does find a substantially different world full of adventure.

As Canadians and Americans compare themselves to each other, much the same experiences are often felt–the familiarity and the fascination with the similar, but the somehow, somewhat, different and intriguing unknown. There are many bases for similarity, though not complete sameness–major institutions, religious traditions, liberal democratic political ideals, geography, British legacy, and immigrant base. The dominant language in both countries is English and both have substantial populations of a second language–French in Canada and Spanish in the U.S. However, Canadians have been variously identified as more conservative, more self-contained, less optimistic, more risk-averse, lacking in self-confidence, more reserved. Americans are said to place more emphasis on individual freedoms and rights, a free enterprise economic system, and a commitment to country and flag (the melting pot view of the assimilation of immigrants). Canadians are more inclined to strong government, peace, law and order, public enterprise, and acceptance of diversity (the cultural mosaic or salad bowl view of immigrant assimilation).

Because of their much smaller population size, it is not surprising to find that Canadians seem to be more obsessed with differentiating themselves from their neighbors. In the last decade, several books have been written by both Americans and Canadians comparing the two countries but usually with the goal of describing Canadians to themselves (see, for example, Berton 1982; Malcolm 1985; Garreau 1981; Gwyn 1985). Essential to the description of Canada and Canadians seems to be that they are "not Americans." The search for a Canadian identity appears to be repeatedly mired in the negatives. Similar experiences can be observed in other situations of smaller and larger neighboring countries (e.g., New Zealand-Australia, Belgium-France in the European Community).

In his book, *The Nine Nations of North America,* Garreau (1981) takes a decidedly different view of the relationship between the two countries. To Garreau, the border between Canada and the United States is useless and nonexistent. His argument is that the true differences among the people of North America are not based on the national borders, but rather on the regional variations in lifestyles, ways of making a living, values, attitudes, and speech patterns that are linked to differences in climate, geography, history, and bases of economic activity. To Garreau, Canada shares five regional identities with the U.S. The only distinct political entity unique to Canada is Quebec, which is a "nation" unto itself.

If Garreau is correct, Americans and Canadians (outside of Quebec) should each view themselves as quite similar to their neighbor. They will emphasize their commonalities in judging each other. According to social psychology theories, people like and admire those with whom they share commonalities. Therefore, similarity judgments should lead to positive attitudes about the products and people of the other country (Hill and Stull 1981; Taormina and Messick 1983).

If people do hold positive attitudes toward their neighboring country and the products produced there, they should welcome closer political, cultural, and economic ties, such as the Free Trade Agreement. In this chapter, we will explore whether or not this is the case by examining research on product-country images. However, before doing so, some background on the agreement is necessary in order to make clear its economic and historic significance, and how it might make the Looking Glass more permeable.

THE FREE TRADE AGREEMENT

Background Concerns and the Importance
of Consumer Attitudes

In 1989, the United States and Canada entered into an historic trade agreement. Since it was signed, remaining tariff barriers between the two countries have been coming down for virtually all consumer and industrial goods and services flowing between the two countries. The major mechanisms protecting each country's domestic markets from their major trading partner are being removed. What will be the likely outcome of this agreement?

Many political, business, and labor leaders on both sides of the border objected to the Canada-U.S. FTA. They argued that domestic markets would be flooded by imports and that thousands of jobs would be lost. Differences in the availability of raw materials, labor cost, technology levels, manufacturing facilities, and distribution efficiency have been cited variously as the source of competitive advantage held by the "other side."

However, it is not simply the existence of discrepant advantages which make or break markets, but also consumers' perceptions of and reactions to these market situations which determine the outcomes in terms of sales and profits. If consumers do not believe that the foreign product is significantly superior to the domestic product in a meaningful way, then there is little reason to believe that domestic markets will be eroded seriously. If obvious advantages for foreign suppliers are counterbalanced by perceptions that domestic suppliers are more accessible because they are nearer, then consumption may not shift. If buyers ultimately act out of a sense of duty to protect jobs at home, then domestic sales may be further secured.

So the effects of the FTA will ultimately rest on the views of consumers about their own products and the products from the other country. What do we know about these views? What do U.S. consumers think and feel about their own domestically produced products and those produced in Canada? What do Canadian consumers think about U.S.-made products versus ones made in Canada? How do these various attitudes relate to buying behavior? Are these views about products related to views about the country and its people?

PCI research can be very helpful in answering many of these questions. Considerable information has been collected over the last 20-25 years in both the United States and Canada, which can provide needed insight. The results of this research are reviewed late in this chapter in order to point out possible shifts in consumption that may occur under conditions of more open markets. Also, research on transborder shopping can provide additional information. Have consumers changed their shopping habits for products in the neighboring country? Information on these two areas of research will be presented following an overview of the FTA, the general history of free trade between the countries, and public and political responses to the latest agreement.

What Is the FTA?

The FTA was concluded under Article XXIV of the General Agreement on Tariffs and Trade (GATT) to replace a multitude of bilateral and ad hoc arrangements that had accumulated between Canada and the United States. The two countries have long been each other's largest trading partner, with almost 80 percent of their mutual trade being duty-free even before the enactment of the FTA. In 1987, Canada sold 76 percent of its exports to the U.S., while the U.S. sold 23 percent of its exports to Canada. The agreement was designed to eliminate trade barriers between the two countries, encourage fair competition within the free-trade area, liberalize cross-border investment, and lay the foundation for further bilateral and multilateral cooperation (External Affairs 1987, p. 9).

In addition to trade in goods, the FTA includes agriculture, services, business travel, and investments, and provides a basis for developing rules to deal with subsidies, dumping, and countervailing measures. Beginning in 1989, the FTA eliminates all tariffs through annual reductions over a 10-year period or less where mutually agreeable (tariffs were eliminated immediately on some goods, e.g., computers, leather, furs, skates, skis, and motorcycles, or over five years for such goods as paper, paint, furniture, and most machinery). Both countries continue to apply their existing tariffs to imports from other countries. Rules of origin have been defined to allow goods to trade under the FTA only if 50 percent or more of the value added occurs in Canada and/or the U.S. The administration of technical standards and labeling requirements remains to be resolved through ongoing negotiations to rationalize and accommodate different product standards for safety, health, and information–sometimes referred to as non-tariff barriers. Canada was able to retain its controlled marketing systems for poultry and dairy products. However, agricultural export subsidies have been eliminated–a first worldwide. Special considerations have been given to trade in other sectors including wine and spirits, energy, and automotive products–the latter to preserve the basis of the 1967 Canada-U.S. Auto Pact.

Most commercial services, with the exception of transportation and telecommunications, and government-administered health, education, and social services, are now open to free trade. While the service sector has become the major growth area in industrialized countries, no framework for structuring their trade, such as the one for goods under the GATT, has existed. Financial institutions come under some special provisions that open up the cross-border activity considerably, but at the same time prevent the institutions of one country from subsuming those of the other. Business investment has also been opened up to allow much freer access. While Canada still retains the right to review the acquisition of Canadian firms by U.S. investors, a much higher review threshold (upwards of $150 million) than before has been established. Also, the FTA allows for liberalization of entry procedures for business people in order to permit the orderly flow of goods and services, and investments. Finally, the basis for a dispute settlement mechanism was established using bilateral panels with binding powers to review complaints from either country about antidumping and countervailing duty decisions that affect trade.

The FTA is a wide-ranging agreement that promises to have demonstrable effects upon the economies and citizens of the two countries. Can the very different population sizes (Canada has a population approximately one-tenth that of the U.S.), combined with the cultural and geographic differences, be accommodated in such a way that no country suffers but, instead, both prosper as the negotiators and legislators of the deal promised? This question can be answered only at a very tentative level as yet. Several areas are relevant: the history of free trade attempts between Canada and the U.S., attitudes and opinions about the agreement from both sides of the border, and indicators of economic activity between the two countries before and after the introduction of the agreement.

History of Free Trade

Free trade was probably practiced by the fur traders and settlers within North America, but the separation of the United States from British rule imposed trade barriers. By 1854, a Reciprocity Treaty was formed between the U.S. and Britain on behalf of Canada (which did not gain the status of a country until 1867), but this was abrogated in 1866 due to hostilities between the U.S. and Britain over the American Civil War. So 1854-1866 was the only period of truly free trade between the two countries before the present agreement. Many efforts were made from the 1870s up to the First World War to return to free trade, but were never successful. In 1911, a comprehensive agreement was concluded, but business people on both sides of the border were nervous about it, and the defeat of the government of the Canadian Prime Minister, Sir Wilfred Laurier, the following year, caused the trade agreement to die before it was implemented. Protectionism increased in both countries until 1935 when a modest but important most-favored-nation agreement was reached. This helped to get Canada out from under the high tariffs imposed in 1930 in the U.S. Smoot-Hawley Tariff Act. For the next 50 years, Canada and the U.S. negotiated various bilateral agreements. In fact, a free trade pact was negotiated secretly in 1947 but was never publicized, as the Canadian Prime Minister at the time decided it was politically unwise to try to introduce such legislation so soon after the war (Gwyn 1985).

After the Second World War both countries cooperated to help found the GATT among 23 nations (now increased to over 95 members). Since that time, both countries have lowered many trade barriers between themselves during each round of GATT negotiations. The net result was that over three-quarters of their mutual trade was duty-free by the 1980s. A major bilateral accord was achieved with the Auto Pact in 1967 which allowed duty-free trade in cars, trucks, buses, and parts with a provision for the proportion of manufacturing that should occur in each country. This Pact is still very important today to the economic prosperity of central Canada and has been maintained as a special area within the current FTA.

In the early 1980s, signs of trade restraint were occurring with increasing frequency on both sides of the border as a result of large trade deficits, particularly in manufactured goods. Canada especially feared diminishing access to U.S. markets, which account for a proportionately far larger share of its total exports than does Canada for the U.S. At first, Canada wanted to negotiate additional bilateral arrangements like the Auto Pact, but the U.S. was not receptive and instead favored a comprehensive agreement such as the one ultimately evolved.

Attitudes Toward Free Trade

Both the present and all previous negotiations have been accompanied by heated political and public debate. This has been particularly true on the Canadian side, where a population one-tenth of that in the U.S. and mostly concentrated along the border has feared being swallowed up economically, and perhaps even culturally and politically. Accounts of negotiations and election campaigns reveal much heated rhetoric (Columbo 1988; Forsey 1987): "Today the Prime Minister has put Canada up for sale" (1891); ". . . I will oppose the veiled treason. . . to lure our people from their allegiance" (1891); ". . . the first step toward annexation" (1911); "No truck or trade with the Yankees!" (1911); "We need more truck and trade with the Yankees" (1966); "This country would become a satellite of the United States" (1987); "The Canadians don't understand what they have signed. In 20 years they will be sucked into the U.S. economy" (1988); or the prophetic statement by Laurier in 1911 upon his defeat and the death of his free trade deal, "Oh men of little faith, that seed will still germinate."

Political debate and partisan positions have been heard by the public at various times. Media coverage and commentary have probably influenced consumer opinion about the benefits of free trade on both sides of the border.

We can only surmise that public attitudes were wide and varied in earlier free trade debates. In the debate of the 1980s, opinion pollsters surveyed both sides of the border as the negotiations took place leading up to the 1989 implementation and after. Not surprisingly, Canadians were much more aware of the impending agreement than were Americans (only 12 percent of Americans in 1986 and less than 40 percent in 1988 had heard of it); however, the vast majority (90 percent) of Americans supported the free trade agreement and believed that both countries would benefit. Canadians were much more skeptical: while 90 percent had heard of the deal by the conclusion of its negotiation, only 40 percent were in favor of it, with 39 percent being opposed and 21 percent undecided (Adams and Dasko 1988). Other pollsters found similar results: consumers generally thought some type of agreement with the U.S. was a good idea, but many were confused or uncertain about the FTA (Howard 1988).

Opinion polls conducted after the first year of implementation revealed that support versus opposition had stayed about the same in Canada (Winsor 1989), while pessimism that the deal had hurt the economy and had not produced any benefits had grown ("Portrait. . ." 1990). However, Americans were much less concerned. Many believed the deal had equal benefit to both countries (42 percent) or benefited Canada more (20 percent), and that it had had no effect on the U.S. (58 percent), while few believed that it had helped the U.S. more (10 percent), and the reminder did not know (28 percent) ("Portrait. . ." 1990).

Economic Indicators

There are no easy measures of the success or failure of the FTA. At the time of writing, only the early stages of duty reduction have occurred, while at the same time national and international events outside of free trade confound the issue. However, these factors do not prevent either the detractors or supporters from stating their opinions. The Canadian Labor Congress and the Pro-Canada Network have implied that there were substantial negative consequences for labor during 1989 due to free trade, quoting as evidence the loss of 72,000 jobs, the slower creation of new jobs than in the previous year, and a 300 percent increase in mergers and takeovers by U.S. firms over 1988 ("Scoreboard. . ." 1990; Howard 1990). Canadian supporters of the FTA quote trade surpluses and positive economic growth in Central Canada compared to that in the states of New York, Michigan, Ohio, and Illinois (Gates 1990), and decry the lack of visibility and notoriety of "good" news, such as the stable unemployment rate and major new investment initiatives by various companies (Crispo 1990). In reality, the jury is still out on the economic effects of the FTA.

However, a strong indication of the likely impacts of the agreement can be determined from attitudes of consumers toward products produced in their own country and across the border. This is explored in the following sections of this chapter.

PRODUCT-COUNTRY IMAGE RESEARCH

In this section, we will turn to PCI research to provide insight into the likely impacts of the FTA. What do consumers in each country think of products from the other relative to products from their own? Are there preferences which would suggest either that markets will remain stable because of strong domestic product biases, or that lifting of the remaining restrictions will open a floodgate of repressed foreign product purchasing?

American Consumer Views of Domestic and Imported Products

American consumers have been interviewed and questioned in more PCI studies than have those of any other country. This reflects the activity of American marketing researchers, the size of this consumer market, and the opinion leadership role of American consumers. American tastes, trends, and preferences have more impact on consumption in the rest of the world than those of consumers of any other nationality.

Table 1 presents an overview of the major studies of Americans. While it is not an exhaustive list of such research, since it is likely that there are several studies which have not received wide circulation in the research literature, it is highly representative and spans enough years to permit the analysis of trends and substantial cross-country comparisons.

The first reported study is that by Reierson in 1966. The methodology

Table 1. U.S. Studies

Author/Year	Sample	Countries	Measurement	Ratings of Products From		
				United States	Canada	Other
Reierson 1966	University students	US. + Canada + others	Qual. of products, classes, & general products	All products ranked first	Highest on none	
Nagashima 1970	Minnesota businessmen	US + others	Product attributes	Highest for reliability, heavy ind., tech adv., mass produced, wide distribution, pride advg, brand names, choice, use of colour. Low on workmanship	N.A.	
Dornoff, Tankersley & White 1974	Cincinnati householders	US + others	General & specific prods	Highest for general, food, fashion (Japan higher in electronics, Germany in mechanical products).	N.A.	
Lillis & Narayana 1974	US & Japan consumers	US + others	Overall product images	Highest for luxury, heavy ind., mass production, appearance (Japan better on prod)	N.A.	More agreement on profiles of Japan and Germany
Abdel-Malek 1975	175 CEO's in US (views of customers)	Canada + US + others	Customer profiles	Highest for affluent, progressive propensity to spend	Highest for predictability, qual. consciousness	
Cattin & Jolibert 1979	Purchasing managers US, France	US + others	Attitude scales Purchase willingness	Highest for luxury, heavy industry, tech. adv., inventively advertised, choice, appearance, design, young, upper class, 2nd on price, distribution, pride	N.A.	92% of U.S. buyers would buy in U.S. if style equal
Damanpour & Hallaq 1981	150 US + 100 Danish households	US + others	20 attitude scales	Highest for 13/20 attributes except price, tech. adv., mass produced, more for men, distribution	N.A.	

Table 1. U.S. Studies (continued)

Author/Year	Sample	Countries	Measurement	Ratings of Products From United States	Canada	Other
Narayana 1981	Consumers in one US city	US + others	Attitude scales	US higher on all	N.A.	
Hampton 1983 (1976 & 1982 studies)	250 residents 152 residents in NW US	US + Canada + others	Attitude to investment & from country	Slightly higher preference for own investment	Slightly lower attitudes declining in 2nd study, less successful	
Dickerson 1982	408 consumers in 10 areas of Eastern U.S.	US + others	Preference for clothing	64% said US clothing better than imports	N.A.	
Niffenegger & Odin 1983	71 car dealers	US + others	Attitudes	US cars higher only for safety, acceleration, power, comfort, luggage space, service avail., choice	N.A.	
Papadopoulos & Heslop 1989	approx. 300 consumers in Ottawa	US + Canada + others	Attitudes	US and Canada equal on reliability - Highest for tech. adv., qual., service, availability, know, prestige, buy, satisfied	- Highest for workmanship performance price/value honest promotion	
Hester & Yuen 1986 (1984/85 Surveys)	Ithaca NY 507 Edmonton 525 NY City 953	US + Canada + others	Awareness of country promotion programs; concern for origin of products		None	19% of Canadians & 39% of Americans cared about origin; 40% aware of promotions
Garland & Crawford 1985	101 US students	US + others	Willingness to buy, satisfaction quality		N.A.	Preference is product specific; willing of (prior purchase, satisfaction,quality perception)

411

Table 1. U.S. Studies (continued)

Author/Year	Sample	Countries	Measurement	Ratings of Products From		Other
				United States	Canada	
Johansson, Douglas, Nonaka 1985	70 US grad. students	US + others	Attitude scales for cars	US cars rated lower than foreign (non-Canadian)	N.A.	
Johansson & Nebenzahl 1986	320 New Jersey consumers	US + others	13 attribute scales US cars	All brands show preference for US production	N.A.	
"Crafted with Pride" series (1986)	4 consumer surveys	US + Canada + others	Attitude to clothing	US clothing is high quality, dependable sizing, reasonable price, US clothing preferred	Can. ranked 5th as source	Only 36% noticed country of origin
Tourism Canada 1986	9,000 in US	Canada + US + others	Attitude to Canada as vacation destination	N.A.	Canada seen as familiar, close, but "somehow different"	
Han & Terpstra 1988	150 mid-western US consumers	US + others	Ratings of TV's and cars on 16 attitude scales	TV/cars only serviceability best (2nd to Japan on TV on almost all other attr.; 3rd on all others for cars)	N.A.	Serviceability and workmanship attitudes sensitive to origin effects
Garland, Barker, & Crawford 1987	Business students in Can., US, other	US + Canada + others	Willingness to buy, qual., satisfaction, value, fairness of exchange; fashion apparel & packaged food	N.A.	N.A.	LISREL models - only signif. path from quality to willingness to buy for Canadian clothing

of that study and the one by Nagashima in 1970 were widely used by subsequent researchers, making comparisons of findings relatively easy. Usually respondents have been surveyed and asked to rate either products in general or specific product categories on a list of bipolar (semantic differential) scales. Samples have been drawn from populations of household consumers, students, or business people.

For each study, Table 1 lists the author, publication year, sample composition, target countries studied (indicating if only the U.S. or U.S. and others, specifically Canada), what was measured, on what dimensions or products the U.S. scored highest, and in what areas Canada, if included, scored higher than the U.S. Therefore, the presentation of the results of the studies is limited to those that have relevance to the impact on U.S. producers of the free trade agreement between the two countries.

A scanning of the results concerning the ranking of products from the United States indicates strong support of these products by American consumers. When domestic products as a general group, rather than specific products, were rated, they were particularly strongly supported (Reierson 1966; Dornoff, Tankersley, and White 1974; Narayana 1981). Clothing products also received strong ratings (Dickerson 1982; Crafted With Pride in U.S.A. 1986). However, there is evidence of weakness of American products in relation to Japanese and German ones in the areas of workmanship (Nagashima 1970) and price (Lillis and Narayana 1974; Cattin and Jolibert 1979 for industrial buyers; Damanpour and Hallaq 1981). Moreover, specific product categories showed repeated, but not necessarily consistent, weakness in ranking, particularly cars (Niffeneger and Odlin 1983; Johansson, Douglas, and Nonaka 1985; Han and Terpstra 1988), and electronic equipment such as TVs (Dornoff, Tankersley, and White 1974; Han and Terpstra 1988). However, it was clearly not Canadian products which were seen as superior to American goods in any of these areas.

So American consumers and industrial buyers can be seen to express strong preferences for American goods and services, in general. Some weaknesses have emerged over time in the perceptions of the quality of workmanship and price, and for certain products where the U.S. has lost world leadership (e.g., in automotive and home entertainment technology). As noted, however, there is strong reported preference for U.S. clothing.

Two points should be recognized. First, the studies reported here are all surveys of attitudes and buying preferences. The relationship of reported attitudes and actual behavior has been called into question in many areas of consumer behavior. In particular, whether or not consumers act on the basis of their attitudes to country-of-origin has been questioned by such researchers as Ettenson, Wagner, and Gaeth (1988) and by Liefeld in another chapter in this book. Experimental studies and conjoint analysis procedures support a link, but at a weaker level than is indicated by the relatively consistent survey findings. Second, most studies have looked only at products in general, and, when specific products have been named in the research, a relatively narrow range of product categories has been explored. The weaknesses of American products have tended to be more obvious if specific products and specific perceptions in relation to products from other specific countries are examined. Therefore, the information most closely related to actual consumption may be lacking from the research stream.

Furthermore, some researchers have noted changes over time in consumer attitudes. For example, earlier studies showed very solid support for domestic products among Americans. Then, studies in the early 1980s suggested considerable softening of domestic strength. Lately, there appears to have been some resurgence of interest, perhaps based on neo-nationalism and protectionism, in buying domestically produced goods. So some instability can be expected in the future.

American Views of Canadian Products

Very few studies have examined views of Americans toward Canadian products. On first thought, this would seem surprising since Canada is the largest trading partner of the U.S. The omission of Canada from studies of the attitudes of U.S. consumers may have several causes. One reason may be that Canada is taken for granted and assumed to be just like the U.S. in quality of manufacture. Second, Canada may not be perceived to be an important threat to U.S. manufacturers who have had significant market share eroded by Japanese and German producers and by low-cost imports from newly industrialized nations. Third, sometimes the Canadian imports come from U.S.-owned subsidiaries, so there is little concern over U.S. imports from these sources.

In the few studies in Table 1 reporting the inclusion of Canada with the U.S., in no case was Canada rated as superior to the U.S. by American consumers or business people. The only exception to this finding was a study in the mid-1980s by Papadopoulos and Heslop (1989), in which consumers gave a higher rating to Canadian over American products for price and value. That study involved surveying of consumers in eight countries. Consumers in almost all countries gave domestic products relatively low ratings in this one category of attributes. Consumers appear to be saying that, taking all things into consideration (e.g., the costs of transportation from international suppliers, tariffs and duties, etc.), they generally feel that domestic products are overpriced.

Also, in this study, American and Canadian products were seen as similar in warranty, servicing, and advertising believability. In this case, it would appear that Americans saw an integration of market systems that allows for the provision of warranty coverage and servicing regardless of country of manufacture. Several major retailers (such as Sears) and distributors operate in both countries and honor warranties regardless of origin. So, such a conclusion on the part of consumers, that it did not matter where the product was made within the two countries, would be partially correct. The most obvious instance where this is true is for automobiles, which have been free-traded for over 25 years.

In terms of advertising, these views of comparability between the two countries are probably a reflection of the high degree of similarity of television programming and commercials. There are differences in the extent of regulation of advertising, leaning toward more stringent regulations in Canada. However, this would not be apparent to Americans.

Since the studies cited did include attitudes to products in general and to specific product categories, they can be examined for evidence concerning the susceptibility of manufacturers in different industries. The product categories studied have included cars, home entertainment and electronic equipment, fashion apparel, packaged foods, and vacations. In none of these product areas was there any preference among American consumers for Canadian over American products or services. In general, the reverse was true. Even in the area of vacation destinations, where a Tourism Canada (1986) study might have expected to find a preference for Canadian outdoor-oriented vacations, this was not to be found. Americans concluded that Canada was "somehow different" but also familiar, and that their own country had many areas just as suitable for wilderness vacations, camping, and nature exploring.

To summarize, Canadian products and services were seen as inferior to American by industrial buyers (Abdel-Malek 1975), and by consumers (see, for example, Garland, Barker, and Crawford 1987; Reierson 1966; Tourism Canada 1986). There seem to be no natural markets ready to fall to foreign competition from Canada under the FTA. The only area of attitudes where Americans may give some edge to Canadian products may be on price and value. However, Canadian costs of production are generally higher than those in the United States due to higher minimum wage regulations, higher tax structures, and higher real estate costs. Therefore, it is highly unlikely that any real and consistent price advantage of Canadian manufacturers could be realized without very substantial economies of scale. Based on differences in historical market sizes, most Canadian manufacturing facilities have lower, not higher production levels than those of American companies.

Canadian Views of Domestic and Imported Products

In contrast to the large number of studies concerning Americans' attitudes to products, there are far fewer studies of what Canadians think about their own and imported products, although there are several (see Table 2.) All but one of these studies were carried out in the 1980s, so there is little historic context and fewer trends are observable.

Three notes should be made regarding methodological differences between the studies in the U.S. versus those in Canada. First, the studies in Canada have almost always used consumer samples, rather than student samples which are convenient but often raise questions about external applicability of results. Second, there is a greater use of experimental designs with choice-related outcome measures rather than surveys measuring overall and attribute-related attitudes. Third, studies of Canadians' views of products from different countries have always included the United States as a target country of interest.

In general, Canadians have reported very mixed feelings about domestic products versus those from other countries. Wall and Heslop (1986) carried out the largest and most representative study of consumers. They found that, in general, Canadian consumers held very positive attitudes toward Canadian products and toward "buying domestic." Attitudes were most favorable among women, those with less than university education, and older consumers. However, the reasons given for buying Canadian were not tied to product superiority or to personal reasons, such as a liking for the products and value for money. Rather, they included such general reasons as the importance to the economy and to save jobs. Similar reasons were given in a Canadian Gallup Poll survey in 1985. Furthermore, women who held the most positive attitudes to Canadian-made goods rated American goods just as highly. Men gave higher ratings to Japanese and West German products over products from both North American countries.

Highest ratings for specific products made in Canada were given to Canadian clothing and footwear. Nevertheless, these products face significant challenge from imported products, particularly in the low-price end from Pacific Rim countries. For many products, Canadian and American goods were given about equal ratings; that is, there was no strong prefer-

Table 2. Canadian Studies

Author/Year	Sample	Countries	Measurement	Ratings of Products From United States	Ratings of Products From Canada	Ratings of Products From Other
McDougall & Rawlings 1979	130 consumers	Can. + ?	Buying preference attitude	N.A.	Prefer to buy Canadian for patriotic reasons but products not best	
Kaynak & Cavusgil 1983	197 consumers in Nova Scotia	Can. + US + others	Pref. for products overall, food, fashion, electr. & h-hold goods	Highest for all but food	Highest for food (Canada 2nd for all others)	
Wall & Heslop 1986	635 consumers	Can. + US. + others	Quality: product characteristics	US and Canada equal in overall quality; US highest for home entertainment products	Canada highest for clothing & footwear	
Papadopoulos & Heslop 1989	approx. 300 consumers in Ottawa	Can.+ US + others	Overall rating, product attributes, purchase satisfaction	US and Canada equal overall; US highest for engineering & design, -price & value, market presence	Canada highest for marketing integrity (warranty, serv., adv.), prestige from/experience in owning (know/buy/satisfied)	
Barker & Robinson 1987	111 consumers in Saskatchewan	Can. + others	20 attitude scales	Highest on tech. sophist. US>Canada on value, necessity, cons. profile	Highest on aware & willing to buy; also Can>US on quality	
Hung 1989	120 consumers in Calgary	Can. + US + others	Importance of product nationality and product attributes, ranking of products	US>Canada on price, quality, & style of all products except clothing; men say US clothing better on price	Canada> US on price & quality of clothing	Origin important 89% clothing. 95% consumer electr., 83% dress shoes, 69% sporting goods
Heslop, Lieleld, & Wall 1987	240 consumers	Can. + US. + others	Intentions to buy, quality, risk value	N.A.	Highest for all quality ratings but most not significantly different from US.	Experimental design
Schellinck 1989	69 consumers	Can + Others	Quality of socks	N.A.	Canadian socks rated 2nd	Experimental design
Ahmed, d'Astous, & Zouiten[1]	90 students	Can + Others	Preference for cars	N.A.	Canadian cars preferred at medium price range only	Conjoint analysis Japanese cars preferred over Canadian ones

1 See Chapter 8, by these authors in this book.

417

ence for domestic products by Canadians, in contrast to the results of studies of Americans.

Barker and Robinson (1987) found similar divisions of support for Canadian and American products among Canadian consumers. Canadian products were rated as somewhat higher in quality, and consumers said they were more aware of them and willing to buy them. However, American products were more favorably assessed for value and technical sophistication.

It should be noted that respondents in the Wall and Heslop (1986) study reported some difficulty in being able to identify those products that were Canadian-made. This inability to separate Canadian from American products could explain why consumers rated them similarly and showed little preference for one over the other. Furthermore, the 1985 Canadian Gallup Poll survey reported that country-of-origin was fourth in importance after quality, price, and style in selection criteria of consumers. Less than half of consumers said that they were concerned enough to check when purchasing. Clothing products were the most frequently (43 percent) checked for country of manufacture. So, according to existing research, Canadian consumers report that, in general, they (1) do not feel it is important to check where a product is made; (2) find it difficult to determine if a product is made in Canada; and (3) are indifferent to whether or not the product is Canadian- or American-made.

Experimental studies, which have tried to measure the direct impact of country-of-origin on selection of products, have found somewhat similar results. The strength of the experimental designs lies in their unobtrusive means of assessing the impact of the country variable. In surveys, consumers may be more likely to report a liking and preference for domestic products if they perceive this to be the socially acceptable response. Indeed, Canadians are entirely aware of the effect of their choices on jobs for Canadians. They may be inclined to underreport their engagement in practices, such as buying foreign products, which jeopardize these jobs. However, experimental designs do not present this dilemma directly. In a well-designed experiment, respondents will not even be aware that the country-of-origin variable is being assessed because the stimulus will not vary within subjects, but rather between subjects.

Heslop, Liefeld, and Wall (1987) reported that consumers were significantly affected by the origin of the product in two of three product tests. For these two products (telephones and billfolds), however, the differences were between products labeled as made in developed versus developing countries, and there were no significant differences found when comparisons were made between Canadian and American products.

Finally, there is one survey-based study that allows for direct comparisons of Canadians and Americans (Papadopoulos and Heslop 1989). All respondents received the same questionnaire asking about general product characteristics for both countries in North America and several others, including their own. Thus, respondents in Canada and the United States were both asked about products made domestically and by their neighbor. The findings of the study regarding American attitudes were reported above. Americans always rated their products higher than Canadian products overall, as well as for all product dimensions studied, with two exceptions: price-value, where Canadian products were judged as superior; and marketing integrity, where American and Canadian products were seen as equal. For the other product dimensions of engineering-design, market presence, prestige of ownership, and experience in buying and use, American products were given higher ratings than Canadian ones.

Canadians, however, were much more generous in their assessment of American-made products. Overall, American goods were judged as comparable to domestic products. Moreover, Canadians said that American goods were superior in terms of engineering-design, price-value and even market presence. In other words, Canadians said American products were of better quality, better value, and were easier to find. The likelihood that they would buy them seems high.

Relative Position Strengths of Canadian and American Producers

The substantial research evidence provides a very clear answer to the question of who should feel the more deleterious effects of the FTA based on consumer preferences. Americans generally prefer domestic goods. Although the solidity of the belief in the superiority of Americans goods has wavered over time and does vary among products, there seems to be a rising tide of nationalism in the U.S. American consumers' pride in their own products is currently increasing, and fear of loss of jobs to foreign suppliers may reinforce the positive attitudes toward domestic goods. Canadian products hold no special appeal over American goods except for some perceived value advantages. If, in fact, there is no clear price differential in favor of Canadian goods, there is nothing to suggest that Americans will find them appealing. Any exceptions can be expected only in the case of relatively selective products uniquely identifiable as Canadian and for which Canadians hold some superior capabilities, such as furs or maple syrup. Some advantage may also come from a lower-valued Canadian dollar.

Canadians, on the other hand, appear very receptive to American goods. They already perceive that these goods are interspersed in their marketplace with those domestically produced and are entirely comparable or superior. Generally, threats to Canadian jobs would be the only reason to restrain consumption of American products. However, McDougall and Rawlings (1979) argue that patriotism is a poor motivator at the checkout and is not likely to be a determinant attitude in product selection. Canadians have little incentive to buy their own products. They are often hard to find, are not clearly superior, and are seen as too expensive.

To reinforce these findings about attitudes and preferences for domestic products, particularly the lack thereof among Canadians, we can turn to an entirely separate set of evidence about Canadian-American consumer behavior. This is concerned with whether consumers *shop* at home versus in the neighboring country.

TRANSBORDER SHOPPING

If consumers choose to leave their own country to shop, they certainly are more likely to buy foreign-made products. Although the FTA has been in effect since 1989, there are still restrictions on what individual shoppers can bring home from the other country. The restrictions are more stringent and the duty-free level much lower for Canadians returning from shopping trips in the United States than for Americans returning home from Canada. This discrepancy, no doubt, results from past evidence of flows and the impact of these flows on domestic producers.

The growing propensity for Canadians living along or near the U.S. border to shop in the U.S. has attracted considerable media attention (Kidd 1990). Significant reciprocal activity with Americans travelling or shopping in Canada has not occurred in recent years. As a result, Canadian retailers near the border have complained that their businesses have suffered severely. Only a few studies have been conducted by the Canadian side to monitor the cross-border shopping activity.

In 1978, Papadopoulos surveyed the outshopping activity of Thunder Bay, Ontario, residents (Papadopoulos 1980). The same survey was repeated in 1986 (Papadopoulos, Heslop, and Phillips 1988), and it was found that little change had taken place in the total amount of outshopping, but that American cities (Duluth and Minneapolis) had decreased somewhat while Canadian destinations (Toronto and Winnipeg) had increased as "most frequent" outshopping trip destinations. However, a more recent analysis of Thunder Bay cross-border shopping activity (Buchanan 1990) revealed that in the intervening years, U.S. shopping destinations had increased again in importance.

Thunder Bay presents an interesting case in outshopping studies because of its geographic isolation (the nearest city is Duluth, Minnesota, which is four driving hours away and has a comparable population size). Is cross-border shopping widespread and/or growing in more concentrated population regions of Canada? It has been only recently that some municipalities, provinces, and federal agencies have tried to quantify the situation. Studies have been conducted by Winter (1990a, 1990b, 1990c) in the Niagara and Windsor areas of Ontario–two highly travelled border crossing areas. Winter (1990b) noted that 7.5 percent of the Canadian population lives within a 15-minute drive of the border. Many residents within this distance were willing to travel across the border to buy convenience items such as beer, basic foods, gasoline, sporting goods, and toys. Winter suggested that the relatively high value of the Canadian dollar ($0.88 U.S. in August 1990) and different tax structures make it worthwhile for border-town Canadians to shop frequently in the U.S. Almost one half of the population lives within one hour of the border, and many of these Canadians are likely to travel to the U.S. for more expensive items, such as clothing and small appliances.

In 1990, Winter speculated that when a value-added tax would be imposed across Canada in 1991 (the 7 percent "Goods and Services Tax," similar to Western Europe's VAT), shoppers would have an incentive of $19-$23 per $100 clothing purchase to shop in the U.S. His prediction was substantiated as early as January 1991, as Canadian consumers immediately responded to the imposition of the new tax in Canada by stepping up transborder shopping. A survey ("Canadians say. . ." 1991) carried out at the U.S.-Canada border in the first month of the new tax noted that half of respondents planned to increase their spending in the U.S. by at least 25 percent. Based on current estimates that Canadians spent $2 billion in the U.S. in 1990, this would mean an increase of about $500 million in lost revenue to Canadian retailers.

What is not clearly known are the reasons for the increase in cross-border shopping by Canadians. Winter's studies suggested that consumers based their decisions on price, selection, and the availability of Sunday shopping in the U.S. border states. Papadopoulos, Heslop, and Phillips (1988) suggest that the entertainment value of a cross-border trip also influences consumer decisions. And Buchanan (1990) suggested that the major factors are the appreciation of the Canadian dollar against the U.S. dollar, substantial price differences on certain merchandise, the perception/existence of greater merchandise selection, aggressive marketing by U.S. merchants, and new and different retail formats in the U.S.

If Americans were also shopping across the border in Canada, there would be little cause for concern on the Canadian side. However, cross-border statistics and tourism data have shown shrinking amounts of U.S. traffic into Canada (MITT 1990; "The wary tourists" 1990), and Canadian retailers report that American tourists complain about high gasoline and food prices.

In summary, the attitudes toward free trade and shopping in the respective neighbor's country are complex, and ongoing research and monitoring are needed. Will cross-border shopping by Canadians continue to escalate? Will American consumers continue to not reciprocate? Many economic and social factors may intervene to affect these current trends, and marketers and retailers on both sides of the border will be challenged to anticipate and maximize the positive effects while minimizing the negative.

All current evidence, both attitudinal and behavioral, would suggest that manufacturers and marketers in the two countries face quite different levels of challenge as a result of the FTA. On the American side of the border, manufacturers appear to be positioned well against Canadian sources (although they certainly face stiff competition from other foreign sources). Canadian producers appear to face the biggest challenges and will have to be particularly creative and aggressive in their marketing strategies. However, such summary impressions may be too simplistic. All may not be so rosy for American producers seeking markets among Canadians, and things may not be so gloomy for Canadians seeking to export to the U.S.

COUNTRY-PEOPLE IMAGES

When consumers enter markets, they buy not only the physical product, but what we call in marketing the "augmented" or "total" product, which, among other elements, includes the images of the people who sell it and the country in which it is made. Consumers buy not just a collection of products, but a lifestyle. Just as company images are considered important determinants of buyer behavior, so country images will affect shoppers' acceptance of goods from various origins.

It is important, therefore, to look not only at what Canadians and Americans think of each other's products, but also what they think of each other and each other's country. These country-people views can directly impact on product quality images, for example, when they deal with the industry base of the country and worker skills of the people. They can also affect consumer behavior indirectly by influencing the willingness to do business, the desire to be associated with the country through its products, the assessment of the suitability of the products depending on the similarities of lifestyles, etc.

Several recent studies have examined the bilateral views of people in the two countries, including a large-scale opinion poll ("Portrait. . ." 1990), the Tourism Canada (1986) study, and the Papadopoulos and Heslop study (1989).

In the latter study, 11 scales were used to ask Americans about Canada and Canadians and the same was done in Canada about the U.S. and Americans. Both respondent groups also assessed the images of Sweden, Japan, and Great Britain. Nine scales were used to ask respondents about their own country and people. The results concerning Canadians' and Americans' views of their own and each other's country and people are reported in Table 3. Canadians' ratings of the United States indicate that they recognized the latter's much more sophisticated industrial base, with less relative emphasis on agriculture, and a substantial proportion of industry devoted to consumer (light) goods production. These findings line up well with perceptions of U.S. products relative to Canadian ones.

Table 3. Canadian and American Views of Countries and People

| | Canadian Views of | | American Views of | |
	Home	U.S.	Home	Canada
Technologically advanced	4.8	6.2	6.2	4.2
Manage economy well	3.6	4.6	4.2	4.0
Agriculture/Manufacturing	2.3*	5.3	4.1	3.3*
Light/Heavy industry	4.0	3.3*	3.2*	4.3
Industrious people	4.7	5.0	5.0	4.7
Admirable role in world politics	5.0	4.4	5.2	4.2
Taste	4.6	4.2*	4.5*	4.5*
Trustworthy	5.6	4.5*	4.7*	5.2
Likeable	5.7	4.5*	5.0	5.2
Want investment from	-	4.2*	-	5.6
Want closer ties with	-	4.2*	-	5.4

Notes. Underlined numbers indicate the highest scores given by the rating country for the five target countries (U.S., Canada, Japan, Sweden, Great Britain). Asterisks indicate the lowest scores given by the rating country for the five target countries.

Canadians saw themselves as far more agrarian and heavy-industry oriented. All this is not very surprising.

However, what may be surprising is that there is also a very strong
message of dislike for Americans. Americans were given the lowest scores
of all countries tested on several scales, including taste, trustworthiness,
likability, and desire for closer ties with and investment from them. There
is a very clear message that Canadian consumers are not very fond of
Americans, and, therefore, less likely to want to do business with them.

Support for these findings is seen in the opinion poll ("Portrait . . ."
1990) which reported that a growing majority of Canadians have rejected
the notion that Americans and Canadians are essentially or mainly the
same. Canadians often pointed to the greater poverty and lack of social
programs in the U.S. as evidence of its less humane nature. When asked to
describe Americans, Canadians were more likely to say something negative than positive (e.g., the most common responses were "snobs,"
"good," "friendly," "pigheaded," "aggressive," "powerful," "obnox-
ious," "indifferent," "stupid," or "rich").

There are very striking contrasts in looking at views held by Americans
toward Canada and Canadians. In the Papadopoulos and Heslop (1989)
study, Canadians were judged, not surprisingly, to be much less industrialized and oriented to consumer goods than Americans. The Tourism Canada (1986) study also notes that the traditional image of Canadians as
dependent on primary resource industries is still common. However, there
is a growing awareness of the urban centers of Canada as desirable places
to visit for city-style recreation.

It is interesting to note in Table 3 that Canada and Canadians were
given top ratings on several of the scales by Americans–often the ones
where Canadians gave Americans the lowest ratings. Americans judged
Canadians to be highly trustworthy and likeable, and they wished to have
closer ties with them, more than with any other of the countries studied.
Americans, therefore, clearly like Canadians and can be expected to want
to do business with them. The opinion poll ("Portrait. . ." 1990) indicated
that Americans see Canadians as not really foreign. When asked to describe Canadians, the most common responses by Americans were that
Canadians were "friendly," "nice," "neighbors," "wonderful," and
"similar."

IMPLICATIONS

The information from product-country attitudes, country-people attitudes, and shopping behavior suggests that there are both opportunities

and areas of concern on both sides of the border under the new FTA. The following paragraphs highlight implications for both American and Canadian producers. Considerations for the latter are given somewhat more emphasis, since (1) the American perspective has been discussed widely throughout the international marketing literature, and (2) the Canadian experience is more relevant to a larger number of countries which share its position as a small nation facing major international challenges.

The generally positive views of Canadians about American products relative to their own, and their lack of commitment to domestic goods, might suggest that American manufacturers are in a daunting position of strength. However, the negative views Canadians hold of Americans can forecast difficulties for Americans involved in personal selling to Canada, and should warn about the dangers of the wholesale transfer of advertising approaches to Canadian media. Advertising campaigns that promote that the product should be bought because it was made in the U.S. will likely be rejected, especially if a strong nationalistic posture is assumed. Canadians are not so flamboyant about their patriotism and would find such messages offensive, even if they held more positive views about America.

In product design and product line development, the substantial differences in tastes and preferences between Americans and Canadians should be clearly recognized. Not all U.S. products will be warmly received in Canada. The size of the Canadian market can still make it a lucrative market segment to exploit. But this must be done with a sensitivity to Canadian interests, and separate market research is needed to understand the different market characteristics.

U.S. firms may find that joint ventures with Canadian firms can provide both the insider's knowledge of Canadian market conditions and the domestic base necessary for acceptance by Canadian consumers. However, in entering into such arrangements, American companies may have to curb an apparent overbearing attitude of "we're all just the same" or the possible advantages will be lost.

American manufacturers may be most successful in building on regional-based strengths. There is considerable evidence that Canadians feel more affinity for Americans who are near-neighbors and who most closely share their lifestyles. Thus, north-south trade flows within limited east-west corridors can be expected to be more successful.

American companies might benefit from efforts to enhance their corporate images, for example, by supporting Canadian institutions (culture, sports, education, etc.). Such philanthropic actions are seen as appropriate in the home country. There is no reason why they would not be replicated in Canada. They would likely stand out with greater effect because they would be unanticipated by Canadians. The resulting goodwill can be expected to go a long way toward improving the image of "corporate America" and its products.

On a macromarketing level, American companies must make their decisions about rationalizing production between the two countries under the FTA with some sensitivity. If large numbers of U.S. companies with Canadian subsidiaries close their Canadian bases, the response to such a collective movement may result in considerable consumer backlash from Canadians.

Canadian manufacturers, on the other hand, will likely look at the views of Canadian products held by consumers on either side of the border as cause for grave concern. The chances of capturing American markets seem very remote. However, expanding the view to include country-people attitudes again suggests important strategies.

The very positive personal views of Canadians held by Americans suggest that Canadians can expect that their best and brightest ideas based on their special capabilities will receive a warm reception from Americans. Similarly, Canadians' lack of strong support for their own domestically produced products does not mean that they prefer to do business with the Americans, as previously noted. Although they are less prone to wave the flag as much as their neighbors, Canadians do like and wish to support the efforts of their own producers, and do not wish to see their distinctive economy or lifestyle lost in the American melting pot. However, Canadian producers will have to learn to distinguish themselves effectively in rather dramatic ways from their American competitors to be successful in American markets and at home. This can be done, of course. Many Canadian firms and industries have been very successful in the United States, ranging from Moosehead beer to Bombardier urban transit systems to children's cultural products, to name but a very few. What is the basic secret of their success?

Moosehead beer built its market niche on a wilderness image and continues to exploit a connection to the environment. Bombardier based its early success on its expertise in snow travel, and grew from there to become a world-class company with expertise in various aspects of complex intra- and inter-urban travel systems. In domestic marketing, Bell Canada in its advertising uses very dramatic symbols, such as Arctic wolves calling across the long empty wilderness, to reinforce the imagery associated with well-known Canadian expertise in long-distance communication. The common element is the building on unique strengths that are well-recognized and part of a consistent attitude set concerning what Canada and Canadians are good at.

So, the PCI research findings noted above, including country-people images, suggest several avenues. When selling in the U.S., Canadian companies, where appropriate, can take advantage of the positive, good neighbor image. When personal selling is a substantial part of marketing, or personal service and trust are key intangible benefits sought, Canadian sellers are in a strong position.

Canadian companies entering U.S. markets can often successfully exploit niche markets that larger U.S. companies ignore. The key is to look for markets where lifestyles and benefits sought will closely match what Canada is seen as good at delivering. *Harrowsmith* magazine, a Canadian success story, recently entered the American market with its "alternative lifestyle" periodical. Its head office is in a small Ontario town and its branch office was set up in a small town in the northeastern United States. The publishers' strategy was to capitalize on similar lifestyle interests in the proximate region in the United States. For American subscribers, a Canadian publisher of a "back-to-the-land-wannabe" magazine is seen as highly credible. Similarly, the Canadian "snowbird" population (tourists and part-time residents flocking south in the winter months) has become of such substantial size in Florida that there are now two operating Canadian news services for them.

The competitive position of Canadian companies is likely to be weak if they try to go head-to-head with large U.S. manufacturing companies which have marketing budgets many times larger. Rather, a flanking strategy addressed to niche markets will be more effective (Canadian specialty wine producers, for example, recognize this and are welcoming the FTA).

The quality image of Canadian products bears direct addressing. This image is not strong globally, and quality and technological sophistication are its weakest parts. Canadian producers need to deal strategically with this problem, both to assist them in succeeding in the U.S. and to help them hold on to their domestic markets. This is a very significant task which will require the dedication of individual producers, collective associations, and the government of Canada. First the quality must be built, and then the message must get out in order to rebuild the image. Altering significantly such widely held images is a long and difficult task. It may be most effectively done by concentrating on key, flagship industries, in a Japanese or South Korean mode. Once a quality image is established in one product or service area, the message can be transferred through logical connections to other related areas.

Canadian producers need to view the challenge of altering American attitudes toward the quality of Canadian products as part of a global strategy. Quality sells everywhere. A narrow focus on the U.S. market would ignore the formation of equally or even more powerful markets elsewhere in the world. Consideration should be given to the strategic staging of market development. In the future, success in U.S. markets will not necessarily be the only or the first necessity for global success.

Negotiations have recently been initiated for a free trade agreement involving the United States, Mexico, and Canada. In this context and in light of the current very large negative trade flow with Mexico, the president of the Canadian Exporters Association highlighted the need for Canadians to become more aggressive in export development (Saunders 1991). In a similar way, Canadian branch plants of American companies should take an aggressive posture when there is talk about rationalizing production and establishing world mandate production facilities. The traditional Canadian approach may be to assume that the Canadian facility is not "in the running." Instead, Canadian managers of American plants north of the border will need to push assertively the advantages of the Canadian alternative.

Finally, some recommendations can be made to politicians from the research findings, which provide important insights that can be used to anticipate voter reactions to political initiatives in opening markets. The Canadian opposition to the FTA is not surprising when the country-people images of Americans are investigated. It is important to be aware of the favorable images that Canadians hold of American products, but interest in the latter does not mean that Canadians will welcome them without reservation. Both product and country-people images can and should be used as input to making relevant decisions. Similarly, U.S. views of Canadians and Canada clearly predict their acceptance of the FTA. In entering into negotiations with Mexico, politicians would be well-advised to tap the attitudes of their citizens concerning the linkages and also concerning the products, countries, and people involved.

Returning once again to Alice for direction, recall that after passing into the Looking Glass World, one of the first things she does is attempt to read a poem in a book. At first the writing is indecipherable. Only when she holds the book up to the looking glass can she read it. The lesson for Canadian and American manufacturers may be that to determine what to do in order to succeed in the "other world" (of the U.S. or Canada, respectively), they have to look back at what it is about themselves that is admired (or disdained) by those "others." This will be the basis for understanding and success ("read the writing in the mirror, rather than on the wall"). It is imperative to use the information from PCI research to provide the needed insights about how others see us.

Upon reading the poem in the book, Alice is at first frightened by the strong, unknown, apparently invincible beast, the Jabberwock:

"Beware the Jabberwock, my son!
The jaws that bite, the claws that catch!"

(Carroll 1946 edition, p. 175)

But the poem goes on to explain how the brave boy manages to slay the beast with his "vorpal sword."

With insights from PCI research (a vorpal sword), the battle can be won–making the Canada-U.S. FTA, in this case, a beneficial experience for producers and their constituents on both sides of the border. Courage, determination, and wit, coupled with a preparedness to mine available knowledge for insight, are all it takes.

REFERENCES

Abdel-Malek, Talaat (1975), "Comparative Profiles of Foreign Customers and Intermediaries." *European Journal of Marketing*, 9(3) 198-214.

Adams, Michael and Donna Dasko (1988, February 24), "U.S. public favors free trade, poll says." *The Globe and Mail*, A1, A5.

Barker, Tansu A. and T. Robinson (1987), "Saskatchewan Consumers' Perceptions of Domestic and Imported Products." In R.E Turner (ed.), *Marketing*, Vol. 8 (Toronto, Ont.: Proceedings of the Administrative Sciences of Canada–Marketing Division, June) 186-195.

Berton, Pierre (1982), *Why We Act Like Canadians*. Toronto, Ont.: McClelland and Stewart.

Buchanan, James R. (1990), "Cross-border Shopping–A National Phenomenon." *Retailing Today*. Toronto: Ernst & Young. 4-5.

Canadian Gallup Poll Ltd. (1985), *A Study on Canadian-Made Products*. Unpublished report, February.

"Canadians say they'll shop more in U.S." (1991, January 17). *The Ottawa Citizen*, D8.

Carroll, Lewis (1946; first published in Great Britain in 1872), *Alice's Adventures in Wonderland and Through the Looking Glass*. New York: The World Publishing Company.

Cattin, Philippe and Alain Jolibert (1979), "An American vs. French Cross-Cultural Study of Five 'Made-in' Concepts." *Proceedings, 1979 Educators' Conference* (Chicago, IL: American Marketing Association) 450-454.

Columbo, John Robert (1988, November 13), "Columbo's collectible quotes about free trade." *The Toronto Star*, B3.

Crafted With Pride in U.S.A. (1986). New York: Crafted With Pride in U.S.A. Council, Inc.

Crispo, John (1990, January 2), "First year of free trade: time for review–never mind debating the pros and cons, just make it work." *The Globe and Mail*, A7.

Damanpour, Faramarz and John H. Hallaq (1981), "A Survey to Evaluate 'Made In' Product Images of Industrial Countries: A Comparison of U.S. and Danish Consumers' Perceptions." Paper presented to the *Conference of The Academy of International Business* (Montreal, Canada, October).

Dickerson, Kitty G. (1982), "Imported Versus U.S.-Produced Apparel: Consumer Views and Buying Patterns." *Home Economics Research Journal*, 10:3 (March) 241-52.

Dornoff, Ronald J., Clint B. Tankersley, and Gregory P. White (1974), "Consumers' Perceptions of Imports." *Akron Business and Economic Review*, 5(2) (Summer) 26-29.

Ettenson, Richard, Janet Wagner, and Gary Gaeth (1988), "Evaluating the Effect of Country of Origin and the 'Made in U.S.A.' Campaign: A Conjoint Approach." *Journal of Retailing*, 64(1): 85-100.

External Affairs Canada (1987), *The Canada-U.S. Free Trade Agreement*. Ottawa, Canada: Department of External Affairs, The International Trade Communications Group.

Forsey, Joan (1987, December 8), "Free trade fuss is re-run of past." *The Globe and Mail*, A7.

Garland, Barbara C. and John C. Crawford (1985), "Satisfaction with Products of Foreign Origin." In C.T. Tan and J.N. Sheth (eds.), *Historical Perspectives in Consumer Research: National and International Perspectives* (Proceedings, Association of Consumer Research International Meeting, Singapore, July 18-20) 160-161.

Garland, Barbara C., Tansu A. Barker, and John C. Crawford (1987), "A Cross-National Test of a Conceptual Framework of Willingness to Buy Products of Foreign Origin." In K.D. Bahn and M.J. Sirgy (eds.), *Third World Marketing Congress* (Barcelona: Academy of Marketing Science, August) 124-130.

Garreau, Joel (1981), *Nine Nations of North America*. Boston: Houghton-Mifflin.

Gates, Bruce (1990, July 25), "Lakes region hive of activity on free trade." *The Financial Post*, 14.

Gwyn, Richard (1985), *The 49th Paradox*. Toronto: McClelland and Stewart Limited.

Hampton, Gerry M. (1983), "Changing Attitudes Toward Canadian Investment in the American Pacific Northwest." In J. Forbes (ed.), *Marketing* (Vancouver, B.C.: Administrative Sciences Association of Canada–Marketing Division, May).

Han, Min C. and Vern Terpstra (1988), "Country-of-Origin Effects for Uni-National and Bi-National Products." *Journal of International Business Studies* (Summer) 235-54.

Heslop, Louise A., John P. Liefeld, and Marjorie Wall (1987), "An Experimental Study of the Impact of Country-of-Origin Information." In R.E. Turner (ed.),

Marketing, Vol. 8 (Toronto, Ont.: Proceedings, Administrative Sciences Association of Canada–Marketing Division, June) 179-185.

Hester, S.B. and M. Yuen (1986), "The Influence of Country of Origin on Consumer Attitude and Buying Behavior in the United States and Canada." In M. Wallendorf and P. Anderson (eds.), *Advances in Consumer Research* (Association for Consumer Research) 538-542.

Hill, C.E. and D.E. Stull (1981), "Sex Differences in Effects of Social Value Similarity in Same Sex Friendship." *Journal of Personality and Social Psychology,* 78, 165-171.

Howard, Ross (1988, February 1), "Pollsters find contradictory reactions to free trade concept, Mulroney pact." *The Globe and Mail,* A5.

Howard, Ross (1990, January 3), "Free trade opponents claim 72,000 jobs lost during pact's first year." *The Globe and Mail,* A12.

Hung, C.L. (1989), "A Country-of-Origin Product Image Study: The Canadian Perception and Nationality Biases." *Journal of International Consumer Marketing,* 1, 3, 5-26.

Johansson, Johny K. and Israel D. Nebenzahl (1986), "Multinational Production: Effect on Brand Value." *Journal of International Business Studies,* 17, 3 (Fall) 101-126.

Johansson, Johny K., Susan P. Douglas, and Ikujiro Nonaka (1985), "Assessing the Impact of Country of Origin on Product Evaluations: A New Methodological Perspective." *Journal of Marketing Research,* XXII: (November) 388-96.

Kaynak, Erdener and S. Tamer Cavusgil (1983), "Consumer Attitudes Towards Products of Foreign Origin: Do They Vary Across Product Classes?" *International Journal of Advertising,* 2 (April/June) 147-157.

Kidd, Kenneth (1990, July 30), "Retailers react to exodus–cross-border shopping rising." *The Globe and Mail,* B1, B2.

Lillis, Charles M. and Chem L. Narayana (1974), "Analysis of 'Made- in' Product Images–An Exploratory Study." *Journal of International Business Studies,* (Spring) 119-127.

Malcolm, Andrew H. (1985), *The Canadians.* Markham, Ont.: Fitzhenry and Whiteside.

McDougall, G.H.G. and B.J. Rawlings (1979), "Canadian Advertising Appeals: Or Will 'Oh Canada' Sell Beer?" *Business Quarterly* (Autumn) 39-45.

MITT (Ministry of Industry, Trade, and Technology of Ontario, 1990), *Cross-border Shopping Status Report.* Toronto: MITT, May.

Nagashima, Akira (1970), "A Comparison of Japanese and U.S. Attitudes Towards Foreign Products." *Journal of Marketing,* 34 (January) 68-74.

Narayana, Chem L. (1981), "Aggregate Images of American and Japanese Products: Implications on International Marketing." *Columbia Journal of World Business,* 16 (Summer) 31-35.

Niffenegger, P. and J. Odlin (1983), "How Good Is the Overseas Competition?: A Survey of Car Dealers in America." *Journal of the Academy of Marketing Science* 21, 3 (Summer) 259-268.

Papadopoulos, Nicolas (1980), "Consumer Outshopping Research: Review and Extension." *Journal of Retailing*, 56 (Winter) 41-58.

Papadopoulos, Nicolas and Louise A. Heslop (1989), "As Others See Us: The Image of Canadian Products Abroad." *Canadian Business Review*, 16, 4 (Winter) 27-31.

Papadopoulos, Nicolas, Louise A. Heslop, and Gerry Phillips (1988), "A Longitudinal Perspective on Consumer Outshopping." In T.A. Barker (ed.), *Marketing*, vol. 9 (Halifax, N.S.: Administrative Sciences Association of Canada–Marketing Division, June) 58-67.

"Portrait of Two Nations–The Two Nations Poll" (1990, June 25). *Maclean's*, 50-53.

Reierson, Curtis C. (1966), "Are Foreign Products Seen as National Stereotypes." *Journal of Retailing*, 42, 3, (Fall), 33-40.

Saunders, John (1991, February 21), "Anxiety build resistance to free trade with Mexico." *The Globe and Mail*, B5.

Schellinck, D.A. (1989), "Determinants of Country of Origin Cue Usage." In Alain d'Astous (ed.), *Marketing*, vol. 10 (Montreal: Admin. Sciences Association of Canada) 268-275.

"Scoreboard according to labor–the jobs move south" (1990, January 2). *The Globe and Mail*, A7.

Taormina, R.J. and D. Messick (1983), "Deservingness for Foreign Aid: Effects of Need, Similarity, and Estimated Effectiveness." *Journal of Applied Social Psychology*, 13, 371- 391.

"The Wary Tourists" (1990, September 3). *Maclean's*, 28-29.

Tourism Canada (1986), *U.S. Pleasure Travel Market: Canadian Potential* (Highlights Report, Ottawa, Tourism Canada).

Wall, Marjorie and Louise A. Heslop (1986), "Consumer Attitudes Toward Canadian-made versus Imported Products." *Journal of the Academy of Marketing Science*, 14(2): 27-36.

Winsor, Hugh (1989, November 21), "FTA vanished from nation's political agenda." *The Globe and Mail*, C1, C8.

Winter, John (1990a, March), *Out-shopping from Niagara Falls, Ontario*. Toronto: John Winter Associates Ltd.

Winter, John (1990b, July), "Vicious Circle at the Border," in *Retailing in Canada*. Toronto: John Winter Associates Ltd.

Winter, John (1990c, August), *Windsor Downtown Market Study*. Toronto: John Winter Associates Ltd.

Chapter 18

Global Promotion of Country Image: Do the Olympics Count?

Eugene D. Jaffe
Israel D. Nebenzahl

INTRODUCTION

The author of a widely used international marketing textbook states that proper use of the marketing mix can improve a country's product or brand image:

> Each of the four P's can be used to attack this [image] problem: product quality can be offered, price can be lower, promotion can build an image, and place (distribution) can support the overall image campaign with information and advice. (Keegan, 1989, p. 377)

However, the effect of advertising and sales promotion on country image has not been measured, or at least has not been reported in the literature. This chapter addresses a question that should be of interest to both practitioners and researchers: What might be the effects, if any, on the images of products, if the country where these products are made receives extensive international publicity because of an event of global interest?

The chapter is based on findings from a survey that was designed to measure the effect of the promotional aspects of the 1988 Olympic games in Seoul on the image of several household electronic products made in South Korea. This country, and this event, lend themselves particularly well for studying the effects of event-related publicity on country and product image, for a number of reasons. As a Newly Industrialized Coun-

---

Both authors contributed equally to this chapter, which draws from an earlier paper presented to the European International Business Association.

try, South Korea does not yet have as mature a presence in international markets as the major industrial nations which have had established images for decades. The products of South Korean companies, and the companies themselves, have begun to be recognized in foreign markets only recently. The Summer Olympics, on the other hand, are a matter of great interest in most countries, receive extensive publicity both before and during the games, and occur only once every four years. Factors such as these suggest that studying the effect of events on country and product images in the context of the 1988 Seoul Olympics is less likely to involve significant "noise," as compared to other potential country/event combinations.

In the first stage of their economic development, most South Korean companies licensed technology from American firms to produce products for sale in the domestic market. Some Korean conglomerates such as Samsung, Hyundai, and Daewoo have reached a second stage which entails exporting to the United States and other overseas markets. To support their export growth, Korean companies invested in marketing and research and development. An example of a company employing this strategy is Samsung Electronics (1987 revenues of $24 billion) which has begun to focus on producing high-quality, high value-added products. For example, Samsung's consumer electronics division ($32 million in sales) exports 70 percent of its production. It began to penetrate foreign markets by supplying color television sets, microwave ovens, and videocassette recorders (VCRs) to American companies such as Sears Roebuck, RCA, and J.C. Penney, who in turn sold the products under their own names. Forty percent of its output was exported under Samsung's own name and the company was planning to increase this figure to 55 percent by the end of 1990. Samsung spends $20 million on advertising in the United States alone. Much of this advertising is aimed at achieving brand recognition (Tanzer 1988).

South Korea's bid for the 1988 Olympic games was intended in large part to improve its image as a developed, stable country, capable of hosting an international event which demands expertise in marketing, finance, management, and organization. In order to finance the games, South Korean multinational companies contributed heavily. In return, the companies were given extensive exposure as official sponsors. For example, Lee Kun-Hee, the Chief Executive Officer of Samsung, an official sponsor of the games, was quoted as saying (Tanzer 1988, p. 86): "The Olympics will be important to raising [Samsung Electronics'] name recognition."

This view makes intuitive sense and also finds support in the literature. Based on a LISREL analysis of data from eight sample/origin country combinations, Papadopoulos, Marshall, and Heslop (1988) have reported a tentative causal link between consumers' beliefs about the degree to which a country "manages its economy successfully" and is "technologically advanced," and the "industriousness" of its people, on the one hand, and their assessment of the country's products, on the other. In this light, it would appear that the belief that the Olympics can help to enhance the image of a country and its products–a belief apparently held by nations which bid to host the games–is well placed.

Since the games were broadcast throughout the world, they afforded an excellent opportunity to improve the host country's and sponsoring companies' images. In order to determine whether the image of South Korean products had changed as a result of consumer exposure to promotion communicated before and during the Olympics, a survey was designed to measure perception of South Korean goods before and after the games. The survey was conducted in Israel during two time periods: two months before and two months after the games.

The Israeli environment was very suitable for such an experiment. South Korean consumer electronic products had just begun to enter the Israeli market prior to the Olympic games. Moreover, no other Korean consumer durable products were sold or promoted in Israel prior to and during the research for this study. Except for the games, there was practically no advertising or sales promotion of any South Korean-made products during the time periods observed. These facts enabled the questioning of respondents in the "before" period who had little if any brand recognition or familiarity with South Korean products. The absence of advertising during the period of the surveys meant that the effect of the promotion of South Korea's image and products by the games was not confounded with any other type of promotion.

Two surveys were undertaken among some 800 respondents selected in two separate samples. As a control, respondents' perceptions of similar products made in Japan and West Germany were measured to determine if any changes had occurred over the time periods observed.

LITERATURE REVIEW

A substantial body of research has indicated that country-of-origin has an effect on product evaluations.[1] Country-of-origin influence has been

---

1. The authors wish to thank David Bennett, graduate student at the School of Business, Carleton University, whose work served as the basis for part of this section.

found for products in general (Nagashima 1977; Wall and Heslop 1986), classes of products (Nagashima 1970; Wall and Heslop 1986), specific types of products (Gaedeke 1973; Heslop, Liefeld, and Wall 1987; Han and Terpstra 1988), consumer products (Schooler 1965; Lillis and Narayana 1974; Bannister and Saunders 1978), and industrial products (White 1979; Chasin and Jaffe 1979, 1987; Cattin, Jolibert, and Lohnes 1982).

Country-of-origin effects exist for products from more developed nations (Nagashima 1970; Cattin, Jolibert, and Lohnes 1982) and less developed countries (Schooler 1965; Chasin and Jaffe 1979, 1987). Some scholars have examined how people evaluate nations cognitively. Wish, Deutsch, and Biener (1970) found four significant evaluation dimensions which they interpreted as Political Alignment and Ideology, Economic Development, Geography and Population, and Culture and Race. Jones and Ashmore (1973) concluded that their respondents evaluated the sample countries primarily on the dimensions of dominant-subordinate; communist-non-communist; and Western culture-non-Western culture.

Robinson and Hefner (1967) found that respondents perceived four factors in their evaluation of countries: affiliation with communism, economic development, geography (European versus Asian), and Spanish influence. Forgas and O'Driscoll (1984) found three dimensions: European-non European; communist-capitalist; and developed-underdeveloped. Thus, it may be assumed that consumers evaluate products on the basis of a number of information cues, a most salient one being country-of-origin.

RESEARCH DESIGN

The country-of-origin effect was measured for products familiar to a broad cross-section of consumers. The product class chosen was consumer electronics, and two products were used as objects in the research: microwave ovens and VCRs. The task that respondents were asked to perform was threefold.

First, respondents gave an overall rating and 12 attribute-specific ratings on six-point semantic differential scales for a class of electronic products made in each of the three subject countries (the scales used are in the Appendix at the end of this chapter). Next, respondents were presented with specific products (e.g., VCR), brands (e.g., Sony), and origin countries (e.g., Japan) and asked to specify how much more or less they would be willing to pay for them when made in a third country (e.g., South Korea). Combinations of products, country-of-origin, and price questions were given for studying shifts of production from West Germany to Japan and South Korea and from Japan to West Germany and South Korea. Two Japanese brands, Sony and Sanyo, and one West German brand, Grundig, were presented as "made in" two countries. Thus, respondents were asked to value Grundig VCRs made in Japan and South Korea, and Sony VCRs made in West Germany and South Korea. Likewise, respondents valued Grundig microwave ovens made in Japan and South Korea and Sanyo microwave ovens made in Japan and South Korea. The research design is shown in Table 1.

Respondents were also asked to state on a seven-point scale how familiar they were with consumer electronic products in general. Respondents were asked the extent to which they were involved in purchasing the electronic products they owned. In the "before" sample, respondents were asked to list the brand (make) and country-of-origin of products they owned within the product categories mentioned above. Finally, in the post-Olympic sample, the frequency and length of time that respondents were exposed to the Olympic games on all major media were recorded.

Sampling Procedure

A multistage area sample was drawn from the Tel Aviv metropolitan area, which numbers some 500,000 residents out of a total Israeli population of four million. This area is highly representative demographically of the entire urban population. Interviewers were given specific addresses and were required to interview an adult member of the household. In case an adult was not present or refused to participate or no one was at home, the interviewer tried next door. Since we were interested in interviewing

Table 1. Research Model: Shift of Brand Production to New Location

Product	Country		
	Japan	West Germany	South Korea
a. VCR			
Initial Location	Sony	Grundig	--
New Location	Grundig	Sony	Sony
			Grundig
b. Microwave oven			
Initial Location	Sanyo	Grundig	--
New Location	Grundig	Sanyo	Sanyo
			Grundig

only those people who were unfamiliar with products made in South Korea, respondents were screened on the basis of whether they had seen any advertisement for South Korean products. If they answered in the affirmative, the interview was terminated and the interviewer tried the next sampling unit.

The "before" sample was the same as the one we used for our methodological analysis, which is also presented in this book (see Chapter 6 by Nebenzahl and Jaffe). Briefly, 526 adults were approached and a net response rate of 78 percent was obtained (106 potential respondents either refused or were rejected due to familiarity with South Korean products, and seven questionnaires were unusable). In total, 413 questionnaires were included in this analysis.

In the second stage, a matched sample of 460 respondents was selected using the same method as for the "before" sample and resulting in 446 usable questionnaires. Initially, 542 adults were approached. Of these, 85 either refused or were rejected because they were familiar with Korean-made products. An additional 11 questionnaires were rejected because they were not filled out properly, giving a net response of 82 percent. A frequency distribution of respondents' socioeconomic characteristics in both samples is shown in Table 2. Both sample distributions were similar. A Chi Square test showed that there were no significant differences between the demographic categories of the two samples.

Data Collection

The questionnaire used in this study was pretested on a small sample before being finalized. Answers to the 13 scale questions (Jaffe and Nebenzahl 1988) were recorded by the interviewer, whereas answers to the open-ended questions were self-administered. At the termination of the interview, respondents were asked to give their name and telephone number so that project directors could later verify that the interview took place and ask some confirmatory questions.

Hypotheses

If the Olympic game promotion resulted in a change in consumer attitudes toward products made in South Korea, we would expect less negative stereotyping of Korean products after the games. At the same time, we would expect that there would be no significant changes in the attitudes toward products made in Japan and West Germany over the two time periods. Therefore:

- H1: There was a significant, positive change in consumer attitudes toward goods made in South Korea after or as a result of the Olympic games.
- H2: There were no significant changes in consumer attitudes toward goods made in Japan and West Germany after or as a result of the Olympic games.

As pointed out before, the Olympic games were utilized to promote South Korea as an advanced, industrialized country. However, since no specific product or attributes were advertised, one would expect that the promotion campaign should affect the overall country image of South

Table 2. Distribution of Samples

	"Before" (N = 413)		"After" (N = 446)	
	N*	%	N*	%
Sex				
Male	245	59.6	254	57.0
Female	166	40.4	192	43.0
Total	411	100.0	446	100.0
Age				
20-30	97	26.1	109	25.5
31-40	150	40.3	170	39.8
41-54	90	24.2	101	23.7
55-64	20	5.4	21	4.9
>65	15	4.0	26	6.1
Total	372	100.0	427	100.0
Education				
Grade School	28	6.9	30	6.7
Some High School	99	24.3	107	24.0
High School Graduate	102	24.9	107	24.0
Post-High School	46	11.2	49	11.1
Some College	43	10.5	48	10.8
College Graduate	91	22.2	104	23.4
Total	409	100.0	445	100.0
Standard of Living**				
Low	8	2.6	8	2.4
Below Average	13	4.3	14	4.2
Average	263	86.8	289	86.0
Above Average	17	5.6	19	5.7
High	2	0.7	6	1.7
Total	303	100.0	336	100.0

*   Excludes non-responses
** Perceived, self-reported

Korea rather than any particular attribute. Thus, one would not expect consumers to discriminate between the particular attributes of products made in South Korea, but rather to provide better ratings of all attributes after the games. On the other hand, one would not expect any such changes in the overall image of West Germany and Japan. These expectations lead to the following hypotheses:

- H3: There is a significant number of attributes of South Korean products that are more positively rated after the Olympics.
- H4: There is no significant number of attributes of products that are made in West Germany and Japan and that are rated more positively after the games.

A positive change in attitudes toward goods made in South Korea should move the preference curve for Korean products to the right. That is, consumers should be willing to pay more for them. At the same time, there should be no significant shift in preference for goods made in Japan and West Germany. Therefore:

- H5: The preference curve for Korean-made products shifts to the right after the Olympic games.
- H6: Preference curves for Japanese- and West German-made products do not shift after the Olympic games.

These hypotheses were tested by comparing the scale profiles and demand schedules for all three countries using t-tests, linear regressions, and sign tests. The results are discussed in the following section.

FINDINGS

Promotional Exposure and Attitude Change

Israelis had ample opportunity to view the Olympic games on television. Every evening, several minutes were devoted to game coverage on the regular half-hour news program. More extensive coverage was given on regularly scheduled sports programs several times a week. In addition, special programming was run in the early evenings and then again from late night to early morning (after midnight). Close to half of the respondents in the second stage survey watched the games to a significant extent (see Table 3).

Table 3. Exposure to Olympic Games'
Coverage on Television

	Scale	no.	%	
Not at all	1	83	18.8	
	2	69	15.6	
	3	78	17.6	52.0
	4	83	18.8	
	5	59	13.3	
Very much so	6	70	15.8	47.9
	Total	442		100.0

Hypotheses 1 and 2 were tested for change in attitudes toward goods made in Japan, West Germany, and South Korea over the period before and after Olympic game coverage on Israeli television. One would expect to find an association between frequency of exposure and attitude change. In order to test this assumption, linear regressions were run using changes in attitudes (scale values) between the two time periods as dependent variables, and the extent to which respondents viewed the games as the independent variable. Similar regressions were run for all three countries.

The results in Table 4 show that in the case of South Korea, Olympic game exposure is statistically significant with all scale variables, except "known to consumers," "price," and "assortment." The affective variables, "proud to own" and "like-dislike," were significant at $p < .01$ and $p < .001$, respectively. The significance of the affective variables shows that attitude change is not only normative, but emotional as well.

These findings suggest that as exposure to the Olympic games was more extensive, respondents' attitudes toward the electronic products made in South Korea improved. It appears that there was some effect on people's perception of overall technological capability, but none on specifics (e.g., price). These results confirm hypothesis H1.

In order to control for chance, similar regressions were run for Japan and Germany. In the case of Japan, only one variable, "reliability," was significantly different after the Olympic games. For Germany, two variables were significantly higher after the Olympic games, namely, "like-dislike" ($p < .01$) and "serviceability" ($p < .001$), while one variable was significantly lower, "performance" ($p < .01$). These findings show that there was little or no relationship between exposure to Olympic game broadcasts and attitudes toward products made in Germany and Japan. This conclusion supports the second hypothesis.

The verification of these two experimental and control hypotheses suggests a strong effect of the games on the image of South Korea. Table 5 shows the changes in scale values for each attribute before and after game

Table 4. Linear Regression Results
for Following Olympic Game Broadcasts on TV

Variables	S. Korea β estimates	t values	Japan β estimates	t values	W. Germany β estimates	t values
1 Known to consumers	--	--				
2 Reliability	.09294	2.199 (.0285)	.13472	3.409 (.0007)		
3 Price	--	--				
4 Performance	.11574	3.091 (.0021)			-.06227	-2.376 (.0180)
5 Hand-made/ Mass produced	.09118	2.353 (.0191)				
6 Quality	.11654	2.838 (.0048)				
7 Innovativeness	.11250	2.650 (.0084)				
8 Proud to own	.09021	2.630 (.0089)				
9 Technology	.08620	2.140 (.0330)				
10 Like/Dislike	.11867	3.750 (.0002)			.10183	2.513 (.0124)
11 Serviceability	.12965	3.349 (.0009)				
12 Assortment	--	--				
Overall	.13222	3.734 (.0002)				

coverage. To further measure the effect of viewing frequency on attitude change, the "after" group was split into two subgroups according to the extent to which they viewed the games. T-tests were calculated for differences in mean scale values between the "before" group and the "after" high-exposure group. For South Korea, there were statistically significant increases in mean scale values for seven of 12 specific attributes.

In the case of Japan, there were only two significant differences in mean scale values; in one of these cases ("assortment") the change was negative, that is, the mean value decreased over time. For Germany, there were two significant changes, both negative ("price" and "innovativeness"). These findings provide further support for hypotheses H1 and H2.

Promotion and the Overall Image of South Korea

So far we have dealt with each attribute of the image of each country separately. To test whether there was a more global shift in the image of

Table 5. Attitude Change Before and After Exposure to Olympic Games

a. South Korea

		Before Olympics (N=409)	After Olympics Low Exposure (N=230)		High Exposure (N=212)	
	Attributes	Mean	Mean	p (2 tail)*	Mean	p (2 tail)*
1	Known to consumers	2.36	2.57	.097	2.70	.008
2	Reliability	3.15	3.17	.826	3.42	.026
3	Price	4.50	4.30	-.076	4.48	-.831
4	Performance	3.48	3.34	-.151	3.70	.042
5	Hand-made/Mass produced	2.34	2.33	-.945	2.40	.535
6	Quality	3.01	3.03	.854	3.32	.011
7	Innovativeness	2.68	2.47	-.072	2.74	.594
8	Proud to own	3.14	3.07	-.518	3.38	.029
9	Technology	3.60	3.63	.755	3.69	.447
10	Like/Dislike	3.28	3.10	-.046	3.39	.238
11	Serviceability	3.37	3.13	-.023	3.39	.856
12	Assortment	3.48	3.84	.003	3.97	.000
	Overall	3.31	3.25	-.561	3.71	.000

* Minus signs signify a decrease in the mean value of a descriptor in the survey after the Olympic Games.

South Korea, without an accompanying shift in the corresponding images of Japan and Germany, a sign test was conducted on the number of positive and negative shifts in the items of each scale after the games. As can be seen in Table 5, in the case of South Korea, 11 attributes out of 12, in addition to the overall descriptor, have improved in the high-exposure group after the Olympic games. Of these, six changes were significant at p < .05. The overall descriptor was highly significant at p < .000. Furthermore, the only exception to these positive changes is statistically insignificant (p < .83).

These results show that the respondents who were highly exposed to the games were not selective in their shifting attitudes but rather perceive the image of South Korea as being overall better, and therefore, gave South Korea higher ratings across the board. Thus, we observe a significant positive shift in the overall image of South Korea.

In the case of Japan, six out of 12 attributes have changed positively, while six changes are negative. Of all changes, both positive and negative, only one is significant at p < .05. Moreover, with p < .97, the overall descriptor is not significant at all. Similarly, in the case of Germany, five attributes have changed positively, while seven changes were negative, none of which is statistically significant. As in the case of Japan, the

Table 5. (continued)   b. Japan

		Before Olympics (N=409)	After Olympics Low Exposure (N=230)		After Olympics High Exposure (N=212)	
	Attributes	Mean	Mean	p (2 tail)*	Mean	p (2 tail)*
1	Known to consumers	5.58	5.49	-.212	5.57	-.814
2	Reliability	5.05	4.74	-.011	5.10	.654
3	Price	4.22	4.10	-.252	4.18	-.730
4	Performance	5.19	5.11	-.330	5.18	-.862
5	Hand-made/Mass produced	3.03	3.06	.858	3.32	.037
6	Quality	4.81	4.78	-.794	4.89	.448
7	Innovativeness	4.79	4.79	.996	4.82	.763
8	Proud to own	4.94	4.60	-.000	4.88	-.524
9	Technology	5.04	5.31	.011	5.24	.076
10	Like/Dislike	4.73	4.52	-.021	4.73	-.964
11	Serviceability	4.40	4.44	.739	4.55	.193
12	Assortment	5.34	5.07	-.003	5.18	-.092
	Overall	5.34	5.37	.701	5.34	.973

*   Minus signs signify a decrease in the mean value of a descriptor in the survey after the Olympic Games.

overall descriptor is not significant. These results for Japan and West Germany are indicative of a random process. Based on these results, we accept hypotheses H3 and H4 and conclude that, as expected, there is a shift in the global country image of South Korea after the Olympics rather than a reevaluation of particular attributes of the country or its products.

Shifts in Country Image and Product Preference

Having found a positive shift in the overall image of South Korea as a producer of electronic products as a result of the Olympic games, we can now address ourselves to the question of how this improved image might have affected the preference for Korean-made products. Hypotheses H5 and H6 expect a shift to the right of the preference curve of Korean-made products, while no such shift should be observed for the products of Japan and West Germany.[2]

Figures 1, 2, 3, and 4 show preference curves for products made in South Korea–Sony and Grundig VCRs, and Sanyo and Grundig microwave ovens–before and after the Olympic games. These curves were

2. For an explanation of how price differences were measured, see our methodology chapter (Chapter 6) in this volume.

Table 5. (continued)   c. West Germany

	Attributes	Before Olympics (N=409) Mean	After Olympics Low Exposure (N=230) Mean	p (2 tail)*	After Olympics High Exposure (N=212) Mean	p (2 tail)*
1	Known to consumers	5.54	5.44	-.256	5.55	.862
2	Reliability	5.38	5.40	.903	5.27	-.338
3	Price	3.40	3.40	.969	3.19	-.108
4	Performance	5.50	5.49	-.897	5.37	-.116
5	Hand-made/Mass produced	4.73	4.46	-.030	4.67	-.609
6	Quality	5.33	5.39	.520	5.42	.343
7	Innovativeness	5.06	4.92	-.126	4.91	-.093
8	Proud to own	5.01	4.82	-.069	4.92	-.342
9	Technology	5.10	5.08	-.862	5.14	.679
10	Like/Dislike	4.52	4.30	-.082	4.58	.625
11	Serviceability	4.96	4.90	-.601	5.00	.668
12	Assortment	4.92	4.80	-.215	4.82	-.350
	Overall	5.52	5.47	-.470	5.47	-.455

* Minus signs signify a decrease in the mean value of a descriptor in the survey after the Olympic Games.

derived from answers given by all respondents in both time periods according to the methodology suggested by Jaffe and Nebenzahl (1989). Clearly, there is little change visible in the position of the curves over the two time periods, with the exception of the Grundig microwave oven.

Would these results change if the analysis excluded those respondents in the "after" period who did not watch the games or did so only rarely? In order to test this assumption, respondents were divided into two groups on the basis of frequency of exposure to the games. As shown in Table 6, respondents who watched the games with relatively high frequency (high exposure) were willing to pay more for each of the four products made in South Korea. For example, those respondents were willing to pay, on the average, NIS1,467 (exchange rate NIS1.5 = $1) for a Sony VCR before the Olympics and NIS1,490 for the same VCR after the Olympics.[3] However, while the prices respondents were willing to pay increased nominally, the increases were not statistically significant.

Comparing these findings with similar products made in West Germany, the results show two decreases in the mean prices respondents are willing to pay over the two time periods. In the case of products made in Japan, respondents were willing to pay more for a Grundig VCR and about

---

3. NIS: New Israeli Shekels.

Figure 1. Preference for Sony VCR Made in S. Korea
Before and After the Olympic Games

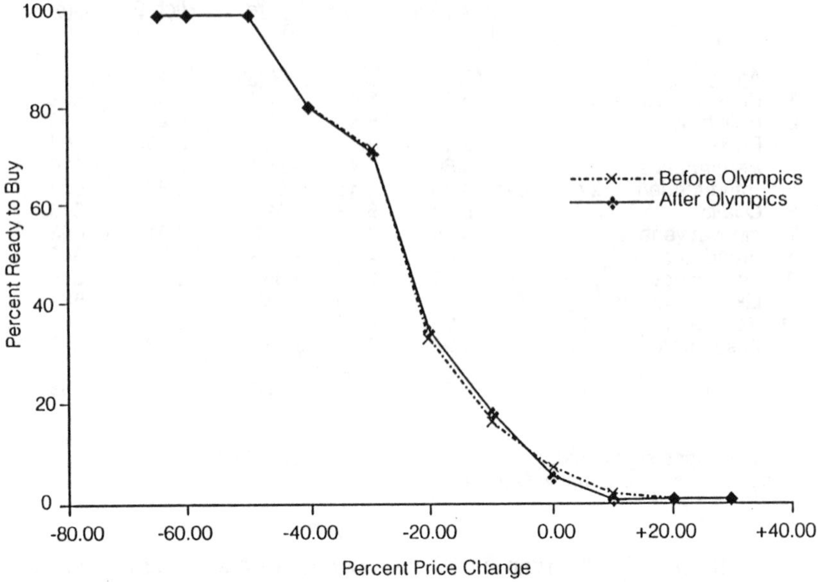

the same price for a Grundig microwave oven. As expected, there were practically no differences in the prices both subgroups (low and high exposure) of respondents were willing to pay for products made in West Germany and Japan.

While individual changes in mean prices were found to be statistically insignificant, a sign test shows that the overall direction of these changes is somewhat significant. In the case of South Korea, four out of four price changes are positive ($p < .0625$). In the case of Japan and Germany taken together, two out of four price changes are positive while two are negative. While these results are not strong, they provide an indication that as country image improves, consumers may be willing to pay somewhat more for the country's products. These results provide some support for hypothesis H5 and confirm hypothesis H6.

IMPLICATIONS

This study has shown that event-related publicity of the sort enjoyed by South Korea as a result of the Olympic games may be utilized to change

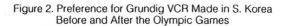

Figure 2. Preference for Grundig VCR Made in S. Korea
Before and After the Olympic Games

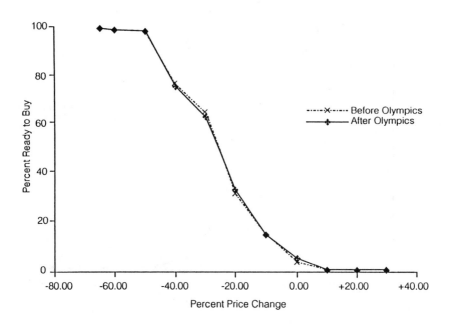

country image. This implies that a macro-governmental approach may serve as an additional strategy in an attempt to improve the image of products originating from a certain country. However, sponsored international or even national events which reach a regional or worldwide audience are infrequent. But due to their large international audience, the impact of sponsored events upon country image may be greater than multidomestic promotional attempts.

If event-related publicity can affect country image, a salient question is: How can it be utilized best to change attitudes? Our study has suggested that changed attitudes toward a country result in parallel affective and cognitive attitudinal changes toward its products as well. If affective and cognitive attitudes toward a country can be changed–as our study has shown–then consumer views toward the country and its products will be modified accordingly. We have found a significant change in the overall image of South Korea as well as in some cognitive attitudes toward its products. The change in attitudes toward South Korea was not brand-spe-

Figure 3. Preference for Sanyo Microwave Oven Made in S. Korea
Before and After the Olympic Games

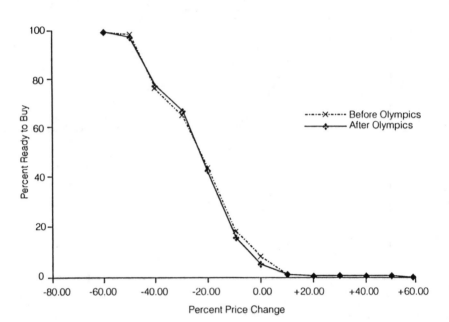

cific but rather overall. Therefore, one can expect that an improvement in country image would be generalized to product categories and brands.

Does a shift in preferences for a country's products signify that potential consumers intend to buy them? This is a very crucial question of country-of-origin and refers to the predictive validity of country image. If promotion can be used to influence buying intentions of domestic products (Han 1988) it can be posited that improved country image will influence consumer behavior as well. Since being introduced into the United States in the 1970s, South Korean consumer electronics manufacturers spent little on advertising, penetrating the market either by selling for private label (e.g., to General Electric and J.C. Penney) or by relying on low prices. Since the 1988 Olympic games, South Korean manufacturers have been spending more on advertising in order to increase consumer awareness and "create the perception that we are more like Sanyo and Sharp" (Foltz 1990). If our findings can be extrapolated to the American market, the Korean attempt by Goldstar, Samsung, and Daewoo to improve brand image is correct.

Figure 4. Preference for Grundig Microwave Oven Made in S. Korea
Before and After the Olympic Games

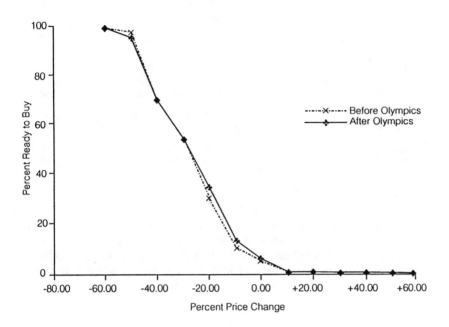

CONCLUSION

This chapter has discussed how it is possible to improve product image through promotion of the image of the origin country. Event-related publicity such as sponsorship, while shown to be an effective tool with which to change country image in the case of South Korea, may be less effective if the country or industry sponsors do not have the organizational abilities needed to control the event. Not only must the event itself be controlled, but the environment as well. Demonstrations, riots, and the like, may be broadcast and negatively influence world opinion, and, of course, country image. Events such as sports or music festivals attract a specific type of audience, and therefore may be more relevant for certain product categories than for others. More research is necessary to indicate the sort of audience that is exposed to such events. Extension of research on corporate sponsorship (Gardner and Shuman 1987; Sandler and Shani 1989) to country image may be appropriate.

Table 6. Mean Price Before & After the Olympics
by Extent of Exposure to Olympic TV Coverage

Brand and Product	Made in -	Mean Price (NIS) "Before"	"After" Exposure Low	High	Relative to High Exposure t-value	p (2 tail)
Sony video	S. Korea	1467	1455	1490	.92	.357
Grundig video	S. Korea	1420	1422	1428	.29	.772
Sanyo microwave	S. Korea	719	704	736	1.08	.281
Grundig microwave	S. Korea	677	683	693	1.02	.310
Sony video	W. Germany	2014	1985	1985	-1.21	.226
Sanyo microwave	W. Germany	1001	973	975	-1.86	.063
Grundig video	Japan	1818	1835	1835	.77	.441
Grundig microwave	Japan	909	914	910	.11	.910

Finally, it should be recalled that the effects of advertising and promotional campaigns, unless continued, decay over time. Therefore, changes in country image associated with events such as the Olympic games must be supported by continued promotional activity. Unless the promotion of South Korea's image in Israel continues, the gains resulting from the Olympic games can be expected to erode over time.

REFERENCES

Bannister, J.P. and J.A. Saunders (1978), "U.K. Consumers' Attitudes Towards Imports: The Measurement of National Stereotype Image." *European Journal of Marketing*, 12, 8, 562-570.

Cattin, Philippe, Alain Jolibert, and Colleen Lohnes (1982), "A Cross-Cultural Study of 'Made In' Concepts." *Journal of International Business Studies* (Winter) 131-141.

Chasin, J.B. and Eugene D. Jaffe (1979), "Industrial Buyer Attitudes Towards Goods Made in Eastern Europe." *Columbia Journal of World Business* (Summer) 74-81.

Chasin, J.B. and Eugene D. Jaffe (1987), "Industrial Buyer Attitudes Towards Goods Made in Eastern Europe: An Update." *European Management Journal*, 5, 3, 180-189.

Foltz, Kim (1990, November 5), "Goldstar Promoting 'User Friendlier' Image." *The New York Times*, 46.

Forgas, J.P. and M. O'Driscoll (1984), "Cross-Cultural and Demographic Differences in the Perception of Nations." *Journal of Cross-Cultural Psychology*, 15 199-222.

Gaedeke, Ralph (1973), "Consumer Attitudes Toward Products 'Made In' Developing Countries." *Journal of Retailing*, 49(2) (Summer) 13-24.

Gardner, M. and P. Shuman (1987), "Sponsorship: An Important Component of the Promotions Mix." *Journal of Advertising*, 16:1, 11-17.

Han, Min C. (1988), "The Role of Consumer Patriotism in the Choice of Domestic versus Foreign Products." *Journal of Advertising Research*, 28(3) (June-July) 25-32.

Han, Min C. and Vern Terpstra (1988), "Country-of-Origin Effects for Uni-National and Bi-National Products." *Journal of International Business Studies*, (Summer) 235-54.

Heslop, Louise A., John P. Liefeld, and Marjorie Wall (1987), "An Experimental Study of the Impact of Country-of-Origin Information." In R.E. Turner (ed.), *Marketing*, Vol. 8 (Toronto, Ont.: Proceedings, Administrative Sciences Association of Canada–Marketing Division, June) 179-185.

Jaffe, Eugene D. and Israel D. Nebenzahl (1988), "On the Measurement of Halo Effect in Country Image Studies." Paper presented at the Annual Meeting of the *European International Business Association* (West Berlin, December).

Jaffe, Eugene D. and Israel D. Nebenzahl (1989), "A Methodological Approach to the Estimation of Demand Functions from Country-of-Origin Effect." *Proceedings, European International Business Association* (Helsinki, December).

Jones, R.A. and R.D. Ashmore (1973), "The Structure of Intergroup Perception." *Journal of Personality and Social Psychology*, 25, 428-438.

Keegan, Warren (1989), *Global Marketing Management*. Englewood Cliffs, NJ: Prentice-Hall, 4th Ed.

Lillis, Charles M. and Chem L. Narayana (1974), "Analysis of 'Made- in' Product Images–An Exploratory Study." *Journal of International Business Studies*, (Spring) 119-127.

Nagashima, Akira (1970), "A Comparison of Japanese and U.S. Attitudes Towards Foreign Products." *Journal of Marketing*, 34 (January) 68-74.

Nagashima, Akira (1977), "A Comparative 'Made In' Product Image Survey Among Japanese Businessmen." *Journal of Marketing*, 41, (July) 95-100.

Papadopoulos, Nicolas, Judith J. Marshall, and Louise A. Heslop (1988), "Strategic Implications of Product and Country Images: A Modelling Approach." *Marketing Productivity* (European Society for Opinion and Marketing Research, 41st Research Congress, Lisbon, September) 69-90.

Robinson, J.P. and R. Hefner (1967), "Multidimensional Differences in Public and Academic Perceptions of Nations." *Journal of Personality and Social Psychology*, 25, 428-438.

Sandler, D. and D. Shani (1989), "Olympic Sponsorship vs. 'Ambush' Marketing: Who Gets the Gold?" *Journal of Advertising Research* (August/September) 9-14.

Schooler, Robert D. (1965), "Product Bias in the Central American Common Market." *Journal of Marketing Research*, II: (November) 394-397.

Tanzer, A. (1988, May 16), "Samsung: South Korean Marches to Its Own Drummer." *Forbes*, 84:89.

Wall, Marjorie and Louise A. Heslop (1986), "Consumer Attitudes Toward Canadian-made versus Imported Products." *Journal of the Academy of Marketing Science,* 14(2): 27-36.

White, Phillip D. (1979), "Attitudes of U.S. Purchasing Managers Toward Industrial Products Manufactured In Selected Western European Nations." *Journal of International Business Studies,* 20 (Spring-Summer) 81-90.

Wish, M., M. Deutsch, and L. Biener (1970), "Differences in Conceptual Structures of Nations: An Exploratory Study." *Journal of Personality and Social Psychology,* 16, 361-373.

Appendix. Scale Items Used in the Study

Known to Consumers	Unknown to Consumers
Reliable	Unreliable
Reasonable Price	Unreasonable Price
Good Performance	Bad Performance
Custom-made Products	Mass Produced Products
High Quality Products	Low Quality Products
Innovative Products	Imitative Products
Proud to Own	Ashamed to Own
Advanced Technology	Backward Technology
Like	Dislike
Frequent Need for Service	Infrequent Need for Service
Large Assortment	Small Assortment
Good Products Overall	Bad Products Overall

Epilogue:
Could You Please Pass the Salt?

Ah, country–or is it origin?–images! We know they are "there," we use them, we debate them, we research them. In some ways, they are the salt that helps to give taste to a meal. It is there, it is used, but most people could live without it if it were not available. In many other cases, and for some market segments in most cases, the image is an integral part of the meal–or even the meal itself.

Producers need to learn when to "pass the salt" around and how much of it to use. And researchers, whether in the private and public sectors or in academic settings, can help them to do so. It is hoped that the 18 chapters and 29 researchers in this book have been a significant step in this direction.

The works in this volume cover the entire spectrum–from research overviews to methodological suggestions, from the images of specific sectors to the images of entire nations, and from the influence of events to the strategic synthesis of origin images with the competitive positions of products in the marketplace.

Some readers may use this integrative knowledge as a means for understanding origin images better, others as a means of improving the effectiveness of international marketing strategies, and others in a variety of other and different ways. As ever-larger numbers of researchers and practitioners become involved in this area, we look forward with anticipation to learning ever more about "the little label that could"–the phenomenon that started out in antiquity, was reborn a century ago as the little "Made-in" sticker, and that now plays such an important role in our personal and professional gestalt.

Index

DUE DATE

APR 2 4 1997			
DEC 1 2 1997			
DEC 0 5 2008			
REC'D DEC 0 1	2008		
REC'D MAR 1 1	2013		
			Printed in USA